FIFTH EDITION

I Never Knew
I Had a Choice

OTHER BOOKS BY GERALD COREY:

Theory and Practice of Group Counseling, 3RD EDITION
(and *Manual*) (1990)

Case Approach to Counseling and Psychotherapy, 3RD EDITION (1991)

Theory and Practice of Counseling and Psychotherapy, 4TH EDITION
(and *Manual*) (1991)

BY GERALD COREY AND
MARIANNE SCHNEIDER COREY:

Groups: Process and Practice, 4TH EDITION (1992)

Group Techniques, 2ND EDITION (1992, with Patrick Callanan and
J. Michael Russell)

Becoming a Helper, 2ND EDITION (1993)

Issues and Ethics in the Helping Professions, 4TH EDITION (1993, with
Patrick Callanan)

FIFTH EDITION

I Never Knew
I Had a Choice

GERALD COREY

*California State University, Fullerton
Diplomate in Counseling Psychology,
American Board of Professional Psychology*

MARIANNE SCHNEIDER COREY

Private Practice

BROOKS/COLE PUBLISHING COMPANY
Pacific Grove, California

I(**T**)**P** ™ The trademark ITP is used under license.

 A CLAIREMONT BOOK

Brooks/Cole Publishing Company
A Division of Wadsworth, Inc.

Printed in the United States of America

10   9   8   7   6   5   4   3   2

Library of Congress Cataloging-in-Publication Data

Corey, Gerald.
    I never knew I had a choice / Gerald Corey, Marianne Schneider
Corey. — 5th ed.
      p. cm.
    Includes bibliographical references and index.
    ISBN 0-534-20166-0
    1. Self-perception. 2. Choice (Psychology) 3. Emotional maturity. 4. Self-actualization
(Psychology) I. Corey, Marianne Schneider, [date] . II. Title.
BF697.5.S43C67 1993
158 — dc20   92-35589

Sponsoring Editor: CLAIRE VERDUIN
Editorial Associate: GAY C. BOND
Production Coordinator: FIORELLA LJUNGGREN
Manuscript Editor: LORRAINE ANDERSON
Permissions Editor: CARLINE HAGA
Interior and Cover Design: VERNON T. BOES
Cover Photo: ED YOUNG
Art Coordinator: LISA TORRI
Interior Illustration: RON GRAUER
Photo Editor: LARRY MOLMUD
Photo Researcher: SUE C. HOWARD
Typesetting: TYPELINK, INC.
Cover Printing: PHOENIX COLOR CORPORATION
Printing and Binding: ARCATA GRAPHICS/FAIRFIELD
(Credits continue on p. 417.)

In memory of our friend Jim Morelock,
a searcher who lived and died
    with dignity and self-respect,
who struggled and questioned,
who made the choice to live his days fully
    until time ran out on him at age 25.

PREFACE

I Never Knew I Had a Choice is intended for college students of any age and for all others who wish to expand their self-awareness and explore the choices available to them in significant areas of their lives. The topics discussed include choosing a personal style of learning; reviewing childhood and adolescence and the effects of these experiences on current behavior and choices; meeting the challenges of adulthood and autonomy; becoming the woman or man one wants to be; balancing work and leisure; maintaining a healthy body, learning how to manage stress, and making the right choices for wellness; appreciating the significance of sexuality, love, and intimate relationships; coping well with feelings of loneliness; understanding and accepting death and loss; and choosing one's values and philosophy of life.

This is a personal book, because we encourage readers to examine the choices they have made and how these choices affect their present level of satisfaction. (It is also a personal book in another sense, inasmuch as we describe our own concerns, struggles, decisions, and values with regard to many of the issues we raise.) The book is designed to be a personal workbook as well as a classroom text. Each chapter begins with a self-inventory that gives readers the chance to focus on their present beliefs and attitudes. Within the chapters, sections called "Time Out for Personal Reflection" offer an opportunity to pause and reflect on the issues raised. Additional activities and exercises, including further reading, are suggested at the end of each chapter for use in the classroom or outside of class. We wish to stress that this is an *unfinished* book, since readers are encouraged to become coauthors in their own personal way through the many opportunities for active involvement.

What are some of the changes from the fourth to this fifth edition? The introductory chapter continues to emphasize the importance of self-exploration and invites students to consider the value and excitement, as well as the commitment and work, involved in learning about oneself, others, and personal growth. However, this edition shows an increased interest in social concerns as a balance to self-interests. Although we still emphasize self-actualization, we have expanded on the counterpoint of actualizing oneself within the framework of one's culture, and we have developed the perspective that self-actualization can occur only if individuals have a sense of social consciousness. New material has been added on the lives of such key figures as Maslow, Rogers, Jung, and Adler — and on the ways that their lives are revealed through their theories and ideas. Cultural identity is discussed throughout the chapters as appropriate, and for each of the topics covered, we have mentioned some of the cultural factors that influence choice and behavior.

Chapters Two and Three provide theoretical material on personality development from a life-span perspective, as well as practical tools to help readers modify the design of their present and future existence in their struggle toward autonomy. Chapter Four continues with a developmental theme but focuses on how life experiences influence beliefs about gender identity. This chapter has been considerably updated to reflect current trends in the women's movement and its effects on both women and men. Chapter Five, "Work and Leisure," discusses college education as work, specific factors in vocational decision making, the relation between personality types and occupational choices, and active career planning for one's chosen lifestyle. It also offers practical guidelines for career decision making and increased coverage of the role of leisure in providing a balance to work. Chapter Six, "Your Body and Wellness," deals with topics such as body image, touch and sensuality, and techniques of coping with stress constructively. New to this edition are the contributions of Dr. Bernie Siegel to the wellness movement. The focus is on challenging readers to look at the value they place on health and well-being rather than merely avoiding illness.

Fewer major changes are evident in Chapter Seven, "Love," although updating was done as appropriate. Chapter Eight, which deals with sexuality, now includes an updated and expanded section on the AIDS crisis and its effects on sexual behavior. New to this chapter is a section on sexual abuse and harassment, which looks at subjects such as incest, date and acquaintance rape, and sexual harassment on the campus and in the workplace.

Chapter Nine, "Relationships and Lifestyles," contains expanded guidelines for meaningful interpersonal relationships. We have broadened the scope of this chapter to include a variety of lifestyles and a broad range of relationships: friendships, couple relationships (including gay and lesbian relationships), and family relationships. New material on effective communication has been included, and the importance of recognizing and dealing with anger and conflict in relationships is emphasized. Chapter Ten, "Loneliness and Solitude," focuses on the creative dimensions of solitude. The remaining two chapters, "Death and Loss" and "Meaning and Values" (Chapters Eleven and Twelve), have been updated and expanded, with new or increased coverage of the following topics: fear of death, the interdependence of life and death, the importance of grieving, suicide, and the choice of experiences for personal growth. The discussion of the role of dreams has been expanded, and the coverage of four perspectives on interpreting and exploring the meaning of dreams has been updated.

Fundamentally, our approach in *I Never Knew I Had a Choice* is humanistic and personal; that is, we stress the healthy and effective personality and the common struggles that most of us experience in becoming autonomous. We especially emphasize accepting personal responsibility for the choices we make and consciously deciding whether and how we want to change our lives.

Although our own approach can be broadly characterized as humanistic and existential, our aim has been to challenge readers to recognize and assess their own choices, beliefs, and values rather than to convert them to a particular point of view. Our basic premise is that a commitment to self-exploration can create new potentials for choice. Many of the clients with whom we work are relatively well-functioning people who desire more from life and who want to recognize and remove blocks to their personal creativity and freedom. It is for people like these that we've written this book.

In talking about the contents of this book with both students and instructors, we have found that students select a personal growth course because of their interest in discovering more about themselves and their relationships with others. Most of them are looking for a *practical* course, one that deals with real issues in everyday living and that will provide an impetus for their own personal growth. Accordingly, we have focused on helping readers recognize blocks to their creative and productive energies, find ways of removing these obstructions, and make conscious choices to modify their attitudes and behaviors.

The experiences of those who have read and used the earlier editions of *I Never Knew I Had a Choice* reveal that the themes explored have application to a diversity of ages and backgrounds. Readers who have taken the time to write us about their reactions say that the book encouraged them to take an honest look at their lives and challenge themselves to make certain changes. Although the book was written primarily for a college market, some students have shared it with friends and relatives.

We wrote this book for use in college courses dealing with the psychology of adjustment, personality development, applied psychology, personal growth, and self-awareness. It has also been adopted in courses ranging from the psychology of personal growth on the undergraduate level to graduate courses that deal with the training of teachers and counselors. Our experience has been that active, open, and personal participation in these courses can lead to expanded self-awareness and greater autonomy in living.

An updated and expanded *Instructor's Resource Manual* accompanies this textbook. It includes sections on test items, both multiple-choice and essay, for every chapter; a student study guide covering all chapters; suggested readings; questions for thought and discussion; numerous activities and exercises for classroom participation; guidelines for using the book and teaching the course; examples of various formats of personal-growth classes; guidelines for maximizing personal learning and for reviewing and integrating the course; and a student evaluation instrument to assess the impact of the course on readers.

ACKNOWLEDGMENTS

We wish to express our deep appreciation for the insightful suggestions made by friends, associates, reviewers, students, and readers. The following people provided helpful reviews for this revision: L. William Cheney of Community College of Rhode Island, James Dailey of Vincennes University, Herb Goldberg of California State University at Los Angeles, Robert Levine of Hillsborough Community College, Robert D. Lock of Jackson Community College, Barbara A. McDowell of California State University at Fullerton, Sebastian Mudry of Manchester Community College, Jana Preble of St. Cloud State University, Shirley Reeves of Volunteer State Community College, Valerie Scott of Upsala College, Bonnie Tyler of the University of Maryland at College Park, and G. Joseph Zieleniewski of the University of Cincinnati.

We are indebted to these close friends and colleagues—J. Michael Russell of California State University, Fullerton; Patrick Callanan, in private practice in Santa Ana, California; Mary Moline of Loma Linda University; and Helga Kennedy, in private practice in Auburn, California—for many provocative discussions concerning the ideas raised in this book. We also thank Debbie De Bue for providing technical assistance and for typing much of the manuscript and Glennda Gilmour for preparing the index.

Finally, as is true of all our books, *I Never Knew I Had a Choice* continues to develop as a result of a team effort, which includes the combined talents of several people in the Brooks/Cole family. It is a delight to work with a dedicated staff of professionals who go out of their way to give their best. We especially appreciate our continuing relationship with Claire Verduin, managing editor and psychology editor, and with Fiorella Ljunggren, production services manager. We thank Lorraine Anderson, the manuscript editor; Vernon Boes, the designer of the book; Lisa Torri, the coordinator of the art program; Larry Molmud, the photo editor; and Sue C. Howard, the photo researcher. We are very grateful to all these people, who continue to devote extra time and effort to ensure the quality of our books.

Gerald Corey
Marianne Schneider Corey

CONTENTS

CHAPTER THREE
Adulthood and Autonomy   65

CHAPTER FOUR
Becoming the Woman or Man You Want to Be   103

CHAPTER EIGHT
Sexuality

CHAPTER NINE
Relationships and Lifestyles

FIFTH EDITION

I Never Knew
I Had a Choice

CHAPTER ONE

Invitation to Personal Learning and Growth

Introduction: Choice and Change

WE *DO* HAVE CHOICES!

If you are interested in examining your life and living by choice, this book is for you. Although many of us want to grow and learn more about ourselves, we may be living in ways that are not fully satisfying. We often complain of feeling powerless, of living by the expectations and designs of others, and of being prevented by external circumstances from making any real change. Statements such as the following reflect this attitude that our destiny has been determined: "If only my partner were more affectionate, I'd feel worthwhile." "I'd like to say what I feel, but I'm afraid I'll lose my friends if I do." "I know I'm shy, but it's too late for me to change because I've been this way since I was a kid." "I would be fine if the people around me were different." "If my parents weren't so critical of me, then I'd feel much better."

Our hope is that this book and this course will inspire you to reflect on the quality of your life and decide for yourself how you want to change. We encourage you to challenge your fears, rather than being stopped by them. Socrates, in his wisdom, said, "The unexamined life is not worth living." As you examine your values and typical behavior, options are likely to open up to you. If you have struggled with various crises in your life, for example, you can come to realize that a crisis represents a significant turning point. The Chinese symbol for *crisis* represents both *danger* and *opportunity*. As you engage yourself in this book, consider ways to use critical life situations as opportunities for personal growth.

It is exciting for us when our students and clients discover that they can be in charge of their own lives to a greater degree than they ever dreamed possible. As one client put it: "One thing I can see now that I didn't see before is that I can change my life if I want to. *I never knew I had a choice!*" This remark captures the central message of this book: we are *not* passive victims of life, we *do* make choices, and we *do* have the power to change major aspects of our lives as we struggle toward a more authentic existence.

ARE YOU READY TO CHANGE?

One way to begin focusing on the quality of your life is by reflecting on such questions as: To what extent do you like the way you are living now? Are there some things in your life that you'd like to change? Do you feel that change is even necessary?

It is not uncommon to hear comments like these: "I don't know if I want to rock the boat. Things aren't all that bad in my life. I'm fairly secure, and I don't want to take the chance of losing this security. I'm afraid that if I start probing around, I may uncover things that will be tough for me to handle." It is not a sign of cowardice to have doubts and fears over changing your stance in the world. In fact, it is a mark of bravery to acknowledge your resistance to change and your anxiety over taking increased control. It is a challenge and a

struggle to take an honest look at your life and begin to live differently. Those who are close to you might not approve of or like your changes, and they might put up barriers to your designing a new life. Your cultural background may have taboos against your assuming a new role and modifying certain values. These factors are likely to increase your anxiety as you contemplate making your own choices, rather than allowing others to choose for you. Self-exploration, being honest with yourself and others, thinking for yourself, and making a commitment to live by your choices entail diligent effort. There is a price for taking charge of your life. There is also a degree of discomfort, and even fear, associated with discovering more about yourself. Some people may prefer to remain unaware, to allow others to choose for them, and to be content with the status quo. Others do question but decide that change is not necessary. After all, there is no command that one *must* change. You need to ask yourself if you are willing to pay the price for taking the personal risks involved in choosing for yourself.

Throughout this book both of us make disclosures about our own lives and our values. It is fitting that we use a personal style and openly share with you how we arrived at some of the beliefs and values we write about. We hope that knowing our assumptions, biases, and struggles will help you evaluate your own position more clearly. We are not suggesting that you adopt our philosophy of life but rather that you ask how the issues we raise concern *you.* It is not our intention to provide simple answers to complex problems. In our view, self-help books that give an abundance of advice about the way you should live are really limiting and can do you a disservice. Our aim is to offer material that will raise questions and lead to thoughtful reflection on your part and meaningful dialogue with others. We encourage you to develop a tolerance for dealing with questions that engage you. Instead of searching for advice or for simple solutions to your problems, we hope that you will increasingly look inside yourself for direction by learning to listen to your inner voice. The focus is on questions such as: What are your answers? How can you trust yourself to discover what is best for you? What are the choices you've made for yourself? What choices do you want to make now? How can you best live with your choices?

WHAT ABOUT OTHER PEOPLE?

We have been saying that making choices for yourself and being in control of your life is important. Yet we are certainly not encouraging you to ignore the reality that you are a social being and that many of your decisions will be influenced by your relationships with significant people in your life. In this book we write about becoming your own person, and at the same time we point out the need to consider others in this quest for self-development. Although we encourage you to make your own decisions and determine who and what you want to be, we also emphasize the importance of the impact that your decisions have on the people around you.

In *Habits of the Heart* the authors assert that the goal for most Americans is to "become one's own person, almost to give birth to oneself" (Bellah, Madsen, Sullivan, Swidler, & Tipton, 1985). But in their many interviews they also found as a common theme the notion that the good life cannot be lived alone, that we do not find ourselves in isolation, and that connectedness to others in love, work, and community is absolutely essential to our self-esteem and happiness: "We find ourselves not independently of other people and institutions but through them. We never get to the bottom of our selves on our own. We discover who we are face to face and side by side with others in work, love, and learning" (p. 84).

We should not expect that others will necessarily change because we do. The focus for change needs to be on ourselves, not others. For one thing, we don't have the power to change other people unless they want to change. Moreover, we can easily encounter any impasse by focusing on all the ways we wish they would change. In her provocative book *The Dance of Anger,* Harriet Goldhor Lerner (1985) makes the point time and again that it is not our task to change how others feel, think, and behave. Many of those who participate in her anger workshops become aware that they are putting their "anger energy" into trying to change the other person. Rather than attempting to remake others into who we think they should be, our job is to clearly state what we think and feel and to make responsible decisions that are congruent with our values. Lerner contends that if our focus in our relationships is on changing other people, the typical result will be a good deal of emotional pain but little change in our situation.

Although we cannot control others, we do have a large degree of control over our own destiny. If we wait for others to become different, or if we blame them for the fact that we're not as happy as we'd like to be, we diminish our power to take full control of our own life. If you want a closer relationship with your father and insist that he talk to you more and approve of you, for example, you are likely to be frustrated. He may not behave the way you want him to, and if you make changing him your central goal, you are keeping yourself helpless in many respects. If you make some significant changes in the way you talk to your father and in the way you treat him, you may be greatly surprised at how much he becomes a different person in your eyes. You will increase your chances of success if *you* do what you want *him* to do.

As this example shows, the idea of personal choice does not imply doing whatever we want without regard for others. Making a commitment to examine our life does not mean becoming wrapped up in ourselves to the exclusion of everyone else. Unless we know and care about ourselves, however, we cannot develop genuinely caring relationships. As we enrich our own life by making constructive choices, we can also improve our interpersonal relationships.

A Model for Personal Growth

One of the obvious benefits of choosing to change your life is that you will grow by exposing yourself to new experiences. It's time we looked more closely at just what personal growth entails. This section contrasts the idea of *growth* with that of *adjustment* and offers a humanistic model of what ideal growth can be. It also deals with divergent perspectives on what constitutes the ideal standard of personal growth.

ADJUSTMENT OR GROWTH?

Although this book deals with topics in what is often called "the psychology of adjustment," we have an uneasy feeling about this common phrase. The term *adjustment* is frequently taken to mean that some ideal norm exists by which people should be measured. This notion raises many problems. You may ask, for example: What is the desired norm of adjustment? Who determines the standards of "good" adjustment? Is it possible that the same person could be considered well adjusted in our culture and poorly adjusted in some other culture?

One reason we resist "adjustment" as a goal of human behavior is that those who claim to be well adjusted have often settled for a complacent existence, with neither challenge nor excitement. Within the limits imposed by genetic and environmental factors, we have many possibilities for creating our own definitions of ourselves as persons. No single standard of measurement exists for identifying universal qualities of the well-adjusted or psychologically healthy person. The concept of adjustment cannot be understood apart from the person-in-the-environment, for cultural values and norms play a crucial role. For example, if you are in your 20s and still living with your parents, some would view this as dependent behavior on your part and think that you should be living apart from your family of origin. Yet, depending on the cultural perspective assumed, some would see this as the expected lifestyle and consider it inappropriate for you to be living on your own.

Instead of talking about adjustment, then, we tend to talk about *growth*. A psychology of growth rests on the assumption that growth is a lifelong adventure, not some fixed point at which we arrive. Personal growth is best viewed as a *process* rather than a goal or an end. A growth-oriented perspective assumes that we will face numerous crises at the various stages of our development. These crises can be challenges to give our lives new meaning. Growth also encompasses our relationships with significant others, our community, and our world. We do not grow in a vacuum but through our engagement with other people. To continue to grow, we have to be willing to let go of some of our old ways of thinking and acting so new dimensions can develop. During your reading and studying, think about the ways in which you've stopped growing and the degree to which you're willing to invest in personal growth. In this regard, some questions to ask yourself are:

- What do you want for yourself, for others, and from others?
- What aspects of your life are working for you?
- What is not working in your life?
- How would you like to be different?
- What are possible consequences if you do or do not change?
- How will your changes affect others in your life?
- What range of choices is open to you at this time in your life?
- How has your culture laid a foundation for the choices that you have made, and how might your cultural values either enhance or inhibit you in deciding on ways you want to be different?

A HUMANISTIC APPROACH TO PERSONAL GROWTH

I Never Knew I Had a Choice is based on a humanistic view of people. A central concept of this approach to personal growth is *self-actualization*. Striving for self-actualization means working toward fulfilling our potential, toward becoming all that we are capable of becoming. Humanistic psychology is based on the premise that this striving for growth exists but is not an automatic process. Because growth often involves some pain and considerable turmoil, many of us experience a constant struggle between our desire for security, or dependence, and our desire to experience the delights of growth.

Although other figures have made significant contributions to humanistic psychology, we have chosen to focus on four key people who devoted much of their professional careers to the promotion of psychological growth and the self-realization process: Abraham Maslow, Carl Rogers, Carl Jung, and Alfred Adler. With these four theorists, it is particularly interesting to note the close parallels between the struggles of their early childhood and the focus of their theories. Based upon a set of life experiences, each of these men made a choice that influenced the development of his theory.

Abraham Maslow recalled that he had a miserable relationship with both of his parents. In fact, given the life he had as a child, Maslow thought that it was surprising that he did not become mentally ill. Shortly after the attack on Pearl Harbor, Maslow was watching a parade and made a choice that would determine the direction of his professional work. He decided that he would study the highest ideals and potentials of humans, which would demonstrate that people are capable of more noble behavior than prejudice, hatred, and war.

In Maslow's background was a concern over taking care of basic survival needs. As you will see, Maslow's theory stresses a hierarchy of needs, with satisfaction of physiological and safety needs being a prerequisite for being concerned about actualizing one's potentials. Self-actualization became the central theme of the work of Abraham Maslow (1968, 1970, 1971). Maslow used the phrase "the psychopathology of the average" to highlight his contention that merely "normal" people may never extend themselves to become what they are capable of becoming. Further, he criticized Freudian psychology for what he saw as its preoccupation with the sick and crippled side of human nature; if our findings are based on a sick population, Maslow reasoned, a sick psychology will emerge. Thus, he believed that too much research was being conducted into anxiety, hostility, and neuroses and too little into joy, creativity, and self-fulfillment.

In his quest to create a humanistic psychology that would focus on our potential, Maslow studied what he called self-actualizing people and found that they differed in important ways from so-called "normals." Some of the characteristics that Maslow found in these people were a capacity to tolerate and even welcome uncertainty in their life, an acceptance of themselves and others, spontaneity and creativity, a need for privacy and solitude, autonomy, a capacity for deep and intense interpersonal relationships, a genuine caring for others, a sense of humor, an inner-directedness (as opposed to the tendency to live by others' expectations), and the absence of artificial dichotomies within themselves (such as work/play, love/hate, and weak/strong).

Carl Rogers (1961, 1980), a major figure in the development of humanistic psychology, focused on the importance of nonjudgmental listening and acceptance as a condition for people to feel free enough to change. It's interesting that Rogers's emphasis on the value of autonomy seems to have grown, in part, out of his own struggles to become independent from his parents. Rogers grew up fearing his mother's critical judgment. In an interview, Rogers mentioned that he could not imagine talking to his mother about anything of significance, because he was sure that she would have some negative judgment. He also grew up in a home where strict religious standards governed behavior. In his early years, while Rogers was at a seminary studying to be a minister, he made a critical choice that influenced his personal life and the focus of his theory. Realizing that he could no longer go along with the religious thinking of his parents, Rogers questioned the religious dogma he was being taught, which led to his emancipation and his psychological independence. As a college student he took the risk of writing a letter to his parents telling them that his views were changing from fundamentalist to liberal and that he was developing his own philosophy of life. Even though he knew that his departure from the values of his parents would be difficult for them, he felt that such a move was necessary for his own intellectual and psychological freedom.

Rogers built his entire theory and practice of psychotherapy on the concept of the "fully functioning person," a concept much like Maslow's self-actualizing person. Fully functioning people tend to reflect and ask basic questions such as: Who am I? How can I discover my real self? How can I become what I deeply wish to become? How can I get out from behind my facade and become myself? Rogers maintained that when people give up their facade and accept themselves, they move in the direction of being open to experience (that is, they begin to see reality without distorting it), they trust themselves and look to themselves for the answers to their problems, and they no longer attempt to become fixed entities or products, realizing instead that growth is a continual process. Such fully functioning people, Rogers wrote, are in a fluid process of challenging and revisiting their perceptions and beliefs as they open themselves to new experiences.

Rogers, in contrast to those who assume that we are by nature irrational and destructive unless we are socialized, exhibited a deep faith in human beings. In his view, people are naturally social and forward-moving, strive to function fully, and have at their deepest core a positive goodness. In short, people are to be trusted, and since they are basically cooperative and constructive, there is no need to control their aggressive impulses.

Carl Jung (1961) made a monumental contribution to the understanding of the human personality. His ideas are more abstract than are Maslow's and Rogers's, yet his pioneering work sheds light on human development, particularly during middle age. Jung's personal life paved the way for the expansion of his theoretical notions. His loneliness as a child is reflected in his personality theory, which focuses on the inner world of the individual. Jung's emo-

tional distance from his parents contributed to his feeling of being cut off from the external world of conscious reality. Largely as a way of escaping the difficulties of his childhood, Jung turned inward and became preoccupied with pursuing his unconscious experiences as reflected in his dreams, visions, and fantasies. At age 81 he wrote about his recollections in his autobiography *Memories, Dreams, Reflections*. He made a choice to focus on the unconscious realm in his personal life, which also influenced the development of his theory of personality.

According to Jung, humans are not merely shaped by past events but strive for progression as well. Part of the nature of humans is to be constantly developing, growing, and moving toward a balanced and complete level of development. For Jung, our present personality is determined both by who and what we have been and by the person we hope to become. The process of self-actualization is oriented toward the future. Jung's theory is based on the assumption that humans tend to move toward the fulfillment or realization of all their capabilities. Achieving individuation, or a fully harmonious and integrated personality, is a primary goal. To come to our full realization, we must become aware of and accept the full range of our being. This means that the public self that we present is only a small part of who and what we are. For Jung, both constructive and destructive forces coexist in the human psyche, and to become integrated we must accept the dark side of our nature with our primitive impulses such as selfishness and greed. Acceptance of our dark side (or shadow) does not imply being dominated by this dimension of our being but simply recognizing that this is a part of our nature.

Along with Maslow, Rogers, and Jung, another pioneer in the humanistic movement of growth psychology was Alfred Adler (1958, 1964, 1969), who made major contributions during Freud's era. In opposition to Freud's deterministic views of the person, Adler's theory stresses self-determination. Adler's early childhood experiences were characterized by a struggle to overcome weaknesses and feelings of inferiority. His family experiences had a major impact on the formation of his theory. The basic concepts of his theory grew out of his willingness to deal with his personal problems. Adler is a good example of a person who shaped his own life as opposed to being determined by his fate.

Adlerian psychologists contend that we are not the victims of fate but are creative, active, choice-making beings whose every action has purpose and meaning. Adler's approach is basically a growth model that rejects the idea that some individuals are psychologically sick. Instead of sickness, Adlerians talk of people being discouraged. Adlerian therapists view their work as providing encouragement so that people can grow to become what they were meant to be. They teach people better ways to meet the challenges of life tasks, provide direction, help people change unrealistic assumptions and beliefs, and offer encouragement to those who are discouraged.

One of Adler's basic concepts is *social interest*, an individual's attitudes in dealing with other people in the world, which includes striving for a better future. Adler equated social interest with identification and empathy with others. For him, our happiness and success are largely related to a sense of belonging and a social connectedness. As social beings we need to be of use to others and to establish meaningful relationships in a community. Adler asserted that only when we feel united with others can we act with courage in facing and dealing with life's problems. Since we are embedded in a society, we cannot be understood in isolation from our social context. Self-actualization is thus not an individual matter; it is only within the group that we can actualize our potentialities. Adler maintained that the degree to which we successfully share with others and are concerned with their welfare is a measure of our maturity. Social interest becomes the standard by which to judge psychological health. M. Scott Peck (1987) captures this idea of social interest: "It is true that we are created to be individually unique. Yet the reality is that we are inevitably social creatures who desperately need each other not merely for sustenance, not merely for company, but for any meaning to our lives whatsoever" (p. 55).

The values underlying one's world view have a bearing on how one views the process of self-actualization. The Western orientation is grounded in individualism, which affirms the uniqueness, autonomy, freedom, and intrinsic worth of the individual and emphasizes personal responsibility for behavior and well-being. The ultimate aim of this orientation is the self-actualization of the individual, or becoming everything that one is potentially able to become. By contrast, the Eastern orientation rests on collectivism, which affirms the value of preserving and enhancing the well-being of the group as the main principle guiding social action. This collective orientation emphasizes unity, unification, integration, and fusion. It does not view self-actualization as the ultimate good. Instead, it emphasizes cooperation, harmony, interdependence, the achievement of socially oriented and group goals, and collective responsibility.

Rather than considering these perspectives as polar opposites, we can conceive of the ideal as involving a synthesis of the best of both world views. This synthesis entails the collective actualization of individuals-in-society and, at the same time, the actualization of the individual. C. H. Patterson (1985) has proposed that the Eastern and Western cultures move toward each other: "Eastern culture must change in the direction of greater concern for individual personal development. Western culture must move in the direction of greater concern for the influence of the individual upon others and upon their development, and of cooperation in fostering personal development in others" (p. 188). An integration of the contributions of Maslow, Rogers, Jung, and Adler provides a useful background to understanding personal growth.

OVERVIEW OF MASLOW'S SELF-ACTUALIZATION THEORY

Maslow postulated a hierarchy of needs as a source of motivation. The most basic are the physiological needs. If we are hungry and thirsty, then our attention is riveted on meeting these basic needs. Next are the safety needs, which include a sense of security and stability. Once our physical and safety needs are fulfilled, we are concerned with meeting our needs for belonging and love, followed by working on our need for esteem, both from self and others. We are able to strive toward self-actualization once these four lower needs are met: physiological, safety, love, and esteem. Maslow emphasized that people are not motivated by all of these five needs at the same time. The key factor that determines which one of these needs is dominant at a given time is the degree to which others are satisfied. This notion is crucial to understand, for some come to the erroneous conclusion that if they were "bright" enough or "good" enough, then they would be further down the road of self-actualization. The truth may be that in their particular cultural, environmental, and societal circumstances these people are motivated to work toward physical and psychological survival, which keeps them functioning at the lower end of the hierarchy.

We can summarize some of the basic ideas of the humanistic approach by means of Maslow's model of the self-actualizing person. He describes self-actualization in his book *Motivation and Personality* (1970), and he also treats the concept in his other books (1968, 1971). Keep in mind that an individual is not much concerned with actualization, nor is a society focused on the development of culture, if the basic needs are not met.

Self-awareness. Self-actualizing people are more aware of themselves, of others, and of reality than nonactualizing people. Specifically, they demonstrate the following behavior and traits:

1. *Efficient perception of reality*
   a. Self-actualizing people see reality as it is.
   b. They have an ability to detect phoniness.
   c. They avoid seeing things in preconceived categories.
2. *Ethical awareness*
   a. Self-actualizing people display a knowledge of what is right and wrong for them.
   b. They have a sense of inner direction.
   c. They avoid being pressured by others and living by others' standards.
3. *Freshness of appreciation.* Like children, self-actualizing people have an ability to perceive life in a fresh way.
4. *Peak moments*
   a. Self-actualizing people experience times of being one with the universe; they experience moments of joy.
   b. They have the ability to be changed by such moments.

Freedom. Self-actualizing people are willing to make choices for themselves, and they are free to reach their potential. This freedom entails a sense of detachment and a need for privacy, a creativity and spontaneity, and an ability to accept responsibility for choices.

1. *Detachment*
   a. For self-actualizing people, the need for privacy is crucial.
   b. They have a need for solitude in order to put things in perspective.
2. *Creativity*
   a. Creativity is a universal characteristic of self-actualizing people.
   b. Creativity may be expressed in any area of life; it shows itself as inventiveness.
3. *Spontaneity*
   a. Self-actualizing people don't need to show off.
   b. They display a naturalness and lack of pretentiousness.
   c. They act with ease and grace.

Basic honesty and caring. Self-actualizing people show a deep caring for and honesty with themselves and others. These qualities are reflected in their interest in humankind and in their interpersonal relationships.

1. *Sense of social interest*
   a. Self-actualizing people have a concern for the welfare of others.
   b. They have a sense of communality with all other people.
   c. They have an interest in bettering the world.
2. *Interpersonal relationships*
   a. Self-actualizing people have a capacity for real love and fusion with another.
   b. They are able to love and respect themselves.
   c. They are able to go outside themselves in a mature love.
   d. They are motivated by the urge to grow in their relationships.
3. *Sense of humor*
   a. Self-actualizing people can laugh at themselves.
   b. They can laugh at the human condition.
   c. Their humor is not hostile.

Trust and autonomy. Self-actualizing people exhibit faith in themselves and others; they are independent; they accept themselves as valuable persons; and their lives have meaning.

1. *Search for purpose and meaning*
   a. Self-actualizing people have a sense of mission, of a calling in which their potential can be fulfilled.
   b. They are engaged in a search for identity, often through work that is a deeply significant part of their lives.
2. *Autonomy and independence*
   a. Self-actualizing people have the ability to be independent.
   b. They resist blind conformity.
   c. They are not tradition-bound in making decisions.
3. *Acceptance of self and others*
   a. Self-actualizing people avoid fighting reality.
   b. They accept nature as it is.
   c. They are comfortable with the world.*

The above profile is best thought of as an ideal rather than a final state that we reach once and for all. Thus, it is more appropriate to speak about the self-actualizing process rather than becoming a self-actualized person.

How do we work toward self-actualization? There is no set of techniques for reaching this goal, but in a sense the rest of this book, including the activities and "Time Out" sections, is about ways of beginning this lifelong quest. As you read about the struggles we face in trying to become all we are capable of becoming, we hope you will begin to see some options for living a fuller life.

*Adapted from *Motivation and Personality*, by A. H. Maslow. Copyright © 1970 by Harper & Row, Publishers, Inc. Used by permission.

Time Out for Personal Reflection

The "Time Out" sections in this book are an opportunity for you to pause and reflect on your own experiences as they relate to the topic being discussed. Unlike most quizzes and tests you have taken, these inventories have no right and wrong answers. Taking them will probably be a different experience for you, and you may have to make a conscious effort to look within yourself for the response or answer that makes sense to you, rather than searching for the expected response that is external to you.

1. To what degree do you have a healthy and positive view of yourself? Are you able to appreciate yourself, or do you discount your own worth? Take this self-inventory by rating yourself with the following code: 4 = this statement is true of me *most* of the time; 3 = this statement is true of me *much* of the time; 2 = this statement is true of me *some* of the time; 1 = this statement is true of me *almost none* of the time.

_____ I generally think and choose for myself.
_____ I usually like myself.
_____ I know what I want.
_____ I am able to ask for what I want.
_____ I feel a sense of personal power.
_____ I am open to change.
_____ I feel equal to others.
_____ I am sensitive to the needs of others.
_____ I care about others.
_____ I can act in accordance with my own judgment without feeling guilty if others disapprove of me.
_____ I do not expect others to make me feel alive.
_____ I can accept responsibility for my own actions.
_____ I am able to accept compliments.
_____ I can give affection.
_____ I can receive affection.
_____ I do not live by a long list of "shoulds," "oughts," and "musts."
_____ I am not so security-bound that I will not explore new things.
_____ I am generally accepted by others.
_____ I can give myself credit for what I do well.
_____ I am able to enjoy my own company.
_____ I am capable of forming intimate and meaningful relationships.
_____ I live in the here and now and do not get stuck dwelling on the past or the future.
_____ I feel a sense of significance.
_____ I am not diminished when I am with those I respect.
_____ I believe in my ability to succeed in projects that are meaningful to me.

Now go back over this inventory and identify not more than five areas that keep you from being as self-accepting as you might be. What can you do to increase your awareness of situations in which you do not fully accept yourself? For example, if you have trouble giving yourself credit for things you do well, how can you become aware of times when you discount yourself? When you do become conscious of situations in which you put yourself down, think of alternatives.

2. Take a few minutes to review Maslow's theory of self-actualization and then consider the following questions as they apply to you:

   • Which of these qualities do you find most appealing? Why?
   • Which would you like to cultivate in yourself?
   • Which of Maslow's ideal qualities do you most associate with living a full and meaningful life?
   • Who in your life comes closest to meeting Maslow's criteria for self-actualizing people?

Are You an Active Learner?

The self-actualization process of growth implies that you will be an *active learner*: that you will assume responsibility for your education, will question what is presented to you, and will apply what you learn in a personally meaningful way. Your schooling experiences may not have encouraged you to learn actively. Instead of questioning and learning to think for yourself, you can easily assume a passive stance by doing what is expected, memorizing facts, and giving back information on tests. This section asks you to review your school experiences and assess whether you are an active learner.

During my own (Jerry's) childhood and adolescence, school was a largely meaningless and sometimes painful experience. In addition, my educational experiences from grammar school through graduate school often taught me to be a passive learner. I learned that pleasing the teacher was more important than pleasing myself; that accepting the opinions of an authority was more valuable than becoming a questioner; that learning facts and information was more valuable than learning about myself; that learning was motivated by external factors; that there was a right answer to every problem; that school life and everyday life were separate; that the sharing of personal feelings and concerns had no place in the classroom; and that the purpose of school was mainly to cultivate the intellect and acquire basic skills, not to encourage me to understand myself more fully and make choices based on this self-awareness. I do think that it is essential to learn basic skills, but I also think that academic learning of content is most fruitful when it is combined with the personal concerns of the learners.

In his thought-provoking book *Freedom to Learn for the 80's*, Rogers (1983) deals with the challenges of the teaching/learning process. He advocates "whole-person learning," in which what is learned becomes a basic part of the person and in which attitudes and values are at least as important as factual knowledge. Several key elements are involved in the personal learning that Rogers proposes: it is self-initiated, in that there is a sense of discovery, reaching out, and comprehending that comes from within the learner. It is pervasive, meaning that it makes a difference in the behavior, attitudes, and personality of the learner. The locus of evaluation is within the learner; that is, the learner determines whether what is being learned is meeting his or her needs. The essence of this kind of whole-person learning lies in its meaning: it is significant and matters to the learner. As such, significant learning is holistic in that it combines the logical and intuitive and the cognitive and feeling dimensions. If you think of learning from this perspective, it becomes a very different matter from simply taking in information that is external to the self, devoid of meaning, and quickly forgotten. A challenge is for you to find ways to bring meaning to your learning, and this is largely done by being active in the process.

You can get the most out of your courses if you develop an active style of learning in which you raise questions and search for answers within yourself. Since this kind of active learning may be different from most of your previous experiences in school, the following "Time Out" will help you review your own experiences as a learner and think about the effects that your education has had on you.

Attempt to determine how some of your present values and beliefs are related to these experiences. You might pause and reflect on a particularly positive school experience and think about how it might be affecting you today. You can do the same for a negative experience with school. If you like the kind of learner you are now, or if you have had mostly good experiences with school, you can build on that positive framework as you approach this course. You can continue to find ways of involving yourself with the material you will read, study, and discuss. If you feel cheated by a negative educational experience, you can begin to change it. *You* can make this class different by applying some of the ideas provided in this chapter. Once you become aware of those aspects of your education that you don't like, *you* can decide to change your style of learning.

Time Out for Personal Reflection

How do you rate your education? In taking this inventory, respond quickly by giving your initial reaction. Indicate your response by circling the corresponding letter. You may choose more than one response for each item, or if none of the responses fit you, you may write your own response on the blank line.

1. How would you evaluate your experience in elementary school?
   a. It was a pleasant time for me.
   b. I dreaded going to school.
   c. It taught me a lot about life.
   d. Although I learned facts and information, I learned little about myself.

   e. _____

2. How would you evaluate your high school experience?
   a. I have mostly favorable memories of this time.
   b. I got more from the social aspects of high school than I did from the educational ones.
   c. I remember it as a lonely time.
   d. I was very involved in my classes.

   e. _____

3. How do you evaluate your present college experience?
   a. I like what I'm getting from my college education.
   b. I see college as an extension of my earlier schooling experiences.
   c. I'm learning more about myself as a result of attending college.
   d. I'm here mainly to get a degree; learning is secondary.

   e. _____

4. To what degree do you see yourself as a "teacher pleaser"?
   a. In the past I worked very hard to gain the approval of my teachers.
   b. I'm now more concerned with pleasing myself than I am with pleasing my teachers.
   c. It's very important to me to please those who are in authority.
   d. Good grades are more important than what I learn.

   e. _____

5. To what degree have you been a questioner?
   a. I generally haven't questioned authority.
   b. I've been an active learner, and I've raised many questions.
   c. Basically, I see myself as a passive learner.
   d. I didn't raise questions earlier in my schooling, but now I'm willing to question the meaning of what I do in school.

   e. _____

6. Have you been motivated externally or internally?
   a. I've been motivated primarily by competition and other forms of external motivation.
   b. I've learned things mainly because of the satisfaction I get from learning.
   c. I see myself as having a lot of curiosity and a need to explore.

d. I've generally learned what I think will be on a test or what will help me get a job.

e. _____

7. To what degree are you a confident learner?
   a. I'm afraid of making mistakes and looking foolish
   b. I often look for the "correct way" or the "one right answer."
   c. I trust my own judgment, and I live by my values.
   d. I think there can be many right answers to a problem.

   e. _____

8. To what degree has your learning been real and meaningful?
   a. School has been a place where I learn things that are personally meaningful.
   b. School has been a place where I mostly perform meaningless tasks and pursue meaningless goals.
   c. I've learned how to apply what I learn in school to my life outside of school.
   d. I've tended to see school learning and real life as separate.

   e. _____

9. To what degree have feelings been a part of your schooling?
   a. School has dealt with issues that relate to my personal concerns.
   b. I've believed that what I feel has no place in school.
   c. The emphasis has been on the intellect, not on feelings.
   d. I've learned to distrust my feelings.

   e. _____

10. How much freedom have you experienced in your schooling?
    a. Schooling has taught me how to handle freedom in my own learning.
    b. I've found it difficult to accept freedom in school.
    c. I've experienced schools as places that restrict my freedom and do not encourage me to make my own choices.
    d. I've experienced schools as sources of encouragement to make and accept my own choices.

    e. _____

Now that you've taken this inventory, we have some suggestions for applying the results to yourself. Look over your responses and then decide which of the following questions might be meaningful follow-up activities for you.

1. How would you describe yourself as a learner during elementary school? during your high school years? as a college student?
2. What effects do you think your schooling has had on you as a person?

3. If you don't like the kind of learner you've been up until now, what can you do about it? What changes would you like to make?
4. What important things (both positive and negative) did you learn about yourself as a result of your schooling?

When you've completed your review of your school experience, you might consider (1) bringing your responses to class and sharing them or (2) using a journal to write down memories of school experiences that have had an impact on you and to keep an ongoing account of significant events in your present learning. Many students find that keeping a journal helps them personalize the topics addressed in this book, and they value looking back over what they wrote earlier. Further suggestions for journal writing are given in the section of this chapter on "How to Use This Book."

Choosing an Active Learning Style

If you became aware in the preceding section that you are not exercising your full power as a learner, you can decide now to be a more active learner. To be challenged to think for themselves and to search within for direction is a new experience for many students. It is unsettling to them when they do not get definite answers to their questions. Such students may have a high need for structure and little tolerance for ambiguity. They have been conditioned to find the "one correct answer" to a problem and have been trained to support whatever statements they make with some authoritative source. Our experience with university students repeatedly shows us how timid many of them are when it comes to formulating and expressing their position on an issue. They are often apologetic for using the word *I* in a paper, even if their viewpoint is backed up with reasoning and material from other sources. Yet many of them are disenchanted with mechanical and impersonal learning, and they truly want to learn how to think through issues and to find meaning in the courses they take. One of the ways to do this involves employing what is known as divergent thinking.

USING DIVERGENT THINKING

In approaching a problem you can use either convergent thinking or divergent thinking. In *convergent thinking* the task is to sort out alternatives and arrive at the best solution to the problem. A multiple-choice test taps convergent thinking, for you must select the one best answer from a list of alternatives given. *Divergent thinking* in contrast, involves coming up with many acceptable answers to the problem. Essay tests have the potential to tap divergent thinking. Your education should value divergent thinking as much as it values convergent thinking. For many subjects there are often multiple

routes that lead to a number of correct answers. Part of being an active learner is having the capacity to raise questions, to brainstorm, and to generate multiple answers to your questions. This process implies personal involvement with the material to be learned. This book is based on divergent thinking, because the themes it addresses do not have simple solutions. It is designed to engage you in exploring how these themes apply to you and to help you find your own answers.

TAKING RESPONSIBILITY FOR LEARNING

At the beginning of a new semester some college students are typically overwhelmed by how much they are expected to do in all their courses while maintaining a life outside of school. One reaction to this feeling of being swamped is to put things off, which typically leads to discouragement, which then results in getting behind with class assignments.

What is most important is that you take responsibility for your own learning. Students who fail to see their own role in the learning process may find others to blame for their failures. If you're dissatisfied with your education, it is appropriate to take a look at yourself and see how much you're willing to invest in making it more vital. Are you just waiting for others to make your learning meaningful? How much are you willing to do to change the things you don't like? Are you accepting your share of responsibility for putting something into the learning process?

Many students who complain among themselves seem unwilling to risk approaching their instructors to talk about their feelings. Of course, not all instructors are open to student input. Yet some of them are receptive to suggestions from students, especially specific ideas for changes.

Regardless of the format or structure of a course, you can actively search for ways of becoming personally involved in the issues it deals with. For example, this book discusses personal topics that have a direct bearing on your life. Whatever the limits set by your instructor, you will have many opportunities to decide how involved to become in these issues. Whether the class is conducted primarily as a lecture, a lecture/discussion, an experiential group with some structure, or an open-ended group, you can decide to be only marginally involved or to actively apply these topics to yourself. During a lecture, for example, you can raise your own questions and think about your daily behavior.

It is also essential that you develop effective study habits and learn basic time management skills. Although acquiring these skills alone does not guarantee successful learning, knowing how to organize your time and how to study can contribute significantly to assuming an active and effective style of learning. In the "Activities and Exercises" section at the end of this chapter you will find the five-step SQ3R technique for studying, reading, and reviewing. Also, the next section contains some specific suggestions for getting the most out of your courses. Take a few minutes now to look at these guidelines for study.

One way to begin to become an active learner is to think about your reasons for taking this course and your expectations concerning what you will learn. The following "Time Out" will help you focus on these issues.

Time Out for Personal Reflection

1. What are your main reasons for taking this course?

   _____

   _____

   _____

   _____

2. What do you expect this course to be like? Check all the comments that fit you.

_____   I expect to talk openly about issues that matter to me.
_____   I expect to get answers to certain problems in my life.
_____   I hope that I will become a more fulfilled person.
_____   I hope that I will have less fear of expressing my feelings and ideas.
_____   I expect to be challenged on why I am the way I am.
_____   I expect to learn more about how other people function.
_____   I expect that I will understand myself more fully by the end of the course than I do now.

3. What do you most want to accomplish in this course?

_____

_____

_____

_____

4. What are you willing to do in order to become actively involved in your learning? Check the appropriate comments.

_____   I'm willing to participate in class discussions.
_____   I'm willing to read the material and think about how it applies to me.
_____   I'm willing to question my assumptions and look at my values.
_____   I'm willing to spend some time most days in reflecting on the issues raised in this course.
_____   I'm willing to keep a journal and to record my reactions to what I read and experience.

Getting the Most from This Course: Suggestions for Personal Learning

Few of your courses deal primarily with *you* as the subject matter. Most of us spend years in acquiring information about the world around us, and we may even equate learning with absorbing facts that are external to us. Although such learning is essential, it is equally important to learn about oneself. To a large degree, what you get from this course will depend on what you're willing to invest of yourself; so it's important that you clarify your goals and the steps you can take to reach them. The following guidelines may help you become active and involved in personal learning as you read the book and participate in your class.

1. *Preparing.* Reading and writing, of course, are excellent devices for getting the most from this class. Many students have been conditioned to view reading as an unpleasant assignment, and they tolerate textbooks as

something to plow through for an examination. As an active learner, however, you can selectively read this book — as well as some of the books you may select from the *References and Suggested Readings* at the end of this book — in a personal way that will stimulate you intellectually and emotionally. Read this book for your personal benefit, and make use of the "Time Out" sections and exercises to help you apply the material to your own life. Writing can also give you a focus. In addition to completing the "Time Out" sections you can take personal notes, keep a log or journal, and write brief reactions about the personal impact of the topics. This can be done in the margins as you read and as you feel affected personally. It is helpful to simply write in a free-flowing and unedited style, rather than attempting to analyze what you write. The idea is simply to keep some record of personally significant issues.

2. *Dealing with fears.* Personal learning entails experiencing some common fears. Some of these are the fear of taking an honest look at yourself and discovering terrible things; the fear of the unknown; the fear of looking foolish in front of others, especially your instructor; the fear of being criticized or ridiculed; and the fear of speaking out and expressing your values. It's natural to experience some fear about participating personally and actively in the class, especially since this kind of participation may involve taking risks you don't usually take in your courses. What is critical is how you deal with any fears you experience. You have the choice of remaining a passive observer or recognizing your fears and dealing with them openly, even though you might experience some degree of discomfort. Facing your fears takes both courage and a genuine desire to increase your awareness of yourself, but by doing so you take a first big step toward expanding the range of your choices.

3. *Deciding what you want for yourself.* If you come to class with only vague ideas of what you want, the chances are that you'll be disappointed. You can increase your chances of having a profitable experience by taking the time and effort to think about what problems and personal concerns you're willing to explore.

4. *Taking risks.* If you make the choice to invest yourself fully in the course, you should be prepared for the possibility of some disruption in your life. You may find yourself changing. It can be a shock to discover that those who are close to you do not appreciate your changes. They may prefer that you remain as you are. Thus, instead of receiving their support, you may encounter their resistance.

5. *Establishing trust.* You can choose to take the initiative in establishing the trust necessary for you to participate in this course in a meaningful way, or you can wait for others to create a climate of trust. Often students have feelings of mistrust or other negative feelings toward an instructor yet avoid doing anything. One way to establish trust is to seek out your instructor and discuss any feelings you have that might prevent you from participating fully in the course. The same applies to any feelings of mistrust you have toward other class members. By expressing your feelings, you can actively help establish a higher level of trust.

6. *Practicing self-disclosure.* Disclosing yourself to others is one way to come to know yourself more fully. Sometimes participants in self-awareness courses or experiential groups fear that they must relinquish their privacy in order to be active participants. However, you can be open and at the same time retain your privacy by deciding how much you will disclose and when it is appropriate to do so. Although it may be new and uncomfortable for you to talk in personal ways to people whom you don't know that well, you can say more than you typically would in most social situations. You will need patience in learning this new communication skill and you will need to challenge yourself to reveal yourself in meaningful ways.

7. *Being direct.* You can adopt a direct style in your communication. You'll be more direct if you make "I" statements than if you say "you" when you really mean "I." For example, instead of saying "You can't trust people with what you feel, because they will let you down if you make yourself vulnerable," substitute "I" for "you." In this way, you take responsibility for your own statement. Similarly, it will help your communication if you make eye contact and speak directly *to* a person rather than *at* or *about* the person.

8. *Avoiding asking questions.* If you want to get the most from your interactions in class, don't adopt a style of asking questions of others. Continually asking questions can lead to a never-ending chain of "whys" and "becauses." Moreover, questioning can be a way of avoiding personal involvement; a question keeps the questioner safe, unknown, and hidden. Instead, we often urge people to reveal their personal reactions that led to the question. For example, behind "Why are you so quiet?" may lie any of the following statements: "I'm afraid of you, and I'd like to know what you think of me." "I don't know what's going on with you, and I'm interested." "I notice that you're not saying much, and I'm afraid you're judging me." "I'm aware that you've been quiet. When I'm quiet I'm usually afraid, and I wonder what you're thinking and feeling."

9. *Listening.* You can work on developing the skill of really listening to what others are saying without thinking of what you will say in reply. The first step in understanding what others say about you is to listen carefully, neither accepting what they say wholesale nor rejecting it outright. *Active listening* (really hearing the full message another is sending) requires remaining open and carefully considering what others say, instead of rushing to give reasons and explanations.

10. *Thinking for yourself.* Only you can make the choice whether to do your own thinking or to let others do your thinking and deciding for you. Many people seek counseling because they have lost the ability to find their own way and have become dependent on others to direct their life and take responsibility for their decisions. If you value thinking and deciding for yourself, it is important for you to realize that neither your fellow students nor your instructor can give you answers.

11. *Avoiding self-fulfilling prophecies.* You can increase your ability to change by letting go of ways in which you've categorized yourself or been categorized by others. If *you* start off with the assumption that you're stupid,

CHANGE THE WAY YOU SEE YOURSELF.

helpless, or boring, you'll probably convince others as well. For example, if you see yourself as boring, you'll probably present yourself in such a way that others will respond to you as a boring person. If you like the idea of changing some of the ways in which you see yourself and present yourself to others, you can experiment with going beyond some of your self-limiting labels. Allowing yourself to believe that a particular change is possible is a large part of experiencing that change. And once you experience *yourself* differently, others might experience you differently, too.

12. *Practicing outside of class.* One important way of getting the maximum benefit from a class dealing with personal learning is to think about ways of applying what you learn in class to your everyday life. You can make specific contracts with yourself (or with others) detailing what you're willing to do to experiment with new behavior and work toward the changes you want to make.

At this point it would be worthwhile to pause and assess your readiness for taking an honest look at yourself. Right now you may not feel motivated to examine the issues explored in the following chapters. You may feel that you don't need to explore these topics, or you may see yourself as being not quite ready. If you do feel some hesitation, leave the door open and give yourself and the course a chance. If you open yourself to change and try the techniques we've suggested, you may well experience a sense of excitement and promise.

How to Use This Book

This book was not written to tell you how you should be; rather, its purpose is to challenge you to think of how you want to be. Once you become aware of the ways in which you function, you will be in a position to decide what you want to do about yourself.

Many of the exercises, questions, and suggested activities will appeal differently to different readers. Considerations such as your age, life experiences, and cultural background will have a bearing on the meaning and importance of certain topics to you. We have written this book from our own cultural framework. Some of the points that we make may seem strange within your cultural context. Most of these topics, however, do seem to be personally significant to most readers, regardless of their background. In our workshops with people from various cultures, we continue to find that many of the issues we explore are common human themes that unite us in our life struggles and that transcend culture. Before you reject these ideas too quickly, reflect on ways that you might be able to adapt them to your own cultural background. We hope you'll treat this book in a personal way. Rather than merely reading it as you do any other text, attempt to apply it to yourself. With this in mind, here are some suggestions:

1. At the beginning of each subsequent chapter is a self-inventory. These inventories are designed to involve you personally with each subject. For the most part, they consist of personal statements to stimulate your thinking about the topics of discussion. We have resisted providing methods of rigidly diagnosing and neatly interpreting the meaning of your responses. There are no "universal norms" that you can compare yourself to on these inventories. Instead, you are encouraged to simply assess your attitudes and beliefs and think about aspects of your life that you might otherwise ignore. You may want to bring your responses to class and discuss your views or compare them with those of others. If you're reading this book alone, you may want to have a close friend or your mate answer some of the questions and react to the statements in the inventories. Doing this is a good way to stimulate meaningful dialogue with a person close to you. It could also be interesting for you to quickly take all of the prechapter self-inventories now and record your responses on a separate sheet. This is a useful means of assessing your current thinking on the topics to be covered. Then retake these inventories as you work through each chapter and compare your an-

swers with your previous responses. At the end of the semester you can look over the inventories and determine the degree to which you have changed your thinking on selected topics.

2. In one sense this is an *unfinished* book. You are challenged to become a co-author by completing the writing of this book in ways that are meaningful to you. In many of the chapters, examples are drawn from everyday life. You can extend the impact of these examples by thinking and writing about how they apply to you. Rather than reading simply to learn facts, take your own position on the issues raised. As much as possible, put yourself into what you read.

3. As you have seen, "Time Out" sections are inserted from time to time. Since these sections are designed to help you focus on specific topics, it will be most valuable if you do these exercises as you read. Actually writing down your responses in the text will help you begin to think about how each topic applies to you. Then you can look for common themes, go back to review your comments, or share them with a few friends or others in class. This process of reflecting and writing can help you get actively involved with the topics. Here again you have many opportunities to become a co-author in finishing this book.

4. At the end of each chapter are additional activities and exercises suggested for practice, both in class and out of class. Ultimately you will be the one to decide which activities you are willing to do. You may find some of the suggested exercises too threatening to do in a class with fifty other students, yet exploring the same activities in a small group in your class could be easier. If small discussion groups are not a part of the structure of your class, consider doing the exercises alone or sharing them with a friend. Don't feel compelled to complete all the activities; select those that have the most meaning for you at this time in your life.

5. One activity we suggest throughout the book is keeping a journal. You might purchase a separate notebook in which to write your reactions. Later, you can look for patterns in your journal; doing so can help you identify some of your critical choices and areas of conflict. We frequently give concrete suggestions of things you might include in your journal, but the important thing is for you to decide what to put in and how to use it. Consider writing about some of the following topics:

- what I learned about others and myself through today's class session
- the topics that were of most interest to me (and why)
- the topics that held the least interest for me (and why)
- the topics I wanted to talk about
- the topics I avoided talking about
- particular sessions (or issues) in the chapter that had the greatest impact on me (and why)
- some of the things I am learning about myself in reading the book
- some specific things I am doing in everyday life as a result of this class

- some concrete changes in my attitudes, values, and behavior that I find myself most wanting to make
- what I am willing to do to make these changes
- some barriers I encounter in making the changes I want to make

It is best to write what first comes to your consciousness. Spontaneous reactions tend to tell you more about yourself than well-thought-out comments.

At this time we suggest that you do the exercise on writing your philosophy of life, which is at the end of Chapter Twelve. It would be good to at least write a rough draft of your life's philosophy early in the course and then to rewrite this exercise toward the end of the course.

Chapter Summary

We do not have to passively live out the plans that others have designed for us, but with awareness we can begin to make significant choices. Taking a stand in life by making choices can result in both gains and losses. Changing long-standing patterns is not easy, and there are many obstacles to overcome, yet a free life has many rewards.

One of these benefits is personal growth. Growth is a lifelong process of expanding our awareness and accepting new challenges. It does *not* mean disregard for others but, rather, implies fulfilling more of our potentials, including our ability to care for others. Four major figures who have made significant contributions to the concept of personal growth in a framework of humanistic psychology are Abraham Maslow, Carl Rogers, Carl Jung, and Alfred Adler. Perhaps the best way to conceptualize personal growth is by considering Maslow's ideal of *self-actualization*. Keep in mind that until our more basic needs have been met, we are not really much concerned about becoming a fully functioning person. If you are hungry or are living in the streets, you are not likely to reflect on the meaning of becoming an actualized individual. Remember also that self-actualization is not something that we do in isolation; rather, it is through meaningful relationships with others and through social interest that we discover and become the person we are capable of becoming. Paradoxically, we find ourselves when we are secure enough to go beyond preoccupation with our self-interest and become involved in the world with selected people. Striving for self-actualization does not cease at a particular age but is an ongoing process. Rather than speaking of *self-actualization* as a product that we attain, it is best to consider the process of becoming a *self-actualizing person*. Four basic characteristics of self-actualizing people are self-awareness, freedom, basic honesty and caring, and trust and autonomy. This course can be a first step on the journey toward achieving your personal goals and living a self-actualizing existence while at the same time contributing to making the world a better place.

Growing obviously entails learning. We've encouraged you to review your school experiences and to make an inventory of the ways in which your present attitudes toward learning have been influenced. Becoming aware of the effects that schooling has had on you gives you the power to choose a new learning style that will make a significant difference in your life and will involve both your thoughts and your feelings. A major purpose of this chapter has been to encourage you to examine your responsibility for making your learning meaningful. It's easy to criticize impersonal institutions if you feel apathetic about your learning. It's more difficult and more honest to look at *yourself* and ask such questions as: When I find myself in an exciting class, do I get fully involved and take advantage of the opportunity for learning? Do I expect instructors to entertain and *teach* me while I sit back passively? If I'm bored, what am I doing about it?

Even if your earlier educational experiences have taught you to be a passive learner and to avoid risks in your classes, awareness of this influence gives you the power to change your learning style. This chapter has invited you to decide how personal you want your learning to be in the course you're about to experience.

Activities and Exercises

1. The following are exercises that you can do at home. They are intended to help you focus on specific ways in which you behave. We've drawn the examples from typical fears and concerns often expressed by college

students. Study the situations by putting yourself in each one and decide how you might typically respond. Then keep an account in your journal of actual instances you encounter in your classes.

   a. *Situation:* You'd like to ask a question in class, but you're afraid that your question will sound dumb and that others will laugh.
      • *Issues:* Will you simply refrain from asking questions? If so, is this a pattern you care to continue? Are you willing to practice asking questions, even though you might experience some anxiety? What do you imagine will happen if you ask questions? What would you like to have happen?
   b. *Situation:* You feel that you have a problem concerning authority figures. You feel intimidated, afraid to venture your opinions, and even more afraid to register a point of view opposed to your instructor's.
      • *Issues:* Does this description fit you? If it does, do you want to change? Do you ever examine where you picked up your attitudes toward yourself in relation to authority? Do you think they're still appropriate for you?
   c. *Situation:* Your instructor seems genuinely interested in the students and the course, and she has extended herself by inviting you to come to her office if you have any problems with the course. You're having real difficulty grasping the material, and you're falling behind and doing poorly on the tests and assignments. Nevertheless, you keep putting off going to see the instructor to talk about your problems in the class.
      • *Issues:* Have you been in this situation before? If so, what kept you from talking with your instructor? If you find yourself in this kind of situation, are you willing to seek help before it's too late?

2. Review Maslow's characteristics of self-actualizing people. Then consider the following questions:

   a. To what degree are these characteristics a part of your personality?
   b. Do you think that Maslow's ideal of self-actualization fits for individuals of all cultural and ethnic groups? Are there any characteristics that are not appropriate for certain cultures?

3. In keeping with the spirit of developing active learning habits, we suggest that you tackle your reading assignments systematically. A useful approach is Robinson's (1970) SQ3R technique (*survey, question, read, recite, review*). It is intended to get you actively involved with what you are reading. The technique does not have to be applied rigidly; in fact, you can develop your own way of carrying it out. This five-step method involves breaking a reading assignment down into manageable units and checking your understanding of what you are reading. The steps are as follows:

   a. *Step 1: Survey.* Rather than simply reading a chapter, begin by skimming it to get a general overview of the material. Look for ways in which the topics are interrelated, strive to understand the organization of the chapter, and give some preliminary thought to the information you are about to read.

b. *Step 2: Question.* Once you get the general plan of the chapter, look at the main chapter headings. What questions do they raise that your reading of the chapter should answer? Formulate in your own words the questions that you would like to explore as you read.

c. *Step 3: Read.* After skimming the chapter and raising key questions, proceed to read one section at a time with the goal of answering your questions. After you've finished a section, pause for a few moments and reflect on what you've read to determine if you can clearly address the questions you've raised.

d. *Step 4: Recite.* In your own words, recite (preferably out loud) the answers to your questions. Avoid rote memorization. Attempt to give meaning to factual material. Make sure that you understand the basic ideas in a section before you go on to the next section. Writing down a few key notes is a good way to have a record for your review later. Then go on to the next section of the chapter, repeating steps 3 and 4.

e. *Step 4: Review.* After you finish reading the chapter, spend some time reviewing the main points. Test your understanding of the material by putting the major ideas into your own words. Repeat the questions, and attempt to answer them without looking at the book. If there is a chapter summary or listing of key terms, be sure to study this carefully. A good summary will help you put the chapter into context. Attempt to add to the summary by listing some of the points that seem particularly important or interesting to you.

4. At the end of each chapter, we identify a few sources of further reading on the topics addressed by each chapter. For a full bibliographic reference for each book, consult "References and Suggested Readings" at the end of this book. For this chapter we highly recommend the following: Peck, *The Different Drum: Community Making and Peace* (1987); Maslow, *Motivation and Personality* (1970); Rogers, *Freedom to Learn for the 80's* (1983).

CHAPTER TWO

Reviewing Your Childhood and Adolescence

Prechapter Self-Inventory

Use the following scale to respond: 4 = this statement is true of me *most* of the time; 3 = this statement is true of me *much* of the time; 2 = this statement is true of me *some* of the time; 1 = this statement is true of me *almost none* of the time.

_____ 1. I'm capable of looking at my past decisions and then making new decisions that will significantly change the course of my life.

_____ 2. "Shoulds" and "oughts" often get in the way of my living my life the way I want.

_____ 3. To a large degree I've been shaped by the events of my childhood and adolescent years.

_____ 4. When I think of my early childhood years, I remember feeling secure, accepted, and loved.

_____ 5. As a child I was taught not to express negative feelings such as rage, anger, hatred, jealousy, and aggression.

_____ 6. I had desirable models to pattern my behavior after when I was a child and an adolescent.

_____ 7. In looking back at my early school-age years, I think that I had a positive self-concept and that I experienced more successes than failures.

_____ 8. I went through a stage of rebellion during my adolescent years.

_____ 9. My adolescent years were lonely ones.

_____ 10. I remember being significantly influenced by peer-group pressure during my adolescence.

Here are a few suggestions for using this self-inventory:

• Retake the inventory after reading the chapter and again at the end of the course, and compare your answers.
• Have someone who knows you well take the inventory for you, giving the responses he or she thinks actually describe you. Then you can discuss any discrepancies between your sets of responses.
• In your class, compare your responses with those of the other members, and discuss the similarities and differences between your attitudes and theirs.

Introduction

As you'll recall from the previous chapter, becoming a fully functioning person can be done only in the context of relationships with others and concern for their welfare. This chapter and the next one lay the groundwork for much of the rest of the book by focusing on our lifelong struggle to achieve psychological emancipation, or autonomy. The term *autonomy* refers to a mature independence *and* interdependence. The autonomous person is able to function without constant approval and reassurance, is sensitive to the needs of others, can effectively meet the demands of daily living, is willing to ask for help when it is needed, and can provide support to others. In essence, autonomy is the ability both to stand alone and to stand by another person. Autonomous individuals are at home with both their inner world and their outer world. Although they are concerned with meeting their needs, they do not do so at the expense of those around them. They are aware of the impact of their behavior on others, and they consider the welfare of others as well as their own self-development. Achieving personal autonomy is a continuing process of growth and learning, not something we arrive at once and for all.

Our attitudes toward our gender-role identity, work, our body, love, sexuality, intimacy, loneliness, death, and meaning—the themes we'll be discussing in future chapters—are largely shaped by our experiences and decisions during our early years. Each period of life has its own challenges and meanings, however, and we continue to develop and change, ideally in the direction of autonomy. Before going on to discuss these specific themes, therefore, we want to look at the developmental stages that make up a complete human life. This chapter will deal with the stages from infancy through adolescence; in Chapter Three we will take up early, middle, and late adulthood.

Stages of Personality Development: A Preview

Much of this chapter describes a model that draws on Erik Erikson's (1963, 1982) theory of human development, and it highlights some major ideas about development from a Freudian psychoanalytic perspective. The father of psychoanalysis, Sigmund Freud, developed one of the most comprehensive theories of personality. He emphasized unconscious psychological processes and stressed the importance of early childhood experiences. According to his viewpoint, our sexual and social development is largely based on the first six years of life. During this time, he maintained, we go through three stages (oral, anal, and phallic). Our later personality development hinges on how well we have resolved the demands and conflicts of each stage. Most of the problems that people wrestle with in adulthood seem to have some relationship to unresolved conflicts dating from their early childhood.

As you will see, Freud developed a model for understanding early development, especially its psychosexual aspects. Erikson built on and extended

ERIKSON'S 8 CRITICAL STAGES OF LIFELONG DEVELOPMENT.

Freud's ideas by stressing the psychosocial aspects of development and by carrying his own developmental theory beyond childhood. Although intellectually indebted to Freud, Erikson suggested that we should view human development in a more positive light, focusing on health and growth. Erikson also emphasized the rational side of human nature, whereas Freud emphasized the irrational aspects of development. Another area of divergence between Erikson's and Freud's perspectives is that psychosocial theory maintains that the ego, not the id, is the life force of human development (Erikson, 1963). (The id is the part of the personality that seeks immediate gratification; the ego is the component of the self that is in contact with the outside world through cognitive processes such as thinking, perceiving, remembering, reasoning, and attending.) Erikson's theory focuses on the emergence of the self and the ways in which the self develops through our interaction with our social and cultural environment. Later in this chapter we go into more detail about the developing of and protecting of the self-concept.

Erikson's theory of development holds that psychosexual and psycho-social growth occur together and that at each stage of life we face the task of establishing an equilibrium between ourselves and our social world. Psycho-social theory stresses the integration of the biological, psychological, and social aspects of development. A combination of the Freudian psychosexual view and this psychosocial view of development provides the conceptual framework required for understanding trends in development; major developmental tasks at each stage of life; critical needs and their satisfaction or frustration; potentials for choice at each stage of life; critical turning points, or developmental crises; and the origins of faulty personality development, which leads to later personality conflicts.

Erikson described human development over the entire life span in terms of eight stages, each marked by a particular crisis to be resolved. You may think of a crisis as a gigantic problem or catastrophic happening. But for Erikson, *crisis* meant a *turning point* in life, a moment of transition characterized by the potential to go either forward or backward in development. At these turning points we can achieve successful resolution of our conflicts and move ahead, or we can fail to resolve the conflicts and regress. To a large extent our life is the result of the choices we make at each stage.

By getting a picture of the challenges at each period of life, we will be able to understand how earlier stages of personality development influence choices that we make later in life. These stages are not precise categories that people fall into neatly. In reality there is great variability among individuals within a given developmental phase. For example, although there are general developmental tasks and problems associated with adolescence, each adolescent reacts to the challenges of this period uniquely. The important point is that there is continuity in life. Our childhood experiences have a direct impact on how we approach the adolescent years. How well we master the tasks of adolescence has a bearing on our ability to cope with the critical turning points of adulthood. If we do not develop a clear sense of identity during adolescence, for example, then finding meaning in adult life becomes extremely difficult. As we progress from one stage of life to the next, we at times meet with roadblocks and detours. These barriers are often the result of having failed to master basic psychological competencies at an earlier period.

Although the life-span perspective presented in these two chapters relies heavily on concepts borrowed from Freud's and Erikson's theories, we also draw on ideas from other writers who describe crises as individuals pass through life's stages: Berne (1975), Elkind (1984), Gould (1978), Mary and Robert Goulding (1978, 1979), Hamacheck (1988, 1990), Havighurst (1972), Ivey (1990), Sheehy (1976, 1981), and Steiner (1975). Table 2-1 gives you an overview of the major turning points in the life-span perspective of human development.

TABLE 2-1   Overview of Developmental Stages

Life Stage	Freud's Psychosexual View	Erikson's Psychosocial View	Potential Problems
Infancy (1st year of life)	*Oral stage.* Most critical stage in terms of later development. Failure to have one's need for basic nurturing met may lead to greediness later on. Material things may become a substitute for love. Infant's nursing satisfies the need for both food and pleasure.	*Infancy.* Basic task is to develop a sense of trust in self, others, and the environment. Infants need a sense of being cared for and loved. Absence of a sense of security may lead to suspiciousness and a general sense of mistrust toward human relationships. Core struggle: *trust* versus *mistrust*.	Later personality problems that stem from infancy can include greediness and acquisitiveness, the development of a view of the world based on mistrust, fear of reaching out to others, rejection of affection, fear of loving and trusting, low self-esteem, isolation and withdrawal, and inability to form or maintain intimate relationships.
Early childhood (ages 1–3)	*Anal stage.* Child experiences parental demands and faces frustration. Toilet training is first experience with discipline. Attitudes toward body and bodily functions are direct results of this period. Problems in adulthood such as compulsive orderliness or messiness may stem from parental disciplinary practice.	*Early childhood.* A time for developing autonomy. Failure to master self-control tasks may lead to shame and doubt about oneself and one's adequacy. Core struggle: *self-reliance* versus *self-doubt*.	Children experience many negative feelings such as hostility, rage, destructiveness, anger, and hatred. If these feelings are not accepted, individuals may not be able to accept their feelings later on.
Preschool age (ages 3–6)	*Phallic stage.* Gender-role identity is a key issue. Child's interest in sexual matters increases; sexual attitudes are formed. Sexual dysfunctions in adulthood often have their roots in early conditioning and experiences.	*Preschool age.* Characterized by play and by anticipation of roles; a time to establish a sense of competence and initiative. Children who are not allowed to make decisions tend to develop a sense of guilt. Core struggle: *initiative* versus *guilt*.	Parental attitudes can be communicated verbally and nonverbally. Negative learning experiences tend to lead to feelings of guilt about natural impulses. Strict parental indoctrination can lead to rigidity, severe conflicts, remorse, and self-condemnation.

(continued) |

TABLE 2-1   Overview of Developmental Stages *(continued)*

Life Stage	Freud's Psychosexual View	Erikson's Psychosocial View	Potential Problems
Middle childhood (ages 6–12)	*Latency stage.* Socialization takes place as children turn outward toward relationships with others. New interests emerge: school, playmates, sports, books. The sexual impulses are relatively quiescent, and social interests become prominent.	*School age.* Central task is to achieve a sense of industry; failure to do so results in a sense of inadequacy. Child needs to expand understanding of the world and continue to develop appropriate gender-role identity. Learning basic skills is essential for school success. Core struggle: *industry* versus *inferiority.*	Problems that can originate during middle childhood include negative self-concept, feelings of inferiority in establishing social relationships, conflicts over values, confused gender-role identity, dependency, fear of new challenges, and lack of initiative.
Adolescence (ages 12–18)	*Genital stage.* Old themes of phallic stage are revived. Interest develops in opposite sex, with some sexual experimentation. Genital stage is the longest, beginning at puberty and lasting until later adulthood. In face of social restrictions and taboos, adolescents can redirect sexual energy by engaging in socially acceptable activities.	*Adolescence.* A critical time for forming a personal identity. Major conflicts center on clarification of self-identity, life goals, and life's meaning. Struggle is over integrating physical and social changes. Pressures include succeeding in school, choosing a job, forming relationships, and preparing for future. Core struggle: *identity* versus *role confusion.*	A time when individual may anticipate an *identity crisis.* Caught in midst of pressures, demands, and turmoil, adolescent often loses sense of self. If *role confusion* results, individual may lack sense of purpose in later years. Absence of a stable set of values can prevent mature development of a philosophy to guide one's life.
Early adulthood (ages 18–35)	*Genital stage* (continues). Core characteristic of mature adult is the freedom "to love and to work." The move toward adulthood involves developing intimacy, freedom from parental influence, and capacity to care for others.	*Young adulthood.* Sense of identity is again tested by the challenge of achieving intimacy. Ability to form close relationships depends on having a clear sense of self. Core struggle: *intimacy* versus *isolation.*	The challenge of this period is to maintain one's separateness while becoming attached to others. Failing to strike a balance leads to self-centeredness or to exclusive focus on needs of others. Failure to achieve intimacy can lead to alienation and isolation.

TABLE 2-1 Overview of Developmental Stages *(continued)*

Life Stage	Freud's Psychosexual View	Erikson's Psychosocial View	Potential Problems
Middle adulthood (ages 35–60)	*Genital stage* (continues).	*Middle age.* Individuals become more aware of their eventual death and begin to question whether they are living well. The crossroads of life; a time for reevaluation. Core struggle: *generativity* versus *stagnation*.	Failure to achieve a sense of productivity can lead to stagnation. Pain can result when individuals recognize the gap between their dreams and what they have achieved.
Late adulthood (age 60 onward)	*Genital stage* (continues).	*Later life.* Ego integrity is achieved by those who have few regrets, who see themselves as living a productive life, and who have coped with both successes and failures. Key tasks are to adjust to losses, death of others, maintaining outside interests, and adjusting to retirement. Core struggle: *integrity* versus *despair*.	Failure to achieve ego integrity often leads to feelings of hopelessness, guilt, resentment, and self-rejection. Unfinished business from earlier years can lead to fears of death stemming from sense that life has been wasted.

Infancy

Developmental psychologists contend that a child's basic task in the first year of life is to develop a sense of trust in self, others, and the environment. Infants need to count on others; they need to sense that they are cared for and loved and that the world is a secure place. They learn this sense of trust by being held, caressed, and taken care of.

Erikson asserted that infants form a basic conception of the social world. He saw their core struggle as *trust* versus *mistrust*. If the significant other persons in an infant's life provide the needed warmth, cuddling, and attention, the child develops a sense of trust. When these conditions are not present, the child becomes suspicious about interacting with others and acquires a general sense of mistrust toward human relationships. Although neither orientation is fixed to one's personality for life, it is clear that well-nurtured infants are in a more favorable position with respect to future personal growth than are their more neglected peers.

A sense of being loved is also the best safeguard against fear, insecurity, and inadequacy. Children who receive love from parents or parental substitutes generally have little difficulty accepting themselves, whereas children who feel unloved and unwanted may find it very hard to accept themselves. In addition, rejected children learn to mistrust the world and to view it primarily in terms of its ability to do them harm. Some of the effects of rejection in infancy include tendencies in later childhood to be fearful, insecure, jealous, aggressive, hostile, and isolated.

At times parents are unduly anxious over wanting to be the perfect mother and father. They spend much time worrying about "doing the right thing at the right time," and they hope to have the "perfectly well-adjusted child." The parents' chronic anxiety can be the very thing that causes difficulties for their sons and daughters, who will soon sense that they must be "perfect children." Children can and do survive "mistakes" that all parents make. When we talk about long-lasting negative effects, what we are talking about is the effect of chronic neglect or chronic overprotection.

According to the Freudian psychoanalytic view, the events of the first year of life are extremely important for later development and adjustment. Infants whose basic needs for nurturing are not met during this time (known as the *oral stage*) may develop greediness and acquisitiveness in later life. Material things thus become substitutes for what the children really want—love and attention from parents. For instance, a person whose oral needs are unmet may become a compulsive eater, in which case food becomes a symbol for love. Other personality problems that might stem from this period include a mistrustful and suspicious view of the world, a tendency to reject affection from others, an inability to form intimate relationships, a fear of loving and trusting, and feelings of isolation.

According to psychoanalytic theorists, we experience a number of critical conflicts before we begin school, and we are presented with several developmental tasks. One task is to develop a sense of trust in the world, which requires that we feel loved and accepted. If love is absent, we will suffer during later years from an inability to trust ourselves and others, a fear of loving and becoming intimate, and low self-esteem. This does not mean that we're doomed if we didn't get our quota of love. Many people reexperience their childhood feelings of hurt and rejection through some form of counseling; in this way, they come to understand that even though they did not feel loved by their parents, this doesn't mean that they are unlovable or that others find them unlovable now.

The case of 9-year-old Joey, the "mechanical boy" described by Bettelheim in *The Empty Fortress* (1967), is a dramatic illustration of how the pain of extreme rejection during infancy can affect us later on. When Joey first went to Bettelheim's school, he seemed devoid of any feeling. He thought of himself as functioning by remote control, with the help of an elaborate system of machines. He had to have his "carburetor" to breathe, "exhaust pipes" to exhale from, and a complex system of wires and motors in order to move. His delusion was so convincing that the staff members at the school sometimes found themselves taking care to be sure that Joey was plugged in properly and that they didn't step on any of his wires.

Neither Joey's father nor his mother had been prepared for his birth, and they related to him as a thing, not a person. His mother simply ignored him; she reported that she had no feeling of dislike toward him but that "I simply did not want to take care of him." He was a difficult baby who cried most of the time, and he was kept on a rigid schedule. He wasn't touched unless necessary, and he wasn't cuddled or played with. Joey developed more and more unusual symptoms, such as head banging, rocking, and a morbid fascination with machines. Evidently, he discovered that machines were better than people; they didn't hurt you, and they could be shut off. During years of intense treatment with Bettelheim, Joey gradually learned how to trust, and he also learned that feelings are real and that it can be worth it to feel.

Another case that illustrates the possible effects of severe deprivation during the early developmental years is that of Sally, who is now in her 40s. She was given up by her natural parents and spent the first decade of her life in orphanages and foster homes. She recalls pleading with one set of foster parents who had kept her for over a year and then said that they had to send her away. As a child Sally came to the conclusion that she was at fault; if her own parents didn't want her, who could? She spent years trying to figure out what she had done wrong and why so many people always "sent her away."

As an adult Sally still yearns for what she missed during infancy and childhood. Thus, she has never really attained maturity; socially and emotionally, she is much like a child. She has never allowed herself to get close to anyone, for she fears that they will leave if she does. As a child she learned to isolate herself emotionally in order to survive; now she still operates on the assumptions that she had as a child. Because of her fear of being deserted, she won't allow herself to venture out and take even minimal risks.

Sally is not unusual. We have worked with a number of individuals who suffer from the effects of early psychological deprivation, and we have observed that in most cases such deprivation has lingering adverse effects on a person's ability to form meaningful relationships later in life. Many people — of all ages — struggle with the issue of trusting others in a loving relationship. They are unable to trust that another can or will love them, they fear being rejected, and they fear even more the possibility of closeness and being accepted and loved. Many of these people don't trust themselves or others sufficiently to make themselves vulnerable enough to experience love.

At this point, you might pause to ask yourself these questions:

• Am I able to trust others? myself?
• Am I willing to open myself — to make myself known to a few selected people in my life?

- Do I basically accept myself as being OK, or do I seek confirmation outside of myself? Am I hungry for approval from others? How far will I go in my attempt to be liked? Do I need to be liked and approved of by everyone? Do I dare make enemies, or must I be "nice" to everyone?
- Am I in any way like Sally? Do I know of anyone who has had experiences similar to hers?

Early Childhood

Freud called ages 1–3 the *anal stage*. The tasks that children must master at this time include learning independence, accepting personal power, and learning to cope with negative feelings such as rage and aggression. Their most critical task is to begin the journey toward autonomy by progressing from being taken care of by others to meeting some of their own physical needs.

In this second stage, children begin to communicate what they want from others. They also face continual parental demands. For instance, they are restricted somewhat from physically exploring their environment, they begin to be disciplined, and they have toilet training imposed on them. According to the Freudian view, parental feelings and attitudes associated with toilet training are highly significant for their children's later personality development. Thus, problems in adulthood such as compulsive orderliness or messiness may be due to parental attitudes during this time. For instance, a father who insists that his son be unrealistically clean may find that the son develops into a sloppy person as a reaction — or that he becomes even more compulsively clean.

Erikson identified the core struggle of early childhood as *autonomy* versus *shame* and *doubt*. Children who fail to master the task of establishing some control over themselves and coping with the world around them develop a sense of shame, and they doubt their capabilities. Erikson emphasized that during this time children become aware of their emerging skills and have a drive to try them out. To illustrate this point, I (Marianne) remember when I was feeding one of our daughters during her infancy. Up to this point Heidi had been a very agreeable child who swallowed all of the food that I put into her mouth. One day, much to my surprise, she spit it right back at me! No matter how much I wanted her to continue eating, she refused. This was one way in which Heidi began asserting herself with me. As my children were growing up, I strove to establish a good balance between allowing them to develop their own identity and at the same time providing them with guidance and appropriate limits.

Parents who squelch any emerging individuality and who do too much for their children hamper their proper development. They are saying, however indirectly, "Let us do this for you, because you're too clumsy, too slow, or

too inept to do things for yourself." Young children need to experiment; they need to be allowed to make mistakes and still feel that they are basically worthwhile. If parents insist on keeping their children dependent on them, the children will begin to doubt their own abilities. If parents don't appreciate their children's efforts, the children may feel ashamed of themselves or become insecure and fearful.

Sometimes children may want to do more than they are capable of doing at their age. For example, the 5-year-old son of a friend of ours went on a hike with his father. At one point the boy asked his father to let him carry a heavy backpack the way the "big people" do. Without saying a word, the father took his backpack off and handed it to his son, who immediately discovered that it was too heavy for him to carry. The boy simply exclaimed, "Dad, it's too heavy for me." He then went happily on his way up the trail. In a safe way the father had allowed his son to discover experientially that he was, indeed, too small. He had also avoided a potential argument with his son.

Young children also must learn to accept the full range of their feelings. They will surely experience rage, hatred, hostility, destructiveness, and ambivalence, and they need to feel that such feelings are permissible and that they aren't evil for having them. Of course, they also need to learn how to express their feelings in constructive ways. In *The Angry Book* Theodore Isaac Rubin (1969) contends that a healthy environment is one in which all emotions, especially anger, are allowed expression. It is important for children to learn that it is acceptable to feel anger and to express it. During early childhood they need to feel loved and accepted with all of their feelings; otherwise they will tend to stifle their anger so as not to lose the love of their parents. According to Rubin, most of us become victims of victims and thus are afraid to express anger. We are ruled by injunctions (messages received from parents) such as "If you get angry, I'll know you don't love me." Our childhood follows us into adulthood, for we can allow only "acceptable" feelings. We learn early to seek universal love and acceptance, and anger is a threat to getting what we want. Often we learn to become "nice guys" by playing a role in early childhood. Yet we pay a steep price for blocking off anger, says Rubin. If we seal off anger, we also manage to destroy that which we most want—love. If patterns of denying anger begin in early childhood, we become the victims of perverted anger. Rubin describes the process of pushing anger into a slush fund, which eventually poisons our system. When our anger cannot be acknowledged or expressed, it becomes toxic and it finds expression in a number of indirect ways (which Rubin describes in detail in his book). One of the results of denying anger is that children begin to numb all of their feelings, including the positive ones such as joy.

In many ways, then, early childhood is a time when we struggle between a sense of self-reliance and a sense of self-doubt. Many people seek professional help precisely because they have a low level of autonomy. They doubt their ability to stand alone, so they depend on others to do for them things they could do for themselves. This applies particularly to some marriages; some people marry so that they will have a mother figure or a father figure to protect them and take care of their needs. Similarly, many of us have grave difficulty in recognizing our anger, even when it is fully justified. We swallow our anger and rationalize away other feelings, because we learned when we were 2 or 3 years old that we were unacceptable when we had such feelings. As children we might have shouted at our parents: "I hate you! I never want to see you again!" Then we may have heard an equally enraged parent reply: "How dare you say such a thing—after all I've done for you! I don't ever want to hear that from you again!" We soon take these messages to mean "Don't be angry! Never be angry with those you love! Keep control of yourself!" And we do just that—keeping many of our feelings to ourselves, stuffing them in the pit of our stomach and pretending we don't experience them. It is not surprising that so many of us suffer from migraine headaches, peptic ulcers, hypertension, and heart disease.

Again, take time out to reflect in a personal way on some of your current struggles in the area of autonomy and self-worth. You might ask yourself:

+ Am I able to recognize my own feelings, particularly if they are "unacceptable" to others? How do I express my anger to those I love? Can I tolerate the ambivalence of feeling love and hate toward the same person?
+ Have I established a good balance between depending on others and relying on myself?
+ Am I able to let others know what I want? Can I be assertive without being aggressive?

The Preschool Years

The preschool years (ages 3–6) are characterized by play and by anticipation of roles. During this time children seek to find out how much they can do. They imitate others; they begin to develop a sense of right and wrong; they widen their circle of significant persons; they take more initiative; they learn to give and receive love and affection; they identify with their own gender; they begin to learn more complex social skills; they learn basic attitudes regarding sexuality; and they increase their capacity to understand and use language.

According to Erikson, the basic task of the preschool years is to establish a sense of competence and initiative. The core struggle is between *initiative* and *guilt*. Preschool children begin to initiate many of their own activities as they become physically and psychologically ready to engage in pursuits of their own choosing. If they are allowed realistic freedom to make some of their own decisions, they tend to develop a positive orientation characterized by confidence in their ability to initiate and follow through. If they are unduly restricted or if their choices are ridiculed, however, they tend to experience a sense of guilt and ultimately to withdraw from taking an active stance. For example, one middle-aged woman still finds herself extremely vulnerable to being seen as foolish. She recalls that during her childhood, family members laughed at her attempts to perform certain tasks. Even now she very vividly carries these pictures in her head and allows them to have some control of her life.

In Freudian theory this is the *phallic stage*, during which children become increasingly interested in sexual matters and begin to acquire a clearer sense of gender-role identity. Before children enter school, they begin to decide how they feel about themselves in their roles as boys and girls. Children exhibit a natural curiosity about sexual matters, and very early in life they form attitudes toward their sexuality and sexual feelings, their bodies, and what they think is right and wrong. Many adults suffer from deep feelings of guilt concerning sexual pleasure or desires. Some have learned that their sexual organs are disgusting; others have traumatic memories associated with sexual intercourse. Much sexual dysfunctioning in adulthood has its roots in early conditioning and experiences. Preschool children begin to pay attention to their genitals and experience pleasure from genital stimulation. They typically engage in both masturbatory and sex-play activities. They begin to show considerable curiosity about the differences between the sexes and the differences between adults and children. This is the time for questions such as "Where do babies come from?" and "Why are boys and girls different?" Parental attitudes toward these questions, which can be communicated nonverbally as well as verbally, are critical in helping children form a positive attitude toward their own sexuality. Since this is a time for conscience formation, one danger is that parents may instill rigid and unrealistic moral standards, which can lead to an overdeveloped conscience. Children who learn that their bodies and their impulses are evil soon begin to feel guilty about them. Carried into adult life, these attitudes can prevent people from appreciating and enjoying sexual intimacy. Another danger is that strict parental indoctrination, which can be accomplished in subtle, nonverbal ways, will lead to an infantile conscience. Children may thus develop a fear of questioning and thinking for themselves, instead blindly accepting the dictates of their parents. Other effects of such indoctrination include rigidity, severe conflicts, guilt, remorse, and self-condemnation.

Children need adequate models if they are to accept their sexual feelings as natural and develop a healthy concept of their body and their gender-role identity. In addition to forming attitudes toward their body and sexuality, they begin to formulate their conceptions of what it means to be feminine or masculine. By simply being with their parents, they are getting some perspective on the way men and women relate to one another, and they are acquiring basic attitudes toward such relationships. They are also deciding how they feel about themselves in their roles as boys and girls. Their learning and decisions during the phallic stage pave the way for the ability to accept themselves as men or women in adulthood. This topic of gender-role identity is developed in depth in Chapter Four.

Pause and reflect on some of your own current struggles with these issues.

• What did you learn from your culture about the way to behave as a woman or a man? What are your standards of femininity or masculinity? Where did you get them?
• Are you comfortable with your own sexuality? with your body? Are there any unresolved conflicts from your childhood that get in the way of your enjoyment? Do your present behavior and current conflicts indicate areas of unfinished business?

The Impact of the First Six Years of Life

In describing the events of the first six years of life, we have relied rather heavily on the psychoanalytic view of psychosexual and psychosocial development, as originally formulated by Freud and later modified by Erikson. You may be asking why we are giving so much emphasis to the events of this period. In working with clients, we continue to realize the influence of these early years on our levels of integration and functioning as adults. Sometimes people ask: "Why look back into my past? I don't see any point in dredging up that painful period, especially since I've worked so hard to get that part of my life under control." Our point is that many of their childhood experiences have a profound impact on both their present and their future.

If during the first six years we reached faulty conclusions based on our life experience, we are likely to still be operating on the basis of them. If we told ourselves as a child that "I can never do enough for my father," we may find that we often feel today that we can never do enough (or be enough) to meet the expectations of those who are significant in our lives. Not only is our current functioning shaped by early interpretations, but our future is, too. Our goals and purposes have some connection with the way we dealt with the issues during the first six years of life. Consider Marty's case. People told Marty as a child that she couldn't do much and therefore shouldn't waste time striving. It would be best if she were simply to be satisfied with what she had. However, she challenged these messages and was intent on proving them wrong. In fact, much of what she does can be understood as attempts to prove that she can do what others were convinced she could never do.

In his book *Making Peace with Yourself*, Bloomfield (1985) writes about personal vulnerabilities and weaknesses, originating during our early years, which he refers to as our *Achilles heel*. Bloomfield believes that each of us has at least one Achilles heel that regularly trips us up. He stresses that if we ignore, suppress, or deny it, it will reappear unexpectedly. Furthermore, a powerful psychological principle is "What we resist persists." The *Achilles syndrome* is the price that we pay for resisting our Archilles heel, and it can manifest itself in many ways. For example, if your Archilles heel is a fear of being rejected in love relationships and ending up a loner, you may avoid becoming intimate with others, and the result is that you wind up alone. If Bloomfield's principle is correct, we do not gain in the long run by hiding and denying our personal vulnerabilities. By refusing to acknowledge our Achilles heel, we actually remain controlled by past weaknesses and insecurities.

This concept of the Achilles heel is similar to Jung's concept of the *shadow* side of personality, which is thought to contain the basic and primitive instincts. Known as our *dark side*, the shadow does need to be understood and restrained. Yet it is a mistake to view this only as our evil side, and even a greater mistake to deny this aspect of our being. The shadow side also is the source of our spontaneity and vitality, and if it is not recognized, our personality becomes dull and lifeless. Furthermore, if we deny this facet, we become controlled by our unconscious material. Paradoxically, if we strive to conquer something inside of us, the very thing conquers us. Simply understanding the many complexities within us, including all of our vulnerabilities, is a source of strength that can lead to wholeness.

In working in personal-growth groups with relatively well-functioning adults who have "normal" developmental issues, we find that a new understanding of their early years often entails a certain degree of emotional pain. Yet by understanding these painful events, they have a basis for transcending them and not being stuck with replaying old self-defeating themes throughout their lifetimes. We don't think that healthy people are ever really "cured" of their Achilles heel or their shadow. For example, if during your preschool years you felt abandoned by the divorce of your parents, you are still likely to have vestiges of fears and hesitations in forming close relationships. Yet you do not have to surrender to these traces of mistrust. Instead, you can gain control of your fears of loving and trusting.

In reviewing your childhood, you may well find some aspects that you like and do not want to change. You may also find a certain continuity in your life that gives you meaning. At the same time, if you are honest with yourself, you are likely to become aware of certain revisions that you would like to make. With this awareness comes the first critical step toward changing.

When we consider the most typical problems and conflicts that we encounter in people in our personal-growth groups, the following areas come to mind: inability to trust oneself and others; inability to freely accept and give love; difficulty in recognizing and expressing the full range of one's feelings; guilt over feelings of anger or hatred toward those one loves; inability or unwillingness to control one's own life; difficulties in fully accepting one's sexuality or in finding meaning in sexual intimacy; difficulty in accepting oneself as a woman or a man; and problems concerning a lack of meaning or purpose in life or a clear sense of personal identity and aspirations. Notice that most of these adult problems are directly related to the turning points and tasks of the early developmental years. The effects of early learning are reversible in most cases, but these experiences, whether favorable or unfavorable, clearly influence how we relate to future critical periods in our lives.

Some people learn new values, come to accept new feelings and attitudes, and overcome much of their past negative conditioning. In contrast, other people steadfastly hang on to the past as an excuse for not taking any action to change in the present. We can't change in a positive direction unless we stop blaming others for the way we are now. Statements that begin "If it hadn't been for . . . ," are too often used to justify an immobile position. For example: "If it hadn't been for the fact that I was adopted and had several foster parents, I'd be able to feel loved now, and I wouldn't be stuck with feelings of abandonment." "If only my parents had done more for me, I could feel a sense of security and trust." "If only my parents had done less for me, I could have grown up independent." "If only my parents had given me a healthy outlook on sex, I wouldn't feel so guilty now about my sexual feelings." Blaming others for our present shortcomings ultimately keeps us trapped and in a position of waiting for "them out there" to change before we can change. Whenever we catch ourselves pointing an accusing finger at someone else, it is a good idea to look at our other fingers that are pointing back to ourselves. Once we are able to see in ourselves the very traits that we accuse others of, and once we suspend a blaming stance, then we make it possible to reclaim responsibility for ourselves, and thus make it possible to take charge of our own lives.

A relevant case is that of Bryan, who used to blame his mother for everything. Because she had dominated his father, he felt that he could not trust any woman now. If he couldn't trust his own mother, he reasoned, then whom could he trust? At 25 he saw himself as fearing independence, and he blamed his mother for his fear. He refused to date, and he tried to convince himself that he did so because his mother had "messed up my life by making me afraid." He continually wanted to use his therapy sessions to dwell on the past and blame his present problems on what his parents had and hadn't done. Through counseling he became aware that his dwelling on his past and his focusing on others were ways in which he was avoiding assuming responsibility for his own life. After actively questioning some of his beliefs about women and about himself, Bryan decided that not all women were like his mother, that he didn't have to respond to women in the way his father had, and that he could change his life now if he was willing to accept the responsibility for doing so.

It may often be important to go through a stage of experiencing anger and hurt for having been cheated in the past, but it is imperative that we eventually claim for ourselves the power we have been giving to the people who were once significant in our lives. Unless we recognize and exercise the power we now have to take care of ourselves, we close the door to new choices and new growth.

Time Out for Personal Reflection

1. Close your eyes and reflect for a moment on your memories of your first six years. Attempt to identify your earliest concrete single memory — something that you actually remember that happened to you, not something that you were told about. Spend a few minutes recalling the details and reexperiencing the feelings associated with this early event.

   a. Write down your earliest recollection: _____

   _____

   _____

   _____

   _____

   b. Do you have any hunches about how this early memory may still be having an impact on the way you think, feel, and behave today?

   _____

   _____

   _____

   _____

2. Reflect on the events that most stand out for you during your first six years of life. In particular, think about your place in your family, your family's reaction to you, and your reactions to each person in your family. What connections do you see between how it felt to be in your family as a child and how you now feel in various social situations? What speculations do you have concerning the impact your family had then and the effect that these experiences continue to have on your current personality?

   _____

   _____

   _____

   _____

   _____

3. Take the following self-inventory. Respond quickly, marking "T" if you believe the statement is more true than false for you as a young child and "F" if it tends not to fit your early childhood experiences.

_____   As a young child I felt loved and accepted.
_____   I basically trusted the world.
_____   I felt that I was an acceptable and valuable person.
_____   I didn't need to work for others' approval.
_____   I didn't experience a great deal of shame and self-doubt as a child.
_____   I felt that it was OK for me to express anger.
_____   My parents trusted my ability to do things for myself.
_____   I believe that I developed a natural and healthy concept of my body and my gender-role identity.
_____   I had friends as a young child.
_____   I felt that I could talk to my parents about my problems.

Look over your responses. What do they tell you about the person you now are? If you could live your childhood over again, how would you like it to be? Record some of your impressions in your journal.

Middle Childhood

During middle childhood (ages 6–12), children face the following key developmental tasks: to engage in social activities; to expand their knowledge and understanding of the physical and social worlds; to continue to learn and expand their concepts of an appropriate feminine or masculine role; to develop a sense of values; to learn new communication skills; to learn how to read, write, and calculate; to learn to give and take; to learn how to accept people who are culturally different; to learn to tolerate ambiguity; and to learn physical skills.

For Freudians this period is the _latency stage_, characterized by a relative decline in sexual interests and the emergence of new interests, activities, and attitudes. With the events of the hectic phallic period behind them, children take a long breathing spell and consolidate their positions. Their attention turns to new fields, such as school playmates, books, and other features of the real world. Their hostile reactions tend to diminish, and they begin to reach out for friendly relationships with others in the environment.

Erikson, however, disagreed with the Freudian view of this period as a time of emotional latency and neutrality. He argued that the middle-childhood years present unique psychosocial demands that children must meet successfully if their development is to proceed. According to Erikson, the major struggle of middle childhood is between _industry_ and _inferiority_. The central task of this period is to achieve a sense of industry; failure to do so results in a sense of inadequacy and inferiority. The development of a sense of industry includes focusing on creating and producing and on attaining goals. Of course, starting school is a critical event of this time. Children who encounter failure during the early grades may experience severe handicaps later on. A child with early learning problems may begin to feel worthless as a person. Such a feeling may, in turn, drastically affect his or her relationships with peers, which are also vital at this time.

Helen's case illustrates some of the common conflicts of the elementary school years. When Helen started kindergarten—a bit too early—she was smaller than most of the other children. Although she had looked forward to beginning school and tried to succeed, for the most part she felt overwhelmed. She began to fail at many of the tasks her peers were enjoying and mastering. School-age children are in the process of developing their self-concept, whether positive or negative, and Helen's view of her capacity to succeed was growing dimmer. Gradually, she began to avoid even simple tasks and to find many excuses to rationalize away her failures. She wanted to hide the fact that she was not keeping up with the other children. She was fearful of learning and trying new things, so she clung to secure, familiar ways. She grew increasingly afraid of making mistakes, for she believed that everything she did had to be perfect. If she did some artwork, for instance, she would soon become frustrated and rip up the piece of paper because her picture wasn't coming out exactly as she wanted it to. Basically, Helen was afraid of putting her potential to the test, and she would generally freeze up when she had to be accountable for anything she produced. Her teachers' consistent evaluation of her was: "Helen is a sensitive child who needs a lot of encouragement and direction. She could do much more than she does, but she quits too soon, because she feels that what she does isn't good enough."

Helen grew to resent the fact that some of her teachers were not demanding much of her because they didn't want to push her. She then felt even more different from her peers, completing the vicious circle. Despite her will to try and her desire to succeed, she was prevented from venturing out by her fears of gambling and making mistakes. When she was in the third grade, she was at least a grade level behind in reading, despite the fact that she had repeated kindergarten. As she began to feel stupid and embarrassed because she couldn't read as well as the other children, she shied away from reading aloud. Eventually, she received instruction in remedial reading in a clinic, and this attention seemed to help. She was also given an intelligence test at the clinic, and the results were "low average." The reading staff and those who tested Helen were surprised, for they saw her as creative, insightful, and much brighter than the results showed. Again, she had frozen up when she felt that she had to perform on a test.

Helen is now in college. She is still anxious about taking tests. Often she does poorly on an examination, not because she does not know the material but because she allows her anxiety to get the best of her. Helen could long ago have given up on school, yet being in a supportive environment, she has been able to continue her education in spite of her fears. Although she is not "cured" of her feelings of inadequacy and self-doubt, she has not allowed these feelings to control her. Instead, she is learning to manage her self-doubts by arguing back to those old voices that tell her that she is basically inadequate.

Helen's case indicates that the first few years of school can have a powerful impact on a child's life and future adjustment to school. Her school experiences colored her view of her self-worth and affected her relationships with other children. At this point ask yourself: Can I identify in any ways with Helen's case? What struggles did I experience in forming my self-concept? Does Helen remind me of anyone I know?

DEVELOPING A SELF-CONCEPT

The term *self-concept* refers to your cognitive awareness about yourself. It is your private mental image of yourself and a collection of beliefs about the kind of person you are (Hamachek, 1988, 1990). This picture includes your view of your worth, value, and possibilities. It includes the way you see yourself in relation to others, the way you'd ideally like to be, and the degree to which you accept yourself as you are. From ages 6 to 12 the view you have of yourself is influenced greatly by the quality of your school experiences, by contact with your peer group and with teachers, and by your interactions with your family. To a large extent your self-concept is formed by what others tell you about yourself, especially during the formative years of childhood. Whether you develop a basically positive or negative outlook on yourself has a good deal to do with what people close to you have expected of you.

This view of yourself has a significant impact on how you present yourself to others and how you act and feel when you are with them. For example, you may feel inadequate around authority figures. Perhaps you tell yourself that you have nothing to say or that whatever you might say would be stupid. Since you have this view of yourself, you behave in ways that persuade people to adopt your view of yourself. More often than not, others will see and respond to you in the way that you "tell" them you are. For this reason, it can be a most useful exercise for you to monitor the messages you are sending to others about yourself and become aware of the patterns that you might be perpetuating. It is difficult for those who are close to you to treat you in a positive way when you consistently discount yourself. Why should others treat you better than you treat yourself? In contrast, people with a positive self-concept are likely to behave confidently, which causes others to react to them positively.

PROTECTING OUR SELF-CONCEPT: THE EGO-DEFENSE MECHANISMS

Freud conceived of ego-defense mechanisms as involving an unconscious process that prevents a person from becoming consciously aware of threatening feelings, thoughts, and impulses. Erikson's psychosocial theory is built around the idea that emotional and social growth progresses through a series of stages, each with its own unique ego accomplishments. His theory provides a natural conceptual framework for understanding the defense of the self (Hamachek, 1988, 1990).

For our purposes, defense mechanisms can be thought of as psychological strategies, such as self-deception and distortion of reality, that we use to protect our self-concept against unpleasant emotions. We use these protective devices at various stages of life to soften the blows of harsh reality. The ego defenses typically originate during our childhood years, and later experiences during adolescence and adulthood reinforce some of these styles of self-defense.

To illustrate the nature and functioning of these ego defenses, we will use the case of Helen discussed earlier. For the most part she made poor adjustments to her school and social life during her childhood years. Other children stayed away from her because of her aggressive and unfriendly behavior. She did not like her elementary school experience, and her teachers were not overly fond of her. Helen's behavioral style in coping with the pressures of school included blaming the outside world for her difficulties. In the face of these failures in life, she might have made use of any one or a combination of the following ego-defense mechanisms.

Repression. The mechanism of repression is one of the most important processes in Freudian theory, and it is the basis of many other ego defenses. By use of it, we exclude threatening or painful thoughts and feelings from awareness. By pushing them into the unconscious, we sometimes manage the anxiety that grows out of situations involving guilt and conflict. Repression may block out stressful experiences that could be met by realistically facing and working through a situation.

In Helen's case, she was unaware of her dependence/independence struggles with her parents; she was also unaware of how her painful experiences of failure were contributing to her feelings of inferiority and insecurity. She had unconsciously excluded most of her failures and had not allowed them to come to the surface of awareness.

Denial. Denial plays a defensive role similar to that of repression, but it generally operates at a preconscious or conscious level. In denial there is a conscious effort to suppress unpleasant reality. It is a way of distorting what the individual thinks, feels, or perceives to be a stressful situation. Helen simply "closed her eyes" to her failures in school. Even though she had evidence that she was not performing well academically, she refused to acknowledge this reality.

Displacement. Displacement involves redirecting emotional impulses (usually hostility) from the real object to a substitute person or object. In essence, anxiety is coped with by discharging impulses onto a "safer target."

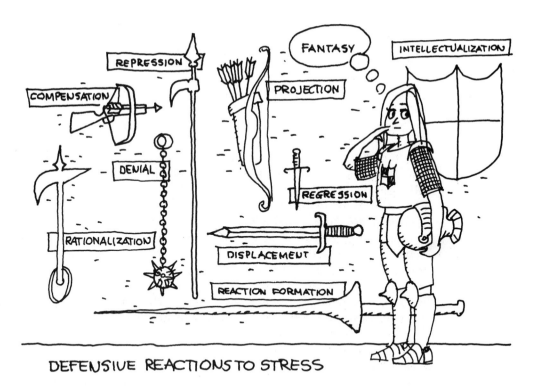

DEFENSIVE REACTIONS TO STRESS

For example, Helen's sister Joan was baffled by the hostility that she received from her. Joan did not understand why Helen was so critical of her every action. Helen probably used Joan as the target of her aggression, especially in light of the fact that Joan did exceptionally well at school and was very popular with her peers.

Projection. Another mechanism of self-deception is projection, which consists of attributing to others our own unacceptable desires and impulses. We are able to clearly see in others the very traits that we disown in ourselves, which serves the purpose of keeping a certain view of ourselves intact. Typically, projection involves seeing clearly in others actions that would lead to guilt feelings in ourselves. Helen tended to blame everyone but herself for her difficulties in school and in social relationships. She complained that her teachers were unfairly picking on her, that she could never do anything right for them, and that other children were mean to her.

Reaction formation. One defense against a threatening impulse is to actively express the opposite impulse. This involves behaving in a manner that is contrary to one's real feelings. A characteristic of this defense is the excessive quality of a particular attitude or behavior. For example, Helen bristled when her teachers or parents offered to give her help. She was convinced that she did not need anyone's help. Accepting their offers would have indicated that she really *was* stupid.

Rationalization. Rationalization involves manufacturing a false but "good" excuse to justify unacceptable behavior and explain away failures or losses. Such excuses help restore a bruised ego. Helen was quick to find many reasons for the difficulties she encountered, a few of which included sickness, which caused her to fall behind in her classes; teachers who went over the lessons too fast; other children who did not let her play with them; and siblings who kept her awake at night.

Compensation. Another defensive reaction is compensation, which consists of masking perceived weaknesses or developing certain positive traits to make up for limitations. The adjustive value in this mechanism lies in keeping one's self-esteem intact by excelling in one area to distract attention from an area in which the person is inferior. The more Helen experienced difficulties at school and with her peers, the more she withdrew from others and became absorbed in artwork that she did by herself at home.

Regression. Faced with stress, some people revert to a form of immature behavior that they have outgrown. In regression, they attempt to cope with their anxiety by clinging to such inappropriate behaviors. Faced with failure in both her social and school life, Helen had a tendency to engage in emotional tirades, crying a lot, storming into her room, and refusing to come out for hours.

Fantasy. Fantasy involves gratifying frustrated desires by imaginary achievements. When achievement in the real world seems remote, some people resort to screening out unpleasant aspects of reality and living in their world of dreams. During her childhood Helen developed a rich fantasy in which she imagined herself to be an actress. She played with her dolls for hours and talked to herself. In her daydreams she saw herself in the movies, surrounded by famous people.

Although the ego-defense mechanisms have some adaptive value, their overuse can become problematic. While it is true that self-deception can soften harsh reality, the fact is that reality does not change through the process of distorting those aspects of it that produce anxiety. When these defensive strategies do not work, the long-term result is an even greater degree of anxiety. The overreliance on these defenses leads to a vicious circle, for as the defenses lose their value in holding anxiety in check, people step up the use of other defenses.

All defenses are not self-defeating, however, and there is a proper place for them, especially when stresses are great. In the face of certain crises, for example, defenses can enable people to cope at least temporarily until they can build up other resources, both from their environment and from within themselves.

Before moving on to the section on adolescence, spend some time reflecting on some of the defenses you used during your childhood years. Do you see any analogies between the defenses you employed as a child and those you sometimes use at this time in your life?

- At the end of a day, think about some of the ways in which you used defenses and ask yourself how these defenses might serve you. Also ask yourself what price you pay for some of them.
- What do you think it would be like if you were to surrender all your defenses? If you decided that you wanted to retain some of them, which ones do you consider truly essential for you?

Adolescence

The years from 12 to 18 constitute a stage of transition between childhood and adulthood. For most people this is a particularly difficult period. It is a paradoxical time: adolescents are not treated as mature adults, yet they are often expected to act as though they had gained complete maturity; they are typically highly self-centered and preoccupied with their subjective world, yet they are expected to cope with the demands of reality and to go outside of themselves by expanding their horizons.

Adolescence is a time for continually testing limits, and there is usually a strong urge to break away from dependent ties that restrict one's freedom. It is not uncommon for adolescents to be frightened and lonely, but they may mask their fears with rebellion and cover up their need to be dependent by exaggerating their degree of independence. Although young people are becoming increasingly aware of the extent to which they are the products of their own family, it seems extremely important for them to declare their uniqueness and establish a separate identity. Much of adolescents' rebellion, then, is an attempt to determine the course of their own lives and to assert that they are who and what they want to be, not what others expect them to be.

In this quest to define themselves, adolescents may tend to dismiss completely anything their parents stand for, because they are insecure about achieving their own sense of uniqueness unless they do. It would be better to recognize that our parents, our family, and our history are a part of us, and that it's unrealistic to think that anyone can completely erase this influence. Instead of totally rejecting parental influences, young people could learn how to incorporate those values that give their life meaning, to modify those values that they deem in need of change, and to reject the ones that they choose not to live by. Those who go to the extreme of attempting to be totally different from their parents are really not free, because they are investing a great deal of energy in proving themselves and by their overreaction are continuing to give their parents undue importance in their life.

DEVELOPING AN IDENTITY

Adolescence is a time for integrating the various dimensions of one's identity that have been achieved in the past. As infants we must learn to trust ourselves and others; as adolescents we need to find a meaning in life and models in whom we believe. As toddlers we begin to assert our rights as independent people by struggling for autonomy; as adolescents we make choices that will shape our future. As preschoolers we try to achieve a sense of competence; as adolescents we explore choices concerning what we want from life, what we can succeed in, what kind of education we want, and what career may suit us.

Adolescence is a critical period in the development of personal identity. For Erikson, adolescents' major developmental conflicts center on the clarification of who they are, where they are going, and how they are going to get there. He sees the core struggle of adolescence as *identity* versus *role confusion*. A failure to achieve a sense of identity results in role confusion. Adolescents may feel overwhelmed by the pressures placed on them; if so, they may find the development of a clear identity a difficult task. They may feel pressured to make an occupational choice, to compete in the job market or in college, to become financially independent, and to commit themselves to physically and emotionally intimate relationships. In addition, they may feel pressured to live up to the standards of their peer group. Peer-group pressure is such a potent force that there is a danger that adolescents will lose their focus on their own identities and conform to the expectations of their friends and classmates. If the need to be accepted and liked is stronger than the need for self-respect, adolescents will most likely find themselves behaving in nongenuine ways, selling themselves out, and increasingly looking to others to tell them what and who they should be.

During adolescence a crucial part of the identity-formation process requires *individuation*. This term refers to the separation from our family system and the establishing of our identity based on our own experiences, rather than merely following our parents' dreams. This process of psychological separation from parental ties is the most agonizing part of the adolescent struggle and lays the foundation for future development. From Carl Jung's perspective, individuation implies a level of self-realization that is not possible until at least middle age. It should be noted that this view of achieving psychological separation from one's family is culturally biased. In some cultures, the wishes of parents are a major influence on the behavior of adult children. Furthermore, becoming psychologically separate from one's family is not seen as a guiding value in certain cultures. Instead, the collective is given far more weight than striving for fulfillment of the individual.

A strain on adolescents' sense of identity is imposed by the conflict between their awareness of expanding possibilities and society's narrowing of their options for action. Adolescents confront dilemmas similar to those faced by old people in our society. Both age groups must deal with finding a meaning in living and must cope with feelings of uselessness. Just as older people may be forced to retire and may encounter difficulty in replacing work activities, young people have not completed the education that will give them entry to many careers, and they generally haven't had the chance to acquire the skills necessary for many occupations. Instead, they are in a constant process of preparation for the future. Even in their family they may feel unneeded. Although they may be given chores to do, many adolescents do not experience much opportunity to be productive.

The question of options is made even more urgent by the myth that the choices we make during adolescence bind us for the rest of our life. Adolescents who believe this myth will be hesitant to experiment and test out many options. Too many young people yield to pressures to decide too early what they will be and what serious commitments they will make. Thus, they may never realize the range of possibilities open to them. To deal with this problem, Erikson suggested a *psychological moratorium*—a period during which society would give permission to adolescents to experiment with different roles and values so that they could sample life before making major commitments.

Adolescents are also faced with choices concerning what beliefs and values will guide their actions; indeed, forming a philosophy of life is a central task of adolescence. In meeting this challenge young people need adequate models, for a sense of moral living is largely learned by example. Adolescents are especially sensitive to duplicity, and they are quick to spot phony people who tell adolescents how they *ought* to live while themselves living in very different ways. They learn values by observing and interacting with adults who are positive examples, rather than by being preached to.

A particular problem adolescents face in the area of values concerns sexual behavior. Adolescents are easily aroused sexually, and everywhere they turn, whether in the media or in real life, they are saturated with sexual stimuli. At the same time, our society formally frowns on engaging in most types of sexual behavior before marriage. The resulting conflict can produce much frustration, anxiety, and guilt. Even apart from moral values with regard to sexuality, adolescents need to assess anew issues related to their gender-role identities. What is a woman? What is a man? What is feminine? What is masculine? What are the expectations we must live up to, and where do they originate? Wrestling with these difficult questions is part of the struggle of being an adolescent.

THE CRISIS OF ADOLESCENCE

In *All Grown Up and No Place to Go*, David Elkind (1984) writes about teenagers in crisis. Elkind believes that in the 1960s teenagers had a clearly defined position in the social structure, for they were the "future leaders" and the "next generation." Society recognized that the transition from childhood to adulthood was challenging and that adolescents needed time, support, and guidance in their striving for maturity. Yet young people today, says Elkind, have lost their once privileged position, because they have had a premature adulthood thrust on them. Although they are not capable of meeting adult responsibilities, today's youth are expected to meet the challenges that life imposes on them with the same degree of maturity once expected only of middle-aged people — and without adequate time for preparation. To complicate the situation, many of these adolescents are without adequate adult role models. Their parents are struggling with the demands of work and home and are attempting to find meaning in their own lives. The reality is that many parents are too preoccupied with their own lives to give young people the time and attention they need. A conflict exists, because even though adolescents are expected to be grown up in so many areas, they are at the same time expected to behave like obedient children. Elkind has captured a central dilemma of today's adolescents when he refers to them as being "all grown up with no place to go."

As you think about all the tasks and demands facing the adolescent, it becomes easy to see that this is typically a turbulent and fast-moving period of life, often marked by feelings of powerlessness, confusion, and loneliness.

It is a time for making critical choices, even the ultimate choice of living fully or bringing about one's own death. It is a time of making choices in almost every area of life — decisions that, to a large extent, define our identity. The following "Time Out" is a chance for you to spend some time reflecting on the choices that you made during your adolescent years, as well as clarifying the impact that these experiences continue to exert on you today.

Time Out for Personal Reflection

At this point it could be useful to review the choices open to adolescents, and especially to think of the choices that you remember having made at this time in your life. How do you think those choices have influenced the person you are today?

1. What major choices did you struggle with during your adolescent years?

   _____

   _____

   _____

   _____

2. How do you think your adolescence affected the person you are today?

   _____

   _____

   _____

   _____

Chapter Summary

A road map giving a general overview of the developmental tasks of the life span reveals that each stage presents certain dangers and opportunities. In a positive sense crises can be seen as challenges to be met rather than catastrophic events that happen to us. In normal development there are critical turning points and choices for each phase. There is continuity in life, for our early experiences influence the choices we make at a later time in our development. No neat delineation exists between one stage and another. Instead, stages blend into one another. We all experience each period of life in our own unique ways.

The struggle toward autonomy, or psychological independence, begins in early childhood, takes on major proportions during adolescence and young adulthood, and extends into later adulthood. The process of individuation, and the value attached to it, are greatly influenced by culture. Actualizing our full potential as a person and learning to stand alone in life, as well as stand beside others, is a task that is never really finished. Although major life events during childhood and adolescence have an impact on the ways that we think, feel, and behave in adult life, we are not helplessly molded and hopelessly determined by such events. Instead, we do choose our attitudes toward these events, which in turn affects how we behave today.

Freud's psychoanalytic view of human development during the first six years of life emphasizes the importance of acquiring a sense of trust toward the world, of learning how to recognize and express the full range of feelings, and of acquiring a healthy attitude toward sexuality and a clear sense of our gender-role identity. His psychosexual perspective shows how our later personality development hinges on the degree to which we have successfully met the demands and conflicts during early childhood.

Erikson built on Freud's basic ideas, and his psychosocial theory offers a more complete and comprehensive perspective of the unique tasks of the entire life span. In his eight stages of development Erikson emphasizes the critical turning points facing us at each transition in our life. At these points we can either successfully resolve the basic conflict or get stuck on the road to development. Again, early choices affect the range of choices open to us later in life.

From infancy through adolescence we are faced with developmental challenges at each stage of life. The basic task of *infancy* is to develop a sense of trust in others and our environment, so we can trust ourselves. Later personality problems that can stem from failure to develop this trust include fearing intimate relationships, low self-esteem, and isolation. *Early childhood* presents the challenge of beginning to function independently and acquiring a sense of self-control. If we do not master this task, becoming autonomous is extremely difficult. During the *preschool years* we are forming our gender-role identity, and ideally we experience a sense of competence that comes with making some decisions for ourselves. Parental attitudes during this period are very powerful and these attitudes are communicated both verbally and nonverbally. Our school experiences during *middle childhood* play a significant role in our socialization. At this time the world is opening up to us, and we are expanding our interests outside of the home. Problems that typically begin at this phase include a negative self-concept, conflicts over values, a confused gender-role identity, a fear of new challenges, and disturbed interpersonal relationships. *Adolescence* is the period when we are forming an identity as well as establishing goals and values that give our life meaning. A danger of this time of life is that we can follow the crowd out of fear of being rejected. If that happens, we fail to listen to ourselves and discover what it is that we want for ourselves.

Each of these developmental phases lays the foundation on which we build our adult personality. As we will see in the next chapter, mastery of these earlier challenges is essential in learning to cope with the problems of adult living.

Activities and Exercises

1. Write an account in your journal of the first six years of your life. Although you may think that you can't remember much about this time, the following guidelines should help in your recall:

   a. Write down a few key questions that you would like answered about your early years.
   b. Seek out your relatives, and ask them some questions about your early years.
   c. Collect any reminders of your early years, particularly pictures.
   d. If possible, visit the place or places where you lived and went to school.

2. Choose from among the many exercises in this chapter any that you'd be willing to integrate into a self-help program during your time in this course. What things are you willing to do to bring about some of the changes you want in your life?

3. Pictures often say more about you than words. What do your pictures tell about you? Look through any pictures of yourself as a child and as an adolescent, and see if there are any themes. What do most of your pictures reveal about the way you felt about yourself? Bring some of these pictures to class. Have other members look at them and tell you what they think you were like then. Pictures can also be used to tap forgotten memories.

4. Select one or more books for further reading on the topics explored in this chapter. We highly recommend the following: Bloomfield, *Making Peace with Yourself: Transforming Your Weaknesses into Strengths* (1985); Elkind, *All Grown Up and No Place to Go* (1984). For a full bibliographic reference for each book, consult "References and Suggested Readings" at the end of this book.

CHAPTER THREE
Adulthood
and
Autonomy

Prechapter Self-Inventory

Use the following scale to respond: 4 = this statement is true of me *most* of the time; 3 = this statement is true of me *much* of the time; 2 = this statement is true of me *some* of the time; 1 = this statement is true of me *almost none* of the time.

_____ 1. For the most part, my values and beliefs are very much like my parents'.

_____ 2. I'm an independent person more than I'm a dependent person.

_____ 3. I think about early messages I received from my parents.

_____ 4. I would say that I have psychologically divorced my parents and become my own parent.

_____ 5. As I get older, I feel an urgency about living.

_____ 6. Much of my life is spent in doing things that I do *not* enjoy.

_____ 7. I look forward with optimism and enthusiasm to the challenges that lie ahead of me.

_____ 8. I expect to experience a meaningful and rich life when I reach old age.

_____ 9. There are many things I can't do now that I expect to do when I retire.

_____ 10. I have fears of aging.

Introduction

This chapter continues our discussion of the life-span perspective by focusing on the transitions and turning points in adulthood. Our childhood and adolescent experiences lay the foundation for our ability to meet the developmental challenges of the various phases of adulthood. Throughout adulthood many choices are still open to us, yet in some ways we continue to be influenced by the decisions and experiences of our childhood and adolescent years. Before taking up early, middle, and late adulthood, this chapter examines how you can become more autonomous. One facet of the struggle toward autonomy involves recognizing the early life decisions you made and realizing that you can change them if they are not appropriate or useful. This change entails questioning some of the messages that you received and accepted during your early childhood. You can also learn to argue with your self-defeating thoughts and beliefs and acquire a more rational, positive, and constructive set of beliefs.

Although this chapter addresses some typical developmental patterns, it should not be thought that everybody goes through these stages in the same way at the same time. Influences in your family and culture account for the manner in which you confront the developmental tasks. It is important that you understand the ways in which your culture and your family-of-origin

experiences have contributed to shaping the person you are. Your passage through adulthood will be characterized by the choices you make in response to demands made on you. It would be a good idea to look for a pattern of choices in your life. You may see that you are primarily adapting yourself to others. Or you may discover a pattern of choosing the path of security rather than risking new adventures. On the other hand, you may be pleased with many of the decisions that you have made. As you think about these choices at critical turning points in your adulthood, look for a unifying theme beginning in childhood. Strive to understand and work through your past so that you do not get bogged down by earlier experiences.

If you are a young adult, you may wonder why you should be concerned about middle age and later life. We invite you to look at the choices you are making now that will have a direct influence on the quality of a later adulthood phase. As you read this chapter, reflect on what you hope to be able to say, when you reach later adulthood, about how you have lived.

The Struggle toward Autonomy

As we leave adolescence and enter young adulthood, our central task is to assume increased responsibility and independence. Although most of us have moved away from our parents physically, not all of us have done so psychologically. To a greater or lesser degree our parents will have a continuing influence on our lives. Cultural factors play a significant role in determining the degree to which our parents influence our lives. This is especially true for certain groups that do not see a value in children's developing a spirit of independence. Instead, they place a prime value on cooperation with others and on a spirit of interdependence. Within some cultures, parents continue to have a significant impact and influence on their children even when they reach adulthood. Respect and honor for parents may be values that are extolled above individual freedom by the adult children.

Regardless of our cultural background, the challenge we face as mature adults is to be aware of the present influence that our parents have on our decisions and behavior. Having reviewed your own childhood and adolescent years in the last chapter, you can probably recognize more clearly the impact of your parents on your life. The struggle toward autonomy entails choosing for yourself and working for your own approval, rather than living your life primarily by your parents' designs and to earn their approval. Being an autonomous person does not mean that you will not share many of your parents' values. We are not suggesting that rebellion against whatever your parents stand for is a sign of being autonomous.

Making decisions about the quality of life you want for yourself and affirming these choices is partly what autonomy is about. Autonomy also entails your willingness to accept responsibility for the consequences of your choices, rather than looking for others to blame if you are not satisfied with the way your life is going. Furthermore, separating from your family and finding your own identity is not something you do at a given time once and for all. The struggle toward autonomy begins in early childhood and continues throughout life.

RECOGNIZING EARLY LEARNING AND DECISIONS

Transactional analysis (TA) offers a useful framework for understanding how our learning during childhood extends into adulthood. TA is a theory of personality and a method of counseling originally developed by Eric Berne (1975) and later extended by practitioners such as Claude Steiner (1975) and Mary and Robert Goulding (1978, 1979). The theory is built on the assumption that adults made decisions based on past premises, premises that were at one time appropriate to their survival needs but may no longer be valid. It stresses the capacity of the person to change early decisions and is oriented toward increasing awareness, with the goal of enabling people to alter the course of their lives. TA teaches people how to recognize the three ego states (Parent, Adult, and Child) in which they function. Through TA, people learn how their current behavior is affected by the rules and regulations they received and incorporated as children and how they can identify the "life script," and also the family script, that determines their actions. These scripts are almost like plots that unfold. Individuals are able to realize that they can now change what is *not* working while retaining that which serves them well.

Ego states: Parent, Adult, and Child. TA identifies three ego states that encompass important facets of personality. According to TA, people are constantly shifting from one ego state to another, and their behavior at any one time is related to the state of the moment.

The *Parent* part of personality represents that which has been incorporated from one's parents and parental substitutes. When we are in the Parent ego state, we react to situations as we imagine our parents might have reacted, or we act toward others the way our parents acted toward us. The Parent contains all the "shoulds" and "oughts" and other rules for living. When we are in that ego state, we may act in ways that are strikingly similar to those of our parents. We are likely to use some of their very words and phrases, and our posture, gestures, tone and quality of voice, and mannerisms may replicate theirs. Such behavior occurs whether the Parent in us is a positive ego state (a Nurturing Parent) or a negative one (a Critical Parent).

The *Adult* ego state is our processor of data. It is the objective part of our personality and gathers information about what is going on. It is not emotional or judgmental but works with the facts and with external reality.

The *Child* ego state consists of feelings, impulses, and spontaneous acts. The Child in each of us is either the "Natural Child," the "Little Professor," or the "Adapted Child." The Natural Child is the spontaneous, impulsive, open, alive, expressive, often charming, but untrained being within each of us. The Little Professor is the unschooled wisdom of a child. It is manipulative, egocentric, and creative. The Adapted Child is the tamed version of the Natural Child, the part of us that learns to accommodate to the expectations of others in order to gain acceptance and approval.

People who participate in TA counseling are taught how to recognize what ego state they are functioning in when they are faced with a problem. In this way they can make conscious decisions about the particular ego state in which they want to function. For example, if Betty becomes aware that she is treating her children in the same critical way in which her own mother responded to her, she is in a position to change her behavior. As Betty becomes more aware of her ego states in various situations, she also becomes more aware of her adaptive behavior (both to her internal Parent and to the outside world). With this awareness she can knowingly choose other options.

The life script. The concept of the life script is an important contribution of TA. A life script is made up of both parental teachings and the early decisions we make as a child. Often, we continue to follow our script as an adult.

Scripting begins in infancy with sutble, nonverbal messages from our parents. During our earliest years we learn much about our worth as a person and our place in life. Later, scripting occurs in both subtle and direct ways. Some of the messages we might "hear" include: "Always listen to authority." "Don't act like a child." "We know that you can perform well, and we expect the best from you, so be sure you don't let us down." "Never trust people; rely on yourself." "You're really stupid, and we're convinced that you'll never amount to much." Often these messages are sent in disguised ways. For example, our parents may never have told us directly that sexual feelings are bad or that touching is inappropriate. However, their behavior with each other and with us may have taught us to think in this way. Moreover, what parents *don't* say or do is just as important as what they say directly. If no mention is ever made of sexuality, for instance, that very fact communicates significant attitudes.

On a broader level than the messages we receive from our parents are the life scripts that are a part of our cultural context. Each culture has a set of values that are transmitted in many ways in the family circle. A few examples of cultural messages pertaining to the family are as follows:

"Older people are to be revered and respected."
"Don't bring shame to the family."
"Don't talk about family matters outside of the family circle."
"Don't demonstrate affection in public."
"Always obey your parents and grandparents."
"The mother is the heart of the family."

"The father is the head of the family."
"Avoid conflict and strive for harmony within the family."
"Never get a divorce."

Our life script, including the messages from both our family of origin and our culture, forms the core of our personal identity. Our experiences may lead us to such conclusions as "I really don't have any right to exist." "I can only be loved if I'm productive and successful." "I'd better not trust my feelings, because they'll only get me in trouble." These basic themes running through our lives tend to determine our behavior, and very often they are difficult to unlearn. In many subtle ways these early decisions about ourselves can come back to haunt us in later life.

A couple of examples may help to clarify how early messages and the decisions we make about them influence us in day-to-day living. In my (Jerry's) own case, even though I now experience myself as successful, for many years of my life I felt unsuccessful and unworthy. I haven't erased my old script completely, and I still experience self-doubts and struggle with insecurities. I don't think that I can change such long-lasting feelings by simply telling myself, "OK, now that I'm meeting with success, I'm the person that I was meant to be." It may be necessary to deal again and again with feelings of being insecure and unworthy. In fact, even striving for and attaining success can be a compulsive way of denying basic feelings of inadequacy. I am convinced that part of the dynamics motivating me toward success are linked to the acceptance I wanted from my parents, especially my father. In many important ways my father did not feel successful, and I believe that on some level my own strivings have been not only to prove my own worth, but also to make up for some of the successes that could have been his. Even though he died twenty-five years ago, on a psychological plane I am still making some attempt to win his acceptance and make him proud of my accomplishments. As a child I did not feel that I was able to do much of anything very well. Although my external reality has certainly changed from the time I was a child to now, I continue to play out some of the underlying patterns. For me this does not mean that I need to put an end to my projects, yet I do want to be aware of who I am in service to and not spend the rest of my life living up to parental expectations. In short, although I believe that I can change some of my basic attitudes about myself, I don't think I can ever get rid of all vestiges of the effects of my early learning and decisions. In general, although we need not be determined by old decisions, it's wise to be continually aware of manifestations of our old ways that interfere with our attempts to develop new ways of thinking and being.

A second illustration of how we can be affected by early decisions concerns a woman we'll call Pamela. Pamela is 38 years old, and she has been in and out of relationships with men. She finds it very difficult to take anything for herself or to experience needing anything from anyone. Instead, she has continually sought ways of being a "giver." She has told herself that she must be strong, that she mustn't allow herself to depend on others, and that she mustn't cry or experience grief. Yet Pamela isn't satisfied to continue living in this way, for she has felt lonely and resentful much of the time. She has typically picked men whom she views as weak — men who can give her nothing but whom she can take care of, thereby satisfying her "giving" needs. She sees the dishonesty in believing that she has been unselfish; she is aware that she has been motivated more by her own need to be *needed* than by her concern for others. Gradually, she has also become aware that her parents used to "tell" her such things as "Always be strong. Don't let yourself need anything from anyone, and in that way you'll never get let down." "Keep your feelings to yourself; if you feel like crying, don't do it in front of others." "Remember that the way to win approval and affection is to do things for others. Always put others before yourself." Pamela's behavior had been determined by these values until she realized that she could change her early decisions. This realization has increased her freedom and pointed the way toward steps she can take in revising some of her decisions.

Injunctions. Let's look more closely at the nature of the early messages (often called injunctions) that we incorporate into our lifestyle. First of all, these injunctions aren't just planted in our heads while we sit by passively. By making decisions in response to real or imagined injunctions, we assume some of the responsibility for indoctrinating ourselves. Thus, if we hope to free ourselves, we must become aware of what these "oughts" and "shoulds" are and of how we allow them to operate in our lives.

The following list, based on the Gouldings' works (1978, 1979), includes common injunctions and some possible decisions that could be made in response to them.

1. *"Don't."* Children who hear and accept this message will believe that they cannot do anything right, and they will look to others to make their decisions for them.
   - *Possible decisions:* "I'm scared of making the wrong decision, so I simply won't decide." "Because I made a dumb choice, I won't decide on anything important again!"
2. *"Don't be."* This lethal message is often given nonverbally by the way parents hold (or don't hold) the child. The basic message is "I wish you hadn't been born."
   - *Possible decisions:* "I'll keep trying until I get you to love me." "If things get terrible, I'll kill myself."
3. *"Don't be close."* Related to this injunction are the messages "Don't trust" and "Don't love."
   - *Possible decisions:* "I let myself love once, and it backfired. Never again!" "Because it's scary to get close, I'll keep myself distant."
4. *"Don't be important."* If you are constantly discounted when you speak, you are likely to believe that you are unimportant.
   - *Possible decisions:* "If, by chance, I ever do become important, I'll never let anyone know it." "I'll keep a low profile."
5. *"Don't be a child."* This message says: "Always act adult!" "Don't be childish and make a fool of yourself." "Keep control of yourself."
   - *Possible decisions:* "I'll take care of others and won't ask for much myself." "I won't let myself have fun."
6. *"Don't grow."* This message is given by the frightened parent who discourages the child from growing up in many ways.
   - *Possible decisions:* "I'll stay a child, and that way I'll get my parents to approve of me." "I won't be sexual, and that way my father won't push me away."
7. *"Don't succeed."* If children are positively reinforced for failing, they may accept the message not to seek success.
   - *Possible decisions:* "I'll never do anything perfect enough, so why try?" "I'll succeed, even if it kills me."
8. *"Don't be you."* This involves suggesting to children that they are the wrong sex.
   - *Possible decisions:* "They'd love me only if I were a boy [girl], so it's impossible to get their love." "I'll pretend I'm a boy [girl]."

9. *"Don't be sane"* and *"Don't be well."* Some children get attention only when they are physically sick or acting crazy.
   • *Possible decisions:* "I'll get sick, and then I'll be included." "I am crazy."
10. *"Don't belong."* This injunction may indicate that the family feels that the child does not belong anywhere.
    • *Possible decisions:* "I'll be a loner forever." "I'll never belong anywhere."

In our work with both undergraduate and graduate students in human services and counseling, we are surprised by the large number of them whose parents are alcoholics. As you will see, certain patterns of injunctions, roles that are learned, and decisions about life often characterize adult children from alcoholic families.

In *It Will Never Happen to Me*, Claudia Black (1987) vividly portrays the life histories of adult children of alcoholics (ACAs), and we have adapted much of the material in this section from her book. Black discusses three central injunctions that she detects over and over in her work with these clients: "Don't talk." "Don't trust." "Don't feel."

With reference to the "Don't talk" message, the family injunction is not to discuss real issues in the family. Children are conditioned to ignore these issues in the hope that the hurt will go away. Children learn not to rock the boat. The key dynamic is denial of the family secret of alcoholism.

In the case of the "Don't trust" message, adult children of alcoholics learn to always be on guard, to rely on themselves, and not to trust others with their feelings. In alcoholic homes children learn that their parents are not consistently available and cannot be relied on for safety. Unfortunately, they carry this pattern of not trusting from their childhood into their adulthood.

In terms of the "Don't feel" message, children develop a denial system to numb their feelings. To bring stability and consistency to their lives, they acquire coping mechanisms. They learn not to share what they feel, because they are convinced that their feelings will not be validated within their family. Gradually, they build walls for self-protection as a way of coping with a feared world. They learn to deny and discount their feelings, they hide their pain, and they do not express what is inside of them. This process of denial interferes in their emotional life when they reach adulthood.

Children raised in alcoholic families enter adulthood with strategies for survival that worked to some degree in their childhood and adolescent years. Over the years they have refined behaviors such as being responsible, adjusting, or placating, as well as not talking, not trusting, and not feeling. On reaching adulthood, most ACAs continue to struggle with problems related to trust, dependency, control, identification, and expression of feelings.

Children tend to adopt certain roles for survival in alcoholic families. In her research and therapeutic work with ACAs, Black has found that later, as adults, they play out the same roles. She writes that the majority of ACAs adopt one or a combination of three roles: the responsible person, the adjuster, or the placater.

First is the role of the *responsible* person. Children who miss their childhood by having to mature very early often take on household and parenting responsibilities for other siblings. When structure and consistency are not provided, these children provide it for themselves. They rely completely on themselves, for they have learned many times over that they cannot count on their parents. Second is the role of the *adjuster*, who makes an early decision that "since I can't do anything about the family situation, I'll adjust to it." As children, adjusters become detached; as adults they have no sense of self, they are not autonomous, and they typically feel that they have few choices. Third is the role of the *placater*, who has become skilled at listening and providing empathy. Placaters have a difficult time in dealing with their own feelings. For example, if they cry, they tend to cry alone.

There are many other forms of dysfunctional behavior in families besides alcoholic patterns. For example, incest victims get the message that what is going on is secret, which can be reinforced with the threat of violence if the child informs. People who experienced incest frequently learn to deny what is taking place, both outside of them and in their inner world as well. They are likely to incorporate shame, guilt, and feelings of self-blame. All of these are manifestations of accepting injunctions on either a verbal or a nonverbal level.

As you can see, these are not rigid categories that box people in but general patterns of learned behavior. The roles that children play in a dysfunctional family tend to evolve from childhood to adulthood. As children, individuals may busy themselves by taking care of others and pleasing others; as adults, they often become professional helpers, and they strive to please their clients. They become carriers of the pain of others. Yet if they don't attend to their own needs and feelings, eventually they burn out. They have a difficult time asking for what they need for themselves, and in their personal relationships they tend to seek out others who are takers.

As a personal example of a struggle with listening to injunctions from both parents and society, I (Marianne) want to share some messages I heard growing up. I was born and spent my childhood and adolescence in a farming village in Germany. Some of the messages I received, though they were not typically verbalized, were: "You can't do anything about it." "Things could be worse, so don't talk so much about how bad things are." "Accept what you have, and don't complain about what you don't have." "Don't be different. Fit in with the community. Do what everybody else does." "Be satisfied with your life."

Although my childhood was very good in many aspects and I was satisfied with part of my life, I still wanted more than I felt I could get by remaining in the village and becoming what was expected of me. It was a continuing struggle not to surrender to these expectations, but having some adult role models who themselves had challenged such injunctions inspired me to resist these messages. As early as age 8 I felt a sense of daring to be different and hoping someday to go to America. Although I doubted myself at times, I still began saving every penny I could lay my hands on. Finally, at the age of 19 I asked my father for permission to take a ship to the United States and surprised him when I told him that I had saved enough money to buy a ticket.

Even though there were many obstacles, I seemed to be driven to follow a dream and a decision that I made when I was only 8. When I did come to America, I eventually fulfilled another dream, and consequently challenged another injunction, by furthering my education. The theme of my struggles during my earlier years was that I was not willing to surrender to obstacles. I argued with myself about simply accepting what seemed like limited choices for a life's design, and in doing so I began writing a new life script for myself. It was important to me not to feel like a victim of circumstances. I was willing to do what was necessary to challenge barriers to what I wanted and to pursue my dreams and goals. Although I fought against these injunctions at an early age, it does not mean that they have gone away forever. I continue to have to be aware of them and not allow them to control me as an adult.

At this point, think about some of the childhood decisions that you made about yourself and about life. For example, you might have made any one of the following early decisions:

"I will be loved only when I live up to what others expect of me."
"I'd better listen to authorities outside of myself, because I can't trust myself to make decent decisions."
"I won't let myself trust people, and that way they won't ever let me down again."

Themes like these that run through your life determine not only your self-image but also your behavior. It is a difficult matter to unlearn some of these self-defeating assumptions and learn new and constructive ones in their place. This is one reason for learning how to critically evaluate questions such as these:

- What messages have I listened to and "bought"?
- How valid are the sources of these messages?
- In what ways do I now continue to say self-defeating sentences to myself?
- How can I challenge some of the decisions I made about myself and make new ones that will lead to a positive orientation?

LEARNING TO DISPUTE SELF-DEFEATING THINKING

As children and adolescents we uncritically incorporate certain assumptions about life and about our worth as a person. Rational-emotive and other cognitive-behavioral therapies are grounded on the premise that emotional and behavioral problems are originally learned by the inculcation of faulty beliefs

SALLY, THE TROUBLE WITH YOU IS...

from significant others during our childhood, as well as by our creative inventing of unrealistic aspirations and self-defeating beliefs by ourselves. We
actively reinstill false beliefs by the processes of self-suggestion and self-
repetition (Ellis, 1988). It is largely our own repetition of early-indoctrinated
faulty beliefs, rather than a parent's repetition, that keeps dysfunctional attitudes alive and functional within us. Self-defeating beliefs are supported and
maintained by negative and illogical statements that we make to ourselves
over and over again: "If I don't win universal love and approval, then I'll
never be happy." "If I make a mistake, that would prove that I am an utter
failure."

Albert Ellis (1988), the developer of rational-emotive therapy (RET),
describes some of the most common ways in which people make themselves
miserable by remaining wedded to their irrational beliefs. Ellis has devised an
A-B-C theory of personality that explains how people develop negative eval-
uations of themselves. He holds that it is our faulty thinking, not actual life
events, that creates emotional upsets and that leads to our misery. He contends that we have the power to control our emotional destiny. He suggests
that when we are upset, it is a good idea to look to our hidden dogmatic
"musts," "oughts," and absolutistic "shoulds." For Ellis, practically all human
misery and serious emotional turmoil is unnecessary.

An example will clarify this A-B-C concept. Assume that Sally's parents
abandoned her when she was a child (A, the activating event). Sally's emotional reaction may be feelings of depression, worthlessness, rejection, and
unlovability (C, the emotional consequence). However, Ellis asserts, it is not
A (her parents' abandonment of her) that caused her feelings of rejection
and unlovability; rather it is her belief system (B) that is causing her low self-
esteem. She made her mistake when she told herself that there must have

been something terrible about her self for her parents not to want her. Her faulty beliefs are reflected through self-talk such as: "I am to blame for what my parents did." "If I were more lovable, they would have wanted to keep me."

According to Ellis (1988, p. 60), most of our irrational ideas can be reduced to three main forms of what he refers to as *mustubation*. The three basic "musts" that create emotional problems are

1. "I *must* perform well and win the approval of important people, or else I am an inadequate person!"
2. "Others *must* treat me fairly and considerately!"
3. "My life *must* be easy and pleasant. I need and *must* have the things I want, or life is unbearable!"

RET is designed to teach people how to *dispute* irrational beliefs such as these. Let's apply RET to Sally's example. She does not need to continue believing that she is basically unlovable. Instead of clinging to the belief that something must have been wrong with *her* for her parents to have rejected her, she can begin to dispute this self-defeating statement and think along different lines: "It hurts that my parents didn't want me, but perhaps *they* had certain problems that kept them from being good parents." "Maybe my parents didn't love me, but that doesn't mean that nobody could love me." "While it's unfortunate that I didn't have parents in growing up, it's not devastating, and I no longer have to be a little girl waiting for their protection."

Ellis stresses that your feelings about yourself are largely the result of the way you think. Thus, if you hope to change a negative self-image, it is essential to learn how to dispute the illogical sentences you now continue to feed yourself and to challenge faulty premises that you have accepted uncritically. Further, you also need to work and practice at replacing these self-sabotaging beliefs with constructive ones. If you wish to study common ways of combating the negative self-indoctrination process, we highly recommend *How to Stubbornly Refuse to Make Yourself Miserable about Anything—Yes, Anything!* (Ellis, 1988).

LEARNING TO CHALLENGE YOUR INNER PARENT

We'd like to expand a bit on the general concepts of transactional analysis and rational-emotive therapy and discuss some related ideas about challenging early messages and working toward autonomy. The term *inner parent* refers to the attitudes and beliefs we have about ourselves and others that are a direct result of things we've learned from our parents or parental substitutes. The willingness to challenge this inner parent is a mark of autonomy. Since being autonomous means that we are in control of the direction of our life, it implies that we have discovered an identity that is separate and distinct from the identities of our parents and of others.

It should be noted that many of the values we incorporated from our parents may be healthy standards for guiding our behavior. No doubt our past has contributed in many respects to the good qualities we possess, and many of the things that we like about ourselves may be largely due to the influence of the people who were important to us in our early years. What is essential is that we look for the subtle ways in which we have psychologically incorporated our parents' values in our life without a deliberate choice.

How do we learn to recognize the influence that our parents continue to have on us? One way to begin is by talking back to our inner parent. In other words, we can begin to notice some of the things we do and avoid doing, and then ask ourselves why. For instance, suppose you avoid enrolling in a college course because you long ago branded yourself "stupid." You may tell yourself that you'd never be able to pass the class, so why even try? In this case an early decision that you made about your intellectual capabilities prevents you from branching out to new endeavors. Rather than stopping at this first obstacle, however, you could challenge yourself by asking: "Who says I'm too stupid? Even if my father or my teachers have told me that I'm slow, is it really true? Why have I accepted this view of myself uncritically? Let me check it out and see for myself."

In carrying out this kind of dialogue, we can talk to the different selves we have within us. You may be struggling to open yourself to people and trust them, for example, while at the same time you hear the inner injunction "Never trust anybody." In this case you can carry on a two-way discussion between your trusting side and your suspicious side. The important point is that we don't have to passively accept as truth the messages we learned when we were children. As adults we can now put these messages to the test.

In his excellent book *Making Peace with Your Parents*, the psychiatrist Harold Bloomfield (1983) makes the point that many of us suffer from psychological wounds as a result of unfinished business with our parents. We often keep the past alive by insisting on blaming them for all of our problems. Instead of pointing the blaming finger at parents, it is a good idea to look at the ways that we can give to ourselves some of the things that we may still expect or hope for from our parents. If we don't get past the blaming, we end up wedded to resentment. As long as we cling to our resentments, expect our parents to be different from who they are, or wait for their approval, we are keeping painful memories and experiences alive. If we harbor grudges against our parents and focus all of our energies on changing them, we have little constructive energy left over to assume control of our own lives. Instead of trying to change them, we can approach them in the very ways that we'd like them to treat us. According to Bloomfield, before we can resolve any conflicts with our actual parents, we first must make peace with our inner parent.

To be at peace with yourself, you need to let go of festering resentments, to work through unresolved anger, and to cease blaming others. These fac-

PLEASE, MOTHER!

tors not only poison relationships but also take a toll on the way you feel about yourself. It is only when you find a sense of inner peace that you can ever hope to make peace with the significant people in your life. You do have a choice about whether you will do what is necessary to find this inner peace that will allow you to make peace with others, or whether you will continue to focus on others as the source of your current problems. Even though your family situation may have been far from ideal, you now have the choice of the attitude that you take toward your past circumstances. If you choose to assume responsibility for the person that you are now, you are also moving in the direction of becoming your own parent.

BECOMING YOUR OWN PARENT

Achieving emotional maturity involves divorcing ourselves from our inner parent and becoming our own "parent." But maturity is not some fixed destination at which we finally arrive; it is, rather, a direction in which we can choose to travel. What are some of the characteristics of the person who is moving toward becoming his or her own parent? There is no authoritative list of the qualities of an autonomous person, but the following characteristics may stimulate you to come up with your own view of what kind of parent you want to be for yourself and what criteria make sense to you in evaluating your own degree of psychological maturity. For each of these characteristics, ask yourself whether it applies to you and whether you agree that it is a mark of one who is becoming independent. We encourage you to add to or modify this list as you see fit.

1. People moving in the direction of autonomy recognize the ways in which their inner parent controls them. They see how they are controlled by guilt or by the promise of love and how they have cooperated in giving parents and parent substitutes undue power in their lives.
2. People moving in the direction of autonomy have a desire to become both free and responsible and to do for themselves what they are capable of doing.
3. People moving in the direction of autonomy have a sense of identity and uniqueness. Rather than looking outside of themselves, they find answers within. Instead of looking to what others expect of them and seeking their approval, they ask: "What can I do that will make me pleased with myself? Who is it that I want to become? What seems right for me? What do I expect of myself?"
4. People moving in the direction of autonomy have a sense of commitment and responsibility. They are committed to some ideals and personal goals that make sense to them. Their sense of commitment includes the willingness to accept responsibility for their actions rather than blaming circumstances or other people for the way their lives are going.
5. The discovery of a meaning or purpose in life is an important mark of independent people. Although this meaning can be derived from many sources, an independent life is characterized by purpose and direction.
6. Autonomous people do not have a need to prove their autonomy. They are willing to consider opinions of their parents or other significant people in the framework of their decision-making process.
7. In addition to pursuing self-interests, autonomous individuals are also concerned with reaching out to others, sharing with them, and giving something of themselves to make society a better place.

To become our own parent, Gould (1978) says, it is essential that we deal with the unfinished business from childhood that periodically intrudes into our adult relationships. Referring to this unfinished business as the "angry demons of childhood consciousness," he asserts that our central developmental task consists of striving for a fuller and more independent *adult consciousness*. We accomplish this transformation from childhood to adult consciousness by reformulating our definition of self, which is a risky and continuing process. Thus, developing a mature personality involves eliminating the distortions of childhood demons and the protective devices we've developed to cope with these demons. Gould captures the essence of this struggle toward autonomy when he says: "As our life experience builds, ideally we abandon unwarranted expectations, rigid rules and inflexible roles. We come to be the owners of our own selves, with a fuller, more independent adult consciousness" (pp. 37–38).

In writing about "becoming your own best parent," Bloomfield (1983) challenges us as *adults* to recognize that we are responsible for satisfying our psychological needs for maintenance, encouragement, and affection. His message is that rather than getting stuck in whining about all the ways our parents did not live up to our expectations, we can learn to give to ourselves what we missed from our parents.

Recall that we have emphasized that you do not find yourself in isolation; rather, the process of self-discovery is bound up with the quality of your relationships to others. Autonomy does not mean being completely independent or not needing others. Becoming your own person does not imply "doing your own thing" irrespective of your impact on those with whom you come in contact. Instead, being autonomous implies that you have questioned the values you live by and made them your own; part of this process includes concern for the welfare of those people whom you love and associate with. Consider these questions as a way of clarifying the meaning autonomy has for you:

- Is it important to you to feel that you are your own person?
- To what degree do you think you can live by your own standards and still be sensitive to the needs and wants of others?
- Are you satisfied with living by the expectations that others have for you?
- Do you want to become more independent, even though there are risks involved? Or do you prefer the security of being what others want you to be?

Time Out for Personal Reflection

The following self-inventory is designed to increase your awareness of the injunctions that you have incorporated as a part of your self-system and to help you challenge the validity of messages that you may not have critically examined.

1. Place a check (√) in the space provided for each of the following "don't" injunctions that you think applies to you.

_____   Don't be you.
_____   Don't think.
_____   Don't feel.
_____   Don't be close.
_____   Don't trust.
_____   Don't be sexy.
_____   Don't fail.
_____   Don't be foolish.
_____   Don't be important.
_____   Don't brag.
_____   Don't let us down.
_____   Don't grow or change.

2. Check the following ways that you sometimes badger yourself with "do" messages.

——————— Be perfect.
——————— Say only kind things.
——————— Be more than you are.
——————— Be obedient.
——————— Work up to your potential.
——————— Be practical at all times.
——————— Listen to authority figures.
——————— Always put your best foot forward.
——————— Put others before yourself.
——————— Be seen but not heard.

List any other injunctions that you can think of that apply to you:

——————————————————————————————————

——————————————————————————————————

——————————————————————————————————

——————————————————————————————————

3. What are some messages you've received concerning

your self-worth? ————————————————————————

your potential to succeed? ————————————————————

your gender role? ——————————————————————

your intelligence? ————————————————————————

your trust in yourself? ————————————————————

trusting others? ————————————————————————

making yourself vulnerable? ————————————————

your security? ————————————————————————

your aliveness as a person? ————————————————

your creativity? ————————————————————————

your ability to be loved? ————————————————————

your capacity to give love? ————————————————

4. Because your view of yourself has a great influence on the quality of your interpersonal relationships, we invite you to look carefully at some of the views you have of yourself and also to consider how you arrived at these views. To do this, reflect on these questions:

a. How do you see yourself now? To what degree do you see yourself as confident? secure? worthwhile? accomplished? caring? open? accepting?

_____

_____

_____

_____

b. Do others generally see you as you see yourself? What are some ways in which others view you differently from how you view yourself?

_____

_____

_____

_____

c. Who in your life has been most influential in shaping your self-concept, and how has he or she (they) affected your view of yourself? (father? mother? friend? teacher? grandparents?)

_____

_____

_____

_____

Early Adulthood

In the previous chapter we discussed the developmental process from infancy through adolescence based on Freud's psychosexual stages and Erikson's psychosocial stages. Inasmuch as Freud deemphasized development in adulthood, this chapter will rely on Erikson's perspective on the core struggles and choices from early adulthood through late adulthood.

The period of early adulthood is ages 18–35. According to Erikson, we enter adulthood after we master the adolescent conflicts over *identity* versus *role confusion*. Our sense of identity is tested anew in adulthood, however, by the challenge of *intimacy* versus *isolation*.

One characteristic of the psychologically mature person is the ability to form intimate relationships. Before we can form such relationships, we must be sure of our own identity. Intimacy involves a sharing, a giving of ourselves, a relating to another out of strength, and a desire to grow with the other person. Failure to achieve intimacy can result in isolation from others and a sense of alienation. The fact that alienation is a problem for many people in our society is evidenced by the widespread use of drugs and by other ways in which we try to numb our sense of isolation. If we attempt to escape isolation by clinging to another person, however, we rarely find success in the relationship.

Erikson's concept of intimacy can be applied to any kind of close relationship between two adults. Relationships involving emotional commitments may be between close friends of the same or the opposite sex, and they may or may not have a sexual dimension. Some of the characteristic behaviors of people who have achieved a sense of intimacy include: establishing a clear sense of their own identity; being tolerant of differences in others; trusting others and themselves in relationships; establishing cooperative, affiliative relationships with others; being willing to give in relationships; believing in the value of mutual interdependence as a way to work through difficulties; being willing to commit themselves to relationships that demand some degree of sacrifice; and being able to form close emotional bonds without fearing the loss of their own identity (Hamachek, 1990).

ENTERING THE 20S

Whereas adolescence is a time of extreme preoccupation with internal conflicts and with the search for identity, your adulthood is a time for beginning to focus on external tasks, such as developing intimate relationships, getting established in an occupation, carving out a lifestyle, and perhaps marrying and starting a family.

During their 20s young people are faced with a variety of profound choices. If you are in this age group, you are no doubt facing decisions about how you will live. Your choices probably include questions such as: Will I choose the security of staying at home, or will I struggle financially and psychologically to live on my own? Will I stay single, or will I get involved in some committed relationship? Will I stay in college full-time, or will I begin a career? If I choose a career, what will it be, and how will I go about deciding what I might do in the work world? If I marry, will I be a parent or not? What are some of my dreams, and how might I make them become a reality? What do I most want to do with my life at this time, and how might I find meaning?

Choices pertaining to work, education, marriage, family life, and a lifestyle are complex and deeply personal, and it is common to struggle over what it is we really want. There is the temptation to let others decide for us or to be overly influenced by the standards of others. But if we choose that path, we remain psychological adolescents at best. We have the choice whether to live by parental rules or to leave home psychologically and decide for ourselves what our future will be. The following personal statements of individuals in their 20s illustrate the struggles of this period. A young man says:

I want to live on my own, but it's very difficult to support myself and go to college at the same time. The support and approval of my parents is surely something I want, yet I am working hard at finding a balance between how much I am willing to do to get their approval and how much I will live by my values. When I look at my parents, it scares me to see how limited their lives are, and I want my life to be different. I love my parents, yet at the same time I resent them for the hold they have on me due to my dependency needs. When I live differently than they think I should, I feel guilty.

Another person in her 20s expresses her desire for intimacy, along with her reservations and doubts:

While I realize that I want to be in a close relationship with a man, I know that I am also afraid of getting involved. I wonder if I want to spend the rest of my life with the same person. One thing that worries me is that if I allow myself to get close, he might leave, and I don't know if I'm ready for that hurt again. At other times I'm afraid I'll never find someone I can love who really loves me. I just don't want to give up my freedom, nor do I want to be dependent on someone.

Steven, age 24, is worried about the prospects of getting employed. "Now that I'm out of college, will I have an opportunity to use what I studied for all these years? Will I be able to get the kind of job I want in these difficult economic times?"

Martha, age 23, typifies young people who are willing to allow themselves to dream and remain open about what they want in life. She is also a good example of Sheehy's (1976) conviction that the choices made during the 20s aren't irrevocable. Martha works for a savings and loan association, and she is about to begin full-time graduate study toward a counseling degree. Here is what she is looking forward to:

At this time in my life I think I have a thousand choices open to me. I don't like my job as a loan officer that much, but it does provide me with security. I never want to stop learning, and I'm sure I want to be a vital person. At some time, though not yet, I'd like to be married. Eventually I'd like kids. I'd like to publish someday, as well as having a counseling practice.

When Martha was asked what she'd like to be able to say in her old age, she replied:

I have a friend whose grandmother was 63 and she rode a pogo stick. I'd like to be as energetic in my old age as I am now. I never want to get bogged down with old ideas. Some people get set in their values, and they just won't change. I always want to evaluate and to be in the process of integrating new values in my life.

When Martha was asked if she saw herself as typical of those her age, her answer was:

Most people between 18 and 23 don't look inward that much. I think they look to other people to make choices for them. I hope I can do what feels right to me at the time. I'm uncertain now about many of my specific goals.

I like taking life as it comes, but by that I'm not talking about being passive. I hope to be open to the possibilities that might eventually open up to me. I don't want to lose myself in someone else, but I would like to share my life with someone else.

Bret is 21, and he is struggling hard to get through college. He has had no help from his parents, and in fact he has been expected to contribute some of his earnings to the family income. While he is attempting to carve out a life for himself, he feels burdened with the responsibility of providing both emotional and financial support for his impoverished family. At times, taking care of both himself and his family seems overwhelming, and he feels like giving up.

TRANSITION FROM THE 20S TO THE 30S

According to Gould (1978), the transition from the late 20s to the early 30s is sometimes characterized by depression. It is a time of changing values and beliefs. For example, men who are switching careers or making changes within a career may be assuming that they will find a new direction in life. When their visions do not materialize, they may lapse into depression. Women who are married and have children may decide to work full-time, and they may find that this choice was not what they were looking for. Gould talks about the 30s as a time for making a new contract — making basic changes in lifestyle, priorities, and commitments. It is during this period of unrest, disillusionment, depression, and questioning that people modify some of the rigid rules of their 20s. They also realize other facts: that their dreams do not materialize if they simply wish for things to happen; that there is no magic in the world; that life is not simple but, in fact, is complicated and bewildering; and that we get what we want not by waiting and wishing passively but by working actively to attain our goals. As we open up in our 30s, a crisis can be precipitated when we discover that life is not as uncomplicated as we had envisioned it to be.

Sheehy (1976) contends that we become impatient with living a life based on "shoulds" when we enter our 30s. Both men and women speak of feeling restricted at this time and may complain that life is narrow and dull. Sheehy asserts that these restrictions are related to the outcomes of the lifestyle choices we made during our 20s. Even if these personal and career choices have served us well during our 20s, in our 30s we become ready for some changes. That is a time for making new choices and perhaps for modifying or deepening old commitments. We are likely to review our commitments to career, marriage, children, friends, and life's priorities. Because we realize that time is passing, we make a major reappraisal of how we are spending our time and energy. Both women and men tend to become more concerned about the biological clock, for they eventually realize that they don't have forever to reach their goals.

The process of self-examination may involve considerable turmoil and crisis. We may find ourselves asking: Is this all there is to life? What do I want for the rest of my life? What is missing from my life now? Thus, a woman who has primarily been engaged in a career may now want to spend more time at home and with the children. A woman who has devoted most of her life to being a homemaker may want to begin a new career outside the home. Men may do a lot of questioning about their work and wonder how they can make it more meaningful. It is likely that they will struggle with the meaning of success. They may be exteriorly focused in measuring success, which puts the source of the meaning of life on quicksand. They are likely to begin to question the price of success. Single people may consider finding a partner, and those who are married may experience a real crisis in their marriage, which may be a sign that they cannot continue with old patterns.

Time Out for Personal Reflection

1. Think about a few of the major turning points in your young adulthood. Write down not more than two turning points, and then state how you think they were important in your life. What difference did your decision at these critical times make in your life?

   Turning point: _____

   Impact of the decision on my life: _____

   _____

   _____

   _____

   _____

   Turning point: _____

   Impact of the decision on my life: _____

   _____

   _____

   _____

   _____

2. Complete the following sentences by giving the first response that comes to mind:

   a. To me, being an independent person means _____

   _____

   b. The things I received from my parents that I most value are _____

   _____

c. The things I received from my parents that I least like and most want to change are _____

_____

d. If I could change one thing about my past, it would be _____

_____

e. My fears of being independent are these: _____

_____

f. One thing I most want for my children is _____

_____

g. I find it difficult to be my own person when _____

_____

h. I feel the freest when _____

_____

Middle Adulthood

The time between the ages of 35 and 60 is characterized by a "going outside of ourselves." It is a time for learning how to live creatively with ourselves and with others, and it can be the time of greatest productivity in our life. For most of us it is also the period when we reach the top of the mountain yet at the same time realize that we must begin the downhill journey. In addition, we may painfully experience the discrepancy between the dreams of our 20s and 30s and the hard reality of what we have achieved.

According to Erikson, the stimulus for continued growth in middle age is the core struggle between *generativity* and *stagnation*. By generativity, Erikson means not just fostering children but being productive in a broad sense — for example, through creative pursuits in a career, in leisure-time activities, in teaching or caring for others, or in some meaningful volunteer work. Two basic qualities of the productive adult are the ability to love well and the ability to work well. Adults who fail to achieve a sense of productivity begin to stagnate, which is a form of psychological death. According to Hamachek (1990), the people who have a sense of generativity tend to focus more on what they can give to others than on what they can get. They are absorbed in a variety of activities outside of themselves, such as contributing to society or in other ways reflecting a concern for others. They display other-centered values and attitudes. They feel a strong inclination to express their talents. In short, they enjoy being productive and creative. In contrast, people who are not able to achieve a sense of generativity become stagnant. This stagnation is manifested by attitudes such as focusing on what they can get from

others, displaying self-centered attitudes and values, by avoiding risks, and by choosing the security provided by a routine existence and showing little interest in making the world a better place.

THE LATE 30S AND THE 40S

When we reach middle age, we come to a crossroads. We reach the midpoint of our life's journey, and even though we are in our prime we begin to realize more acutely that life has a finishing point and that we are moving toward it. Between the ages of 35 and 45 our physical powers may begin to falter, and the roles that we have used to identify ourselves may lose their meaning. We may begin to question what else is left to life and to reexamine or renew our commitments. We face both dangers and opportunities. There are many dangers of slipping into deadening ruts and failing to make changes to enrich our life. There are also opportunities for choosing to rework the narrow identity of the first half of our lives.

During middle age we realize the uncertainty of life, and we discover more clearly that we are alone. We stumble on masculine and feminine aspects of ourselves that had been masked. We may also go through a grieving process, because many parts of our old self are dying. This process does allow us to reevaluate and reintegrate an identity that is new and emerging, as opposed to an identity that is the sum of others' expectations. A few of the events that might contribute to the midlife crisis are:

- We may come to realize that some of our youthful dreams will never materialize.
- We may begin to experience the pressure of time, realizing that now is the time to accomplish our mission.
- Coping with the aging process is difficult for many; the loss of some of our youthful qualities can be hard to face.
- The death of our parents drives home a truth that is difficult for many to accept; ultimately, we are alone in this life.
- There is the realization that life is not necessarily just and fair and that we often do not get what we had expected.
- There are marital crises and challenges to old patterns. A spouse may have an affair or seek a divorce.
- Our children grow up and leave home at this time. People who have lived largely for their children now may face emptiness.
- We may lose our job or be demoted, or we may grow increasingly disenchanted with our work.
- A woman may leave the home to enter the world of work and make this her primary interest.

Along with these factors that can precipitate a crisis, we may have the following choices available to us at this time:

- We can decide to go back for further schooling and gear up for a new career.
- We can choose to develop new talents and embark on novel hobbies, and we can even take steps to change our lifestyle.
- We can look increasingly inward to find out what we most want to do with the rest of our life and begin doing what we say we want to do.

According to Carl Jung, we are confronted with major changes and possibilities for transformation when we begin the second half of life between 35 and 40. Jung's therapy clients consistently revealed signs of experiencing a pivotal middle-age life crisis. Although they may have achieved worldly success, they typically were challenged with finding meaning in projects that had lost meaning. Many of his clients struggled to overcome feelings of emptiness and flatness of life.

Jung believed that major life transformations are an inevitable and universal part of the human condition at this juncture in life. He maintained that when the zest for living sags, this can be a catalyst for necessary and beneficial changes. To undergo such a transformation requires the death of some aspect of our psychological being, so that new growth can occur that will open us to far deeper and richer ranges of existence. To strive for what Jung called *individuation* — a condition of integration of the unconscious with the conscious and of psychological balance — people during their middle-age years must be willing to let go of preconceived notions and patterns that have dominated the first part of their lives. Their task now is to be open to the unconscious forces that have been influencing them all of their lives and to deepen the meaning of their lives.

For Jung, people can bring unconscious material into awareness by paying attention to their dreams and fantasies and by expressing themselves through such avenues as poetry, writing, music, and art. Individuals need to recognize that the rational thought patterns that drove them during the first half of life represent merely one way of being. At this time of life, they must be willing to be guided by the spontaneous flow of the unconscious, if they hope to achieve an integration of all facets of their being, which is part of psychological health (Schultz, 1990).

You may be some distance away from middle age, but we hope you don't stop reading at this point, determined that this will never happen to you! Now may be a good time for you to reflect on the way your life is shaping up and to think about the person you'd like to be when you reach middle age. To help you in making this projection, it could be useful to consider the lives of people you know who are over 40. Do you have any models available in determining what direction you will pursue? Are there some ways you'd not want to live? Also, consider the following brief statements made by middle-aged people.

A man says that it's difficult to always be striving for success, and he shares some of his loneliness:

> So much of my life has been bound up in becoming a success. While I am successful, I continually demand more of myself. I'm never quite satisfied with anything I accomplish, and I continually look ahead and see what has to be done. It's lonely when I think of always swimming against the tide, and I fear getting dragged into deep water that I can't get out of. At the same time, I don't seem to be able to slow down.

A woman says that she has stayed in a miserable marriage for 23 years. She finally recognizes that she has run out of excuses for staying. She must decide whether to maintain a marriage that is not likely to change much or decide on ending it.

> I'm petrified by the idea that I have to support myself and that I'm responsible for my own happiness—totally. All these years I've told myself that if *he* were different, I'd feel much more fulfilled than I do in life. I also had many reasons that prevented me from taking action, even when it became very clear to me that he wasn't even slightly interested in seeing things change. I'm not afraid to go out and meet people on a social basis, but I'm terrified of getting intimately involved with a man on a sexual or emotional basis. When I think of all those years in an oppressive marriage, I want to scream. I know I've kept most of these screams inside of me, for I feared that if I allowed myself to scream I'd never stop—that I might go crazy. Yet keeping my pain and tears inside of me has made my whole body ache, and I'm tired of hurting all the time. I want something else from life besides hurt!

THE 50s

In the 50s people often begin the process of preparing for older age. Many are at their peak in terms of status and personal power. This can be a satisfying time of life, because now they do not have to work as hard as they did in the past, nor do they have to meet others' expectations. They can enjoy the benefits of long struggle and dedication, rather than striving to continually prove themselves. It is likely that rearing of children and work are moving toward a culmination. Adults at this stage often do a lot of reflecting, contemplating, refocusing, and evaluating of themselves, so that they can continue to discover new directions. The challenge of this time period is to strive for self-motivation, self-determination, and self-acceptance. This is a continuation of the process of integration that began at midlife. This integration is facilitated by accepting reality such as the aging process, life goals that have not materialized, and any past regrets.

For her popular book *Pathfinders*, Sheehy (1981) conducted extensive interviews with people around the United States. She found that the 50s can be a very satisfying period of adulthood provided the earlier developmental tasks have been resolved. Some of the new potentials listed by Sheehy (p. 228) are: a relaxation of roles; increased assertiveness in women; freedom to express one's opinions; an increase of leisure and money; a greater tolerance for others; greater opportunities for companionship with one's mate; opportunities to develop new relationships with children; and chances to contribute to the community.

At the time of this writing, I (Jerry) am 55 and I am finding it an optimal time for review of priorities. For the past thirty years or so, I have devoted most of my time to accomplishing professional goals. I have experienced a culmination of many of these goals, and now I am being challenged to discover other ways of defining and expressing myself. Although I could continue for the next thirty years on the path I've been pursuing, there may be other callings that I have not really allowed myself to consider. There is a part of me that could settle for what I have, and there is another part of me that wonders who and what I can become if I remain open to possibilities. Increasingly, I am aware that there are resources in my inner world yet to tap, at the same time that I am devoting most of my energy to achieving goals in the outer world.

CHANGING CAREERS IN MIDLIFE

The awareness of options can be an important asset at midlife. Most of the people we know have changed their jobs several times; you might think about whether this pattern fits any people you know. And whether or not you've reached middle age, you might ask yourself about your own beliefs and attitudes toward changing careers. Although making large changes in our lives is rarely easy, it can be a good deal harder if our own attitudes and fears are left unquestioned and unexamined.

A common example of midlife change is the woman who decides to return to college or the job market after her children reach high school age. Many community colleges and state universities are enrolling women who realize that they want more fulfillment at this time in their life. They may still value their work at home, but they are looking forward to developing new facets of themselves.

This phenomenon is not unique to women. Many men are deciding in middle age to quit a job they've had for years, even if they're successful, because they want new challenges. Men often define themselves by the work they do, and work thus becomes a major source of the purpose of their life. If they feel successful in their work, they may feel successful as persons; if they become stagnant in work, they may feel that they are ineffectual in other areas.

People sometimes decide on a career change even as they approach late adulthood. Reverend Thomas Bonacum, also known as "Father Tom," made a significant change of careers after the death of his wife of thirty-five years. With the support and encouragement of his four grown children, he entered the seminary in his late 50s and was ordained as a Catholic priest at age 60.

In his earlier days he was drafted into the army at age 21 and became a drill instructor. After leaving the army, Father Tom completed his degree in engineering, which led to a job as an industrial engineer. A few years later he was laid off and then joined the police department. During the time he was a police officer, he returned to college to get another degree in criminal justice. He became a police sergeant and eventually taught criminal justice for four years in the police academy during his twenty-two years in police work.

At age 73, Father Tom is now a paster of two churches and is well liked and respected by his parishioners. Because of his varied and rich life experiences, people find it easy to relate to him. He is able to empathize with both the joys and the struggles of his parishioners.

Father Tom is an example of a person who was able to translate a dream into reality. When he graduated from high school, he tried to become a priest but discovered that he wasn't ready for some of the people in church, and they were not ready for him. He exemplifies a man who was willing to make career changes throughout his life and who dared to pursue what might have seemed like an impossible career choice. Many of us would not even conceive of such a drastic career change, yet Father Tom not only entertained this vision but also realized his dream.

For many it may be extremely risky and seemingly unrealistic to give up their job, even if they hate it, because it provides them with a measure of financial security. This is especially true during economically difficult times. The costs involved in achieving the optimal job satisfaction may be too high. People might choose to stay with a less-than-desirable career yet at the same time discover other avenues for satisfaction. People who feel stuck in their jobs would do well to ask themselves these questions: Does the personal dissatisfaction outweigh the financial rewards? Is the price of mental anguish, which may have resulted in physical symptoms, worth the price of keeping this job? We explore these questions in Chapter Five ("Work and Leisure").

Time Out for Personal Reflection

If you have reached middle age, think about how the following questions apply to you. In your journal you might write down your reactions to a few of the questions that have the most meaning for you. If you haven't reached middle age, think about how you'd like to be able to answer these questions when you reach that stage in your life. What do you need to do now in order to have your expectations met? Do you know a middle-aged person who serves as a role model for you?

- Is this a time of "generativity" or of "stagnation" for you? Think about some of the things you've done during this time of life that you feel the best about.
- Do you feel productive? If so, in what ways?
- Are there some things that you'd definitely like to change in your life right now? What prevents you from making these changes?
- What questions have you raised about your life during this time?
- Have you experienced a midlife crisis? If so, how has it affected you?
- What losses have you experienced?
- What are some of the most important decisions that you have made during this time of your life?
- Are you developing new interests and talents?
- What do you look forward to in the remaining years?
- If you were to review the major successes of your life to this point, what would they be?

Late Adulthood

After about the age of 60 our central developmental tasks include the following: adjusting to decreased physical and sensory capacities, adjusting to retirement, finding a meaning in life, being able to relate to the past without regrets, adjusting to the death of a spouse or friends, accepting inevitable losses, maintaining outside interests, and enjoying grandchildren.

Late adulthood is a time for reflection and integration. Many physical and psychological changes occur as we approach old age. How we adapt to such changes is influenced by past experiences, coping skills, beliefs about changing, and personality traits. At this time, work, leisure, and family relationships are major dimensions of life.

According to Erikson, the central issue of this age period is *integrity* versus *despair*. Persons who succeed in achieving ego integrity feel that their lives have been productive and worthwhile and that they have managed to cope with failures as well as successes. They can accept the course of their lives and are not obsessed with thoughts of what might have been and what they could or should have done. They can look back without resentment and regret and can see their lives in a perspective of completeness and satisfaction. They accept themselves for who and what they are, and they also accept others as they are. They believe that who they are and what they have become are to a great extent the result of their choices. They approach the final stage of their lives with a sense of integration, balance, and wholeness. Finally, they can view death as natural, even while living rich and meaningful lives to the day they die.

Unfortunately, some elderly people fail to achieve ego integration. Typically, such people fear death. They may develop a sense of hopelessness and feelings of self-disgust. They approach the final stage of their lives with a sense of personal fragmentation. They often feel that they have little control over what happens to them. They cannot accept their life's cycle, for they see whatever they have done as "not enough" and feel that they have a lot of unfinished business. They yearn for another chance, even though they realize that they cannot have it. They feel inadequate and have a hard time accepting themselves, for they think that they have wasted their lives and let valuable time slip by. These are the people who die unhappy and unfulfilled.

We often imagine that people in their 80s and 90s tend to live in rest homes and convalescent homes. We forget that many people of advanced age live by themselves and take care of themselves quite well. For instance, I (Marianne) occasionally visit one of Jerry's aunts who is 90 years old. We always have good discussions about the past as well as the present. She has an incredible memory and shows interest in what is happening in the world. She remains active by gardening, sewing, and taking care of her household. During each visit, she proudly displays the fruits from her garden. She follows a daily routine that she seems to enjoy. At times she resists fully accepting her limitations, but eventually she is willing to receive the help needed to make her life more comfortable. For example, at one time she fought her family when they wanted to give her a lifeline system (a system the elderly can use to signal a need for help). Eventually she did accept the offer and she recently enthusiastically explained how the system works as well as telling me with a smile that this gives her adult children peace of mind. She has a deep religious faith, which has given her the strength to cope with many of the hardships that she has had to endure. Another source of vitality is her involvement with her children, grandchildren, and great grandchildren. I always walk away from these visits feeling uplifted, positive about aging, and saying to myself, "I hope I will feel as positive about life should I be fortunate enough to reach 90."

Old age does not have to be something that we look forward to with horror or resignation; nor must it be associated with bitterness. However, many elderly people in our society do feel resentment, because we have generally neglected them. Many of them are treated as members of an undesirable minority and are merely tolerated or put out to pasture in a convalescent home. Their loss is doubly sad, because the elderly can make definite contributions to society.

Elderly people have a vast wealth of life experiences and coping skills, which they are likely to share with others if they sense that others have a genuine interest in them. They can draw upon their past experiences as they are deciding on ways to respond to the circumstances of later life. Many elderly persons are still very capable, yet the prejudice of younger adults keeps them from fully using their resources. Perhaps because we are afraid of aging and mortality, we "put away" the elderly so that they won't remind us of our future.

STEREOTYPES OF AGING

Ageism predisposes us to discriminate against old people by avoiding them or in some way victimizing them because of their age alone. Some of the stereotypes associated with older people that need to be challenged are as follows:

• All elderly eventually become senile.
• Old people are nonproductive and cannot contribute to society.
• Most old people are depressed.
• Retirement is just a step away from death.
• It's disgraceful for an old person to remarry.
• Old people are not creative.
• Growing old always entails having a host of serious physical and emotional problems.
• Older people are set in their ways, stuck in following rigid patterns of thinking and behaving, and are not open to changing.
• When people grow old, they are no longer capable of learning or contributing.
• Old people are no longer beautiful.
• An elderly person will die soon after his or her mate dies.
• Most elderly persons are lonely.
• Old people are no longer interested in sex.

These are just some of the negative perceptions and stereotypes of older people that are common in our society. These myths can render older people helpless if they accept them. The attitude an older person has about aging is extremely important. Like adolescents, the aged may feel a sense of useless-ness because of others' views of them. Then it is easy for them to accept the myths of others and turn them into self-fulfilling prophecies.

Again, although you may not have reached old age, we hope that you won't brush aside thinking about your eventual aging. Your observations of old people whom you know can provide you with information about what it is like to grow older. From these observations, you can begin to formulate some picture of the life you'd like to have as you get older.

RETIREMENT

Retirement is arriving earlier for many people, and it is not uncommon for people to retire in their 50s. Some look forward to this time so that they can take up new projects; others fear this prospect, for they wonder how they will spend their time if they are not working. The real challenge of this period, especially for those who retire early, is to find a way to remain active in a meaningful way. Some people consciously choose early retirement because they have found more significant and valuable pursuits. For other people, however, retirement does not turn out as expected, and it can even be trau-matic. Some questions to raise are: How can people who have relied largely on their job for meaning or structure in their lives deal with having much time and little to do? Must they lose their sense of purpose and value apart from their occupation? The topic of finding meaning through one's work is explored in Chapter Five, which deals with work and leisure.

A couple who did not deal well with retirement are Jane and Bill. Both had very active careers and retired relatively early. They began to spend most of their time with each other. After about two years they grew to dislike each other's company. Because they were fighting so often, they rarely socialized. They both began to have physical symptoms and became overly preoccupied with their health. Jane chronically complained that her husband did not talk to her, to which he usually retorted, "I have nothing to say, and you should leave me alone." They were referred by their physician for marital counsel-ing. One of the outcomes of this counseling included the securing of part-time work for both Bill and Jane. They found that by spending time apart, they had a greater interest in talking to each other about their experiences at work. They also began to increase their social activities and started to de-velop some friendships, both separately and together. Both of them recog-nized and were able to put into words that they had retired too early from life.

What happens to us when we retire depends to a great extent on how well we've resolved the conflicts and issues of the previous stages in our life. It's very unfortunate that so many of us live for the future, deluding ourselves into thinking that we will find what we want once we retire. We may find that if we haven't achieved a sense of creativity, identity, and purpose in our earlier years, we'll feel a sense of inadequacy, emptiness, and confusion once retirement arrives. If we haven't defined for ourselves during our years on the job the place that work has in our life and the meaning we find away from the job, we'll be poorly equipped to find meaning in later life.

Just because people no longer work at a job does not mean that they have to cease being active. Many options are open to retired people who would like to stay active in meaningful ways. This is the time for them to get involved with the projects that they have so often put on the back burner because of their busy schedules. What is essential is for retirees to keep themselves vital as physical, psychological, and social beings. Following are some of the ways in which retired people have stayed involved:

• going back to school to take classes simply for interest or to prepare themselves for a new career
• becoming an integral part of community activities
• sharing their expertise, experiences, and wisdom with others, either on a paid or on a voluntary basis
• becoming more interested in and caring for their grandchildren
• taking trips to places that they have wanted to see
• visiting relatives and friends
• taking time for more physical activity
• cultivating hobbies that they have neglected
• joining a senior citizens' center

This list is not exhaustive, and you can probably add to it. Retirees do have choices to create meaning in their lives. They may discover that retirement is not an end but rather a new beginning. We conclude this chapter with a brief example of a person who is leading a simple and meaningful life in her old age. This woman, who is 89 years old, has lived alone since her husband died. She has a routine that involves keeping up her house, talking with friends, watching her favorite shows on television, and doing chores. When her grandchildren ask her if she isn't lonely, she quickly responds by letting them know that she enjoys her solitude and that her days are full. She likes not having to answer to anyone but herself, and she looks forward to each day. She doesn't brood over the past, nor does she wish that things had been different. Instead, she accepts both her accomplishments and her mistakes, and she still derives pleasure in being alone, as well as in being with those she loves.

Time Out for Personal Reflection

1. If you haven't yet reached old age, imagine yourself doing so. Think about your fears and about what you'd like to be able to say about your life — your joys, your accomplishments, and your regrets. To facilitate this reflection, you might consider the following questions:

- What do you most hope to accomplish by the time you reach old age?
- What are some of your greatest fears of growing old?
- What kind of old age do you expect? What are you doing now that might have an effect on the kind of person you'll be as you grow older?
- Do you know some elderly person who is a role model for you?
- What are some things you hope to do during the later years of your life? How do you expect that you will adjust to retirement? What meaning do you expect your life to have when you reach old age?
- How would you like to be able to respond to your body's aging? How do you think you'll respond to failing health or to physical limitations on your lifestyle?
- Assume that you will have enough money to live comfortably and to do many of the things that you haven't had time for earlier. What do you think you'd most like to do? With whom?
- What would you most want to be able to say about yourself and your life when you become elderly?

In your journal you might write down some impressions of the kind of old age you hope for, as well as the fears you have about growing older.

2. What can you do at this time in your life to anticipate and prepare for retirement?

_____

_____

_____

_____

_____

3. Do you know any retired people? If so, do you think they are leading happy lives? In what ways have they found or failed to find fulfillment in this stage of life?

_____

_____

_____

_____

_____

Chapter Summary

Adulthood involves the struggle for autonomy. One part of this quest is learning to challenge our inner parent and doing what is necessary to become our own parent in a psychological sense.

Transactional analysis can help us recognize early learning and decisions. Our life script is made up of both parental messages and decisions we make in response to these injunctions. The events of childhood and, to some extent, adolescence contribute to the formation of our life script, which we tend to follow into adulthood. By becoming increasingly aware of our life script, we are in a position to revise it. If we determine that earlier decisions are archaic, we can then redecide. Instead of being hopelessly "scripted" by childhood influences, we can use our past to change our future. In short, we can shape our destiny rather than being passively shaped by earlier events.

Our quest for autonomy and maturity is truly a lifelong endeavor. Each stage of adulthood presents us with different tasks; meeting the developmental tasks of later life hinges on successfully working through earlier issues.

During early adulthood it is important to learn how to form intimate relationships. To develop intimacy we must move beyond the self-preoccupation that is characteristic of adolescence. This is also a time when we are at our peak in terms of physical and psychological powers and can direct these resources to establish ourselves in all dimensions of life. Choices that we make pertaining to education, work, and lifestyle will have a profound impact later in life.

As we approach middle age, we come to a crossroads. The midlife crisis is filled with potential for danger and for new opportunities. At this phase we can assume a stance that "it's too late for change," or we can make significant revisions. There are opportunities to change careers, to find new ways to spend leisure time, and to find other ways of making a new life.

Later life can be a time of real enjoyment, or it can be a time of looking back in regret to all that we have not accomplished and experienced. It is important to recognize that the quality of life in later years often depends on the choices we made at earlier turning points in life.

To review the tasks and the choices of each period of the entire life span, we recommend that you go back to the overview table presented in Chapter Two and think about the continuity of the life cycle. Now that you have studied each stage of life, reflect on the meaning of these stages to you. If you have not yet arrived at a particular stage, think about what you can do at this time to assure the quality of life you'd like in a future phase.

The experiences and events that occur during each developmental stage are crucial in helping to determine our attitudes, beliefs, values, and actions regarding the important areas of our life that will be discussed in the chapters to come: gender-role identity, work, the body, love, sexuality, intimate relationships, loneliness and solitude, death and loss, and meaning and values. For this reason we've devoted considerable attention to the foundations of life choices. Understanding how we got where we are now is a critical first step in deciding where we want to go from here.

Activities and Exercises

1. Do you believe that you're able to make new decisions? Do you think that you're in control of your destiny? In your journal write down some examples of new decisions — or renewals of old decisions — that have made a significant difference in your life.

2. Mention some critical turning points in your life. Draw in your journal a chart showing the age periods you've experienced so far and indicate your key successes, failures, conflicts, and memories for each stage.

3. After you've described some of the significant events in your life, list some of the decisions that you have made in response to these events. How were you affected by some of these milestones in your life? Then think about what you've learned about yourself from doing these exercises. What does all of this tell you about the person you are today?

4. Many students readily assert that they are psychologically independent. If this applies to you, think about some specific examples that show that you have questioned and challenged your parents' values and that you have modified your own value system.

5. To broaden your perspective on human development in various cultural or ethnic groups, talk to someone you know who grew up in a very different environment from the one you knew as a child. You could find out how his or her life experiences have differed from yours by sharing some aspects of your own life. Try to discover whether there are significant differences in values that seem to be related to the differences in your life experiences. This could help you to reassess many of your own values.

6. Talk with some people who are significantly older than you. For instance, if you're in your 20s, you could interview a middle-aged person and an elderly person. Try to get them to take the lead and tell you about their lives. What do they like about their lives? What have been some key turning points for them? What do they most remember of the past? You might even suggest that they read the section of the chapter that pertains to their present age group and react to the ideas presented there.

7. Select one or more of the following books for further reading on the topics explored in this chapter: Bloomfield, *Making Peace with Your Parents* (1983); Ellis, *How to Stubbornly Refuse to Make Yourself Miserable about Anything—Yes, Anything!* (1988).

CHAPTER FOUR

Becoming the Woman or Man You Want to Be

Prechapter Self-Inventory

Using the following scale to respond: 4 = this statement is true of me *most* of the time; 3 = this statement is true of me *much* of the time; 2 = this statement is true of me *some* of the time; 1 = this statement is true of me *almost none* of the time.

_____   1. It is important to me to be perceived as feminine (masculine).
_____   2. I have a clear sense of what it means to be a man (woman).
_____   3. It is relatively easy for me to be both logical and emotional, tough and tender, objective and subjective.
_____   4. I have trouble accepting both women who show masculine qualities and men who show feminine qualities.
_____   5. It is difficult for me to accept in myself traits that are often associated with the other sex.
_____   6. I welcome the change toward more flexibility in gender roles.
_____   7. I think I'm becoming the kind of woman (man) I want to become, regardless of anyone else's ideas about what is expected of my sex.
_____   8. I'm glad that I'm the gender that I am.
_____   9. I feel discriminated against because of my sex.
_____   10. My parents provided good models of what it means to be a woman and a man.

Introduction

Kevin, a client in one of our therapeutic groups, gradually became aware of the costs of living by traditional gender-role expectations and began to widen his behavioral repertoire. To a great extent he had been a product of his social and cultural conditioning. His view of himself as a man stemmed from years of traditional child-rearing practices, which were continued in school and reinforced by his culture. For a long time he did not even realize that he was being restricted psychologically by the expectations for his gender. This dawning awareness came to him mainly because of a crisis that faced him in midlife. He was shocked when his father had a heart attack, and he realized the toll that living by traditional roles had taken on his father.

The crisis was the impetus that helped Kevin make some choices about changing his future. He began to look at the impact that his definition of maleness was having on all aspects of his life. He realized that he had never questioned his attitudes about gender-role behavior and that he was behaving unconsciously and automatically rather than by choice. To become a more expressive man, he had to struggle against years of conditioning that presented a highly restricted range of acceptable responses. Although he increased his level of consciousness intellectually through reading and personal counseling, he had trouble catching up emotionally and behaviorally with what he knew. In other words, his intellectual enlightenment did not easily lead to his feeling and acting differently.

All of us are partially the product of our cultural conditioning. Behavior depends not on sex but on prior experience, learned attitudes, cultural expectations, sanctions, opportunities for practice, and situational demands. We learn behavior that is appropriate for our sex by interacting in society. Socialization or enculturation is a process of learning those behaviors that are appropriate to a sex, an age, or a class. Learning about gender differences does not cease with childhood; rather, it is a lifelong process. We never stop acquiring cultural meaning and directions (Lott, 1987).

This chapter invites you to examine those factors that have directly and indirectly shaped your gender-role identity. With an increased awareness you will be in a better position to assess both the positive and the negative effects that your gender-role socialization is having on all aspects of your life. This context will provide a basis for deciding what changes, if any, you want to make.

In summary, we encourage you to think critically about gender-role stereotypes and to form your own standards of what it means to be a woman or a man. You will need to acquire patience and appreciate the difficulties involved in overcoming certain ingrained attitudes. The real challenge is to translate new attitudes into new ways of behaving.

Male Roles

Many men in our society live a restricted and deadening life because they have accepted cultural myths about what it means to be a male. Unfortunately, too many men are caught in rigid roles and expect sanctions when they deviate from what is supposedly "manly." In this way they become so involved in the many roles they are playing that they eventually become strangers to themselves. They no longer know what they are like inside, because they put so much energy into maintaining an acceptable male image.

In an article on rethinking masculinity, Kimmel (1987b) asserts that we are living in an era when the definition of the term *masculine* is in transition. The women's movement and the gay liberation movement have suggested that the traditional view of masculinity is in desperate need of overhaul. Men are now exploring new options in their work, are developing a wider repertoire of emotions, and are giving themselves more latitude in their expression.

THE ALL-AMERICAN MALE

What is the stereotype of the all-American male, and what aspects of themselves do many males feel they must hide in order to conform to it? In general, the stereotypical male is cool, detached, objective, rational, worldly,
competitive, and strong. A man who attempts to fit the stereotype will suppress most of his feelings, for he sees the subjective world of feelings as being
essentially feminine. A number of writers have identified the characteristics
of a man living by the stereotype and also those he may attempt to suppress or
deny (Basow, 1992; Goldberg, 1976, 1979, 1987; Jourard, 1971; Kimmel,
1987a, 1987b; Lerner, 1985; Lott, 1987; Mornell, 1979). Keep in mind that
this discussion is about the stereotypical view of males, and certainly many
men do not fit this characterization. It would be a mistake to conclude that
this picture is an accurate portrayal of the way most men are. But the following list of characteristics outlines the limited view of the male role that many
men have accepted, to a greater or lesser degree:

- *Emotional unavailability.* A man tends to show his affection by being a
  "good provider." Frequently, he is not emotionally available to his female
  partner, and because of this, she complains that she feels shut out by him.
  He also has a difficult time dealing with her feelings. If she cries, he becomes uncomfortable and quickly wants to "fix her" so that she will stop
  crying.
- *Independence.* Rather than admitting that he needs anything from anyone,
  he may lead a life of exaggerated independence. He feels that he should be
  able to do by himself whatever needs to be done, and he finds it hard to
  reach out to others by asking for emotional support or nurturing.
- *Aggressiveness.* He feels that he must be continually active, aggressive,
  assertive, and striving. He views the opposites of these traits as signs of
  weakness, and he fears being seen as soft.
- *Denial of fears.* He won't recognize his fears, much less express them. He
  has the distorted notion that to be afraid means that he lacks courage, so
  he hides his fears from himself and from others. He lacks the courage to
  risk being seen as frightened.
- *Protection of his inner self.* With other men he keeps himself hidden, because they are competitors and in this sense potential enemies. With
  women, he doesn't disclose himself because he is afraid that they will think
  of him as unmanly if they see his inner core. A woman may complain that
  a man hides his feelings from her, yet it is probably more accurate to say
  that he is hiding his own feelings from himself. Because he would find the
  range of feelings to be terrifying, he has unconsciously sealed off most of
  his feelings.
- *Invulnerability.* He cannot make himself vulnerable, as is evidenced by his
  general unwillingness to disclose much of his inner experience. He won't

let himself feel and express sadness, nor will he cry. To protect himself, he becomes emotionally insulated and puts on a mask of toughness, competence, and decisiveness.

• *Lack of bodily self-awareness.* He doesn't recognize bodily cues that may signal danger. He drives himself unmercifully and views his body as some kind of machine that won't break down or wear out. He may not pay attention to his exhaustion until he collapses from it. Goldberg (1976) contends that "the male has become an artist in the creation of many hidden ways of killing himself" (p. 189).

• *Remoteness with other men.* Although he may have plenty of acquaintances, he doesn't have very many male friends whom he can confide in. It is not uncommon for men to state that they don't have a single male friend with whom they can be intimate. He can talk to other men about things but finds it hard to be personal.

• *Drivenness to succeed.* He has been socialized to believe that success at work is the measure of his value as a man. He hides from failure and thinks he must at all times put on the facade of the successful man. He feels he's expected to succeed and produce, to be "the best," and to go ahead and stay ahead. He measures his worth by the money he makes. Based on his feelings of inferiority and insecurity, he is driven to prove his superiority. He has to win at all times, regardless of the costs, which means that someone else has to lose.

• *Denial of "feminine" qualities.* Because he plays a rigid male role, he doesn't see how he can be a man and at the same time possess (or reveal) traits that are usually attributed to women. Therefore, he is highly controlled, cool, and detached, and he shuts out much of what he could experience, which results in an impoverished life. He finds it difficult to express warmth and tenderness, especially public displays of tenderness or compassion. Because he won't allow the feminine experience to be a part of his life, he disowns any aspects within himself that he does not perceive to be manly.

• *Avoidance of physical contact.* He has a difficult time touching freely or expressing affection and caring to other men. He thinks that he should touch a woman only if it will lead to sex, and he fears touching other men because he doesn't want to be perceived as a homosexual.

• *Rigid perceptions.* He sees men and women in rigid categories. Woman should be weak, emotional, and submissive; men are expected to be tough, logical, and aggressive. He does not give himself much latitude to deviate from a narrow band of expression.

• *Devotion of work.* He puts much of his energy into external signs of success. Thus, little is left over for his wife and children.

In our work with men we find that many of them show a variety of these characteristics. In the safe environment that group therapy can provide, we also see a strong desire in these men to modify some of the ways in which they feel they *must* live. They are willing to take the risk of expressing and exploring feelings on a range of topics. For instance, they are willing to let the other group members know that they do not always feel strong and that they are scared at times. As trust builds within the therapeutic group, the men become increasingly willing to share deep personal pain and longings. They struggle a great deal not only in showing to others their tender side but also in accepting this dimension of themselves. It takes some time for them to get beyond their embarrassment at owning feelings such as love, compassion, rejection, sadness, fear, joy, and anger. As these men become more honest with women, they typically discover that women are more able to accept, respect, and love them. The very traits that they often fear to reveal to women are the characteristics that draw others closer to them. This often results in removing some of the major barriers that prevent intimacy between the sexes.

THE PRICE OF REMAINING IN TRADITIONAL ROLES

What price must a man pay for denying most of his inner self and putting on a false front? First, he loses a sense of himself because of his concern with being the way he thinks he should be as a male. Writing on the "lethal aspects of the male role," Sidney Jourard (1971) contends that men typically find it difficult to love and be loved. They won't reveal themselves enough to be loved. They hide their loneliness, anxiety, and hunger for affection, thus making it difficult for anyone to love them as they really are. Part of the price these guarded males pay for their seclusion is that they must always be vigilant for fear that someone might discover what is beneath their armor.

Another price that men pay for living by stereotypical standards is susceptibility to stress-related disorders. Although men have recently been paying more attention to their physical health, evidence continues to show that they have higher rates of stress and ailments related to stress than do women (Kimmel, 1987b). (An exception is those women who are striving to compete in heretofore "male" arenas.) This point reaffirms a key idea that we will explore further in Chapter 6: the truth is in one's body. Stress will take its toll on the body, as evidenced by a wide range of psychosomatic disorders. When denial and stress are chronic, the body will not lie but will show signs of wear and tear. Unfortunately, many men do not respect these messages until the damage to their bodies is severe.

Herb Goldberg (1976) cites evidence in his book *The Hazards of Being Male* that men die at an earlier age than women do and suffer more cardiovascular problems, that boys do worse than girls in school, that men are

involved in more crime than women are, and that the male suicide rate is higher than the female rate. Goldberg asserts that all the statistics that point to the hazards of being male actually constitute a description of the crises faced by males in our society.

In a later book, *The New Male*, Goldberg (1979) develops the idea that if men continue to cling to the traditional masculine blueprint, they will end their lives as pathetic throwaways. He describes such men as alive at 20, machines at 30, and burned out by 40. During their 20s most of their energies are directed toward "making it" while denying important needs and feelings. At 20 these men are typically urgently sexual, restless and passionate about converting their ideas into reality, eager to push themselves to their limits (if they recognize any), curious and adventurous, and optimistic about the possibilities for living. In his early 20s the traditional male is driven by societal pressures to prove his manliness, long before he is aware of who he is and what it is that he really wants for himself. Therefore, he locks himself into a cage and becomes trapped in his life situation, with few apparent choices. At 30 he has convinced himself that he is not a person but a machine that has to function so the job can get done. By his 40s he may experience a "male menopause" as his functioning begins to break down. Goldberg sees this decline as the result of years of repression and emotional denial, which make him a danger to both himself and others.

How might emotional denial make a man dangerous to others? One way is in domestic violence and spouse abuse. In our view, much of the violence by men toward the women in their lives is a result of faulty beliefs, injunctions, and assumptions about what it means to be a man. Men who buy this faulty thinking see themselves as destined to use power to control women. A man who is prone to resorting to violence is using his power over a woman because he is afraid of her. He cannot accept any hint of his being weak, which could be reflected in his inability to control her. Thus, he overcompensates by dominating and using force to exert his will. What we think is crucial to understand is this man's inability to accept the feminine within *himself*. Because he hates what he fears in himself and because it is mirrored by the woman, he attempts to destroy and conquer her. His physically abusive behavior is not a sign of his strength but is grounded in the weakness that he disowns. Yet that which he attempts to conquer will eventually conquer him.

Groups have been designed to help men who are physically violent. In their group for the treatment of men who batter, Grusznski and Bankovics (1990) have found that for many of these men, violence has been their only way of dealing with stressful situations. The group experience teaches men to recognize how their behavior and attitudes, such as the need for power and control over women at all costs, result in problems for both them and their partners. These groups allow men to challenge and change some of their destructive ways and to incorporate alternatives to violent behavior.

According to Weiten and his colleagues (1991), the principal costs to men of remaining tied to traditional gender roles are excessive pressure to succeed, inability to express emotions, and sexual difficulties. If you are a man, ask yourself to what degree you are tied into your socialization regarding expected male patterns. The chances are that you have been an active agent in your own gender-role socialization. Now might be a good time to reevaluate the costs associated with your gender-role identity and to consider in what ways, if any, you may want to alter your picture of what it means to be a man. If you are a woman, reflect on how you have been affected by the roles that the men in your life have subscribed to and ways you may want to change in relation to men.

CHALLENGING TRADITIONAL MALE ROLES

In his most recent book, *The Inner Male*, Goldberg (1987) acknowledges that the options of behaving in less traditional ways have increased. Yet he adds that

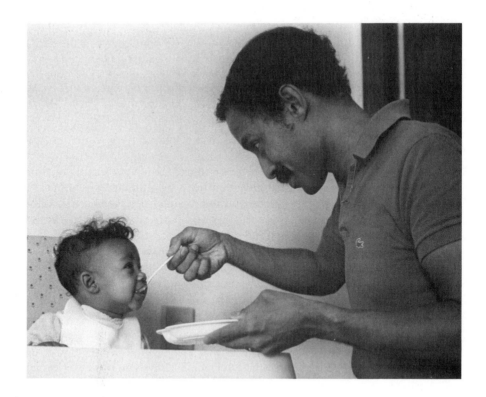

new pressures are pushing men to move back into traditional role-playing behavior and that men pay a steep price for moving too far beyond society's expectations for them. Overall, however, there is a new social atmosphere that makes it easier for men to let go of ritualistic macho behavior patterns that are self-destructive.

In his updated discussion of the challenges facing contemporary males, Goldberg predicts that the psychological growth and evolution of males will involve a lessening of the rigid defensiveness that filters and distorts their experience. As men loosen up their self-destructive notions and behaviors, they will be able to reconnect with themselves and others. In mapping the territory for the journey toward becoming a freer male, Goldberg maintains that psychological evolution will alter the traditional way in which men relate to one another. They will no longer need to be guarded, self-protective, and distrustful.

As Goldberg notes, more and more men appear to be challenging the conditioning that directs them to fall passively into a rigid role. Leroy, who participated in one of our personal-growth groups, is an example of an individual who is willing to break out of rigid patterns of behavior adopted to conform to society's view of a real man. Leroy told us the following:

I was a driving and driven man who was too busy to smell the flowers. My single goal in life was to prove myself and become a financial and business success. I was on my way to becoming the president of a corporation, and I was thinking that I had it made. When I got my W-2 form, I became aware that I had made more money than was in my plan for success, yet I had had a miserable year. I decided that I wanted to experience life, to smell more flowers, and to not kill myself with a program that I had never consciously chosen for myself.

Leroy's decision did not come easy. It was, and continues to be, a real struggle for him to admit that he is only human. It is not easy for him to allow himself to experience and express feelings, yet he is making fine strides at becoming a sensitive, caring, and expressive man. He is actively talking back to inner voices that tell him he *must* keep driving himself, he *must* constantly set and achieve new goals, and he does not have the time to enjoy and savor life. For him a turning point was landing in the hospital and almost dying. This jarred him into accepting that he was not an indestructible machine. Commenting on the impact of this experience, he said:

To me, life was a constant struggle, and I could never let down. Life was a series of performances that involved me pleasing others and then waiting for the applause to come. The applause was never enough, because I prostituted myself. I was always disappointed by the applause, because I felt empty when the applause would die down. So I continued to push myself to give more performances. But out of my illness I began to look at my life and slow down, and I realized there is a world out there that does not solely involve my work. I decided to work no more than 50 hours a week; before getting sick I was working 70 to 90 hours a week. With that extra time, I decided to smell life—there are a lot of roses in life, and the scent is enticing and exciting to me. I'll thrive on it as long as I can breathe it.

At 48, Leroy showed the courage to reverse some of the self-destructive patterns that were killing him. He began deciding for himself what kind of man he wanted to be, rather than living by an image of the man that others thought he should be.

Leroy says that he likes roses because of the scent, even though they do have thorns that hurt. He is now convinced that the scent more than compensates for the thorns. While he experiences more emotional pain than he ever allowed himself to feel before, he also experiences joy and sharing that he never knew before. He and his wife, Angie, lived separately for nearly two years, which apparently helped each of them clarify what they wanted. Although both of them experienced some loneliness, they found inner strength and discovered that they could exist without each other. This time alone helped Leroy take a look at his priorities and clarify some options. Eventually he initiated steps that resulted in the two of them living together again. This time both were stronger as individuals and also had more to give to each other. At the time they decided to live as a couple again, they also got involved in marital counseling as a way of helping them to define a new relationship. They still have their differences, yet they can talk about them, and neither insists that the other fit the picture of the "ideal person."

Leroy continues to be aware of choosing a less stressful lifestyle than the one he had before his illness. By resisting the pressures of becoming a "corporation man," he paid the price of losing his job—and, later, another one. Although he was unemployed for some time, Leroy is now quite satisfied in his work. Even though he is working hard, he does not feel as driven as before. Both he and Angie have busy work schedules, yet they make sure to arrange for time with each other and with their friends. When difficulties arise, they generally deal with them immediately, rather than ignoring them. They recently went on a vacation, and when they got to the airport they became aware that neither of them had brought any work along, even though they had not discussed leaving their work behind.

ARE MEN CHANGING?

How much are the traditional notions of what a man is supposed to be really changing? Are different models available to men that allow them a wider range of feelings and behavioral traits? We think that there are some trends that support Goldberg's predictions about the evolution of male consciousness toward a lessening of rigid defensiveness.

Men are showing a clear interest in men's consciousness-raising workshops. The interest in the men's movement is evidenced by a 1991 *Newsweek* cover story on men's groups as a way for men who are leading lives of quiet desperation to share their stories ("Drums, Sweat, and Tears," 1991). This article reports that hundreds of men's groups are springing up in the country—163 in the Northeast alone. There is a great increase in the number of conferences, workshops, retreats, and gatherings for men. This movement was the subject of Bill Moyers's 1990 PBS television documentary "A Gathering of Men."

Two key books have recently been published that provide impetus for the men's movement. One is the poet Robert Bly's best-selling book *Iron John* (1990). According to Bly, men suffer from "father hunger," which results in unhappiness, emotional immaturity, and a search for substitute father figures. Bly writes and talks about the ways that having an absent, abusive, or

alcoholic father results in the wounding of the sons. Another best-selling book is Sam Keen's *Fire in the Belly: On Being a Man* (1991), which describes what men lack. Keen talks about the importance for men of writing their autobiographies in ways that help them become aware of their family scripts and move away from the myths that formed their socialization. These two books, along with Bill Moyers's interviews with Robert Bly and Sam Keen, have promoted an interest in exploring men's issues in conferences and workshops. Writers have emphasized that love has often failed men because they have expected the women in their lives to heal their boyhood wounds caused by their fathers. Those who do the wounding must be the ones who do the healing. One of the bases of men's gatherings is to share common struggles, reveal their stories, and find healing in the men's collective. The fact that men from all walks of life are becoming interested in talking about their socialization from boyhood to manhood indicates that many men are rebelling against the steep price they have paid for subscribing to traditional role behavior. Writers also focus on the lack of adequate male models to demonstrate healthy male behavior.

Fortunately, television sometimes portrays a different vision of what it means to be male besides the macho stereotype. Just today I (Jerry) happened to catch the televised halftime event of the basketball game between the Los Angeles Lakers and the Boston Celtics. The event was honoring the accomplishments of Magic Johnson, the star player of the Los Angeles Lakers who was retiring from basketball because of his having contracted the AIDS virus. What struck me was Magic's ability to show the depth of his feelings in front of the thousands of fans gathered in the Forum and to the millions of viewers around the world. As he was being honored, tears were streaming down Magic's cheeks. Although he appeared physically uncomfortable with the praise and kindness that was being heaped upon him, he appeared to allow himself to feel deeply. He had the courage to express his tenderness and love to his fellow players, to a number of people who had made a significant difference in his life, and especially to his father, mother, wife, and son. To his father, he expressed his love for teaching him the value of working hard. He told his mother that what he received from her was her heart. He let his wife know that he used to think of himself as a strong man, yet he now sees her as a hundred times stronger as a woman than he is as a man.

Magic allowed himself to be deeply emotionally affected and to out-wardly express what was in his heart. He lovingly embraced a number of his fellow players, defying the myth that "real men" don't hug one another. He also defied the myth that men are cool and detached. His genuineness, grace, sensitivity, and spontaneity moved those who viewed this event. Many in the audience allowed their tears of sadness and joy to show. I was affected emotionally and also found it hopeful that a different model of masculinity was being presented to so many.

Female Roles

Like men, women in our society have suffered from gender stereotypes. There is evidence that gender roles and stereotypes lead to a variety of nega-tive outcomes with respect to one's self-concept, psychological well-being, and physical health (Basow, 1992). A major effect of gender stereotyping is that people tend to adapt their behavior to fit gender-role expectations. In the case of women, their socialization has encouraged them to lower their aspirations in terms of achievement in the competitive world. Many women are concerned that they will be perceived as unfeminine if they strive for success with too much zeal. This rigid viewpoint is changing as many women actively fight the stereotype of the passive, dependent, and unaccomplished female. Lerner (1985) maintains that the culturally prescribed roles for women discourage them from competing with men or expressing anger to them. Like men, women pay a price for living by narrowly defined rules of what women should be. One of these prices is the conflict about achievement that many women experience. Typically, if women do strive toward career aspirations, they also carry the responsibilities of parent and spouse (Weiten et al., 1991).

TRADITIONAL ROLES FOR WOMEN

Elements of the traditional gender stereotypes of women are still too prevalent in our culture. Basow (1992) cites considerable research evidence supporting the existence of gender stereotypes. Women, more so than men, are seen as exhibiting the qualities of warmth, expressiveness, and nurturance. Other characteristics that fit the portrait of femininity include lack of an aggressive and independent spirit, tendency to be emotional and not rational, passivity and submissiveness, proneness toward a home orientation, proneness to tears and feeling easily hurt, excitability in minor crises, indecisiveness, tactfulness, religiosity, and interest in relationships. The costs for women of traditional gender roles are diminished aspirations, frustration associated with the housewife role, and ambivalence about sexuality (Weiten et al., 1991).

In pointing out how inaccurate gender stereotypes are when it comes to individuals, Basow (1992) writes that "(1) people cannot be viewed simply as collections of consistent traits, because situations also are important; (2) males and females specifically cannot be viewed as having unique traits that are opposite each other; and (3) whatever attributes are thought of as distinctly masculine or feminine are also possessed by at least some members of the other sex" (p. 9). Basow emphasizes that gender stereotypes are powerful forces of social control. Women and men can choose to be socially acceptable by conforming to such stereotypes, or they can make the choice of rebelling and dealing with the consequences of being socially unacceptable.

If you are a woman, ask yourself to what degree you are tied into your socialization regarding expected female patterns. As is the case with men, you have likely been an active agent in your own gender-role socialization. Now might be a good time to reevaluate the costs associated with your gender-role identity and to consider in what ways, if any, you may want to alter your picture of what it means to be a woman. If you are a man, reflect on how you have been affected by female roles and ways you may want to change in relation to women. Ask yourself about the ways that you might have more flexibility as a man if women had a wider range of traits and behaviors available to them.

CHALLENGING TRADITIONAL FEMALE ROLES

There are signs that women are increasingly recognizing the price that they have been paying for staying within the limited boundaries set for them by their culture. We are realizing that gender stereotypes influence societal practices, discrimination, individual beliefs, and sexual behavior itself. Sensitizing ourselves to the process of gender-role development can help us make choices about modifying the results of our socialization. Women are beginning to take actions that grow out of their awareness.

SIMILARITIES BETWEEN WOMEN & MEN GREATLY OUTWEIGH THE DIFFERENCES.

The changing structure of gender relations has altered what women expect of men and the role that men play in women's lives. According to Kathleen Gerson (1987), the so-called traditional family has given way to a variety of family and household forms. It now becomes difficult to argue that the traditional division of labor between the sexes is natural, inevitable, and morally superior. There is no single standard for family life. Among the new options are equity in parenting and freedom from family commitments. Gerson writes that the larger social changes are promising women new sources of power but also bringing about new insecurities. In her book *Composing a Life*, Mary Catherine Bateson (1990) claims that the guidelines for composing a life are no longer clear for either sex. Especially for women, it is not possible to use previous generations as a model. For women, some of the most basic concepts — work, home, love, and commitment — used to design a life have changed their meanings.

It is clear, then, that despite the staying power of gender stereotypes, increasing numbers of women are rejecting limited views of what a woman is expected to be. They are discovering that they can indeed have many of the traits traditionally attributed to them yet at the same time take a new view of themselves. Today's women are pursuing careers that in earlier times were closed to them. They are demanding equal pay for equal work. Many women are making the choice to postpone marriage and child rearing until they have established themselves in careers, and some are deciding not to have children. Choosing a single life is now an acceptable option. In dual-career marriages there is considerable sharing of responsibilities that previously were allocated to one sex or the other. Women are assuming positions of leadership in government and business. There are signs that they are questioning many of the attitudes they have incorporated and are resisting the pressures to conform to traditional gender-role behaviors. In particular, many women are challenging the pressures put on them to find their satisfactions exclusively or primarily in marriage and the raising of a family.

WOMEN AND WORK CHOICES

The number and proportion of women employed in the workplace is predicted to increase. More than 60 percent of all adult females are expected to participate in the labor force by the year 2000. Although in the past a home and a family largely contributed to giving women an identity, more and more women are now looking to an occupation outside of the home as a major source of their identity (Lock, 1992a). Many women work not only out of choice but also out of necessity. Some feel the pressure of taking care of the home and holding down an outside job to help support the family. And many single parents must work. Consider the case of Deborah, who after her divorce said, "I know I can survive, but it's scary for me to face the world alone. Before, my job was an additional source of income and something I did strictly out of choice. Now a job is my livelihood and the means to support my children."

According to Naisbitt and Aburdene (1990), occupational options for women are increasing. Seventy-nine percent of women with no children under age 18 are currently working outside the home. Women are now exploring a wide variety of choices besides those that have been viewed as appropriate for them. They are joining the labor force, going back to college, and entering professional schools. Women are studying medicine, business, and law. More women are assuming leadership roles. They work in two thirds of all new jobs created. And women are beginning new businesses twice as often as men do.

Naisbitt and Aburdene (1990) have predicted that the 1990s will be the decade of women's leadership in the world of work. Below are some of their findings and specific predictions:

- Women are starting new businesses twice as fast as men do.
- In the 1990s it will be increasingly recognized that women and men function equally well as business leaders; consequently, women will take on leadership roles that were denied to them in the past.
- In the 1990s the numbers of female physicians and attorneys will increase substantially, as will their influence.
- In the not-too-distant future, people will look back with some wonderment on the days when women were excluded from the higher echelons of business and political leadership, much as we do now when we look back on the days when women were not permitted to vote.

How is this widening of vocational options for women affecting men? Naisbitt (1984) observed that as women continue to exercise personal options, choices also open up for men. Some men now have the freedom to become full-time fathers or students or to share jobs with their wives. Naisbitt writes that traditional family life, which depended on the woman's subordinating her individual interests and making her children and husband her priority, is not destined to return anytime soon.

According to Carney and Wells (1991), surveys indicate that social change is accelerating as different options are becoming available to women and many women want to combine a career with a marriage and a family. The challenge for these women is learning how to balance the difficult demands involved in a two-career family. Increasingly, there is a trend for couples to postpone having children so that the woman can get established in her career. Many women who have made the personal and financial investment of preparing for a career are open to taking a maternity leave and returning to work.

Other women are making the choice to find their fulfillment primarily through the roles of wife, mother, and homemaker. Such women are not assuming these roles because they feel that they *must* or because they feel that they cannot enter the world of work; they *want* to devote most of their time to their family. Such women often struggle with feeling that they *should* want a career outside of the home, for they have heard so much about finding satisfaction in that way. Yet they see their work in the home, and they do not feel incomplete without an outside career. They need to learn how to feel comfortable with their choice. One woman whom we know, Valerie, illustrates the importance of accepting her choice, in spite of reactions from others that she should not settle for being "merely" a mother. Valerie was very professionally involved until she had two children. At this time, she has decided to put her full energies into being a mother and a wife. Even though she feels comfortable with her choice, she frequently hears from people who know her: "Why do you want to stay home with your kids? Is that enough for you?"

WOMEN IN DUAL-CAREER FAMILIES

As we mentioned, one of the realities of our time is that more married women now have full-time jobs outside of the home. Although having a career meets the needs of many women who want something more than taking care of their families, it drastically increases their responsibilities. Unless their husbands are willing to share in the day-to-day tasks of maintaining a home and rearing children, these women often experience fragmentation. Some women burden themselves with the expectation that they should perform perfectly as workers, mothers, and wives. The "superwoman's

syndrome" is described by Carol Orsborn (1986) in her book *Enough Is Enough*. Orsborn herself became one of these superwomen. She describes herself at age 37 as an unqualified success on every front, a woman of the 1980s who had proven that she could have it all. Yet her life was being ruined. Like other superwomen, she could point to her accomplishments, which were many. She was the president of her own company, a published journalist, a brown belt in karate, a devoted wife, and a mother of two. In her struggle for perfection in all areas of her life, however, she became aware that she was losing her own sense of identity. Such women need to reevaluate their priorities and decide how they want to live. Eventually, many of them realize that they simply cannot continue to balance their career with their home responsibilities, and they finally exclaim that enough is enough! For women who are trying to do it all, Betty Friedan's advice is worth considering: "Yes, women can have it all, but just not all at once."

Marsha, a physician, is another woman who is facing the challenge of a dual career. She holds a teaching position at a hospital. In addition to practicing medicine, she must teach interns, keep current in her field, and publish. Marsha enjoys all of these activities, yet they all produce pressure. She adds to this pressure by telling herself that she must be an outstanding practitioner, teacher, and researcher and must also be fully available as a mother and a wife. She feels pressure from her husband, Moe, to assume the bulk of the responsibility for taking care of their son and maintaining the household. With some difficulty Moe could arrange his schedule to take an increased share of the responsibility, but he expects Marsha to consider his professional career above her own. Marsha leaves her job early each day to pick up her son from the day-care center. She fights traffic and gets herself worked up as she tries to get to the center before it closes. It is clear that Marsha puts herself under a great deal of stress in holding up all her roles. She has both family and work pressures, and these pressures take a toll on her physical and psychological well-being.

Some women experience a lack of support and an actual resistance from the men in their lives when they do step outside of traditional roles and exercise some of their options. Although Marsha did not get much resistance from her husband about maintaining her career, she got very little active support to make it possible for her to balance her double life. The power resided in her husband, and she was expected to make decisions that would not inconvenience him greatly. Basow (1992) notes that since men typically have been the dominant sex, with most of the power, it is difficult for them to share this power with women. Those husbands who see themselves as liberated are put to the test when they are expected to assume an increasing share of the responsibilities at home. They may say that they want their wives to "emerge and become fulfilled persons," and yet they may also send messages such as "Don't go too far! If you want, have a life outside of the home, but don't give up any of what you are doing at home." A woman who has to fight her husband's resistance to her changes may have an even more difficult fight with herself. Both husband and wife may need to reevaluate how realistic it is to expect that she can have a career and also assume the primary responsibility for the children, along with doing all the tasks to keep a home going. Both parties need to redefine and renegotiate what each is willing to do and what each considers essential.

Other visions of fatherhood are emerging that call for fathers to join mothers as equal partners in child care. Consider the case of Belinda and Bert as an alternative to Marsha and Moe. Belinda is a professional woman with a husband and three young children. Bert, unlike Moe, continues to show a great deal of interest in his wife's personal and professional advancement. She often tells her colleagues at work how much support she gets from him. When he was offered a higher paying job that entailed a move to another state, he declined the offer after a full discussion with his wife and children.

They decided that the move would be too disruptive for all concerned. During the times when Belinda is experiencing the most pressure at work, Bert is especially sensitive and takes on more responsibility for household chores and for taking care of their children. This is an example of a dual-career couple who have created a more equitable division of responsibilities.

DIFFICULTIES AND FEARS

In her popular book *The Cinderella Complex*, Colette Dowling (1981) clearly describes women's struggles in achieving independence and their accompanying fears. Women, like men, have been subject to conditioning for many years, and they experience anxiety when they step out of well-defined roles governing their behavior. For example, many women are still not able to enjoy their achievements because of their fear of being perceived as "unfeminine." One of the themes in Dowling's book is that women have not kept pace on an emotional level with what they know intellectually about living more freely. Although they may *think* independently, they often *feel* emotionally dependent.

In the counseling field we find that many women hear "inner voices" that get in the way of enjoying their work and striving for success. What they tell themselves is a reflection of the messages they were given as children. They simply were not reinforced for professional achievements when they first began their careers, and now they have difficulties in recognizing their own merits as professional persons.

Just as a woman can question the traditional female stereotype, she can also question the myth that a successful and independent woman doesn't need anyone and can make it entirely on her own. This trap is very much like the trap that many males fall into and may even represent an assimilation of traditionally male values. Ideally, a woman will learn that she can achieve independence, exhibit strength, and succeed while at times being dependent and in need of nurturing. Real strength allows either a woman or a man to be needy and to ask for help without feeling personally inadequate.

We have experienced the particular difficulties a woman has while working in a husband-and-wife team. We often present workshops at professional conventions. We are comfortable with the way we work together, and each of us can appreciate and enjoy the other's style. In fact, we often get very positive feedback about the way we work with each other. Yet we have noticed Marianne must work harder for the recognition she gets than does Jerry. We often find that people refer to our mutual projects, such as books that we co-author, as "Jerry's books." This response comes not only from men but also from women. When we begin a workshop, there is a tendency for people to look at Jerry as the "expert" and "authority" on our subject. It is only as we have more contact with our audience that many of them are willing to include Marianne as an equal professional and recognize her contributions. In situations such as this, as difficult as they might be, Marianne tends to avoid a defensive stance yet finds ways to assert herself professionally. It is interesting that even among well-educated mental-health professionals, gender biases do exist.

ONE WOMAN'S STRUGGLE

Susan is one of the many women who are struggling to break out of rigid traditional roles and move toward greater independence. In high school she was an exceptional student and had aspirations to go to college, but she was discouraged by her family. Instead, they encouraged her to marry the "nice guy" she had been dating through high school, letting her know that she would risk losing him if she went off to college. Susan's parents maintained that he could provide a good future for her and that it was not necessary for her to pursue college or a career. Without much questioning of what she was told, she got married and had two children. To an outside observer it appeared that she had a good life, that she was well provided for, and that she and her husband were getting along well. In reflecting over the history of her marriage, Susan remembers first feeling restless and dissatisfied with her life when her children went to school. Her husband, David, was advancing in his career and was getting most of his satisfaction from his work. Around him, she felt rather dull and had a vague feeling that something was missing from her life. She had never forgotten her aspiration to attend college, and she eventually enrolled. Although David was not supportive initially, he later encouraged her to complete her education. But he made it perfectly clear that he expected her not to neglect her primary responsibilities to the family.

As Susan pursued her college education, she often had to make difficult choices among multiple and sometimes conflicting roles. She was an excellent student, she loved her association with her peers, and she sometimes felt guilty about how much she enjoyed being away from her family. For the first time in her life she was being known as Susan and not as someone's daughter or wife. Although at times David felt threatened by her increasing independence from him, he did like and respect the person she was becoming. Neither of them talked about divorce, yet she felt reassured that she was staying with him out of choice and that she wanted him more than she needed him.

Susan's situation illustrates that women who for many years have followed traditional roles can successfully shed them and define new roles for themselves. Some of the themes that she, and many women like her, struggle with are dependence versus independence, fear of success, looking outside of one's self for support and direction, expecting to be taken care of, and questioning the expectations of others.

Time Out for Personal Reflection

1. Dowling's *The Cinderella Complex* describes women's hidden fear of independence and the roots of their inner conflicts as they struggle toward liberation. What follows are some of the points she makes in her book. After reading each statement, place an "A" in the blank if you agree more than you disagree with it; place a "D" in the blank if you disagree more than you agree with it.

_____ Liberated women are able to move toward the things that are satisfying to them and away from those that are not.

_____ Women in our society have been conditioned to fear success.

_____ Many women are actually afraid of independence.

_____ Women have typically been brought up thinking that asserting themselves is unfeminine.

_____ Women's performance anxiety relates to their feeling inadequate and defenseless in the world.

_____ Although women have a tendency to try to solve their problems by changing things externally (getting married, finding a new job, fighting for women's rights), such external changes will not help them change self-destructive attitudes within themselves.

_____ Women who want to achieve a better self-image must begin by recognizing what's going on inside of them.

_____ Women will not experience real change and genuine emancipation until they combat the anxieties that are preventing them from feeling competent and whole as persons.

_____ Ultimately, women will not achieve genuine liberation from anyone other than themselves.

2. The central message of Dowling's book is that psychological dependency, or the wish to be taken care of by others, is the major force holding women down today. The author's thesis is that like Cinderella, women are still waiting for something or someone external to transform their lives. What are your reactions to this thesis? What path do you think women need to take to free themselves from the restrictions of their gender-role socialization and to achieve psychological independence?

Liberation for Both Women and Men

Some forces in contemporary society contribute to keeping women isolated, either in a nuclear family or alone in an apartment. Society has attempted to convince women that they are in competition with one another for men.

However, the women's movement has been instrumental in showing them how to deal with this isolation and to see through the myths that reduce their personal power (Lott, 1987). *Power* is a word now used by more women with less self-consciousness and apology. Lott asserts that women are less constrained by gender ideology and freer to choose options largely because of the feminist movement. The focus of the movement is that women must be respected and allowed to develop as full human beings. According to Lerner (1985), women can be pioneers in the process of personal and social change. They can use their anger to create new and more functional relationships. It is especially important that they avoid getting trapped in blaming and focusing on others. To do this, it is helpful to have support from other women. "Our challenge is to listen carefully to our own anger and to use it in the service of change" (p. 224).

The increasing liberation of women has also stimulated some degree of liberation of men. This trend is underscored by Basow's (1992) contention that a goal worth striving for is allowing people to be fully human and to bring about changes in our society that will reflect that humanity. She states: "Eliminating gender stereotypes and redefining gender in terms of equality does not mean simply liberating women, but liberating men and our society as well" (Basow, 1992, p. 359).

Goldberg (1976) contends that increasingly women are refusing to conspire with men in fostering the stereotype of themselves as weak, helpless, and designed primarily to take care of a family. Goldberg views this assertiveness on the part of women as liberating not only for themselves but for men as well, because it frees men from the need to live up to the macho image. When both men and women are free of restrictive roles and thus free to be the persons they *can* be, they develop authentic relationships with each other based on their individual strengths instead of on a game in which one must be weak so that the other can be strong.

Gerson (1987) contends that men cannot remain insulated from the changes taking place in women's lives and will be forced to adjust to new social circumstances. Men have also begun to realize the steep price of gender expectations, and there is now the movement we mentioned earlier for the liberation of men and for a nonpatriarchal society (Lott, 1987).

In his lectures on the men's movement and in his book *Iron John*, Robert Bly (1990) addresses the subject of men learning to experience and express their feelings. He believes that the time is ripe for a new vision of masculinity. In the preface to *Iron John*, he writes:

> We are living at an important and fruitful moment now, for it is clear to men that the images of adult manhood given by the popular culture are worn out; a man can no longer depend on them. By the time a man is thirty-

five he knows that the images of the right man, the tough man, the true man which he received in high school do not work in life. Such a man is open to new visions of what a man is or could be. (p. ix)

According to Bly, the Industrial Revolution meant that the father was largely absent from the home and no longer assumed a role in teaching his son about manhood. Most boys do not have adequate role models upon which to base the development of their gender identity. Bly addresses the devastating effects of remote fathers and mourns the disappearance of male initiation rites in our culture. He believes that because boys are cut off emotionally from their fathers, they eventually become men who are cut off from the wellsprings of their own feelings. Bly sees it as important for men to express their deep grief over not bonding with the father. In his own case, Bly detached from his own feelings because of his lack of connection with his alcoholic father. It was not until he was in his late 30s that he was able to initiate emotional contact with his father. He saw the importance of connecting to the father energy, which often takes the form of a younger man forming a relationship with an older male. For men to be able to appreciate women's nature more fully, they must first understand and respect themselves as men.

In the therapeutic groups that we conduct, we continue to find that many men feel hurt over not having had the relationships they would like to have had with their fathers. As the world is changing and gender roles for men are giving way to new forms, many fathers are unable to prepare their sons for these transformations. Men are often angry at their fathers for not having taught them to express affection, failing to realize that their fathers also did not learn this in growing up. We encourage these men to assume the responsibility to change some of the notions that have been passed down for generations, which no longer fit in today's world. We see it as essential that they not get stuck in a blaming stance and that they realize that they have a choice to be different and can begin by approaching and treating their fathers in a different way. Whether or not their fathers ever fulfill their expectations of what they would have hoped for, it is still possible for men to be the kinds of men they would like to be.

Women and men need to remain open to each other and to change their attitudes if they are interested in releasing themselves from stereotyped roles. People of both genders seem to be in a transitional period in which they are redefining themselves and ridding themselves of old stereotypes; yet too often they are needlessly fighting with each other when they could be helping each other be patient as they learn new patterns of thought and behavior. As men and women alike pay closer attention to attitudes that are deeply ingrained in themselves, they may find that they haven't caught up emotionally with their intellectual level of awareness. Although we might well be "liberated" intellectually and *know* what we want, many of us have difficulty in *feeling* OK about what we want. The challenge is getting the two together.

Alternatives to Rigid Gender-Role Expectations

The prevalence of certain male and female stereotypes in our culture doesn't mean that all men and women live within these narrow confines. Nevertheless, many people uncritically accept rigid definitions of their roles, and even liberated people are probably affected by some vestiges of sexual stereotypes. Fortunately, there is much challenging of traditional perspectives among the college students we come in contact with. For instance, more and more men are apparently realizing that they can combine self-confidence, assertiveness, and power with tenderness, warmth, and self-expressiveness.

The alternative to living according to a stereotype is to realize that we can actively define our own standards of what we want to be like as women or as men. We don't have to blindly accept roles and expectations that have been imposed on us or remain victims of our early conditioning, or of our own self-socialization as well. We can begin to achieve autonomy in our sexual identity by looking at how we have formed our ideals and standards and who our models have been; then we can decide whether these are the standards we want to use in defining our gender-role identity now.

ANDROGYNY AS AN ALTERNATIVE

For us, one appealing alternative to rigid gender stereotypes is the concept of *androgyny*, or the coexistence of male and female personality traits and characteristics in the same person. Androgyny refers to the flexible integration of strong "masculine" and "feminine" traits in unique ways: androgynous people are able to recognize and express both the "feminine" and "masculine" dimensions. We all secrete some male and some female hormones, and we also have both feminine and masculine psychological characteristics. Carl Jung developed the notions of the *animus* and *anima*, which refer to the (usually hidden) masculine and feminine aspects within us. Taken together, the animus and the anima reflect Jung's conception of humans as androgynous. Since women share some of the psychological characteristics of men (through their animus), and since men possess some feminine aspects (through their anima), both can better understand the opposite sex. Jung was very insistent that women and men must express both dimensions of their personality. Failure to do so means that part of our nature is denied, which results in one-sided development. Becoming fully human implies accepting the full range of our personality characteristics.

Basow (1992) writes in *Gender: Stereotypes and Roles* that androgyny does not mean being neuter or imply anything about one's sexual orientation. Instead, the concept describes the degree of flexibility a person has regarding stereotypic gender-role behaviors. Androgynous individuals are able to adjust their behavior to what the situation requires in integrated and flexible ways. They are not bound by rigid, stereotyped behavior. Androgynous people have a wider range of capacities than those who are entrapped by gender-typed expectations. They can give expression to the rich ranges within themselves, depending on what a situation calls for. Thus, they may perceive themselves as being both understanding, affectionate, and considerate *and* self-reliant, independent, and firm. The same person has the capacity to be an empathic listener to a friend with a problem, a forceful leader when a project needs to be moved into action, and an assertive supervisor.

Lott (1987, p. 259) captures the essence of androgyny by calling it a move toward a human perspective. Because *masculine* and *feminine* imply a false dichotomy, Lott urges the discontinuation of these terms. Teachable behaviors of humans do not belong exclusively to either gender, for both genders show wide individual differences along all behavioral dimensions. Instead, it is better to consider the conditions under which people learn to be assertive, expressive, and compassionate. In reality, we are multidimensional beings, and polarities of behavioral traits are rare.

One of the reviewers of this book informed us that her students tend to be threatened by our presentation of androgyny as an alternative to traditional gender roles. That reviewer prefers to explain that males and females possess all characteristics, but society has labeled some as "male" and others as "female." This causes people to deny some of these characteristics within themselves because they are seen as belonging to the opposite sex. Regardless of what labels are used, we still maintain that people do have both feminine and masculine aspects within them, and that to become fully human we need to realize the rich and complex dimensions of our being. Another alternative to traditional roles is a transcendence perspective, which suggests that to be fully human we must go beyond the limitations of gender stereotypes and rigid gender roles.

GENDER-ROLE TRANSCENDENCE

According to Basow (1992), androgyny may be one step on the path to transcending gender roles, yet it is not the only nor necessarily the best way for personal change to occur. In writing about transcending gender stereotypes and roles, Basow indicates that we need to define healthy human functioning independently of gender-related characteristics. She believes that the ultimate goal is to move beyond gender roles by transcending traditional gender-role polarities to reach a new level of synthesis. In this view the world is not divided into polarities of masculinity and femininity; rather, people have a range of potentials that can be adapted to various situations. When transcendence occurs, people feel the freedom to be individuals in their own right, and they feel evaluated on their own terms. As Basow puts it: "When gender transcendence occurs, people can be just people—individuals in their own right, accepted and evaluated on their own terms" (p. 327). When individuals go beyond the restrictions imposed by gender roles and stereo-types, they experience a sense of uniqueness because each person has different capabilities and interests. The transcendence model implies that personality traits should be divorced from biological sex. Those who advocate gender-role transcendence claim that this practice will enable individuals to free themselves of linking specific behavior patterns with a gender. They argue that if there were less emphasis on gender as a means of categorizing traits, then individuals would be freer to develop their own unique potentials (Weiten et al., 1991).

Time Out for Personal Reflection

1. The following statements may help you assess how you see yourself in relation to gender roles. Place a "T" before each statement that generally applies to you and an "F" before each one that generally doesn't apply to you. Be sure to respond as you are now, rather than as you'd like to be.

_____   I'd rather be rational than emotional.
_____   I'm more an active person than a passive person.
_____   I'm more cooperative than I am competitive.
_____   I tend to express my feelings rather than keeping them hidden.
_____   I tend to live by what is expected of my sex.
_____   I see myself as possessing both masculine and feminine characteristics.
_____   I'm afraid of deviating very much from the customary gender-role norms.
_____   I'm adventurous in most situations.
_____   I feel OK about expressing both negative and positive feelings.
_____   I'm continually striving for success.
_____   I fear success as much as I fear failure.

Now look over your responses. Which characteristics, if any, would you like to change in yourself?

_____

_____

_____

2. What are some of your reactions to the changes in women's view of their gender role? What impact do you think the feminist movement has had on women? on men?

_____

_____

_____

_____

_____

3. What do you think of the concept of androgyny? Would you like to possess more of the qualities you associate with the other sex? If so, what are they? Are there any ways in which you feel limited or restricted by rigid gender-role definitions and expectations?

_____

_____

_____

_____

_____

Chapter Summary

The gender-role standard of our culture has encouraged a static notion of clear roles into which all biological males and females must fit. Masculinity has become associated with traits that imply power, authority, and mastery; femininity has become associated with traits that suggest passivity and subordination. Yet the concepts of masculinity and femininity are not biologically derived but historically and socially conditioned (Kimmel, 1987b).

Many men have become prisoners of a stereotypical role that they feel they must live by. Writers who address the problems of traditional male roles have focused on characteristics such as independence, aggressiveness, worldliness, directness, objectivity, activity, logic, denial of fears, self-protection, lack of emotional expressiveness, lack of bodily awareness, denial of "feminine" qualities, rigidity, obsession with work, and fear of intimacy. Fortunately, an increasing number of men are challenging the restrictions of these traditional roles. Books on men's issues have recently appeared that describe the challenges men face in breaking out of rigid roles and redefining themselves in new ways.

Women, too, have been restricted by their cultural conditioning and by accepting gender-role stereotypes that keep them in an inferior position. Adjectives often associated with women include *gentle, tactful, neat, sensitive, talkative, emotional, unassertive, indirect,* and *caring.* Too often women have defined their own preferences as being the same as those of their partners, and they have had to gain their identity by protecting, helping, nurturing, and comforting. Women have a long legacy of being responsible for the feelings of others; they also have deep-seated anger about culturally prescribed positions (Lerner, 1985). Despite the staying power of these traditional female role expectations, more and more women are rejecting the limited vision of what a woman is "expected" to be. Like men, they are gaining increased intellectual awareness of alternative roles, yet they often struggle emotionally to *feel* and *act* in ways that differ from their upbringing. The challenge for both sexes is to keep pace on an emotional level with what they know intellectually about living more freely.

We described androgyny as one path toward uprooting gender-role stereotypes. However, it is not the only way, or even the best way, to bring about this change. Ideally, you will be able to transcend rigid categories of "femininity" and "masculinity" and achieve a personal synthesis whereby you can behave responsively as a function of the situation. The real challenge is for you to choose the kind of woman or man you want to be and not be determined by passive acceptance of a cultural stereotype or blind identification with some form of rebellion. In asking you to examine the basis of your gender-role identity and your concept of what constitutes a woman or a man, we stress that you can ultimately decide for yourself what kind of person you want to be, instead of following the expectations of others.

In this chapter we've encouraged you to think about your attitudes and values concerning gender roles and to take a close look at how you developed them. Granted that there are definite cultural pressures to adopt given roles as a woman or a man, you are not hopelessly cemented into a rigid way of being. You can challenge those role expectations that seem restricting to you, and you can then determine if the costs of having adopted certain roles are worth the potential gains.

Activities and Exercises

1. Write down the characteristics you associate with being a woman (or feminine) and being a man (or masculine). Then think about how you acquired these views and to what degree you're satisfied with them.

2. The chapter has developed the idea that many men and women are challenging traditional roles. Based on your own observations, to what extent do you find this to be true? Do your friends typically accept traditional roles, or do they tend to challenge society's expectations.

3. Interview some people from a cultural group different from your own. Describe some of the common gender stereotypes mentioned in this chapter, and determine if such stereotypes are true of the other cultural group.

4. Make a list of gender-role stereotypes that apply to men and a list of those that apply to women. Then select people of various ages, and ask them to say how much they agree or disagree with each of these stereotypes. If several people bring their results to class, you might have the basis of an interesting panel discussion.

5. For a week or two, pay close attention to the messages that you see transmitted on television, both in programs and in commercials, regarding gender roles and expectations of women and men. Record your impressions in your journal.

6. Select one or more of the following books for further reading on the topics explored in this chapter: Basow, *Gender: Stereotypes and Roles* (1992); Bly, *Iron John: A Book About Men* (1990); Goldberg, *The Hazards of Being Male* (1976); Goldberg, *The New Male* (1979); Goldberg, *The Inner Male: Overcoming Roadblocks to Intimacy* (1987); Keen, *Fire in the Belly: On Being a Man* (1991); Thompson, *To Be a Man: In Search of the Deep Masculine* (1991).

CHAPTER FIVE

Work

and

Leisure

Prechapter Self-Inventory

Use the following scale to respond: 4 = this statement is true of me *most* of the time; 3 = this statement is true of me *much* of the time; 2 = this statement is true of me *some* of the time; 1 = this statement is true of me *almost none* of the time.

_____ 1. I'm in college because it's necessary for the career I want.

_____ 2. My primary reason for being in college is to grow as a person and fulfill my potential.

_____ 3. I'm attending college to give me time to decide what to do with my life.

_____ 4. I wouldn't work if I didn't need the money.

_____ 5. Work is a very important means of expressing my self.

_____ 6. I expect to change jobs several times during my life.

_____ 7. A secure job is more important to me than an exciting one.

_____ 8. If I'm unhappy in my job, it's probably my fault, not the job's.

_____ 9. I expect my work to fulfill many of my needs and to be an important source of meaning in my life.

_____ 10. I want work to allow me the leisure time that I require.

Introduction

Freud sees the goals of *lieben und arbeiten* as core characteristics of the healthy person; that is, "to love and to work" and to derive satisfaction from loving and working are of paramount importance. As you will see, work has an impact on many of the topics discussed in this book. The quality of the balance between work and leisure can contribute to our personal vitality or can be a stressful experience that ultimately results in burnout.

Work is a good deal more than an activity that takes up a certain number of hours each week. If you feel good about your work, the quality of your life will improve. If you don't like your job and dread the hours you spend on it, your relationships and your feelings about yourself are bound to be affected. In their *Wellness Workbook*, John Travis and Regina Sara Ryan (1988) write that work and play "are the stuff of our lives," since in most of our waking hours we are generally doing one or the other. They advocate that it is more important to become aware of what we are doing and to perhaps change our attitudes toward work and play than to change *what* we do for work or play.

We want to express our appreciation to Robert D. Lock, of Jackson Community College, and also to Jim Morrow, of Western Carolina University, who reviewed this chapter and provided us with useful feedback. We have included many of their ideas in this revised chapter.

"You may want to stop long enough to examine the roles working and playing take in your life. If they do not enhance it, you may want to make some changes" (p. 148). It is certainly worth the effort to think about ways to improve the quality of the many hours you devote to work and to leisure in your daily life.

If you have not yet begun a career, you can increase the relevance of this chapter by examining your expectations about work. Make an assessment of your personal interests, needs, values, and abilities, and begin the process of matching these personal characteristics with occupational information and trends in the world of work. In *Taking Charge of Your Career Direction*, Lock (1992a) acknowledges that choosing an occupation is not easy. Externally, the working world is constantly changing; internally, there are changes in your expectations, needs, motivations, values, and interests. Deciding on a career involves integrating the realities of these two worlds. Lock emphasizes the importance of *actively choosing* a career.

> You must accept the responsibility of choosing an occupation for yourself and then be willing to live with the consequences of that decision. These words are easily said but difficult to practice. There will be times when you want to escape the responsibility that freedom of choice brings, but no good counselor, parent, friend, or test interpreter will allow you to abdicate that responsibility. (p. 5)

One way to assume an active role in deciding on a career is to talk to people in your immediate environment about their job satisfaction. If you let others' expectations or attitudes determine how you feel about your work, however, you'll surrender some of your autonomy. Consequently, it's important to sort out your own attitudes about a career.

Before continuing with this chapter, let's clarify the terms *career*, *occupation*, and *job*. A *career* can be thought of as your life's work. A career spans a period of time that involves one or several occupations. It is the sequence of a person's work experience over time. An *occupation* is your vocation, profession, business, or trade. You may have several changes in occupation during your lifetime. A *job* is your position of employment within an occupation, and over a period of time you may have several jobs within the same occupation (Lock, 1992a).

Your College Education as Your Work

You may already have made several vocational decisions and held a number of different jobs, or you may now be in the process of exploring career options or preparing yourself for a career. If you are in the midst of considering what occupations might best suit you, it would be helpful to review the meaning that going to college has for you now. There is doubtless some relationship between how you approach your college experience and how you will some-day approach your career.

School is probably your primary line of work for the present. Ask yourself questions such as: Why am I in college? Is it my choice or someone else's choice for me? Do I enjoy most of my time as a student? Is my work as a student satisfying and meaningful? Would I rather be somewhere else or do-ing something other than being a student? If so, why am I staying in college?

According to research evidence studied by Herr and Cramer (1988), the reasons for choosing college are many and varied. Yet the studies suggest that student motivations can be summarized under the following three categories:

- *The self-fulfillers.* If you are in this category, your primary concern is search-ing for a personal identity and using your college experience as a means of self-fulfillment. Your expectation is that school will provide a supportive environment for self-expansion through academic pursuits.
- *The careerists.* If you are in this category, you view yourself as attending college mainly for vocational reasons. School is a means to an end rather than an end in itself. Although you may have other motivations, they are secondary to your major goal of adequately preparing yourself for a selected occupation.
- *The avoiders.* The decision to go to college is sometimes more of an avoid-ance maneuver than a conscious striving for a career goal or for self-development. You may be in college largely as a result of pressure from parents or peers. You also may not be quite certain what you want to do with your life and may hope that you can clarify your thoughts. Some attend college as a delaying tactic. Others are interested primarily in the social life.

Herr and Cramer maintain that many students in each of these catego-ries can ultimately benefit from career counseling. Self-fulfillers may eventu-ally realize that even though personal growth is a laudable goal, they will have to work. Careerists may discover that an original career choice is inap-propriate and that they need to search for other alternatives. Avoiders even-tually realize that they cannot endlessly put off their career choice. Whatever your motivation for going to college, career-development assistance can pro-vide you with the needed tools for making the best decisions over a period of time.

In Chapter One we asked you to review the impact of your experiences in elementary school and secondary school on yourself as a learner. If you saw yourself as a passive learner, you were encouraged to take steps to become an active and involved one. This would be a good time to review the goals that you set and determine how well you are progressing toward them. If you established a contract to take increased responsibility for your own learning and to get personally involved in this book and the course, reevaluate how you are doing. Perhaps this is an ideal time to set new goals, to modify your original goals, or to try new behavior in reaching your goals.

If you like the meaning your college experience has for you, as well as your part in creating this meaning, then you are likely to assume responsibility for making your job satisfying. If you typically do more than is required as a student, you are likely to be willing to go beyond doing what is expected of you in your job. If you are the kind of student who fears making mistakes and will not risk saying what you think in class, you may carry this behavior into a job. You may be afraid of jeopardizing your grades by being assertive, and someday you may very well be unassertive in the work world out of fear of losing your job or not advancing. If you are taking on too many courses and other projects, planning poorly, procrastinating, getting behind, and then feeling utter frustration and exhaustion by a semester's end, might you not display this same behavior in your occupation? Make an honest inventory of your role as a student. If you are not satisfied with yourself as a student, the situation is surely far from being hopeless. If you decide that your present major is not what really interests you, you are no more wedded to your course of study than you are to one particular job in the future. Determine for yourself why you are in college and what you are getting from it and giving to the project.

Choosing an Occupation or Career

What do you expect from work? What factors do you stress in selecting a career or an occupation? In working with college students, we find that many of them haven't really thought seriously about why they are choosing a given vocation. For example, parental pressure or encouragement is the major reason for the choice of some. Others have idealized views of what it would be like to be a lawyer, an engineer, or a doctor. Many of these people haven't looked at what they value the most and whether these values can be attained in their chosen vocation. John Holland's (1985) theory of career decision making is based on the assumption that career choices are an expression of personality: "The choice of an occupation is an expressive act that reflects the person's motivation, knowledge, personality, and ability. Occupations represent a way of life, an environment rather than a set of isolated work functions or skills" (p. 8).

BEING ACTIVE IN CAREER PLANNING

One of the major factors that might prevent you from becoming active in planning for a career is the temptation to put off doing what needs to be done to *choose* your work. If you merely "fall into" a job, you will probably be disappointed with the outcome.

Naisbitt and Aburdene (1990) indicate that the fast pace of social and technological change will continue to force people to adapt to a changing world of work. They mention that the average American who enters the work force today will change careers, not just jobs, three times. Some experts tell people that they can expect to have five different careers during their working years. This means that people who are entering the work force in the 1990s need to have more than specific knowledge and skills. Most importantly, they need to be able to adapt to change and to find a variety of ways to express their talents through their careers. It is a process that changes over time and, one career may pave the way to another one. Thus, it could well be a mistake to think about selecting *one* occupation that will last a lifetime. Instead, it may be more fruitful to think about choosing a general type of work or a broad field of endeavor that appeals to you. You can consider your present job or field of study a means of gaining experience and opening doors to new possibilities, and you can focus on what you want to learn from this experience. It can be liberating to realize that your decisions about work can be part of a developmental process and that your jobs can change as you change or can lead to related occupations within your chosen field.

THE DANGERS OF CHOOSING AN OCCUPATION TOO SOON

So much emphasis is placed on what you will do "for a living" that there is a real danger of feeling compelled to choose an occupation or a career before you're really ready to do so. In our society there is pressure from an early age to grow up. The encouragement to identify with some occupation begins in childhood with the often-heard question "What are you going to be when you grow up?" (Part of the implication of this question is that we're not grown up until we've decided to *be* something.) If freshman year in high school isn't too early to start worrying about acceptance to college, then no grade is too early to start worrying about acceptance to the right high school! Carney and Wells (1991) write that society expects young people to identify their values, choose a vocation and a lifestyle, and then settle down. The implication is that once young people make the "right decision," they should be set for life. Yet deciding on a career is not that simple.

One of the dangers in focusing on a particular occupation too soon is that students' interest patterns are often not sufficiently reliable or stable in high school or sometimes even in the college years to predict job success and satisfaction. Furthermore, the typical student does not have enough self-knowledge or knowledge of educational offerings and vocational opportunities to make realistic decisions. The pressure to make premature vocational decisions often results in choosing an occupation in which one does not have the interests and abilities required for success. At the other extreme, however, are those who engage in delay, defensive avoidance, and procrastination. An individual on this end of the scale drifts endlessly and aimlessly, and life may be pretty well over when he or she asks, "Where am I going?" It is clear that either extreme is dangerous. We need to be cautious in resisting pressures from the outside to decide too quickly on a life's vocation, yet we also need to be alert to the tendencies within ourselves to expect that what we want will come to us easily.

FACTORS IN VOCATIONAL DECISION MAKING

Making vocational choices is a process spanning a considerable period rather than an isolated event. Researchers in career development have found that most people go through a series of stages in choosing the occupation or, more typically, occupations that they will follow. As you recall from our discussion of the stages of the life span, various factors emerge or become influential during each phase of development. The following factors have been shown to be important in determining a person's occupational decision-making process: self-concept, motivation, achievement, occupational attitudes, abilities, interests, values, socioeconomic level, parental influence, ethnic identity, gender, and physical, mental, emotional, and social handicaps. In choosing your vocation (or evaluating the choices you've made previously), you may want to consider which factors really mean the most to you. Let's consider some of these factors, keeping in mind that vocational choice is a process, not an event.

Self-concept. Some writers in career development contend that a vocational choice is an attempt to fulfill one's self-concept. People with a poor self-concept, for example, are not likely to envision themselves in a meaningful or important job. They are likely to keep their aspirations low, and thus their achievements will probably be low. They may select and remain in a job that they do not enjoy or derive satisfaction from, based on their conviction that such a job is all they are worthy of. In this regard, choosing a vocation can be thought of as a public declaration of the kind of person we see ourselves as being. Casey and Vanceburg (1985) capture in a poetic way the notion that how we view ourselves has a great deal to do with how others perceive and treat us: "Our self-perception determines how we present ourselves. The posture we've assumed invites others' praise, interest, or criticism. What others think of us accurately reflects our personal self-assessment, a message we've conveyed directly or subtly."

Motivation and achievement. Setting goals is at the core of the process of deciding on a vocation. If you have goals but do not have the energy and persistence to pursue them, then your goals will not materialize. Your need to achieve, along with your achievements to date, are related to your motivation to translate goals into action plans. In thinking about your career choices, let yourself identify those areas where your drive is the greatest.

Also, reflect on any of your specific achievements. What have you accomplished that you feel particularly proud of? What are you doing now that moves you in the direction of achieving what is important to you? What are some of the things you dream about doing in the future? Thinking about your goals, needs, motivations, and achievements is a good way to get a clearer focus on your career direction.

Occupational attitudes. Research indicates that the higher the educational requirements are for an occupation, the higher is its status or prestige (Isaacson, 1986). We develop our attitudes toward the status of occupations by learning from the people in our environment. Typical first graders are not aware of the differential status of occupations, yet in a few years these children begin to rank occupations in a manner similar to that of adults. Some research has shown that positive attitudes toward most occupations are common among first graders but that these preferences narrow steadily with each year of school (Nelson, 1963). As students advance to higher grades, they reject more and more occupations as unacceptable. Unfortunately, they rule out some of the very jobs from which they may have to choose if they are to find employment as adults. It is difficult for people to feel positive about themselves if they have to accept an occupation they perceive as low in status.

Abilities. Ability or aptitude has received as much attention as any of the other factors deemed significant in the career decision-making process, and it is probably used more often than any other factor. Your abilities involve those things that you are able to do. *Ability* refers to your competence in an activity; *aptitude* is your ability to learn. There are both general and specific abilities. Scholastic aptitude, often called general intelligence or IQ, is a general ability typically considered to consist of both verbal and numerical aptitudes. Scholastic aptitude is particularly significant, because it largely determines who will be able to obtain the levels of education required for entrance into the higher status occupations. Your abilities can be measured and compared with the skills required of various professions and academic areas that are of interest to you.

Interests. Your interests reflect your experiences or ideas pertaining to work-related activities that you like or dislike. Interest measurement has become popular and is used extensively in career planning. Vocational planning should give primary consideration to interests. It is important to first determine your areas of vocational interest, then to identify occupations for which these interests are appropriate, and then to determine those occupations for which you have the abilities required for satisfactory job performance. Occupational interest surveys can be used to compare your interests with those of others who have found job satisfaction in a given area. These comparisons can help you identify general occupational areas where your interests overlap with those of people who have found success in a particular occupation (Carney & Wells, 1991). As important as it is to follow your interests, you need to know that simply because you are interested in a job does not necessarily mean that you have the ability needed for it.

There are several interest inventories that you might want to take as a way of assessing your vocational interests. These are the Strong Interest Inventory, the Kuder Occupational Interest Inventory, and the Myers-Briggs Type Indicator. This last instrument assesses types of human personality. If you want further information about such inventories you can contact the counseling center at your college.

Values. Your values indicate who and what you are as a person. Values are what is significant to you, and they also influence what you want from life. It is important for you to assess, identify, and clarify your values so that you will be able to match them with your career. After you have considered how your interests and abilities match with possible career choices, it is then helpful to explore your values. An inventory of your values can reveal the pattern behind the aspects of life that you prize and will also enable you to see how your values have emerged, taken shape, and changed over time. For purposes of this discussion, values can be classified in three general areas: (1) spiritual/ religious, (2) family/interpersonal, and (3) money/material possessions. Refer to the "Activities and Exercises" in this chapter for a self-assessment of your work-related values.

Your *work values* pertains to what you hope to accomplish through your role in an occupation. Work values are an important aspect of your total value system, and knowing those things that bring meaning to your life is crucial if you hope to find a career that has personal value for you. Because certain work values are related to certain occupations, they can be the basis of a good match between you and a position. Most career guidance centers in colleges and universities now offer one or more computer-based programs to help students decide on a career. One popular program is known as the System of Interactive Guidance and Information, more commonly referred to as SIGI. This program assesses and categorizes your work values in these ten areas: income, prestige, independence, helping others, security, variety, leadership, leisure, working in one's field of interest, and early entry. Taking the SIGI will aid you in identifying specific occupations that you might want to explore. SIGI Plus is an updated version of the original SIGI.

You might consider scheduling an appointment in the career counseling center at your college to participate in a computer-based occupational guidance program. In addition to SIGI, other programs are the Career Information System (CIS), the Guidance Information System (GIS), Choices, and Discover. Each of these programs develops lists of occupations to explore. There are other instruments that assess values. One is the Allport, Vernon, and Lindzey Study of Values; another is Super's Work Values Inventory. It may be well worthwhile to meet with a career counselor to discuss the value assessment instruments, and the follow-up counseling as well, but could be of use to you. As you will see, it is both realistic and useful to think of an occupation that is consistent with your personal orientation to life, which is described next.

PERSONALITY TYPES AND CHOOSING A CAREER

Holland (1985) has developed an approach to occupational theory that identifies worker personality types. He assumes that it is important for the work environment to match one's personality type. His typology is widely used as the basis for books on career development, vocational tests used in career counseling centers, and self-help approaches for deciding on a career. Because of his influence on vocational theory, it is essential that you read the following section carefully and that you take the time to think about your own personal orientation to life.

The following discussion of the six personality types is the work of Jim Morrow, who is a professor of counseling at Western Carolina University in North Carolina. Over a period of time he has refined the description of Holland's personality types through the process of giving his graduate students this descriptive survey of these six types.

The Realistic personality type. Realistic persons are attracted to outdoor, mechanical, and physical activities, hobbies, and occupations. They like to work with things, objects, and animals rather than with ideas, data, and people. They tend to have mechanical and athletic abilities and are usually strong and well-coordinated. They like to construct, shape, and restructure things around them and to repair and mend things. They like to use equipment and machinery and to see tangible results from their efforts. Although they are persistent and industrious builders, they are seldom creative and original ones, preferring instead to use familiar methods and to follow established patterns. They view themselves as practical, strong, stable, and physically skilled.

They tend to think in terms of absolutes and to have a low tolerance for ambiguity. They have a straightforward and uncomplicated view of life and prefer not to deal with abstract, theoretical, and philosophical issues and problems. They are materialistic and have traditional and conservative values and attitudes.

They do not have strong interpersonal and verbal skills and are uncomfortable in social situations in which attention is directed at or centered on them. They find it difficult to give emotional expression to their feelings and tend to be regarded as shy.

The Investigative personality type. Investigative persons are naturally curious and inquisitive. They have a need to understand, explain, and predict the things that go on around them. They are scholarly and scientific in their attempts to understand things and tend to be pessimistic and critical when nonscientific, simplistic, or supernatural explanations are suggested by others. They tend to become engrossed in whatever they are doing and may appear to be oblivious to everything else around them. They are independent and like to work alone. They prefer neither to supervise others nor to be supervised.

They are theoretical and analytic in outlook and find abstract and ambiguous problems and situations challenging. They observe, assess, evaluate, and theorize in order to solve problems. They are original and creative and often find it difficult to accept traditional attitudes and values. They avoid highly structured situations with externally imposed rules but are themselves internally well-disciplined, precise, and systematic in thought and action.

They have confidence in their intellectual abilities but often feel inadequate in social situations. They tend to lack leadership and persuasive skills and to be reserved and formal in interpersonal relationships. They typically find it difficult to express themselves emotionally and may not be considered friendly.

The Artistic personality type. Artistic persons are very creative, expressive, original, intuitive, and individualistic. They like to be different and strive to stand out from the crowd. They like to express their personalities by creating new and different things with words; with music; with materials, through painting, crafting, and the like; and with physical expressions, as in acting and dancing. They want attention and praise for their artistic endeavors but are very sensitive to criticism. They tend to be uninhibited and nonconforming in dress, speech, and action. They prefer to work without supervision.

They are impulsive in outlook. They place great value on beauty and esthetic qualities and tend to be emotional and complicated. They prefer abstract tasks and unstructured situations. They find it difficult to function effectively in highly ordered and systematic situations.

They seek acceptance and approval from others but often find the demands of close interpersonal relationships so stressful that they avoid them. They compensate for their resulting feelings of estrangement or alienation by relating to others primarily through the indirect medium of their art. They tend to be imaginative and introspective.

The Social personality type. Social persons are friendly, enthusiastic, and outgoing. They are cooperative and enjoy working with and being around other people. They are understanding and insightful concerning the feelings and problems of others. They like to be helpful to others by serving in facilitative roles such as those of teachers, mediators, advisers, or counselors.

They have social skills, express themselves well, and are persuasive in inter-personal relationships. They like attention and enjoy being at or near the center of the group.

They are idealistic, sensitive, and conscientious in their outlook on life and in their dealings with others. They like to deal with philosophical issues such as the nature and purpose of life, religion, and morality. They dislike working with machines, tools, and data and at highly organized, routine, and repetitive tasks.

They see themselves as having social and educational skills but as lacking in mechanical and scientific abilities. They get along well with others and find it natural to express their emotions. They are tactful in relating to others and are considered to be kind, supportive, and caring.

The Enterprising personality type. Enterprising persons are outgoing, self-confident, persuasive, and optimistic. They like to organize, direct, manage, and control the activities of groups to attain personal or organiza-tional goals. They are ambitious and like to be in positions of authority. They place a high value on status, power, money, and material possessions. They like to feel that they are in control of situations and are responsible for mak-ing things happen. They are energetic and enthusiastic in initiating and supervising the activities in which they engage. They like to influence the opinions and actions of others and to hold positions of leadership.

They are adventurous and impulsive. They are assertive and verbally persuasive in bringing others around to their point of view. They enjoy social gatherings and like to associate with well-known and influential people. They like to travel and explore and often have exciting and expensive hobbies.

They see themselves as popular and as having leadership and speaking abilities. They tend to dislike activities requiring scientific abilities and systematic and theoretical thinking. They avoid activities that require attention to detail and adherence to a set routine.

The Conventional personality type. Conventional persons are well organized, persistent, and practical in their approach to life. They enjoy clerical and computational activities performed according to set procedures. They are dependable, efficient, and conscientious in accomplishing their tasks. They enjoy the security of belonging to groups and organizations and make good team members. They are status-conscious but usually do not aspire to positions of highest authority and leadership. They are most comfortable working in situations and at tasks in which they know what is expected of them.

They tend to be conservative and traditional in values and attitudes. They usually conform to expected standards and follow the lead of those in positions of authority, with whom they identify. They like to work indoors in pleasant surroundings and place value on material comforts and possessions.

They are self-controlled and low-key in the expression of their feelings. They avoid intense personal relationships in favor of more casual ones. They are most comfortable in familiar situations and in the company of persons they know well. They like for things to go as planned and prefer not to have their routines changed or upset.

Relationships among the personality types. As you were reading the six personality types, you probably noticed that each type shares some characteristics with some of the other types and also is quite different from some of the others. To help you compare and contrast the six types, Holland's "hexagon," which illustrates the order of the relationships among the types, is shown here.

Each type shares some characteristics in common with those types adjacent to it on the hexagon. Each type has only a little in common with those types two positions removed from it, and it is quite unlike the type opposite it on the hexagon. For example, the Investigative type shares some characteristics in common with the Realistic and Artistic types, has little in common with the Conventional and Social types, and is quite different from the Enterprising type. If you read the descriptions of the six types once more with the hexagon in mind, the relationships among the types will become clearer.

People who feel that they resemble two or three types that are not adjacent on the hexagon may find it difficult to reconcile the conflicting elements in those type descriptions. It is important to remember that the descriptions provided are for "pure" types and that very few people resemble a single type to the exclusion of all others. It is necessary and appropriate to eliminate from the descriptions of the types that best fit you those specific elements that are not compatible with each other.

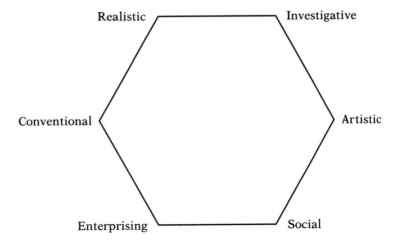

Holland suggests that you compare your personal traits with the characteristics of each of the six types. Using his model, it is possible to find a general area of work that most matches your personal qualities, interests, and values. The following "Time Out" assists you in assessing your personality type, and it also encourages you to have someone you know assess you. We highly recommend that you take the time to complete this exercise, which has been developed and class-tested by Jim Morrow.

Time Out for Personal Reflection

This exercise helps you become familiar with Holland's personality types.

1. Read the descriptions and other information furnished about Holland's six personality types at least two or three times.
2. Which of the six personality types best describes you? No one type will be completely "right" for you, but one of them will probably sound more like you than the others. Consider the overall descriptions of the types, and don't concentrate on just one or two of the characteristics of a type. As soon as you are satisfied that one type describes you better than the others, write that type down on the space for number 1 below.
3. Which of the six types next best describes you? Write that type down in the space for number 2. Continue this process until you have listed all of the types. You may find it difficult to decide on the last two or three because of their lack of resemblance to you.
4. Next, give the descriptions of the six types to someone who knows you very well. Ask them to read the descriptions carefully and order them

in terms of their resemblance to you, just as you have done. Do not show or tell them how you rated yourself.

5. After the other person finishes rating you, compare your own rating with theirs. Do not be concerned about the last two or three types listed by each of you; it's the first two or three that are important. If there is not close agreement among the first two or three types on both lists, ask the other person to give examples of your behaviors that prompted his or her ratings. The other person may not have rated you very accurately, or your behavior may not portray you to others as you see yourself. The purpose of this exercise is to familiarize you with Holland's personality types. It may have a "bonus" effect of better familiarizing you with yourself. In any event, it should assist you in using Holland's personality types to better understand individuals' characteristics for use in career planning.

Your rating of yourself:

Rating by someone who knows you well:

1. _____   1. _____

2. _____   2. _____

3. _____   3. _____

4. _____   4. _____

5. _____   5. _____

6. _____   6. _____

The Process of Deciding on a Career

In addition to making a visit to your counseling center for information about testing and counseling for career development, we strongly advise you to do some reading about the career decision-making process. Entire books are devoted to deciding on a career. We highly recommend *What Color Is Your Parachute?* (Bolles, 1992); *Occupational Information Overview* (Sharf, 1993); *Discover the Career within You* (Carney & Wells, 1991); and three by Robert Lock (1992a, 1992b, & 1992c): *Taking Charge of Your Career Direction, Job Search,* and *Student Activities for Taking Charge of Your Career Direction and Job Search.* Lock describes a systematic, rational approach to the process of career decision making, and Carney and Wells focus on specific skills needed for career planning. Bolles provides many practical suggestions on ways to decide on a vocation. Besides books, you will find some useful information in the following three resource guides put out by the U. S. Department of Labor: *Dictionary of Occupational Titles* (4th edition), *Guide for Occupational Exploration* (2nd edition), and *Occupational Outlook Handbook* (current edition).

The steps presented below are a modification of ideas found in the six books we've recommended. This process shows that selecting a career is more than a simple matter of matching information about the world of work with your personal characteristics. You will find it useful to go through the following steps, or at least some of the steps, several times. For example, gathering and assessing information is a continual process, rather than a step to be completed.

1. *Begin by focusing on yourself.* Identify your interests, abilities, values, beliefs, wants, and preferences. Keep these questions in mind: Who are you? How do you want to live? Where do you want to live? What kind of environment do you envision in your occupation? Whom will you spend your time with? The awareness that comes from focusing on yourself may arouse anxiety; gaining a clear perspective takes time.

2. *Generate alternative solutions.* This stage is closely related to the next two. Rather than first narrowing down your options, consider a number of alternatives or different potential occupations that you are drawn to. In this step it is wise to consider your work values and interests, especially as they apply to Holland's six personality types.

3. *Gather and assess information about the alternatives generated.* Be willing to research the occupations that attract you. Read about their educational requirements and their positive and negative characteristics. Talk to as many people as you can who are involved in them. Examine the social, political, economic, and geographic environment as a basis for assessing the factors that influence your career choice.

4. *Weigh and order your alternatives.* After you arrive at your list of alternatives, spend adequate time prioritizing them. Consider the practical aspects of your decisions, such as: Where do I most want to live? What values do I place on money and material goods? What are my values pertaining to family and time with friends? How much leisure is available to me in this job? What do I most want the outcome of my decision to be? Integrate occupational information and the wishes and views of others with your knowledge of yourself.

5. *Make the decision and formulate a plan.* Remember that although you are ultimately responsible for deciding what path to follow, you are not riveted to your decision forever. It is best to think of a career as representing a series of decisions at various turning points. In formulating a plan, read about the preparation required for your chosen alternative.

6. *Carry out the decision.* After deciding, take practical steps to make your vision become a reality. Realize that committing yourself to implement your decision does not mean that you will have no fears. The important thing is not to allow these fears to keep you frozen. Thus, you will never know if you are ready to meet a challenge unless you put your plan into action. Part of the way you can carry out a decision is to learn how to sell yourself. To market your skills to employers, you need to learn how to identify employment sources, prepare resumes, and meet the challenges of job interviews. One

excellent way to acquire these marketing skills is by reading books such as the six listed earlier. Another resource is specific courses and workshops on job marketing skills that are available through the career guidance office at your college.

7. *Get feedback.* After taking practical steps to carry out your decision, you will need to determine whether your choices are viable for you. Both the world of work and you will change over time, and what may look appealing to you now may not seem appropriate at some future time. Remember that career development is an ongoing process, and it will be important to commit yourself to repeating at least part of the process as your needs change or as occupational opportunities open up or decline.

In short, you stand a greater chance of being satisfied with your work if you put time and thought into your choice and if you actively take steps to find a career or an occupation that will bring enrichment. Consider the suggestion given by Bolles (1978):

> You are in charge of your life. No matter how many forces there may be which seem to influence or even dictate part of your life, there is always that part over which you have control. You can increase that control. If you decide what it is that you want out of your Learning, and out of your Working, and out of your Playing, you will be infinitely less *powerless* and "*victimizable.*" (p. 58)

Time Out for Personal Reflection

This is a survey of your basic attitudes, values, abilities, and interests in regard to occupational choice.

1. Rate each item, using the following code: 1 = this is a *most important* consideration; 2 = this is *important* to me, but not a top priority; 3 = this is *slightly important*; 4 = this is of *little or no importance* to me.

_____   financial rewards
_____   security
_____   challenge
_____   prestige and status
_____   the opportunity to express my creativity
_____   autonomy—freedom to direct my project
_____   opportunity for advancement
_____   variety within the job
_____   recognition
_____   friendship and relations with co-workers
_____   serving people
_____   a source of meaning
_____   the chance to continue learning
_____   structure and routine

Once you've finished making the above assessment, review the list to determine the three most important values you associate with selecting a career or occupation.

_____

_____

_____

2. In what area(s) do you see your strongest abilities?

_____

_____

_____

3. What are a few of your major interests?

_____

_____

_____

_____

4. Which one value of yours do you see as having some bearing on your choice of a vocation?

_____

_____

_____

_____

5. At this point, what jobs do you see as most suitable to your interests, abilities, and values?

_____

_____

_____

_____

Choices at Work

In this section the unifying theme is that we have choices within the careers we select. Just as choosing a career is a process, so is creating meaning in our work. If we grow stale in our job or do not find an avenue of self-expression through the work we do, we eventually lose our vitality. This section looks at ways to find meaning in work and at approaches to keeping our options open.

THE DYNAMICS OF DISCONTENT IN WORK

It is certainly true that if you're dissatisfied with your job, one recourse is to look for a new one. Change alone, however, might not produce different results. In general, it's a mistake to assume that change necessarily cures dissatisfactions, and this very much applies to changing jobs. To know whether a new job would be helpful, you need to understand as clearly as you can why your present job isn't satisfactory to you. Consequently, it's important to consider some of the external factors that can devitalize you in your job and the very real pressures your job often creates. It is also critical to deal with those factors *within yourself* that lead to discontent at work. The emphasis of our discussion will be on what *you* can do about changing some of these factors in the job and in yourself.

You may like your work and derive satisfaction from it yet at the same time feel drained because of irritations produced by factors that aren't intrinsic to the work itself. Such factors may include low morale among fellow workers or actual conflict and disharmony among them; authoritarian supervisors who make it difficult for you to feel any sense of freedom on the job; or organizational blocks to your creativity. There are also countless pressures and demands that can sap your energy and lead you to feel dissatisfied with your job. These include having to meet deadlines and quotas; having to compete with others instead of simply doing your best; facing the threat of losing your job; feeling stuck in a job that offers little opportunity for growth or that you deem dehumanizing; dealing with difficult customers or clients; and having to work long hours or perform exhausting or tedious work. A stress that is particularly insidious — because it can compound all the other dissatisfactions you might feel — is the threat of cutbacks or layoffs, an anxiety that becomes more acute when you think of your commitments and responsibilities. In addition to the strains you may experience on the job, there may also be the daily stress of commuting to and from work. You may be tense before you even get to work, and the trip home may only increase the level of tension or anxiety you bring home with you. One real problem for many is that relationships with others are negatively affected by this kind of pressure. In one suburb, a new train route carries workers from their homes to downtown. This scenic ride gives them a chance to read, look out the window, or just reflect, instead of having to endure a solitary battle with traffic. This train ride provides for more personal time. If your work is draining and de-energizing, you may have little to give your children, spouse, and friends, and you may not be receptive to their efforts to give to you.

All the factors mentioned above can contribute to a general discontent that robs your work of whatever positive benefits it might otherwise have. In the face of such discontent you might just plod along, hating your job and spoiling much of the rest of your life as well. The alternative is to look at the

specific things that contribute to your unhappiness or tension and to ask yourself what you can do about them. You can also ask what you can do about your own attitudes toward those pressures and sources.

CREATING MEANING IN WORK

Work can be a major part of your quest for meaning, but it can also be a source of meaninglessness. Work can be an expession of yourself; it can be, as Gibran says, "love made visible" (1923, p. 27). It can be a way for you to be productive and to find enjoyment in daily life. Through your work you may be making a significant difference in the quality of your life or the lives of others, and this may give you real satisfaction. But work can also be devoid of any self-expressive value. It can be merely a means to survival and a drain on your energy. Instead of giving life meaning, it can actually be a destructive force that contributes to burnout and even an early death. Ask yourself: Is my work life-giving? Does it bring meaning to my life? If not, what can I do about it? Is my most meaningful activity—my true work—something I do away from the job?

If you find your work meaningless, what can you do about it? What can you do if, instead of energizing you, your job drains you physically and emotionally? What are your options if you feel stuck in a dead-end job? Are there some ways that you can constructively deal with the sources of dissatisfaction within your job? When might it be time for you to change jobs as a way of finding meaning?

One way of dealing with the issue of meaninglessness and dissatisfaction in work is to look at how you really spend your time. It would be useful to keep a running account for a week to a month of what you do and how you relate to each of your activities. Which of them are draining you, and which are energizing you? While you may not be able to change everything about your job that you don't like, you might be surprised by the significant changes you can make to increase your satisfaction. People often adopt a passive and victimlike position in which they complain about everything and dwell on those aspects that they cannot change. Instead, a more constructive approach is to focus on those factors within your job that you *can* change.

Perhaps, too, you can redefine the hopes you have for the job. Of course, you may also be able to think of the satisfactions you'd most like to aim for in a job and then consider whether there is a job that more clearly meets your needs and what steps you must take to obtain it. You might be able to find ways of advancing within your present job, making new contacts, or acquiring the skills that eventually will enable you to move on.

Although making changes in your present job might increase your satisfaction in the short term, the time may come when these resources no longer work and you may find yourself stuck in a dead-end job that leads toward frustration. The option of changing jobs as a way to create meaning for you does exist, yet you will have to be prepared to pay the required price. Changing jobs might increase your satisfaction with work, but changing jobs after a period of years can entail even more risk and uncertainty than making your first job selection.

It's important to realize that you may be enthusiastic about some type of work for years and yet eventually become dissatisfied because of changes that occur within you. With these changes comes the possibility that a once-fulfilling job will become monotonous and draining. If you outgrow your job, you can learn new skills and in other ways increase your options. Because your own attitudes are crucial, when a feeling of dissatisfaction sets in, it's wise to spend time rethinking what you want from a job and how you can most productively use your talents. Look carefully at how much the initiative rests with *you*—your expectations, your attitudes, and your sense of purpose and perspective.

The Place of Work and Leisure in Your Life

One way of looking at the place that work and leisure occupy in your life is to consider how you divide up your time. In an average day most people spend about eight hours sleeping, another eight hours working, and the other eight hours in routines such as eating, traveling to work, and leisure. If your work is something you enjoy, then at least half of your waking existence is spent in meaningful activities. Yet if you dread getting up and hate going to work, those eight hours can easily have a negative impact on the other eight hours that you are awake.

WORK AND THE MEANING OF YOUR LIFE

If you expect your work to be a primary source of meaning but feel that your life isn't as rich with meaning as you'd like, you may be saying, "If only I had a job that I liked, *then* I'd be fulfilled." This type of thinking can lead you to believe that somehow the secret of finding a purpose in your life depends on something outside yourself. In his book *The Doctor and the Soul*, Viktor Frankl (1965) notes that the fault may be in the person rather than in the work: "The work in itself does not make the person indispensable and irreplaceable; it only gives him the chance to be so" (p. 95). He describes a patient who found her life meaningless. He pointed out to her that her attitude toward her work and the manner in which she worked were more important than the job itself. He showed her that the way a person approaches a job and the special things he or she does in carrying it out are what make it meaningful.

If you decide that you must remain in a job that allows little scope for personal effort and satisfaction, you may need to accept the fact that you won't find much meaning in the hours you spend on the job. It's important, then, to be aware of the effects that your time spent on the job have on the rest of your life and to minimize them. More positively, it's crucial to find something outside the job that fulfills your need for recognition, significance, productivity, and excitement. By doing so, you may develop a sense of your true work as something different from what you're paid to do. You may even come to think of your job as providing the means for the productive activities you engage in away from the job, whether they take the form of hobbies, creative pursuits, volunteer work, or spending time with friends and family. The point is to turn things around so that you are the master rather than the victim of your job. Too many people are so negatively affected by their job that their frustration and sense of emptiness spoil their eating, leisure time, family life, sex life, and relationships with friends. If you can reassume control of your own attitudes toward your job and find dignity and pride elsewhere in your life, you may be able to do much to lessen these negative effects. Seeking counseling is one means to achieve greater control of your life.

LEISURE AND THE MEANING OF YOUR LIFE

Work alone does not generally result in fulfillment. Even rewarding work does take energy, and most people need some break from it. Leisure is "free time," the time that we control and can use for ourselves. Freedom and autonomy are at the root of leisure. Whereas work requires a certain degree of

perseverance and drive, play requires the ability to let go, to be spontaneous, and to avoid getting caught in the trap of being obsessed with what we "should" be doing. Leisure implies flowing with the river rather than pushing against it and making something happen. Compulsiveness dampens the enjoyment of leisure time, and planned spontaneity is almost a contradiction in terms. Carr (1988) writes of work and leisure from a developmental perspective: "Like a symphony, we can blend education, work, and leisure rather than live them as separated stages in the life cycle. Lifelong learning, lifelong working, and lifelong leisure begin in the early years, continue in the middle years, and end only at death" (p. 165).

Brennecke and Amick (1980) also make a strong case for a life of balance between work and leisure: "The puritan attitude of work or sin should be replaced with a new ethic that calls for a healthy balance between work and leisure. The work-sin ethic denies humanness and makes workhorses or machines out of organisms that have the potential to be something more than mere machines" (p. 181). This feeling that we "should" be productive is rooted in the work ethic that views free time as wasteful. The Puritan admonition is that "the idle mind is the devil's workshop." Our acceptance of the work ethic makes it difficult for us to believe and act as though we have a right to leisure time. The ancient Greeks viewed leisure time as essential for self-understanding, introspection, and personal growth. Within this framework leisure provides opportunities for achieving inner potential, for expressing ourselves, and for experiencing a rich and meaningful existence.

The balance between work and leisure can be very different for different people. Some people schedule leisure activities in such a manner that they actually miss the point of recreation. There are those people who "work hard at having a good time." Others become quickly bored when they are not doing something. For Bob and Jill, leisure is more of a burden than a joy. They say they like a weekend trip to the river. He is a laborer, she is a hairstylist, and both of them work hard all week. Their "vacation" includes driving in a car with two whiny children who constantly ask when they will get there. Bob battles traffic jams and actually feels more stressed once he returns home from the river. They need to assess whether their leisure is providing them with what they want.

As a couple, we (Jerry and Marianne) attribute different meanings to our leisure time. Jerry tends to plan most of the things in his life, including his leisure time. I (Jerry) often combine work and leisure. Until recently, I seemed to require less leisure than some people, because most of my satisfactions in life came from my work. Many of my "hobbies" are still work-related, and although my scope tends to be somewhat narrow, this has been largely by choice. I am aware that I have had trouble with unstructured time. I am quite certain that leisure has represented a personal threat, as if any time unaccounted for is not being put to the best and most productive use. Just within this last year, I am learning how to appreciate the reality that time is not simply to be used in doing, producing, accomplishing, and moving mountains. Although it is a lesson that I am learning relatively late in life, I am increasingly relishing times of being and experiencing, as well as time spent on accomplishing tasks. Experiencing sunsets, watching the beauty in nature, and being open to what moments can teach me are ways of using time that I am coming to cherish. Although work is still a very important part of my life, I am realizing that this is only a *part* of my life, not the totality of it. In essence, I am learning the importance of making time for leisure pursuits, which are essential for revitalization.

Marianne, on the other hand, wants and needs unstructured and spontaneous time for unwinding. I (Marianne) am uncomfortable when schedules are imposed on me. I don't particularly like to make detailed life plans, for

W-O-R-K — W-O-O-R-R-K !
... I GOTTA HAVE W-O-R-K !!!

this gets in the way of my relaxing. Although I plan for trips and times of recreation, I don't like to have everything I am going to do on the trip planned in advance. I like the element of surprise. It feels good to flow with moments and let things happen, rather than working hard at making things happen. Also, I don't particularly like to combine work and leisure. For me, work involves considerable responsibility, and it is hard for me to enjoy leisure if it is tainted with the demands of work, or if I know that I will soon have to function in a professional role.

Brennecke and Amick (1980) write about using leisure time for *re-creation*, which includes self-restoration, reenergizing, rebuilding, relaxing, and refreshing ourselves. They emphasize that re-creation and play, whether solitary or social, are basic elements in enriching human experience, for such activities replenish one physically, psychologically, socially, and spiritually. Travis and Ryan (1988) define recreation as "play in the fullest sense of the term: to make new, to vitalize again, to inspire with life and energy" (p. 148). There are many routes to this re-creation of self, a few of which are engaging in sports, spending time with friends, getting out into nature, meditating, and being alone. Just as work has a purpose, so does leisure. Leisure also can include involvement with the community. It can be a time to acquire new learning and also to contribute to others by teaching them what we know, an opportunity to give back to society what we have received from it (Carr, 1988, p. 165).

The objectives of planning for a career and planning for creative use of leisure time are basically the same: to help us develop feelings of self-esteem, reach our potential, and improve the quality of our life. If we do not learn how to pursue interests apart from work, we may well face a crisis when we retire. In fact, there are some writers who have cited evidence that many people die soon after their retirement (Joy, 1990; Siegel, 1988, 1989). If we do plan for creative ways to use leisure, we can experience both joy and continued personal growth.

A COUPLE WHO ARE ABLE TO BALANCE WORK AND LEISURE

What follows is an example of how work and leisure can be combined. We see Judy and Frank as having found a good balance. Although they both enjoy their work, they have also arranged their life to make time for leisure.

Judy and Frank were married when she was 16 and he was 20. They now have two grown sons and a couple of grandchildren. At 59 Frank works for an electrical company as a lineman, a job he has held for close to 35 years. Judy, who is now 55, delivers meals to schools.

Judy went to work when her two sons were in elementary school. Although she felt no financial pressure to do so, she took the job because she liked the extras that their family could afford with her salary. Because she was efficient as a homemaker, she felt that her days would not be filled with housework alone. She was interested in doing something away from home. Judy continues her work primarily because she likes the contact with both her co-workers and the children and adolescents whom she meets daily. She has a good way with children, and they respond well to her. She values the impact that she is able to have on them and the affection she receives from them. If she had her preference, she'd work only three days a week instead of the five she now does. She would like more time to enjoy her grandchildren and would like a longer weekend.

Frank is satisfied with his work, and he looks forward to going to the job. Considering that he stopped his education at high school, he feels he has a good job that both pays well and offers many fringe benefits. Although he is a bright person, he expresses no ambition to increase his formal education. A few of the things that Frank likes about his work are the companionship with his co-workers, the physical aspects of his job, the security it affords, and the routine. As a mechanically inclined person, he is both curious about and challenged by how things work, what makes them malfunction, and how to repair them. He fixes things not only on his job but also at home and for his neighbors.

Judy and Frank have their separate interests and hobbies, yet they also spend time together. Both of them are hardworking, and they have achieved success financially and personally. They feel pleased about their success, since they can see the fruits of their labor. They spend most of their weekends at their mountain cabin, which both of them helped build. He fishes, hikes, jogs, rides his motorcycle, cuts wood, fixes the house, visits with friends, and watches ball games on TV. She is talented in arts and crafts, repairing the cars, housepainting, and preparing delicious meals. Together they enjoy their grandchildren, their friends, and themselves.

Judy and Frank enjoy their work life and their leisure life, both as individuals and as a couple. A challenge that many of us will face is finding ways of using our leisure as well as they do. In a high-technology age, the question of how we can creatively use our increased leisure time must be addressed. Just as our work can have either a positive or a negative influence on our life, so, too, can leisure.

Time Out for Personal Reflection

1. Mention a few of the most important benefits that you get (or expect to get) from work or college.

   _____

   _____

   _____

   _____

2. How do you typically spend your leisure time?

   _____

   _____

   _____

   _____

3. Are there any ways that you'd like to spend your leisure time differently?

   _____

   _____

   _____

   _____

4. What nonwork activities have made you feel creative, happy, or energetic?

   _____

   _____

   _____

   _____

5. Could you obtain a job that would incorporate some of the activities you've just listed? Or does your job already account for them?

_____

_____

_____

_____

6. What do you think would happen to you if you couldn't work? Write what first comes to mind.

_____

_____

_____

_____

Chapter Summary

Some people are motivated to go to college because it offers opportunities for personal development and the pursuit of knowledge; others are in college primarily to attain their career objectives; and some go because they are avoiding making other choices in their lives. Clarifying your own reasons for being in college can be useful in the process of long-range career planning.

Choosing a career is best thought of as a process, not a one-time event. The term *career decision* is misleading, because it implies that we make one choice that we stay with permanently. Most of us will probably have several occupations over our lifetime, which is a good argument for a general education. If we prepare too narrowly for a specialization, that job may become obsolete, as will our training. In selecting a career or occupation, it is important to first assess our attitudes, abilities, interests, and values. The next step is to explore a wide range of occupational options to see what jobs would best fit our personality. Becoming familiar with Holland's six personality types is an excellent way to consider the match between your personality style and the work alternatives you are considering. There are clear dangers in choosing an occupation too soon, because our interests do change as we move into adulthood. Another danger is passively falling into a job, rather than carefully considering where we might best find meaning and satisfaction.

Because we devote about half of our waking hours to our work, it behooves us to actively choose a form of work that can express who we are as a person. Much of the other half of our waking time can be used for leisure. With the trend toward increased leisure time, cultivating interests apart from work becomes a real challenge. Just as our work can profoundly affect all aspects of our life, so, too, can leisure have a positive or negative influence on our existence. Our leisure time can be a source of boredom that drains us, or it can be a source of replenishment that energizes us and enriches our life.

Although work can be an important source of meaning in our life, it is not the job itself that provides this meaning. The satisfaction we derive depends to a great extent on the way we relate to our job, the manner in which we do it, and the meaning that we attribute to it. Perhaps the most important idea in this chapter is that we must look to ourselves if we're dissatisfied with our work. It's easy to blame outside circumstances when we feel a lack of purpose and meaning. Even if our circumstances are difficult, this kind of stance only victimizes us and keeps us helpless. We can increase our power to change these circumstances by accepting that we are the ones responsible for making our life and work meaningful, instead of expecting our job to bring meaning to us. This theme is illustrated by the Serenity Prayer, which is certainly worth reflecting on to determine the sphere of our responsibility: "God grant me the serenity to accept the things I cannot change, the courage to change the things I can, and the wisdom to know the difference."

Activities and Exercises

1. Interview a person you know who dislikes his or her career or occupation. You might ask questions such as the following:
   - "If you don't find your job satisfying, why do you stay in it?"
   - "Do you feel that you have much of a choice about whether you'll stay with the job or take a new one?"
   - "What aspects of your job bother you the most?"
   - "How does your attitude toward your job affect the other areas of your life?"

2. Interview a person you know who feels fulfilled and excited by his or her work. Some questions you might ask are:
   - "What does your work do for you? What meaning does your work have for the other aspects of your life?"
   - "What are the main satisfactions for you in your work?"
   - "How do you think you would be affected if you could no longer pursue your career?"

3. You might interview your parents and determine what meaning their work has for them. How satisfied are they with the work aspects of their lives? How much choice do they feel they have in selecting their work? In what ways do they think the other aspects of their lives are affected by their attitudes toward work? After you've talked with them, determine how your attitudes and beliefs about work have been influenced by your

parents. Are you pursuing a career that your parents can understand and respect? Is their reaction to your career choice important to you? Are your attitudes and values concerning work like or unlike those of your parents?

4. If your college has a vocational counseling program available to you, consider talking with a counselor about your plans. You might want to explore taking vocational interest and aptitude tests. If you're deciding on a career, consider discussing how realistic your vocational plans are. For example,

   • What are your interests?
   • Do your interests match the careers you're thinking about pursuing?
   • Do you have the knowledge you need to make a career choice?
   • Do you have the aptitude and skills for the careers you have in mind?
   • What are the future possibilities in the careers you're considering?

5. If you're leaning toward a particular occupation or career, seek out a person who is actively engaged in that type of work and arrange for a time to talk with him or her. Ask questions concerning the chances of gaining employment, the experience necessary, the satisfactions and drawbacks of the position, and so on. In this way, you can make the process of deciding on a type of work more realistic and perhaps avoid disappointment if your expectations don't match reality.

6. If you are selecting a career, give time to evaluating your values to determine how you can best match them to some form of work that will be satisfying for you. A comprehensive *self-assessment* of values involves several factors discussed by Mencke and Hummel (1984):

   • Make an inventory of your lifestyle values. How important to you is having time for your personal life? What priority do you place on money and advancement? Are you more attracted by taking risks for possible advancement or by job security? How will your preferences for geographic location fit your career choices?
   • Assess your values with regard to other people. What value do you place on interaction with co-workers? What kind of stimulation is important to you? Is support essential? Do you enjoy working with people? What do you receive from helping others?
   • Assess your values with respect to level of responsibility. Do you prefer being a leader, or a follower? In defining your work-related values, how important is degree of influence? promoting a cause? contributing to society? autonomy? structure? freedom?
   • Make an assessment of your intellectual values. Are you primarily interested in thinking and in solving problems? Do you like to acquire new skills? Do you have a talent for organizing events, people, activities, or academic material? Do you expect to see measurable outcomes of your efforts?

Review your priorities, looking for a pattern in your values. You can then use the value summary to evaluate some of the career options you are considering. One way of doing this is by listing your career possibilities on a sheet of paper. On this same sheet list the values you hold to be most central to your future satisfaction. Then evaluate the degree to which each of the careers you have listed is likely to satisfy the values you have identified.

7. Select one or more of the following books for further reading on the topics explored in this chapter: Bolles, *What Color Is Your Parachute?* (1992); Carney and Wells, *Discover the Career within You* (1991); Lock, *Taking Charge of Your Career Direction* (1992).

CHAPTER SIX

Your Body and Wellness

Prechapter Self-Inventory

Use the following scale to respond: 4 = this statement is true of me *most* of the time; 3 = this statement is true of me *much* of the time; 2 = this statement is true of me *some* of the time; 1 = this statement is true of me *almost none* of the time.

_____ 1. Touching and being touched are important to me.

_____ 2. At times I use drugs or alcohol to help me through difficult times, but I don't abuse these substances.

_____ 3. Being upset or under stress can make me feel physically ill.

_____ 4. The way I take care of my body expresses the way I feel about myself.

_____ 5. My lifestyle is a stressful one.

_____ 6. It's relatively easy for me to fully relax.

_____ 7. When I look in the mirror, I feel comfortable with my physical appearance.

_____ 8. When something ails me, I tend to want to treat the symptom rather than looking for the cause.

_____ 9. Making basic changes in my lifestyle to improve my health is not something I often think about.

_____ 10. The way I live, I sometimes worry about having a heart attack.

Introduction

Your body is the primary subject of this chapter, yet it is close to impossible to talk about choices that result in maintaining a healthy body without also discussing the role that emotions and stress play in the state of our physical being. Therefore, we take a holistic focus.

We begin the chapter by exploring the topic of accepting responsibility for your general state of wellness. We focus on ways that your self-image is influenced by your perception of your body. We explore how your bodily identity, which includes the way you experience yourself and express yourself through your body, manifests beliefs, decisions, and feelings about yourself. If you look at your body, you'll see that it reflects some significant choices. Do you take care of the physical you? How comfortable are you with your body? How do your feelings and attitudes about it affect your choices in areas such as self-worth, sexuality, and love? How aware are you of the impact that your emotional state has on your physical state?

Stress and its effects on your body are another central topic of this chapter. Living in contemporary society, we cannot eliminate stress, yet we can monitor its physical and psychological impact. We can become aware of destructive reactions to stress and learn constructive ways to deal with it.

The goal of "wellness" is explored as a lifestyle choice that enhances body and mind. We take up subjects such as making decisions about diet and exercise and ultimately accepting responsibility for your body. Although you might readily say that you desire the state of wellness as a personal goal, you might have experienced frustrations and discouragement in attaining this goal. Wellness is not something that merely happens to you. It is the result of being consciously aware of what your physical and psychological well-being entails and making the commitment to bring it about. Furthermore, wellness is more than the absence of illness. In many ways, the medical model ignores wellness and focuses on the removal of symptoms, which results in a negative view of health. Relatively few physicians ask their patients questions about aspects of their lifestyles that may have contributed to their health problems.

An honest examination of the choices you are making about your body and your overall wellness can reveal a great deal concerning your feelings about your life. If you aren't taking care of your body, what beliefs and attitudes may be getting in the way? What resources do you require to begin modifying those parts of your lifestyle that affect your bodily well-being?

Wellness and Life Choices

The concept of wellness fits into a holistic view of health. Traditional medicine focuses on identifying symptoms of illness and curing disease. By contrast, *holistic health* focuses on every facet of human functioning. It emphasizes the intimate relationship between our body and all the other aspects of ourselves—psychological, social, and spiritual. And it stresses positive health rather than merely the absence of disabling symptoms. Just as there are many degrees of being ill, there are degrees of wellness.

In their *Wellness Workbook*, Travis and Ryan (1988) describe wellness as a bridge that is supported by two piers, self-responsibility and love. They write that self-responsibility and love flow from the appreciation that we are not merely separate individuals, nor are we simply the sum of separate parts. Instead, we are integrated beings, and we are united in one energy system with everything else in creation. For them, health is best conceived of on an illness-wellness continuum that ranges from premature death on one side to high-level wellness on the other side. In their preface (p. xiv), the authors further capture the essence of wellness:

- Wellness is a choice—a decision you make to move toward optimal health.
- Wellness is a way of life—a lifestyle you design to achieve your highest potential for well-being.
- Wellness is a process—a developing awareness that there is no end point but that health and happiness are possible in each moment, here and now.

- Wellness is an efficient channeling of energy—energy received from the environment, transformed within you, and sent on to affect the world outside.
- Wellness is the integration of body, mind, and spirit—the appreciation that everything you do and think and feel and believe has an impact on your state of health.
- Wellness is the loving acceptance of yourself.

In his excellent book *Stress Management for Wellness*, Schafer (1992) emphasizes that the concept of wellness is much more than the absence of illness. Wellness entails living at one's highest possible level as a whole person. People who are functioning at optimal level are characterized by the absence of illness and low illness risk, maximum energy, full enjoyment of life, the capacity to make the most of their abilities, satisfying relationships, and a commitment to the common good. According to Schafer, behavioral-medicine studies clearly demonstrate that wellness is acquired and maintained by healthful daily habits, some of which are sleep, diet, exercise, ways of dealing with anger and tension, work satisfaction, and the presence of energizing visions for oneself and the world. His guiding philosophy about wellness can be summarized in the following four basic suggestions (p. 511):

- Allow yourself to have visions and dreams, some of which have social significance or will benefit others in significant ways.
- Be willing to work hard, sometimes with others, to make these dreams and visions a reality.
- Balance hard work with play, care of the body and spirit, and intimate relationships.
- Enjoy the process of living.

We think Schafer's points are worth considering and trying to implement in our daily lives.

WELLNESS AS AN ACTIVE CHOICE

As the preceding discussion of Travis and Ryan's (1988) and Schafer's (1992) books indicates, wellness entails a lifelong process of taking care of our needs on all levels of functioning, and it implies that we see ourselves as constantly growing and developing. Well people are committed to creating a lifestyle that contributes to taking care of their physical selves, challenging themselves intellectually, expressing the full range of their emotions, finding rewarding interpersonal relationships, and searching for a meaning that will give direction to their lives.

A combination of factors contributes to our sense of well-being. Thus, a holistic approach must pay attention to our lifestyle, including a range of specific factors: how we work and play, how we relax, how and what we eat, how we think and feel, how we keep physically fit, our relationships with

others, and our spiritual needs. One of our friends, Ronnie Coley, captures
the essence of living a balanced life when he talks about the importance of
REDS (rest, exercise, diet, and spirituality) as the key to health. We agree
with his assumption that if you pay attention to the balance among these four
critical areas, then the general result is wellness.

Dr. Bernie Siegel, a psychologically and spiritually oriented physician,
promotes a similar viewpoint in his lectures and his books. Siegel believes
that illness serves some function, and that illness makes sense if we look at
what is going on with people who become physically sick. He investigates the
quality of their psychological and spiritual lives as the key to understanding
the mystery of illness and fostering health. From Siegel's (1988) perspective,
when we are not meeting our emotional and spiritual needs, we are setting

ourselves up for physical illness. Happy people don't get sick. In his work with cancer patients, Siegel finds that one of the most common precursors of cancer is a traumatic loss or a feeling of emptiness in one's life. He also finds that depressed people, who are "going on strike from life," are at much greater risk for contracting cancer than are nondepressed people. One of his patients who developed cancer shortly after her children left home wrote to him, "I had an empty place in me, and cancer grew to fill it" (Siegel, 1988, p. 81). As a physician, Siegel views his role not simply as finding right treatments for disease, but also as helping his patients resolve emotional conflicts, find an inner reason for living, and release the healing resources within.

The popularity of Siegel's books and videotapes is a sign of the times that points to the power within us to keep ourselves well and to heal ourselves. There are scores of self-help books and home videos on the subjects of stress management, exercise, meditation, diet, nutrition, weight control, control of smoking and drinking, and wellness medicine. There is a definite consciousness about the values of preventive medicine, as can be seen by the many wellness clinics, nutrition centers, and exercise clubs. We find our clients becoming much more conscientious about taking care of themselves. For more than twenty years we have worked with people in groups, and we find that fewer and fewer of them are smoking.

It is beyond the scope of this book to prescribe a lifestyle that will lead to wellness. Our purpose is to introduce you to the issues involved in wellness and lifestyle choices, to encourage you to think about the priority you are placing on physical and psychological well-being, and to invite you to consider if there are any changes you want to make.

ONE MAN'S WELLNESS PROGRAM

To make this discussion of wellness concrete, we'll provide a case illustration of a client, whom we'll call Kevin, who was in one of our therapeutic groups. We mentioned Kevin earlier in the chapter on gender roles (Chapter Four). When we first met him in the group, he struck us as being closed off emotionally, rigid, stoical, and defensive. For many years he had thrown himself completely into his work as an attorney. Although his family life was marked by tension and bickering with his wife, he attempted to block out the stress he was experiencing at home by burying himself in his law cases and by excelling in his career.

When Kevin reached middle age, he began to question how he wanted to continue living. One of the catalysts for his self-searching was a series of heart attacks that his father suffered. He watched his father decline physically, and this jolted him into the realization that both his father's time and his own time were limited. Later Kevin went for a long-overdue physical examination and discovered that he had high blood pressure, that his cholesterol level was abnormally high, and that he was at relatively high risk of having a heart attack himself. He also learned that several of his relatives had died of heart attacks, and he decided that he wanted to reverse what he saw as a self-destructive path. After consultations and discussions with his physician, Kevin decided to change his patterns of living in several ways. He was overeating, his diet was not balanced, he was consuming a great deal of alcohol to relax, he didn't get enough sleep, and he was "too busy" to do any physical exercise. His new decision involved making contacts with friends. He learned to enjoy playing tennis and racquetball on a regular basis. He took up jogging and reported that if he had not run in the morning, he felt somewhat sluggish during the day. He radically changed his diet in line with the suggestions from his physician. As a result, he lowered both his cholesterol level and his blood pressure without the use of medication; he also lost twenty pounds and worked himself into excellent physical shape.

Kevin's wellness program did not stop with enhancing his physical being. His tolerance for mediocre family relationships lessened. He and his wife got involved in marital counseling to learn how to bring out the conflicts that were dividing them and how to express their reactions to each other. Previously he had kept most of his feelings to himself and had merely grown silent when he felt unappreciated by his wife. His counseling sessions gave him some tools for expressing his frustrations and conflicts openly. Eventually, his three sons, his wife, and Kevin had a series of family-therapy sessions. He acknowledged that the home atmosphere had been characterized by tension and that he had wanted simply to escape from this stress-producing environment. Now he hoped to face the problems that were keeping the family members strangers to one another. For the first time in his life he allowed himself to *express* his caring to his sons and his wife, he let them know how powerless he felt at times to change the home situation, and he felt his sadness and wept. He no longer wanted to be the strong person who could prove that he was unaffected by whatever went on at home. He continued to reach out to his sons, and he made more time to play as well as work. As he learned how to be more emotionally expressive, he reported that he felt more alive physically.

Let's underscore a few key points in Kevin's case. First of all, he took the time to reflect seriously on the direction he was going in life. He did not engage in self-deception; rather, he admitted that the way he was living was not healthy. On finding out that heart disease was a part of his family history, he did not shrug his shoulders and assume an indifferent attitude. Instead, he made a decision to take an active part in changing his life on many levels. He cut down on drinking and relied less on alcohol as an escape. He changed his patterns of eating, sleeping, and exercise, which resulted in his feeling better physically and psychologically. Although he was still committed to his law practice, he pursued it less compulsively. He realized that he had missed play in his life, and he sought a better balance between work and play.

With the help of counseling, Kevin realized the high price he was paying for bottling up emotions of hurt, sadness, anger, guilt, and joy. Although he did not give up his logical and analytical dimensions, he added to his range as a person by allowing himself to express what he was feeling. He learned that unexpressed emotions would find expression in some form of physical illness or symptom. Kevin learned of the value of taking his emotions seriously, rather than denying them. He continued to question the value of living exclusively by logic and calculation, in both his professional and his personal life. As a consequence, he cultivated friendships and let others who were significant to him know that he wanted to be closer to them. Kevin could have asked his physician for a prescription and could have assumed a passive stance toward curing his illness. Instead, he was challenged to review his life to determine what steps he could take to get more from the time he had to live. A person who knew him only casually commented one day that he seemed so much different than he had a year before. She remembered him as being uptight, unfriendly, uncommunicative, angry-looking, and detached. She was surprised at his changes, and she used adjectives such as *warm*, *open*, *relaxed*, *talkative*, and *outgoing* to describe him.

ACCEPTING RESPONSIBILITY FOR YOUR BODY

As we mentioned earlier, the American public is becoming increasingly informed about exercise programs, dietary habits, and ways to manage stress. More health insurance companies are providing payment for preventive medicine as well as remediation; one does not need to look far to find a preventive health clinic. Many communities provide a wide variety of programs aimed at helping people improve the quality of their lives by finding a form of exercise that suits them.

Major health insurance companies take surveys of their clients' lifestyles to identity positive and negative habits that affect their overall health. One of our daughters signed up for health insurance with a major company. She was asked to fill out a series of surveys at regular intervals to monitor her health practices. This company also presented her with a book describing many common health problems and ways to prevent them. This move is certainly motivated by the company's desire to reduce payments to subscribers. However, another of their motivations might well be a desire to assist people in developing sound health habits that will lead to the prevention of serious health problems.

Doctors often find that many of the people they see are more interested in getting pills and in removing their symptoms than in changing a stressful lifestyle. Some of these patients tend to see themselves as victims of their ailments rather than as responsible for them. Some physicians resist prescribing pills to alleviate the symptoms of what they see as a problematic lifestyle. Psychologically oriented physicians emphasize the role of *choice* and *responsibility* as critical determinants of our physical and psychological well-being. In their practices they challenge their patients to look at what they are doing to their body through their lack of exercise, the substances they take in, and other damaging behavior. While they may prescribe medication to lower a person's extremely high blood pressure, they also inform the patient that medications can do only so much and that what is needed is a radical change in lifestyle, and that the patient shares the responsibility with the physician for maintaining wellness.

The popular book *Worst Pills, Best Pills* (by Sidney Wolfe and his colleagues, 1988) and others like it offer information to consumers about the uses and potentially harmful side effects of medications. This assists consumers in sharing the responsibility with their physicians for the proper use of medicine. Consumers are encouraged to question physicians about the medications they prescribe. While many people prefer to turn over complete authority for their health care to their physicians, the books on the market give signs that many people are taking a more active role and assuming more responsibility in their health care.

It makes a world of difference whether you see yourself as a passive victim or an active agent in the maintenance of your body. If you believe that you simply catch colds or are ill-fated enough to get sick and if you don't see what you can do to prevent bodily illnesses, then your body is controlling you. But if you recognize that the way you are choosing to lead your life (including accepting responsibility for what you consume, how you exercise, and the stresses you put yourself under) has a direct bearing on your physical and psychological well-being, then you can be in control of your body. If you listen to yourself, you will be able to make choices about your health care that enhance the quality of your life. At this time in your life, how would you answer this central question: Do I control my body, or does my body control me?

Time Out for Personal Reflection

1. The following are some common rationalizations that people use for not changing patterns of behavior that affect their bodies. Look over these statements and decide what ones, if any, you use. What others do you sometimes use that are not on this list?

_____ I don't have the time to exercise every day.

_____ No matter how I try to lose weight, nothing seems to work.

_____ I sabotage myself, and others sabotage me, in my attempts to lose weight.

_____ I'll stop smoking as soon as my life becomes less stressful.

_____ When I have a vacation, I'll relax.

_____ Even though I drink a lot (or use other drugs), it calms me down and has never interfered with my life.

_____ I need a drink (or a marijuana cigarette) to relax.

_____ Food isn't important to me; I eat anything I can grab fast.

_____ I simply don't have the time to eat three balanced meals a day.

_____   Food has gotten so expensive, I just can't afford to eat decent meals anymore.

_____   If I stop smoking, I'll surely gain weight.

_____   I simply cannot function without several cups of coffee.

_____   If I don't stop smoking, then I might get lung cancer or die a little sooner, but we all have to go sometime.

What other statements could you add to this list?

_____

_____

_____

_____

2. Complete the following sentences with the first word or phrase that comes to mind:

a. One way I abuse my body is _____

b. One way I neglect my body is _____

c. When people notice my physical appearance, I think that _____

_____

d. When I look at my body in the mirror, I _____

e. I could be healthier if only _____

f. One way I could cut down the stress in my life is _____

_____

g. If I could change one aspect of my body it would be my _____

h. One way that I relax is _____

i. I'd describe my diet as _____

j. For me, exercising is _____

Your Bodily Identity

We are limited in how much we can actually change our body, but there is much we can do to work with the material we have. First, however, we must pay attention to what we are expressing about ourselves through our body, so that we can determine whether we *want* to change our bodily identity. This involves increasing our awareness of how we experience our body through, for instance, touch and movement. As you read this section, reflect on how well you know your body and how comfortable you are with it. Then you can decide about changing your body image — for example, by losing or gaining weight.

EXPERIENCING AND EXPRESSING YOURSELF THROUGH YOUR BODY

Some of us are divorced from our body; it is simply a vehicle that carries us around. If someone asks us what we are thinking, we are likely to come up with a quick answer. If asked what we are experiencing and sensing in our body, however, we may be at a loss for words. Yet our body can be eloquent in its expression of who we are. Much of our life history is revealed through our body. By looking at some people's faces we are able to see evidence of stress and strain. There are those who speak with a tight jaw and who seem to literally choke off feelings. Others typically walk with a slouch and shuffle their feet, expressing their hesitation in presenting themselves to the world. Their bodies may be communicating their low self-esteem and their fear of interacting with others. As you look at your body, what feelings do you have? What story does your body tell about you?

The following are some ways that our bodies express ourselves:

- The eyes can express life or emptiness.
- The mouth can be too tight or too loose.
- The neck can hold back expressions of anger or crying, as well as holding onto tensions.
- The chest can develop armor that inhibits the free flowing of crying, laughing, and breathing.
- The diaphragm can restrict the expression of rage and pain.
- The abdomen can develop armor that is related to fear of attack.
- The pelvis can be rigid and asexual, or it can become a source of intense pleasure.

Unexpressed emotions do not simply disappear. The chronic practice of "swallowing" emotions can take a physical toll on our body and manifest itself in physical symptoms such as severe headaches, ulcers, digestive problems, and a range of other bodily dysfunctions. In counseling clients we often see a direct relationship between a person's physical constipation and his or her emotional constipation. When people are successful in expressing feelings of hurt and anger, they often comment that they are finally no longer physically constipated. If we seal off certain emotions, such as grief and anger, we also keep ourselves from experiencing intense joy. Later in this chapter we address in greater detail how emotions and stress are related to heart disease.

Experiencing your body. In looking at a certain woman we may be impressed with how rigid her body appears. She walks around very stiffly. It is as if she feels disassociated from various body parts. She is rarely conscious of how different parts of her body feel. By contrast, we can look at another person and notice that she moves about with ease, her movements express harmony, and she appears to be comfortable with her body.

One way of becoming more aware of experiencing our body is by paying attention to our senses of touch, taste, smell, seeing, and hearing. Simply pausing and taking a few moments to be aware of how our body is interacting with the environment is a helpful way of learning to make better contact. For example, how often do you allow yourself to really taste and smell your food? How often are you aware of the tension in your body? How many times do you pause to smell and touch a flower? How often do you listen to the chirping of birds or the other sounds of nature? If these simple pleasures are important to us, we can increase our sensory experience by pausing more frequently to fully use all of our senses.

Enjoying our physical self is something that we often fail to make time for. Treating ourselves to a massage, for example, can be exhilarating and can give us clues to how alive we are physically. Dancing is yet another avenue through which we can enjoy our physical selves and can express ourselves spontaneously. Dance is a popular way to teach people through movement to "own" all parts of their body and to express themselves more harmoniously. These are a few paths to becoming more of a friend and less of a stranger to our body. We can express our feelings through our body if we allow ourselves to be in tune with our physical self.

The importance of touch. Some people are very comfortable with touching themselves, with touching others, and with being touched by others. They require a degree of touching to maintain a sense of physical and emotional well-being. Other people show a great deal of discomfort in touching themselves or allowing others to be physical with them. They may bristle and quickly move away if they are touched accidentally. If such people are embraced by another, they are likely to become rigid and unresponsive. For instance, in Jerry's family of origin there was very little touching among members. He found that he had to recondition himself to feel comfortable with being touched by others and in touching others. In contrast, Marianne grew up in a German family characterized by much more spontaneous touching. Between the two of us there are differences in the amount of touching that we seek and require.

Another example of attitudes toward touching is that of Marisa, a college student. She came from a family that freely touched, and she liked to touch and be touched. Marisa found out the hard way that not all people were as comfortable with touching as she was. When she spontaneously touched her female roommates, she noticed their discomfort and felt rebuffed. When they finally discussed the issue, she discovered that her roommates had misinterpreted her touching as a sign of sexual advances.

Some time ago I (Marianne) was teaching in Hong Kong and became friends with a college counselor. One day while we were walking, she spontaneously interlocked her arm with mine. Then she quickly pulled it back, looked embarrassed, and apologized profusely. Her apology went something like this: "I am very sorry. I know that you in America do not touch like this." I let her know that I, too, came from a culture where touching between females was acceptable and that I had felt very comfortable with her touching me. We discovered that we had had similar experiences of feeling rejected by American women who misunderstood our spontaneous touching.

For many cultures, touching is a natural mode of expression; for others, touching is minimal and is regulated by clearly defined boundaries. Some cultures have taboos against touching strangers, against touching people of the same sex, against touching people of the opposite sex, or against touching in certain social situations. In spite of these individual and cultural differences, studies have demonstrated that physical contact is essential for healthy development of body and mind. Harlow and Harlow (1966) studied the effects of material deprivation on monkeys. In these experiments the monkeys were separated from their mothers at birth and raised in isolation with artificial mothers. When young monkeys were raised under conditions of relatively complete social deprivation, they manifested a range of symptoms of disturbed behavior. Infant monkeys reared in isolation during the first six months after birth showed serious inadequacies in their social and sexual behavior later in life. There are critical periods in development when physical stimulation is essential for normal development. Touching is important for developing in healthy ways physically, psychologically, socially, and intellectually.

In writing about touch deprivation, Travis and Ryan (1988) contend that it leads to a sense of alienation from ourselves and isolation from others. They point out that such deprivation results in boredom and lack of energy for life in general, sexual dysfunction, and unsatisfying relationships.

YOUR BODY IMAGE

We rarely come across people who are really satisfied with their physical appearance. Even when people receive compliments about the way they look, they may be quick to respond with "Thank you, but I need to lose some weight"; or "I need to gain some weight"; "I could be in better shape"; "I need to exercise some more"; "I feel a little flabby right now." It seems as though everyone is striving for the "perfect body," yet few people achieve it.

Your view of your body and the decisions you have made about it have much to do with the choices that we will study in the rest of this book. In our view people are affected in a very fundamental way by how they perceive

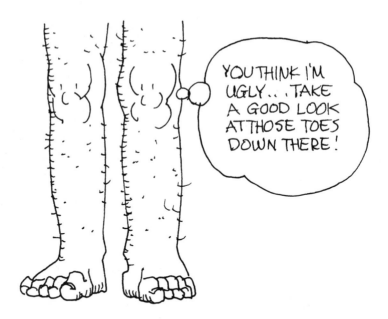

their body and how they think others perceive it. If you feel basically unattractive, unappealing, or physically inferior, these self-perceptions are likely to have a powerful effect on other areas of your life.

For example, you may be very critical of some of your physical characteristics; you may think that your ears are too big, that you're too short, or that you're not muscular enough. Or you may have some of these common self-defeating thoughts:

- "If I were thin, I would have self-worth."
- "Unless I have the perfect body, others will reject me."
- "I'm basically fat and ugly."
- "I'm not in control of my life."

Perhaps some part of you believes that others will not want to approach you because of your appearance. If you *feel* that you are basically unattractive, you may well tell yourself that others will see your defects and will not want to be with you. In this way you may contribute to the reactions that others have toward you by the messages you send them. You may be perceived by others as aloof, distant, or judgmental. Even though you may want to get close to people, you may also be frightened of the possibility of being rejected.

If something like this is true of you, we challenge you to look at the part you may be playing in contributing to the reactions you get from others. How does your state of mind influence both your view of yourself and the view others have of you? Do you take even less care of your body because you're unhappy with it? Why should others approach you, if you continue to tell them that you are not worth approaching? Will others think more of you than you think of yourself?

You may say that there is little you can do to change certain aspects of your physical being, such as your height or basic build. Yet you *can* look at the attitudes you have formed about these physical characteristics. How important are they to who you are? How has your culture influenced your beliefs about what constitutes the ideal body?

We are also prone to develop feelings of shame if we unquestioningly accept certain cultural messages about our body. As children and, even more so, as adolescents many of us learn to associate parts of our body with shame. Small children may be oblivious to nudity and to their bodies, but as they run around nude and are made the objects of laughter and jokes by other children and by adults, they gradually become more self-conscious. Sometimes the sense of shame remains with people into adulthood. The following brief cases represent some typical difficulties:

• Donna painfully recalls that during her preadolescence she was much taller and more physically developed than her peers. She was often the butt of jokes by both boys and girls in her class. While she is no longer taller than most people around her, she still walks stoop-shouldered, for she still feels self-conscious and embarrassed about her body.

• In a group counseling session, Tim finally shares his concern over the size of his penis, which he thinks is small. His anxiety about this has caused him extreme embarrassment when he has showered with other men, and it has inhibited him in his sexual relations. He is convinced that women will laugh at him and find him sexually inadequate. He is very surprised and relieved when several other male members let him know that they also have had these concerns.

• Herbert, a physically attractive young man, is highly self-conscious about his body, much to the surprise of those who know him. He seems to be in good physical condition, yet he gets very anxious when he gains even a pound. As a child he was overweight, and he developed a self-concept of being the "fat kid." Even though he changed his physique years ago, the fear of being considered fat still lurks around the corner.

Consider whether you, too, made some decisions about your body early in life or during adolescence that still affect you. Did you feel embarrassed about certain of your physical characteristics? As you matured physically, these characteristics might have changed — or become less important to others — yet you may still be stuck with some old perceptions and feelings. Even though others may think of you as an attractive person, you may react with suspicion and disbelief, for you continue to tell yourself that you are in some way inferior. Your struggle in changing your self-concept may be similar to that of Donna, Tim, or Herbert.

WEIGHT AND YOUR BODY IMAGE

From years of experience in reading student journals and counseling clients, we have concluded that many people are preoccupied with maintaining their "ideal weight." Although there are people who view themselves as too skinny and who are striving to gain weight, many more are looking for effective ways to lose weight. You may be one of these people and may find that your weight significantly affects the way you feel about your body. Perhaps you have said:

• "I've tried every diet program there is, and I just can't seem to stick to one."
• "I've lost extra pounds many times, only to put them on again."
• "I'm too occupied with school to think about losing weight."
• "I love to eat and I hate to exercise."
• "I don't particularly like the way I look, but it takes too much effort to change it."

It may help to examine how unrealistic societal standards regarding the ideal body can lead to the perpetual feeling that you are never physically adequate. For example, our society places tremendous pressure on women to be thin. Messages from the media often equate thinness and beauty. The price women who accept these cultural norms often pay is depression and loss of self-esteem. Some women are driven by perfectionistic standards to eating disorders. Anorexia and bulimia are frequently linked to the internalization of unrealistic standards that lead to negative self-perceptions and negative body images.

We have noticed in our travels to Germany how standards of ideal weight can differ from culture to culture. The same thin person who is viewed as attractive in the United States might well be seen as undernourished, skinny as a rail, and even somewhat sickly in Germany. A person with a certain amount of weight is generally considered attractive and healthy looking in Germany. Toward the end of a visit to her hometown, Marianne knows that it is time for her to lose weight when people there tell her, "You look good and well-nourished."

The real issue here is being and feeling healthy and deciding for oneself what that entails. Learn to assess yourself and the way you feel about your body, but as Bloomfield (1985) warns, avoid getting trapped in self-destructive modes of judgment and criticism. He offers several suggestions: Assess what you want. Are there any changes that you would like to make pertaining to your body? Assess the price of changing. What are you willing to do to change?

Although weight is a significant health factor, your nutritional and exercise habits are also crucial to your overall well-being. Rather than too quickly deciding that you need to either gain or lose weight or to change your nutritional habits, it is a good idea to consult with your physician or one of the nutrition centers in your area. If you decide that you want to change your weight, there are many excellent support groups designed for this purpose, as well as self-help programs. The counseling centers at many colleges offer groups for weight control and for people with eating disorders.

A basic change in attitude and lifestyle is important in successfully dealing with a weight problem. Overweight people do not eat simply because they are hungry. They are typically more responsive to external cues in their environment. One of these is the acquiescence of well-meaning friends, who may joke with them by saying: "Oh, don't worry about those extra pounds. What's life without the enjoyment of eating? Besides, there's more of you to love this way!" This kind of "friendship" can make it even more difficult to discipline ourselves by watching what and how much we eat.

In our counseling groups we often encourage people who view themselves as having a weight problem to begin to pay more attention to their body and to increase their awareness about what their body communicates to them and to others. A useful exercise has been to ask them, "If your body had a voice, what would it be saying?" The following are examples of what their bodies might communicate:

- "I don't like myself."
- "My weight will keep me at a distance."
- "I'm making myself ill."
- "I'm burdened."
- "I don't get around much anymore!"
- "I'm basically lazy and self-indulging."
- "I work very hard, and I don't have time to take care of myself."

If you determine that you do not like what your body is saying, it is up to you to decide what, if anything, you may want to change. Should you decide that you don't want to change, this is a choice that you need not be defensive about. There is no injunction that you *must* change.

If you have not liked your physical being for some time but have not been able to change it, there may be some subtle reasons for your difficulty. There may be certain "payoffs" to being overweight, even if they are negative. Here are some possible reasons why people get and stay overweight:

- An overweight son or daughter may keep weight on as a way of getting constant parental attention, even if that attention consists of nagging over what he or she is eating.
- A girl may gain weight during adolescence because her father is threatened by her physical attractiveness.
- Overweight people may convince themselves that they are being rejected for their obesity and thus not have to look at other dimensions of themselves.
- Some who are afraid of getting close to others may use their weight as a barrier.
- Those who are afraid of their sexuality and where it might lead them often gain weight as a way to keep themselves safe from sexual involvement.

Are any people you know, including yourself, overweight for these reasons? Others may nag you to do something about your weight. They may be well intentioned, yet you may resist their efforts because of the payoffs you are receiving. Ultimately, it is you who must decide what you want to do about your body. To assist you in assessing your current weight and in taking actions to control it, refer to the section on assessment and control of your weight in the "Activities and Exercises" at the end of the chapter.

Time Out for Personal Reflection

1. What are your attitudes toward your body? Take some time to study your body, and become aware of how you look to yourself and what your body feels like to you. Try standing naked in front of a full-length mirror, and reflect on some of these questions:

   • Is your body generally tight or relaxed? What parts tend to be the most unrelaxed?
   • What does your face tell you about yourself? What kind of expression do you convey through your eyes? Are there lines on your face? What parts are tight? Do you force a smile?
   • Are there any parts of your body that you feel ashamed of or try to hide? What aspects of your body would you most like to change? What are the parts of your body that you like the best? the least?

2. After you've done the exercise just described (perhaps several times over a period of a few days), record a few of your impressions below, or keep an extended account of your reactions in your journal.

   a. How do you view your body, and how do you feel about it?

   _____

   _____

   _____

   b. What messages do you convey to others about yourself through your body?

   _____

   _____

   _____

   c. Are you willing to make any decisions about changing your body?

   _____

   _____

   _____

3. If you decide to stand naked in front of a mirror, go through each of your body parts and "become each part," letting it "speak." For example, give your nose a personality, and pretend that your nose could speak. What might it say? If your legs were to speak, what do you imagine they'd say? (Do this for every part of your body, even if you find yourself wanting to bypass certain parts. In that case you might say: "I'm an ugly nose that doesn't want any recognition. I'd just like to hide, but I'm too big to be inconspicuous!")

4. If you are overweight, is your weight a barrier and a burden? For example, consider whether your weight is keeping you from doing what you want to do. Does it keep certain people away from you? You might pick up some object that is equivalent to the extra pounds you carry with you, let yourself hold this object, and then put it down and begin to experience the excess weight of your body.

5. Imagine yourself looking more the way you'd like to. Let yourself think about how you might be different, as well as how your life would be different.

The Body and Stress

Stress is an event or series of events that leads to strain, both bodily and psychological. Everyday living involves dealing with frustrations, conflicts, pressures, and change. At certain times in our life, moreover, most of us are confronted with severely stressful situations that are difficult to cope with, such as the death of a family member or a close friend, the loss of a job, a personal failure, or an injury. Even changes that we perceive to be positive, such as getting a promotion or moving to a new location, can be stressful and often require a period of adjustment. If stress is severe enough, it takes its toll on us physically and psychologically.

Siegel (1988) indicates that the level of stress is largely determined by cultural factors. Those cultures that emphasize competition and individualism produce the most stress. The cultures that place a high value on cooperation and collectivism produce the least stress and also have the lowest rates of cancer. These latter cultures involve close-knit communities in which supportive relationships are the norm, where the elderly are respected and given an active role, and where religious faith is valued. Siegel is convinced that chronic patterns of intense stress lead to lowering of the efficiency of the body's disease-fighting cells. His work with cancer patients has taught him that stresses resulting from traumatic loss and major life changes are in the background of most of those who get cancer. He adds, however, that not everyone who suffers stressful changes in lifestyle develops an illness. Siegel writes that the deciding factor seems to be how people cope with the problems and stresses they face. What seems particularly important is the ability to express one's feelings about situations, rather than denying that these feelings exist or swallowing one's feelings.

In most places in the modern world stress is an inevitable part of life. Perhaps we cannot eliminate stress, but we can learn how to manage it. We don't have to allow ourselves to be victimized by its psychological and physiological effects. It is true that there are external sources of stress, yet how we perceive and react to them is subjective and internal. By interpreting the events in our lives, we define what is and is not stressful, and thus we determine our levels of stress adaptation. Therefore, the real challenge is to learn how to recognize and deal constructively with the sources of stress, rather than trying to eliminate them.

SOURCES OF STRESS

Environmental sources. Many of the stresses of daily life come from external sources. Consider for a moment some of the environmentally related stresses that you face at the beginning of a semester. You are likely to encounter problems just in finding a parking place on campus. Perhaps you must stand in long lines and cope with many other delays and frustrations. Some of the courses you need may be closed; simply putting together a decent schedule of classes may be next to impossible. There may be difficulties in arranging your work schedule to fit your school schedule, and these difficulties can be compounded by the external demands of friends and family and other social commitments. Financial problems and the pressure to work so that you can support yourself (and perhaps your family, too) make being a student a demanding task.

Our mind and body are also profoundly affected by more direct physiological sources of stress. Illness, exposure to environmental pollutants, improper diet, lack of exercise, poor sleeping habits, and abusing our bodies in any number of other ways — all of these take a toll on us.

Psychological sources. Stress is a subjective phenomenon, in that how we label, interpret, think about, and react to those events that impinge on us has a lot to do with determining it. In discussing the psychological sources of stress, Weiten, Lloyd, and Lashley (1991) identify frustration, conflict, change, and pressure as the key elements. As we consider each of these sources of stress, think how they apply to you and your situation.

Frustration results from a blocking of your needs and goals. External sources of frustration, all of which have psychological components, include failures, losses, accidents, delays, hurtful interpersonal relationships, loneliness, and isolation. Additionally, internal factors can hinder you in attaining your goals. These include a lack of basic skills, physical handicaps, a lack of belief in yourself, and any self-imposed barriers that you may create that block the pursuit of your goals. What are some of the major frustrations you experience, and how do you typically deal with them?

Conflict, another source of stress, occurs when two or more incompatible motivations or behavioral impulses compete for expression. Conflicts can be classified as approach/approach, avoidance/avoidance, and approach/avoidance (Weiten et al., 1991).

- *Approach/approach conflicts* occur when a choice must be made between two or more attractive or desirable alternatives. Such conflicts are inevitable because we have a limited time to do all the things we would like to do and be all the places we'd like to be. An example of this type of conflict is being forced to choose between two or more job offers, all of which have attractive features.
- *Avoidance/avoidance conflicts* arise when a choice must be made between two or more unattractive or undesirable goals. At times you may feel caught "between a rock and a hard place." These conflicts are the most unpleasant and the most stressful. You may have to choose between being unemployed and accepting a job that you do not like, neither of which appeals to you.
- *Approach/avoidance conflicts* are produced when a choice must be made between two or more goals, each of which has attractive and unattractive elements. For example, you may be offered a challenging job that appeals to you but that entails much traveling, which you consider a real drawback.

How many times have you been faced with two or more desirable choices and forced to choose one path? And how many times have you had to choose between unpleasant realities? Perhaps your major conflicts involve your choice of a lifestyle. For example, have you wrestled with the issue of being independent or blindly following the crowd? of living a self-directed life or living by what others expect of you? Consider for a few minutes some of the major conflicts you've recently faced. How have these conflicts affected you? How do you typically deal with the stress you experience over value conflicts?

Change can be a source of stress, especially life changes that involve major adjustments in one's living circumstances. Holmes and Rahe (1967) and their colleagues did a classic study on the relationship between stressful life events and physical illness. Their assumption is that changes in personal relationships, career changes, and financial changes are often stressful, even if these changes are positive. Disruptions in the routines of life can lead to stress. However, the demands for adjustment to these life changes are more important than the type of life changes alone. The Holmes and Rahe Social Readjustment Rating Scale is included in the "Activities and Exercises" at the end of this chapter.

Pressure, which involves expectations and demands for behaving in certain ways, is part of the "hurry sickness" of modern living. We may respond to the pressures placed on us by others at home, school, and work and in our social lives. Also, we continually place internally created pressures on ourselves. Many people are extremely demanding of themselves, driving themselves and never quite feeling satisfied that they've done all they could or should have. There are pressures that people face in performing roles and responsibilities, as well as in conforming to expectations. Striving to live up to the expectations of others, coupled with self-imposed perfectionistic demands, is a certain route to stress. If you find yourself in this situation, consider some of the irrational and unrealistic beliefs that you might be living by. Are you overloading your circuits and heading for certain burnout? What ways do you push yourself to perform, and for whom? To what degree do you demand perfection from yourself? How do you experience and deal with the pressure in your daily life?

EFFECTS OF STRESS

Stress produces adverse physical effects, for in our attempt to cope with everyday living our body experiences what is known as the "fight-or-flight" response. Our body goes on constant alert status, ready for aggressive action to combat the many "enemies" we face. If we subject it to too many stresses, the biochemical changes that occur during the fight-or-flight response may lead to a situation of chronic stress and anxiety. This causes bodily wear and tear, which can lead to a variety of what are known as *psychosomatic*, or *psychophysiological*, disorders. These are real bodily disorders manifested in disabling physical symptoms yet caused by emotional factors and the prolonged effects of stress. These symptoms range from minor discomfort to life-threatening conditions; most commonly they take the form of peptic ulcers, migraine and tension headaches, asthma and other respiratory disorders, high blood pressure, skin disorders, arthritis, digestive disorders, disturbed sleeping patterns, poor circulation, strokes, cancer, and heart disease. It can be helpful to explore how some of your physical symptoms actually serve a purpose. You can ask yourself how your life might be different if you weren't ill.

Dr. Allan Abbott and his wife, Katherine, spent some time treating primitive people in Peru. This experience stimulated their interest in the ways in which stress affects our body. The Abbotts became especially interested in coronary-prone behavior, which is so characteristic of the North American way of life, when they observed that stress was not a part of the lives of these people. While the leading causes of death in North America are cardiovascular diseases and cancer (diseases the Abbotts relate to stress), they rarely cause the death of Peruvian Indians.

In Allan Abbott's view our bodies are paying a high price for the materialistic and stressful manner in which we live. As a family-practice specialist, he has come to believe that about 75 percent of the physical ailments he treats are psychologically induced or related to stress. As an aside, he asserts that 90 percent of what he does as a physician that makes a significant difference is psychological in nature, rather than medical. According to him, belief in the doctor and in the process and procedures a doctor employs has a great deal to do with curing patients. Taking a blood test, having an X ray done, getting a shot, and simple conversation with the physician are factors that appear to make patients improve. Indeed, faith healers work on this very principle of the role of belief and its effect on the body.

In agreement with Abbott is Albrecht (1979), who writes that many physicians have commented that 80 percent of their patients have emotionally induced disorders. A number of physicians treat their patients with medications such as as tranquilizers, stomach remedies, sleeping pills, and pain killers. Instead of dealing with those factors that are producing the disorders, namely the lifestyles of the patients, they treat the symptoms.

The psychiatrist and founder of reality therapy William Glasser (1985) maintains that psychosomatic illness is a creative process. In other words, in a chronic illness for which there is no known physical cause our bodies are involved in a creative struggle to satisfy our needs. Glasser's advice is that since there is no specific medical treatment for psychosomatic disorders, the best course of action is to attempt to regain effective control over whatever is out of control in the person's life. He does not like phrases such as *getting depressed*, *getting angry*, *having a headache*, and *feeling anxiety*. Instead, he substitutes words such as *depressing*, *angering*, *headaching*, and *anxietying*. He emphasizes that these are behaviors that people choose in an attempt to meet their needs and wants. Thus, people do have some control over what they continue to choose to do. Although it may be difficult to directly control their feelings and thoughts, Glasser maintains that they have control over their behavior. If they change their behavior, they increase the chances that their feelings and thoughts will also change.

In his book *Joy's Way*, Brugh Joy (1979) describes how a life-threatening illness was the catalyst for him to call an end to a prosperous and growing private practice as a physician and a position as a clinical professor of medicine. He dropped a role that had brought him a great deal of success and security but that had also sickened him in some key respects. After giving up traditional medicine, Joy traveled through Europe, Egypt, India, and Nepal for nine months on his own pilgrimage toward spiritual reawakening, which led to his physical and psychological healing. Joy returned to California to open a center in the desert where he would teach groups of people how to engage wider ranges of their consciousness, which could lead to major life transformations. Along with certain other physicians, such as Bernie Siegel, Joy believes that we become sick because of the stresses associated with psychological and spiritual anomalies. From Joy's perspective, people generally become sick for one of two reasons: either because they are leading a highly restricted life that is too small for the person they potentially could become, or because they are leading a life that is too expansive, or one where they are trying to be and do more than is possible for them.

In his recent book, *Avalanche*, Joy (1990) further elaborates on the meaning of physical illness and death. For example, when their last child is leaving home, some mothers may develop a life-threatening illness, primarily because they have based their existence on their family and cannot view themselves as separate from this entity. Some men who face retirement, with the potential loss of power, may become ill. Joy and other physicians have observed "a tendency for spouses to die within a two-year period following the death of a husband or wife. In such cases the surviving partner is unable to engage a sense of self that can sustain life without the other person" (p. 65). It is clear that there is an intimate connection between the body and the mind, and that emotional restriction can lead to sickness.

In our counseling practice we see evidence of this connection between stress and psychosomatic ailments. We continue to work with people who deal with their emotions by denying or repressing them or finding some other indirect channel of expression. Consider Lou's situation. He is a young man who suffered from occasional asthmatic attacks. He discovered, during the process of therapy, that he became asthmatic whenever he was under emotional stress or was anxious. To his surprise he found that he could control his symptoms when he began to express his feelings and talk about what was upsetting him. While continuing to receive medical supervision for his asthma, he improved his physical condition as he learned to more fully explore his emotional difficulties. As he let out his anger, fear, and pain, he was able to finally breathe freely again.

There are other examples of how our body pays the price for not coping with stress adequately: Julie suffered from migraines, especially at those times when she felt the pressure to excel. Her tension literally gave her a headache. Luis was on a variety of medications. His physician told him he could decrease the dosage as needed, yet he never did. With intensive personal therapy he began expressing a range of feelings that he had kept bottled up. As he learned how to release some of these buried feelings, he began to realize that holding them in was costing him his life. These examples could be multiplied, but they serve to make the point that many physical symptoms decrease or disappear as people learn how to identify and appropriately express feelings. Of course, it is essential for many of them to do therapeutic and emotionally corrective work, because merely having insight and letting out feelings are not enough.

HIGH STRESS AND YOUR HEART

Friedman and Rosenman (1974) pioneered the study of a certain personality structure, which they called Type A, that leads to a stressful lifestyle and, in turn, to coronary disease. It seems clear that Type A people actually create much of the stress they experience by their beliefs, self-talk, and behavior.

What are the main characteristics of the Type A personality? The primary behavioral characteristics are a *time urgency*, a *preoccupation with productivity and achievement*, a *chronic activation*, and a *competitive drive*. Type A people are characterized by behaviors that seem to result from "hurry sickness." They are chronically harried, are constantly in competition with the clock, and strive to do more and more in less and less time. These individuals

typically move, walk, talk, and eat rapidly. They overemphasize words in their speech and are often impatient in conversations. They tend to interrupt others or will finish sentences for people who they think are speaking too slowly. They have a difficult time waiting. They typically change lanes on the freeway so that they can make up a few car lengths. They are constantly trying to work and move faster than others. Their general impatience is seen by their attempt to do two or more things at once, which is referred to as *multiphasia*. They may eat and read, eat lunch while walking from one place to the other, read while they are sitting on the toilet, or even think of work when they are having sex. Typically, people with the Type A behavior pattern overschedule activities and then become tense when they don't complete the unrealistic tasks they have set for themselves. By assuming too many responsibilities, they become trapped in several stressful situations at once.

Type A people operate on the assumption that their personal worth depends largely on what they produce and that their success depends on being able to accomplish herculean feats. These beliefs tend to lead to behaviors such as hostility, aggressiveness, competitiveness, and impatience. They continually create new demands for themselves, and when anything blocks their striving toward their ambitions, they become irritated and overreact to the hassles of everyday life. Of course, along with these self-imposed demands comes increased stress. There is a pervasive sense of guilt when they are not being productive. Relaxation and vacations are difficult for them, because they are often thinking of all the work they could be doing instead of "wasting time" by nonproductively playing!

In a major paper on the relationship of Type A behavior and coronary artery disease, the president of the American Psychological Association, Logan Wright (1988), discusses how Type A tendencies may corrupt the coronary arteries. In some individuals self-induced stress causes vasoconstriction in peripheral areas of the body and also accelerates the heart rate. The analogy used is that of a car with the brakes on and the accelerator being pushed to the floor. It is assumed that people who drive themselves in this manner cause "wear and tear" on their coronary arteries, which eventually results in heart disease.

Based on his research, Wright discusses some important conclusions for the layperson. From his perspective, job involvement alone does not appear to cause coronary disease. In fact, genuine involvement in work can be a source of meaning in one's life. What is damaging is the desperate striving to accomplish too much in too short a time. Wright's view is consistent with recent research findings, reported by the news media, indicating that it is the hostile and aggressive behavior associated with fierce competitive striving that results in an early death from a heart attack. Apparently, the key to reducing coronary risk lies not in working less but in changing those attitudes that lead to hostility and aggression. Wright proposes that it would be a good idea to find a way to keep the "baby" (drive, ambition, and the resulting accomplishments) while throwing out the "bath water" (urgency, chronic activation, and the resulting heart disease). He believes that the challenge is to examine our values and make some basic changes in our lifestyles. He suggests that we need to learn to run the race of life like a marathon rather than a series of 100-yard dashes.

DESTRUCTIVE REACTIONS TO STRESS

Reactions to stress can be viewed on a continuum from being effective and adaptive, on one end, to being ineffective and maladaptive, on the other. If your reactions to stress are ineffective over a long period of time, this failure typically results in physical and psychological harm. Ineffective ways of dealing with stress include defensive behavior and the abuse of drugs and alcohol. Burnout is a common outcome of ineffectively coping with stress.

Defensive behavior. If you experience stress associated with failure in school or work or in some aspect of your personal life, you may react by attempting to defend your self-concept by denying or distorting reality. Although defensive behavior does at times have adjustive value and does result in reducing the impact of stress, such behavior can actually increase levels of stress in the long run. If you are more concerned with defending your bruised ego than with coping with reality, you are not taking the steps necessary to reduce the source of stress. It is a good idea to review the discussion of the ego-defense mechanisms in Chapter Two.

Drugs and alcohol. Many people are conditioned to take an aspirin for a headache, to take a tranquilizer when they are anxious, to rely on stimulants to keep them up all night at the end of a term, and to use a variety of drugs to reduce other physical symptoms and emotional stresses. Recently, I (Jerry) took a vigorous bike ride on rough mountain trails with a group. I returned home with a headache, which is a condition that afflicts me only occasionally. Instead of recognizing that I had overexerted myself and needed to take a rest, my immediate reaction was to take aspirin and proceed with my usual work for the day. My body was sending me an important signal, which I was ready to ignore by numbing. Perhaps many of you can identify with this tendency to quickly eliminate symptoms, rather than recognizing them as a sign of the need to change certain behaviors. Americans rely heavily on drugs to alleviate symptoms of stress, rather than looking at the lifestyle that produces this stress.

Most of us use drugs in some form or another. We are especially vulnerable to relying on drugs when we feel out of control, for drugs offer the promise of helping us gain control of our life. Consider some of the ways that we attempt to control problems by relying on both legal and illegal drugs. If we are troubled with shyness, boredom, anxiety, depression, or stress, we may become chemically dependent to relieve these symptoms. A drawback to depending on these substances to gain control of our life is that through them we numb ourselves physically and psychologically. Instead of paying attention to our bodily signals that all is not well in our life, we deceive ourselves by believing that we are something that we are not. When drugs are used excessively as a way to escape from painful reality, this use compounds our problems rather than solving them. As tolerance is built up for these substances, we tend to become increasingly dependent on them to anesthetize both physical and psychological pain. Yet once the effects of the drugs wear off, we are still confronted by the painful reality that we sought to avoid. According to Glasser (1985), if we continue to use any addicting drug, no matter how good we feel, we will always lose more and more control of our life. In his book *Control Therapy* he develops the thesis that chemical dependency gets in the way of satisfying basic human needs for love, power, fun, and freedom. When using drugs and alcohol serves the function of distorting reality, we are preventing ourselves from finding direct and effective means of coping with stress. The problem here is that stress is now controlling us, instead of our controlling stress.

Alcohol is perhaps the most widely used and abused drug of all. It is also the most dangerous and debilitating of drugs. This is true not only because of its effects on us physically and psychologically but also because it is legal, accessible, and socially acceptable. Glasser (1985) asserts that alcohol is an integral and glorified aspect of our culture: "Alcohol is the get-things-done, take-control drug, and to deal with it well is a sign of strength and maturity. Because it enhances the sense of control, we welcome it instead of fearing it as we should" (p. 132).

As you read this section, you may be asking yourself whether you have a problem with using substances as a way of coping with stress. For example, you may be worried about the effects that drinking has on you. Perhaps the most difficult aspect of making this self-assessment is simply being honest with yourself. In the final analysis, people who use any drug must honestly consider what they are getting from it as well as the price they are paying for their decision. They must determine for themselves whether the toll on their physical and psychological well-being is too high.

Burnout as a result of continual stress. The phenomenon of burnout is receiving increasing attention. What is burnout? What are some of its causes? What can be done to prevent it? How can it be overcome?

Burnout is a state of physical, emotional, intellectual, and spiritual exhaustion. It is the result of repeated pressures, often associated with intense involvement with people over long periods of time. People who are burned out have depleted themselves on all levels of human functioning. Although they have been willing to give of themselves to others, in the process they have forgotten to take care of themselves. They generally feel negative about themselves and others. People who tend to burn out typically strive for unrealistic goals, which leads to a chronic state of feeling frustrated and let down. Burnout is characterized by feelings of helplessness and hopelessness.

Burnout is a problem for workers and for students as well. Students say that burnout often catches them by surprise. They often do not recognize the general hurry of their lifestyle, nor do they always notice the warning signs that they have pushed themselves to the breaking point. Many students devote the majority of their time to school and work while neglecting to maintain their friendships, to make quality time for their family, or to take time for their own leisure pursuits. Semester after semester they crowd in too many units, convincing themselves that they must push themselves so that they can graduate and then start making money. Sometimes they do not realize the price they are paying. Eventually they become apathetic, just waiting for a semester to end. They are physically and emotionally exhausted and often feel socially cut off.

In the previous chapter we talked about the dynamics of discontent in one's job. If we feel trapped by meaningless work, especially if we do not have a variety of leisure pursuits that give us meaning, there is a high potential for burnout. For example, doing the same routine, distasteful work eventually exacts a toll. If we are giving and extending ourselves but getting very little in return for our investment, our energy eventually dries up. Unless we replenish the well that we dip into for others, we will have very little to offer them.

So what can we do if we feel a general sense of psychological and physical exhaustion? Christina Maslach (1982), a psychologist who has extensively studied burnout, maintains that there are many constructive approaches. Once we recognize our state and seriously want to change it, the situation is not hopeless. Maslach provides many excellent suggestions: Instead of working harder, we can "work smarter," which means changing the way we approach our job so that we suffer less stress. Setting realistic goals is another coping skill. We can also work at conquering feelings of helplessness, since such feelings lead to frustration and anger, which in turn result in our becoming exhausted and cynical. We can learn to relax, even if such breaks are short. Instead of taking all the problems we encounter personally, we can condition ourselves to assume a more objective perspective. Most important, we can learn that caring for ourselves is every bit as important as caring for others. In the next section we will consider other constructive approaches to dealing with stress.

Although learning coping skills to deal with the effects of burnout is helpful, our energies are best directed toward preventing the condition. The real challenge is to learn ways of structuring our life so that we can stay alive as a person as well as a worker (or student). Maslach (1982) asserts that the key to prevention is early action. She stresses using solutions before there is a problem. This includes becoming sensitive to the first signs of burnout creeping up on us. Finding ways to energize ourselves is critical as a preventive measure. This is where learning how to use leisure to nurture ourselves is so important. Each of us can find a different path to staying alive personally. The point is to slow down and monitor the way we are living so that we will discover that path.

CONSTRUCTIVE REACTIONS TO STRESS

To cope with stress effectively you first need to face up to the causes of your problems, including your own part in creating them. Instead of adopting destructive reactions to stress, you can use task-oriented, or constructive, approaches aimed at realistically coping with stressful events. Weiten and his colleagues (1991) describe constructive coping as behavioral reactions to stress that tend to be relatively healthy or adaptive. He lists the following characteristics of constructive coping: it involves a direct confrontation with a problem; it entails staying in tune with reality; it is based on an accurate and realistic appraisal of a stressful situation, rather than on a distortion of reality; it involves learning to recognize and inhibit harmful emotional reactions to stress; it entails a conscious and rational effort to evaluate alternative courses of action; and it is not dominated by wishful or irrational thinking. This section focuses on several positive ways to deal with stress: dealing with self-defeating thoughts and messages, acquiring a sense of humor, leading a low-stress lifestyle, meditating, relaxing, and getting therapeutic massage.

Dealing with self-defeating thoughts and messages. In Chapter Three we discussed ways to challenge parental injunctions, cultural messages, and early decisions. Those same principles can be effectively applied to coping with the negative impact of stress. The basic notion here is that most of our stresses result from our beliefs about the way life is or should be. For example, the pressures we experience to perform and to conform to external standards are greatly exacerbated by self-talk such as "I must do this job perfectly well." The cognitive techniques that we described in Chapter 3 can help us uproot certain faulty beliefs that are based on "shoulds," "oughts," and "musts." If we are successful in changing some of our self-defeating beliefs about living up to external expectations, then we are in a position to behave in ways that produce less stress. Even if it is not always possible to change a difficult situation, we are able to modify our beliefs about the situation. Doing so can result in decreasing the stress we experience.

Acquiring a sense of humor. Workshops and conferences on humor, aimed at teaching people ways of having fun and learning to laugh, are becoming popular. It is a sad commentary that we have to be taught how to laugh because this no longer seems to come naturally to us. Unfortunately, too many of us take ourselves far too seriously and have a difficult time learning how to enjoy ourselves. If we are overly serious, then there is very little room for expressing the child within us. Laughing at our own folly, our own inconsistencies, and at some of our pretentious ways can be highly therapeutic. Taking time for play can be the very medicine that we need to combat the negative forces of stress. If we learn to "lighten up," the stresses that impinge upon us can seem far less pressing. We like the way that Siegel (1988) encourages people to give fun a high priority in life. Siegel reports that laughter actually promotes healing forces within our bodies, and as such, humor can be a powerful antidote to physical illness and stress. He writes: "Each of us must take the time to find humorous books or movies, play the games we enjoy, tell jokes to friends, doodle, or have fun with coloring books, whatever the choice is of the child inside you" (Siegel, 1988, p. 146).

Developing a Type B personality. Earlier we described how a high-stress lifestyle often has an adverse effect on one's heart. The best long-range way to deal constructively with stress is to make substantial changes in one's way of living. Friedman and Ulmer (1985) talk about the Type B personality, which in many ways is the opposite of the Type A orientation. Type B people are not slaves of time and are not preoccupied with achievements and aggressive competition. When they work, they do so in a calm and unhurried manner. They are able to relax and have fun without feeling guilty. They are able to play without the need to win at any cost. Friedman and Ulmer emphasize the importance of being honest with yourself in making an assessment of your behavior.

If you recognize that you are more of a Type A person than you'd like, and if *you* think it is important that you change your behavior and thus reduce your stress, you can consider steps to make these changes. The first step is to realize that Type A is apparently not an "incurable disease." Many people have succeeded in making drastic changes in their lifestyles and have greatly reduced Type A behaviors. Unfortunately, many of them had to first be jolted by a heart attack to take a serious look at the price of their hard-driving, competitive, aggressive, and stressful way of being. If you decide that it is worth it to move in the direction of becoming more of a Type B person, there is no need to wait until you become physically and psychologically debilitated.

Transforming yourself from a Type A person entails learning a balance in life, especially a balance between work and play. It involves changing attitudes and beliefs so that you do not react so intensely to situations and thus cause stress. Most of all, it demands that you accept full responsibility for how you are living. A place to begin would be Charlesworth and Nathan's (1984) comprehensive and useful book *Stress Management*, which presents some fine strategies for changing. Another book to read is Friedman and Ulmer's (1985) *Treating Type A Behavior and Your Heart*. Both books make it clear that recognizing your Type A behaviors and learning to manage the resulting stress is not a one-time task but an ongoing effort.

From a personal perspective, I (Jerry) know how difficult it is to make the transformation from Type A to Type B. I can't cram my life with activities all year, fragmenting myself with many stressful situations, and then expect a "day off" to rejuvenate my system. Even though I'm a somewhat slow learner in this respect, I'm coming to recognize the need to find ways of reducing, if not eliminating, many of those situations that cause stress and to deal differently with the stresses that are inevitable. It has been useful for me to identify thought patterns, beliefs, and expectations that lead to stress. Furthermore, I am increasingly making decisions about ways of behaving that can result in either stress or inner peace. For example, before accepting work projects, I carefully weigh the cost-benefit ratio and also remind myself that I can never find enough time to do everything that interests me. Recently, I began the practice of morning meditation as a way to clear my mind and get centered, as well as making time for several breaks for refocusing throughout the day. These new changes are helping me gain more control over stress.

We suggest that you make time for quiet reflection to consider the priority you may want to give to learning relaxation exercises, practicing some form of meditation, getting adequate sleep, having a sound diet, keeping physically fit, and making other conscious choices that lead to a low-stress lifestyle.

Meditation. Meditation is another constructive reaction to stress. This method of getting personally focused is enjoying an increased popularity among people of all ages. For some people it still has an aura of mysticism, and they may shy away from it because it seems intricately bound up with elaborate rituals, strange language, strange clothing, and abstract philosophical and spiritual notions. But you don't have to wear exotic garb and sit in a lotus position to meditate. Simply sitting quietly and letting your mind wander or looking within can be a simple form of meditation.

In writing about meditation, Joy (1979) points out that meditation is an empowering process that we can learn if we are willing to allow time for the experience. He adds that there are as many different ways to meditate as there are meditators. Some people allow an hour each morning for silence and internal centering. Others find that they can enter meditative states while walking, jogging, bike riding, or doing T'ai Chi.

For much of our waking time, we are typically thinking and engaged in some form of verbalization or inner dialogue. In fact, many of us find it difficult to quiet the internal chattering that typically goes on inside our head. We are not used to attending to one thing at a time or fully concentrating on a single action. Oftentimes we miss the present moment by thinking about what we did yesterday or what we will do tomorrow or next year. Meditation is a tool, or a means to the end of increasing awareness, becoming centered, and achieving an internal focus. In meditation our attention is focused, and we engage in a single behavior. Our attention is cleansed of preconceptions and distracting input so that we can perceive reality more freshly. Although there is a narrowing of the focus of attention, the result is an enlarged sense of being.

Meditation is effective in creating a deep state of relaxation in a fairly short time. The meditative state not only induces profound relaxation but also reduces physical and psychological fatigue. Its beneficial effects are numerous, and it has been shown to relieve anxiety and stress-related disease. People who consistently practice meditation show a substantial reduction in the frequency of stress-related symptoms. Meditators reduce their blood pressure, both during practice and over the long term (Mason, 1985).

Dr. Herbert Benson (1976) describes a simple meditative technique that has helped many people cope with stress. In Benson's studies the subjects achieved a state of deep relaxation by repeating a mantra (a word used to focus one's attention, such as *om*). He describes the following three factors as crucial to inducing this state:

- Find a quiet place with a minimum of external distractions. The quiet environment contributes to the effectiveness of the repeated word or phrase by making it easier to eliminate distracting thoughts.
- Find an object or mantra to focus your attention on, and let thoughts simply pass by. What is important is to concentrate on one thing only and learn to eliminate internal mental distractions as well as external ones.
- Adopt a passive attitude, which includes letting go of thoughts and distractions and simply returning to the object you are dwelling on. A passive attitude implies a willingness to let go of evaluating yourself and to avoid the usual thinking and planning.

Some will argue that they can't find the time for morning meditation. However, if we do not carve out time for this centering activity, it is likely that we will be bounced around by events that happen to us throughout the day. If you are interested in making meditation part of your daily pattern, there are many excellent books that can help you learn to meditate effectively, but discipline and consistent practice are required. Most writers on meditation recommend sessions before breakfast and before dinner, lasting for at least twenty minutes. They often suggest that a sitting position is more conducive than lying in bed. Some write that meditating on an empty stomach is the most conducive to deep meditative states. They also agree that exercises must be practiced for at least a month for meditation's more profound effects to be experienced. Mason (1985) allows three to eight weeks. In his book *Guide to Stress Reduction*, Mason describes several types of meditation, including Zen meditation, Shavasana (a breathing exercise that comes from the yogic tradition), mantra-repeating meditations (such as Transcendental Meditation), and visual-focus-point meditations. Most of them take about twenty minutes. Davis, Eshelman, and McKay (1980) also describe a variety of methods of meditation and urge readers to select one or more that suit them.

Relaxation. Mason (1985) suggests that we have a right to relax and to feel good. We do not have to settle for a range of psychosomatic complaints such as indigestion, backaches, insomnia, and headaches as part of our lifestyle. If we can genuinely learn to relax and take care of ourselves in positive and nurturing ways, the benefits will enhance our lives and those of the people who live with us. Mason writes:

> Twenty minutes of deep relaxation will aid your mental growth, improve your physical health, emotional stability, and possibly even increase your spiritual awareness. You will use your energy more efficiently, and have more time for your family, friends and yourself. You will be on a more even keel, not on the roller-coaster of life with its traumatic ups and downs. This does not lessen the great joys of life, but allows you to progress more evenly with less backsliding and distress. (p. vi)

Before you continue reading, take a few moments to relax and to think about how you relax. Do you engage in certain forms of relaxation on a regular basis? What do you consider relaxing? Look over the following list, and decide which forms of relaxation are for you. Think about the quality of each form of relaxation and how often you use it:

- sitting in a quiet place for as few as ten minutes a day and just letting your mind wander
- listening to music and fully hearing and feeling it (without making it the background of another activity)
- sleeping deeply and restfully
- being involved in a hobby that gives you pleasure
- engaging in sports that have the effect of calming you
- asking for and receiving a massage
- taking longer than usual in lovemaking
- walking in the woods or on the beach
- closing your eyes and listening to the sounds in nature
- listening to the sounds of your breathing
- practicing some form of meditation each day
- relaxing in a hot tub
- allowing yourself to have fun with friends
- regularly practicing muscle-relaxation exercises
- practicing some form of self-hypnosis to cut down stress and outside distractions.

In our complex society many of us encounter obstacles in allowing ourselves to fully relax. Even if we take a few moments in a busy schedule to unwind, our mind may be reeling with thoughts of past or future events. Another problem is simply finding a quiet and private place where we can relax and a time when we will be free from interruptions. Perhaps an important lesson to learn is how to let go for even a few minutes, to learn to unwind while waiting in a line or riding on a bus. Refer to the "Activities and Exercises" for a relaxation exercise that you can apply as a constructive way of coping with stress.

Therapeutic massage. In many European countries, and in Eastern cultures as well, massage is a well-known art that many people participate in as a way of enhancing health. In fact, physicians often prescribe therapeutic massage and mineral baths as one method of coping with the negative effects of stress. Unfortunately, massage has sometimes been linked to selling sex, especially through some massage parlors. Be aware that massage is one legitimate route to maintaining wellness but use caution in selecting a reputable practitioner.

Earlier we talked of the need for touch to maintain the well-being of our body and mind, and we also mentioned how our body tells the truth. Massage is one way of meeting the need for touch; it is also a way to discover where

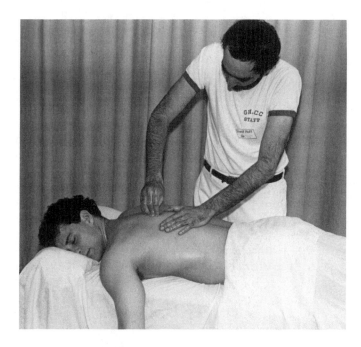

and how we are holding in the tension produced by stressful situations. Practitioners who have studied physical therapy and therapeutic massage say that the body is the place where changes need to be made if long-lasting psychological changes are hoped for. According to Schutz (1972), the body is the source of change because all of our experiences are recorded there and are available for recall through various methods such as deep massage. The nervous system, the muscles, the way the body is held, the patterns of breathing, aberrations of circulation and digestion, patterns of illnesses, and facial expressions—all of these contain the emotional memories of our past experiences. Therefore, by learning to become aware of our bodily states, especially areas where we tend to hold in tension, we are also able to expand our awareness of how we are reacting to both our external and internal worlds. Schutz asserts that attention to these bodily phenomena often gives us insight into our present feeling states and is also helpful in breaking through impasses (or places where we are psychologically stuck).

Therapeutic massage is an excellent way to develop awareness of the differences between tension and relaxation states to release the muscular tightness that so often results when we are encountering stress. It is also a good way to learn how to receive the caring touch of another. A specialized body technique that is somewhat like a very deep massage is known as "Rolfing." This technique, developed by Dr. Ida Rolf, is also called "structural integration." Rolfing consists of deep body manipulation aimed at restructuring and realigning the body to its normal position. Over a period of time, through chronic muscle tensions and the structural adaptations produced by these tensions, the body strays from its proper position. It literally gets out of alignment. The process of structural integration partly consists of breaking up connective tissue and aligning body parts. Rolfing consists of a series of about a dozen sessions, each focusing on a specific region of the body. It is often a painful process, both physically and emotionally. The physical hurt results from the breaking up of muscular tensions. As the physical structure is being worked on, it is not uncommon for people to experience intense emotions and deep crying, since pressure on certain points can trigger past memories.

The combination of Rolfing and massage can do a lot to help us constructively cope with stress. A while back, I (Jerry) developed occasional headaches, especially during periods of stress. I was ignoring some bodily signs until the headaches convinced me that I needed to reduce the sources of my stress. Interestingly, after going through the Rolfing series and continuing with maintenance sessions, I very rarely get the headaches. With the aid of both Rolfing and therapeutic massage, I have become much better at detecting those times when tension begins to build up in my neck and shoulders. During the past few years both of us have experienced Rolfing and therapeutic massage. When we are on the table, the practitioner can generally tell us where the trouble spots are in our bodies. Through regular Rolfing and massage sessions we are confronted with the ways in which we are not adequately dealing with daily stresses.

WHAT PATTERNS ARE YOU WILLING TO CHANGE?

Remember that you are a whole being, which implies an integration of your physical, emotional, social, mental, and spiritual dimensions. If you neglect any one of these aspects of your self, you will feel the impact on the other dimensions of your being. For example, the way in which you process the stress of daily living has a lot to do with your mental attitude, yet stress affects you physically as well as psychologically. At this time you might think again about how well you are taking care of yourself physically. Ask yourself the degree to which you are committed to a wellness perspective. Consider the value you place on taking good care of yourself through practices such as meditation, relaxation exercises, receiving therapeutic massages, paying attention to your spiritual life, participating in meaningful religious activities, maintaining good nutritional habits, getting adequate sleep and rest, participating in a regular exercise program, and so forth. Ask yourself whether your daily behavior gives evidence that you value your physical and psychological health. Once you make this assessment of your health habits and your approach to life, we strongly encourage you to consider implementing Bernie Siegel's five-part therapeutic program that he describes in his book *Peace, Love, and Healing.* Siegel started a form of individual and group therapy known as Exceptional Cancer Patients. As a result of his work with this population, Siegel believes that he has learned a great deal about how to live to the fullest and how people can tap their own healing potential. Siegel recommends following this five-part program on a daily basis as a way to become what he calls an "exceptional human being":

• Keep a daily journal in which you write about your feelings and dreams.
• Join a therapy group that meets on a weekly basis where you can receive support, confrontation, and discipline.
• Make it a practice to meditate, do visualization (imagine yourself as being the way you would like to be), pray, reflect, or listen to quiet music as a way to break up the activities of your day four to six times. Make the time to refocus and get centered several times each day.
• Live one hour at a time. Paying attention to your feelings and reactions will eventually teach you that you are in charge of your feelings.
• Twice a day for fifteen minutes sit or stand naked in front of a mirror and work with the feelings that emerge for you.

Siegel believes that only truly exceptional human beings will commit themselves to the time and work involved in this therapeutic program aimed at change. He writes: "Once you do all of these things, however, you find that you begin to live more and more in the moment, and life becomes a series of moments that you are in charge of. Then joy will enter your life and you will be in heaven without dying" (Siegel, 1989, p. 226).

Chapter Summary

The purpose of this chapter has been to stimulate you to think about how you are treating your body and how you can take control of your physical and psychological well-being. Even if you are not presently concerned with the problems of stress, drug abuse, or weight control, you may have discovered certain attitudes about your body that are self-defeating. A theme of this chapter has been to examine what might be keeping you from really caring about your body or acting on the caring that you say you have. The basic choice is more than a matter of smoking or not smoking, of exercising or not exercising; the basic choice concerns how you feel about yourself and about your life. By accepting responsibility for the feelings and attitudes you have developed about your body, you begin to free yourself from feeling victimized by your body.

One enemy of your overall well-being is excessive stress. A constructive way of dealing with stress is within the framework of wellness and making decisions about changing some of the ways that you are living. You cannot realistically expect to eliminate stress from your life, but you can modify your way of thinking and your behavior patterns to reduce stressful situations and manage stress more effectively.

Conquering stress highlights the importance of a willingness to accept responsibility for what you are doing to your body. A central message is to listen to your body and respect what you hear. By taking time you can experience the world around you through your senses of seeing, hearing, smelling, tasting, and touching. You can also become less of a stranger to your body through relaxation, dance, and movement. Touch is particularly important. For healthy development, both physical and emotional, you need both physical and psychological contact.

When you look at your body in the mirror, what does this reflection tell you about the degree to which you value your body? Your body presents an image, both to yourself and to others, of how you view yourself. Your body image is not something you are born with. You acquire your attitudes about your body in the context of your culture. You can challenge some of the attitudes you have picked up, especially if they are self-critical. This may be a good time for you to think about the ways in which your perceptions of your body affect these other areas of your life. Your ability to love others, to form nourishing sexual and emotional relationships with others, to work well, to play with joy, and to fully savor each day depends a great deal on both your physical and psychological health. Do you shy away from the opposite sex because of your fears about how others will react to your physical being? Is it possible that you keep yourself in a self-imposed prison, unwilling to initiate positive contact with other people, simply because you assume that they won't like the way you look? Does your body express your feelings of tenderness, anger, enthusiasm, and so on, or does it tend to be rigid and under control? By examining these and similar questions, you can widen the brackets of freedom in these other areas of your life.

This chapter ends with an invitation for you to make an honest assessment of how you see your body and how you feel about it, as well as the many ways in which your views influence your behavior. Your subjective evaluation of your body is at least as powerful as your objective physical traits — and it is open to change.

Activities and Exercises

1. In your journal, record for a week all your activities that are healthy for your body as well as those that are unhealthy. It could be valuable to record things such as what you eat, stress patterns, smoking and drinking, sleeping habits, exercise, relaxation, and so forth. After you've done this for a week, look over your list and determine whether there are areas that you'd be willing to work on during this semester.

2. Keep an account in your journal of the stressful situations that you encounter for about a week or so. After each entry you might note items such as these: To what degree was the situation a stressful one because of your thoughts, beliefs, and assumptions about the events? How were you affected? Do you see any ways of dealing with these stresses more effectively?

3. Another way of monitoring stress in your life is to review the following Social Readjustment Rating Scale and evaluate the degree to which life changes

Social Readjustment Rating Scale*

Life Change	Scale of Impact (LCUs)
Death of spouse	100
Divorce	73
Marital separation	65
Jail term	63
Death of close family member	63
Personal injury or illness	53
Marriage	50
Dismissal from job	47
Marital reconciliation	45
Retirement	45
Change in health of family member	44
Pregnancy	40
Sexual difficulties	39
Gain of a new family member	39
Business readjustment	39
Change in financial state	38
Death of a close friend	37
Change to a different line of work	36
Change in number of arguments with spouse	35
Mortgage or loan for major purchase	31
Foreclosure of mortgage or loan	30
Change in responsibilities at work	29
Son or daughter's leaving home	29
Trouble with in-laws	29
Outstanding personal achievement	28
Wife's beginning or quitting work	26
Starting or completing school	26
Change in living conditions	25
Revision of personal habits	24
Trouble with boss	23
Change in work hours or conditions	20
Change in residence	20
Change in school	20
Change in recreation	19
Change in church activities	19
Change in social activities	18
Mortgage or loan for lesser purchase	17
Change in sleeping habits	16
Change in number of family get-togethers	15
Change in eating habits	15
Vacation	13
Christmas	12
Minor violation of the law	11
Total LCUs	____

*Reprinted with permission from *Journal of Psychosomatic Research,* 11, 213–218, T. H. Holmes and R. H. Rahe, "The Social Readjustment Rating Scale," Copyright 1967, Pergamon Press, Inc.

have affected you. The scale was developed by Holmes and his colleagues (1967, 1970) as an objective method of measuring the stress resulting from life events. Stress is measured in terms of "life change units" (LCUs). Each life change is given a numerical value. For example, pregnancy is assigned 40, change in school is given 20, change in sleeping habits is given 16, and so on. To determine the severity of stress that you have experienced, total up the LCUs that relate to you. Keep in mind that it is the demand to adjust that a life change places on you that is important, rather than the type of life change alone. Holmes and his colleagues found a strong relationship between the likelihood of physical illness and the total LCU score. Their results suggested that a score in the 200s was associated with about a 50 percent chance of illness and that a score above 300 was associated with about an 80 percent chance of illness. It is important that you interpret your score in the context of a rough estimate of the stresses you have experienced by changing life situations, rather than using your score as an exact measure. There is a great deal of individual variability with respect to the impact of specific life events. If your score indicates that you have been subjected to a high degree of stress, it is a good idea to consider ways in which you can reduce your exposure to stress and more efficiently deal with the stress that is inevitable in your life.

4. One of the best and most practical ways of dealing with stress is by daily practice of a relaxation exercise such as the one described below. You can practice relaxation in many situations, and doing so can help you assume control of your own behavior, instead of letting yourself be controlled by situations that produce tension within you. For a period of at least a week (and preferably much longer), engage in relaxation training for approximately 20 to 30 minutes daily. The purpose of the exercise is to teach you to become more aware of the distinction between tension states and relaxation states. A further objective is to reduce unnecessary anxiety and tension. The strategy for achieving muscular relaxation is to repeatedly tense and relax various muscle groups. To deepen your relaxation, auxiliary techniques such as concentrating on your breathing and imagining yourself in peaceful situations can eventually be added. Here are some guidelines for your relaxation exercise. Make sure that you're in a peaceful setting and in a relaxed position. Tighten and relax the various parts of your body, beginning with your upper extremities and progressing downward to your lower extremities.

   a. Clench your fists tightly — so tightly that it hurts. Let go of the tension and relax.
   b. Stiffen the lower part of the arm. Tense it. Feel the tension. Let go of the tension.
   c. Tense the upper part of the arm. Tighten it until it begins to hurt. Relax it.
   d. Repeat the last two steps for your other arm.
   e. Wrinkle up your forehead. Wrinkle it tighter and tighter. Then relax and smooth it out. Picture your entire forehead and scalp becoming smoother and more relaxed.
   f. Raise your eyebrows as high as you can. Hold this position. Relax.

g. Close your eyes as tightly as you can. Feel the tension. Close them even tighter, and feel that tension. Let go, and feel the relaxation around your eyes.

h. Wrinkle your nose as tightly as you can. Relax.

i. Clench your jaw, and bite your teeth together hard. Feel the pressure. Increase the tension in your jaw. Let your jaw and mouth become increasingly relaxed. Enjoy this relaxation.

j. Smile in an exaggerated way, and hold it. Let go. Purse your lips as tightly as you can. Tighten your mouth muscles, and feel the tension in your entire face. Let go of the tension. Relax.

k. The exercise progresses with the neck, shoulders, and upper back; then the chest, abdomen, and lower back; then the rest of the body, down to the toes; and finally the entire body. During the entire exercise, keep your eyes gently closed. Cover all the major muscle groups. For each group, tense the muscles for several seconds and then relax them. Note the difference between the tension and relaxation states, and repeat the tension/release cycles at least once or twice for each muscle group.

With practice, you can become aware of tension in every part of your body, and you can learn to relax all the areas of your body, separately or together, without first having to tense them. Ultimately, the goal is to teach you to control your tension states by choosing to switch to a deep muscular-relaxation state. Even closing your eyes for a few moments, concentrating on your breathing and the tension within your body, and telling yourself to "let go" are valuable tools in dealing with stress when you feel its effects on your body. It may take several weeks of practice to really feel the tension in your body and to release it. However, once you master some skills of progressive relaxation, it will be possible to relax your entire body in a few moments.

5. Select one or more of the following books for further reading on the topics explored in this chapter: Siegel, *Love, Medicine, and Miracles* (1988); Siegel, *Peace, Love and Healing* (1989); Mason, *Guide to Stress Reduction* (1985); Travis and Ryan, *Wellness Workbook* (1988). Within the chapter we gave a number of other suggestions of readings on topics such as stress management, relaxation, and meditation.

CHAPTER SEVEN

Love

Prechapter Self-Inventory

Use the following scale to respond: 4 = this statement is true of me *most* of the time; 3 = this statement is true of me *much* of the time; 2 = this statement is true of me *some* of the time; 1 = this statement is true of me *almost none* of the time.

_____ 1. Loving more than one person of the opposite sex diminishes my capacity to be deeply involved with another person.

_____ 2. I have a fear of losing others' love.

_____ 3. When I experience hurt or frustration in love, I find it more difficult to trust and love again.

_____ 4. I make myself known in significant ways to those I love.

_____ 5. I find it difficult to express loving feelings toward members of the same sex.

_____ 6. I am as afraid of being accepted by those I love as I am of being rejected.

_____ 7. I have to take some risks if I'm to open myself to loving.

_____ 8. In my loving relationships there is complete trust and an absence of fear.

_____ 9. I accept those whom I love as they are, without expecting them to be different.

_____ 10. I need constant closeness and intimacy with those I love.

Introduction

In this chapter we invite you to look carefully at your style of loving by examining your choices and decisions concerning giving and receiving love. People often say that either they have love in their life or they don't. We assume in this chapter that you have the capacity to become better at loving. You can look at the situations that you create for yourself and then consider how conducive these are to the sharing of love. You can also look at your attitudes toward love. Some of the questions we examine are: How are love, sexuality, and intimacy interrelated? What is the difference between authentic love and inauthentic love? Is love active or passive? Do we fall in and out of love? How much are we responsible for creating a climate in which we can love others and receive love from them? Do we have romantic and unrealistic ideals of what love should be? If so, how can we challenge them? In what ways does love change as we change? What are the myths surrounding love? Is it worth it to love?

Freud defined the healthy person as one who can work well and love well. Like work, love can make living worthwhile, even during bleak times. We can find meaning in actively caring for others and helping them make their

lives better. Because of our love for others or their love for us, we may be enabled to continue living, even in conditions of extreme hardship. Thus, Frankl (1963) noted that in the Nazi concentration camp where he was imprisoned, some of those who kept alive the images of those they loved and retained some measure of hope survived the ordeal, while many who lost any memories of love perished. From his experiences Frankl concluded that "the salvation of man is through love and in love" (p. 59).

In his discussion of the nature of love in *The Road Less Traveled*, Scott Peck (1978) defines love as "the will to extend one's self for the purpose of nurturing one's own or another's spiritual growth" (p. 81). He also identifies a number of characteristics of love. One of these qualities is extending ourselves by acting with courage. Love involves risk, especially the risk of loss or rejection. The act of reaching out to another person entails the possibility of that person's moving away, leaving you more painfully alone than you were before. Loving and living a full life may include pain, but the alternative is choosing not to live or to love fully. Love also involves commitment, which is the foundation of any genuinely loving relationship. Although commitment does not guarantee a successful relationship, it is perhaps one of the most important factors in nurturing and fostering a relationship. Another major characteristic of genuine love is separateness, so that the identity of those in the relationship is maintained and preserved. Love is also an exercise of free choice, for people who love each other are able to live without each other yet choose to live together. When we speak of love relations, we refer to the various kinds of love, such as love between parent and child, love between siblings, friendships, and romantic relationships. Although some differences characterize the various types of love, the characteristics we just mentioned are common to all forms of genuine love.

One of the purposes of this chapter is to help you clarify your views and values pertaining to love. As you read, try to apply the discussion to your own experience of love, and consider the degree to which you're now able to appreciate and love yourself. We encourage you to review your own need for love as well as your fears of loving. If you do so, you are likely to recognize whether there are barriers within yourself that prevent you from experiencing the level of love you're capable of.

Our Need to Love and to Be Loved

To fully develop as a person and enjoy a rich existence, we need to care about others and have them return this care to us. A loveless life is characterized by a joyless isolation and alienation. Our need for love includes the need to know that in at least one other person's world, our existence makes a difference. If we exclude ourselves from physical and emotional closeness with others, we pay the price in emotional and physical deprivation, which leads to isolation.

People express their need to love and to be loved in many ways, a few of which are revealed in the following statements:

- "I need to have someone in my life I can actively care for. I need to let that person know he [she] makes a difference in my life, and I need to know I make a difference in his [her] life."
- "I want to feel loved and accepted for who I am now, not for what the other person thinks I should be in order to be worthy of acceptance."
- "Although I enjoy my own company, I also have a need for people in my life. I want to reach out to certain people, and I hope they'll want something from me."
- "I'm finding out that I need others and that I have more of a capacity to give something to others than I thought I had."
- "I'm beginning to realize that I need to learn how to love myself more fully, for up until now I've limited myself by discounting my worth. I want to learn how to appreciate myself and accept myself in spite of my imperfections. Then maybe I'll be able to really believe that others can love me."
- "There are times when I want to share my joys, my dreams, my anxieties, and my uncertainties with another person, and at these times I want to feel heard and understood."

Of course, there are many ways to harden ourselves so that we won't experience a need for love. We can close ourselves off from needing anything from anybody; we can isolate ourselves by never reaching out to another; we can refuse to trust others and to make ourselves vulnerable; we can cling to an early decision that we are basically unlovable. It's important to recognize, however, that *we* make these decisions about love — and *we* pay the price. In whatever way we deaden ourselves to our own need for love, the question is whether the safety we achieve is worth the price we pay for it.

Barriers to Loving and Being Loved

MYTHS AND MISCONCEPTIONS ABOUT LOVE

Many misconceptions inhibit our ability to love fully and to receive love from others. We must first recognize those myths that we may have unconsciously bought into, before we are able to substitute for them realistic views of the nature of love. Our culture, especially the media, influences the way that we conceive of love. If we hope to challenge myths, we will have to take a critical look at the messages that we have received from society about the essence of love. In the following pages we present our views of the more common beliefs that need to be challenged.

The myth of eternal love. Some people assume that if the romance in the relationship fades, this is a sure sign that love never really existed. The notion that love will endure forever without any change is unrealistic. While

DO YOU GUARANTEE THAT ?

love can last over a period of time, it is to be expected that it will take on different forms as the relationship matures. Love assumes many complexions and involves both joyful experiences and difficulties. The intensity and degree of your love change as you change. You may experience stages of love with one person, deepening your love and finding new levels of richness; there is also the chance that you and your partner will grow in different directions or outgrow the love you once shared.

The myth that love is fleeting. On the opposite end of the spectrum is the notion that love is strictly temporary. For example, Joel found himself in love with different women as often as his moods changed. One day he would claim that he loved Sabrina and wanted to be committed to her in an exclusive relationship. But in a short while he would grow tired of Sabrina, find himself in love with Peggy, and maintain that he wanted an intense relationship with her. For him, love was strictly a here-and-now feeling. We don't believe that such changeable feelings constitute real love. In most intense, long-term relationships there are times when the alliance is characterized by deadness, frustration, strife, or conflict. There are inevitably times when we feel "stuck" with a person, and at such times we may consider dissolving the relationship. If our attitude is "I'll stay while things are rosy, but as soon as things get stormy or dull, I'll split and look elsewhere for something more interesting," then it's worth asking what kind of love it is that crumbles with the first crisis. From our perspective, authentic love means recognizing when we're stuck in an unsatisfying place but being willing to challenge the reasons for this and caring enough about the other person to stay and work on breaking through the impasse. Love involves a commitment, which is a choice of working at a relationship even though there are difficulties to be resolved.

The myth that love implies constant closeness. Betina and Luis dated throughout junior high and high school, and they went to college together because they could not tolerate any separation. They are making no friends, either with the same or opposite sex, and they show extreme signs of jealousy when the other indicates even the slightest interest in wanting to be with others. Rather than creating a better balance of time with each other and time with others, the only alternative they see is to terminate their relationship. The mistaken assumption that they are operating on is that if they loved each other, then they would be fused into one being. According to Bellah, Madsen, Sullivan, Swidler, and Tipton (1985), the ideal love relationship is one involving intimacy, mutuality, sharing, and commitment. The authors add that there is an ability to express one's individuality and freedom, so that the sense of sharing and togetherness does not swallow up the parties involved, making them lose sight of their own uniqueness as persons.

Many of us can tolerate only so much closeness, and at times we are likely to need some distance from others. Gibran's words in *The Prophet* are still timely: "And stand together yet not too near together: For the pillars of the temple stand apart, and the oak tree and the cypress grow not in each other's shadow" (1923, p. 17).

There are times when a separation from our loved one can be very healthy. At these times we can renew our need for the other person and also allow ourselves to become centered again. If we fail to separate when we feel the need to do so, we'll surely strain the relationship. As an example consider the case of Martin, who refused to spend a weekend without his wife and children, even though he said he wanted some time for himself. The myth of constant closeness and constant togetherness in love prevented him from taking private time. It might also have been that the myth covered up certain fears. What if he discovered that his wife and children could manage very well without him? What if he found that he couldn't stand his own company for a few days and that the reason for "togetherness" was to keep him from boring himself?

As a couple, we (Marianne and Jerry) sometimes travel separately. At times Marianne goes to Germany by herself for a visit. In the past some of the townspeople have let her know that they thought our marriage must be in trouble if we were not always together. Once Marianne and her mother went on a cruise together for a week and many people wondered why Marianne would go on a vacation without her husband. When Jerry travels alone, whether for personal or professional reasons, he rarely is asked why he is not with his wife. This notion that couples should be inseparable is certainly influenced by what society considers appropriate gender-role behavior. The truth is that we enjoy traveling together and also without each other.

The myth that we fall in and out of love. A common notion is that people "fall" in love, that they passively wait for the right person to come along and sweep them off their feet. Part of this misconception is the belief that when love strikes, it is so powerful that it renders people helpless and unable to control what they do. According to this view, love is something that happens *to* pepole. This myth keeps people from assuming personal responsibility for their behavior and decisions. In contrast, we view love as being *active*, something that people themselves create. *They* make love happen.

For Peck (1978), falling in love is invariably temporary, for eventually people will fall out of love if the relationship continues long enough. Buscaglia (1972) also criticizes the phrase "to *fall* in love." He contends that it's more accurate to say that we *grow* in love, which implies an activity of choosing: "Love is active, not passive. It is continually engaged in the process of opening new doors and windows so that fresh ideas and questions can be admitted" (p. 69). In *The Art of Loving*, Fromm (1956) also describes love as active: "In the most general way, the active character of love can be described by stating that love is primarily *giving*, not receiving" (p. 22). Although the notion of falling in love is popular, most serious writers on the subject deny that it can be the basis for a lasting and meaningful relationship.

People often say "I love you" and at the same time are hard pressed to describe the active way in which they show this love. Words can easily be overused and become hollow. The loved one may be more convinced by actions than by words. In our professional work with couples, we find that one person may rant and rave about his or her partner's shortcomings. We often ask, "If the situation is as bad as you describe, what keeps you together as a couple?" To this question people often reply that they love the other person. Yet they are slow in identifying ways that they show what their love actually means, and they go on to blame their partner for whatever is awry in their relationship.

In summary, active love is something that we can choose to share with others. We don't lose love by sharing it but, rather, increase it. This thought leads to the next myth.

The myth of the exclusiveness of love. Sometimes you may think of love as something you possess in a limited quantity that you must carefully dole out and conserve. You may believe that you are capable of loving only one other person — that there is one right person for you and that your fate is to find this singular soul. One of the signs of genuine love is that it is expansive rather than exclusive. By opening yourself to loving others, you also open yourself to loving one person more deeply.

In some senses, though, we may choose to make our love exclusive or special. For example, two persons may choose not to have sexual relationships with others, because they realize that doing so might interfere with their capacity to freely open up and trust each other. Nevertheless, their sexual exclusivity does not have to mean that they cannot genuinely love others as well.

Jealousy is an issue that can be mentioned here. For example, Joe may feel insecure if he discovers that his wife, Carol, has friendships with other men. Even if Carol and Joe have an agreement not to have sexual relationships with others, Joe might be threatened and angry over the fact that Carol wants to maintain these friendships with other men. He may wrongly reason: "What is the matter with me that Carol has to seek out these friends? Her interest in other men is a sign that something is wrong with me!" On the other hand, it is wrong to equate an absence of jealousy with an absence of love. The kind of jealousy that is based on ownership of the other is really not flattering. In Joe's case, his jealousy is probably rooted in his feelings of inferiority and the threat posed to him because of the reality that Carol wants to include others in her life. However, Carol might be upset if Joe did not display any jealousy toward her, insisting that this meant that he was indifferent to her or that he had come to take her for granted. The motivations for jealousy need to be understood.

The myth that true love is selfless. Lily is a mother who has always given to her children. She never lets them know that she needs anything from them, yet she confides to her friends that she is very hurt that the children do not seem to appreciate her. She complains that if she did not initiate visits with them, they would never see her. She would never say anything about her feelings to her children, nor would she ever tell them that she would like for them to contact her. She harbors the myth that if they really loved her, they would know what she needed without her having to ask for it.

Such people as Lily are "selfish givers"; that is, they have a high need to take care of others, yet they appear to have little tolerance in accepting what others want to give to them. "Selfish givers" create an inequality, and others tend to feel guilty because as receivers they do not have a chance to reciprocate. Although these receivers may feel guilty and angry, their feelings do not seem appropriate to them, for how could they have angry feelings toward those who do so much for them? Mothers such as Lily are often guilty of giving but not being good receivers. The giver has established an imbalance of giving and taking. Givers may feel resentment toward those who are always taking from them, not recognizing how difficult they are making it to receive.

We may have been conditioned to believe that genuine love implies that we forget ourselves. It is a myth that true love means giving selflessly. For one thing, love also means *taking*. If you cannot allow others to give to you and cannot take their expressions of love, you are likely to become drained or to become resentful of your continual giving. For another thing, in giving to others we do meet many of our own needs. There is not necessarily anything wrong in this, as long as we can admit it. For example, a mother who never says no to any demands made by her children may not be aware of the ways in which she has conditioned them to depend on her. They may be unaware that she has any needs of her own, for she hides them so well. In fact, she may set them up to take advantage of her out of her need to feel significant. In other words, her "giving" is actually an outgrowth of her need to feel like a good mother, rather than an honest expression of love for her children.

Giving to others or the desire to express our love to others is not necessarily a problem. However, it is important that we recognize our own needs and consider the value of allowing others to take care of us and return the love we show to them. One of us (Marianne) is learning the importance of letting others return favors. It has always been easy for me to show others kindness and take care of others, yet it has been a struggle for me to be on the receiving end. An example of how I am learning to let others give to me is a recent party that we gave for one of our daughters. My old pattern would be to do everything by myself and not take the chance of imposing on others by asking for assistance. This time I asked my brother to shop for groceries and cook a meal for twenty people and I asked a friend if she would be willing to let us use her house as a meeting place. To my surprise, not only did they not feel any imposition, but they expressed delight that I made these requests and were pleased to reciprocate. I continue to learn that it takes a concerted effort to challenge ingrained beliefs about being a selfless giver. One way that I am able to give to others is by letting others take care of me at times.

The myth that love and anger are incompatible. Many people are convinced that if they love someone, this necessarily implies that they cannot get angry at them. If they get angry, therefore, they tend to deny these feelings or to express them in indirect ways. Unfortunately, either of these paths can lead to the deterioration of the relationship. Indeed, in her book *The Dance of Anger*, Lerner (1985) develops the thesis that learning how to deal directly and honestly with anger is one of the most essential tasks in intimate relationships.

Rubin (1969), in *The Angry Book*, has done a good job of showing that denied anger results in the death of a relationship. Because love requires a real self and a real exchange with another self, anger needs to be dealt with when it is felt. It is important to realize that anger and love cannot be compartmentalized, for if you negate anger, you also negate love. Rubin develops the idea that it is the blocking of anger that actually destroys love. If you deny anger, then you must use a number of strategies to push these feelings into the "slush fund of perverted emotions," which can eventually run over. Anger that is not expressed tends to possess us. It is difficult to feel loving toward others if we harbor unexpressed grudges. These unresolved issues tend to poison the relationship.

SELF-DOUBT AND LACK OF SELF-LOVE

Despite our need for love we often put barriers in the way of our attempts to give and receive love. One common obstacle consists of the messages we sometimes send to others concerning ourselves. If we enter relationships convinced that nobody could possibly love us, we will give this message to others in many subtle ways. We thus create a self-fulfilling prophecy, whereby we make the very thing we fear come true by telling both ourselves and others that life can be no other way.

If you are convinced that you're unlovable, your conviction is probably related to decisions that you made about yourself during your childhood or adolescent years. At one time, perhaps, you decided that you wouldn't be loved *unless* you did certain expected things or lived up to another's design for your life. Here, for example, is one such decision: "Unless I produce, I won't be loved. To be loved, I must produce good grades, become successful, and make the most of my life." Such a decision can make it difficult to convince yourself later in life that you can be loved even if you're not productive.

Jay decided as a child that he would do whatever it took to meet the expectations of others and to gain their acceptance. He gives his all to please people and to get them to like him, yet he has few friends. Through his actions of desperately trying to win people over, he pushes them away even more. Although he feels that he is doing everything right, people don't like the way he behaves around them. He is constantly depressed and complains about how hard life is for him. He seeks sympathy and receives rejection. He needs continual reassurance that he is lovable, yet when he does get acceptance and reassurance, he negates it. He seems to work on convincing people that he is really unlovable, and eventually people who know him get frustrated and end up rebuffing him. He may never realize that he is the one who has created a cycle of his own rejection. In some important ways he continues to live by the theme that no matter what he does or how hard he tries, people will still not like him, much less love him.

Sometimes people have a difficult time believing that they are lovable for who they are, and they may discount the love that others give them as being contingent on a single characteristic of their personality. For example, think for a moment of how many times you have completed this sentence in any of the following ways: "People love me only because I am . . . pretty, bright, and witty; good in sports; a good student; a fine provider; attractive; accomplished; cooperative and considerate; a good father [mother]; a good husband [wife]." If you limit your ability to receive love from others by telling yourself (and by convincing others) that you are loved primarily for a single trait, it would be healthy to challenge this assumption. For example, if you say "You only love me because of my body," you might try to realize that your body is *one* of your assets. You can learn to appreciate this asset without assuming that it is all there is to the person you are. If you have trouble seeing any desirable characteristics besides your physical attractiveness, you are likely to give others messages that your primary value is bound up in appearances. Ideally, you will come to accept that being a physically attractive person

"NO ONE COULD POSSIBLY LOVE ME..."

makes it easier for others to notice you and want to initiate contact with you. However, you don't need to limit yourself by depending exclusively on how you look, for you can work at developing other traits. The danger here consists of relying on physical attractiveness as a basis for building and maintaining a relationship. If you rely exclusively on physical attractiveness as a source of gaining love from others (or from yourself), your ability to be loved is in a tenuous state.

In my own life, I (Jerry) have had to struggle for a long time to recognize and accept my lovability. It would be easy for me to say "People love me only because I'm productive — because I write books, am an energetic teacher, am a good organizer, work hard, and because of my accomplishments." It is only recently that I have begun to entertain the notion that who and what I am is far greater than all the things I *do* professionally. I continue to learn that my compulsive energy and drive often put distance between those people who love me (and those I love) and myself. One insight that came to me is that the very thing I sometimes believe I *must* do or be in order to be loved actually gets in the way of others' loving me. I am discovering that my basic worth is not measured by what I accomplish and that there are many lovable dimensions within me if I allow them expression.

We sometimes imagine that other people have expectations we must meet in order to be loved. This obstructs our ability to love and receive love. In his inspirational book *God's Love Song*, the Reverend Sam Maier (1991) admits that it was a difficult struggle for him to assume responsibility for himself instead of striving for love from others by living up to what they expected of him. He writes:

> As a child I was trained to receive satisfaction from meeting other people's expectations of what I should do and be. My parents expected me to behave in certain ways and I tried to please them. My teacher made demands on me and I tried to oblige. When I began my life work, my congregation had expectations of my performance and I tried hard to measure up. The person

who barked the loudest made me jump the highest. I was doing as I was told. I was not responsible for myself. I was meeting the demands of other people. I was a child. (p. 95)

I (Jerry) can relate to Sam Maier's struggle to not buy love and acceptance by meeting the expectations of others. For much of my life, I have been concerned with doing what was expected of me, especially in striving for accomplishments. In my early years I felt that I did not belong, that I was not too useful, and that I did not have much significance. A pattern of my life has been creating my identity through my work, which has led to a sense of being wanted, accepted, and appreciated. I might well have confused the outcomes of my work with being lovable and worthwhile. I think it's essential for me to remember that the difficulty I sometimes have in feeling worthy apart from my productivity is not a condition that I will ever "cure," but it is a pattern that I can recognize and it is possible for me to create a new perspective. Furthermore, it is possible for me to continue to involve myself in productive projects and at the same time feel that if I am not doing something productive at the moment, I am still worthwhile.

OUR FEAR OF LOVE

There are other barriers to love besides a lack of self-love. Despite our need for love, we often fear loving and being loved. Our fear can lead us to seal off our need to experience love, and it can dull our capacity to care about others. Love doesn't come with guarantees; we can't be sure that another person will always love us, and we do lose loved ones. As Hodge (1967) insists, we can't eliminate the possibility that we will be hurt if we choose to love. Our loved ones may die or be injured or become painfully ill; they may simply be mistrustful of our caring. In Hodge's words: "These are painful experiences, and we cannot avoid them if we choose to love. It is part of the human dilemma that love always includes the element of hurt" (p. 266).

There are some common fears of risking in love. Most of them are related to rejection, loss, the failure of love to be reciprocated, and uneasiness with intensity. Some of them might be expressed as follows:

- "Since I once got badly hurt in a love relationship, I'm not willing to take the chance of trusting again."
- "I fear allowing myself to love others because of the possibility that they will be seriously injured, contract a terrible illness, or die. I don't want to let them matter that much; that way, if I lose them, it won't hurt as much as if they really mattered."
- "My fear is that love will never be as good as I imagine it to be."
- "I'm afraid of loving others because they might want more from me than I'm willing to give, and I might feel suffocated."
- "I'm afraid that I'm basically unlovable and that when you really get to know me, you'll want little to do with me."

- "Emotional closeness is scary for me, because if I care deeply for a person and permit him [her] to care about me, then I'm vulnerable."
- "One great fear is that people in my world will be indifferent to me — that they simply won't give a damn about my existence."
- "In many ways it's easier for me to take rejection than acceptance. It's hard for me to accept compliments or to be close and intimate. If people tell me that they want to care for me, I feel I've taken on a burden, and I'm afraid of letting them down."
- "I've never really allowed myself to look at whether I'm lovable. My fear is that I will search deep within myself and find little for another to love. What will I do if I discover that I'm grotesque, or hollow and empty, or incapable of giving or receiving?"

Time Out for Personal Reflection

1. Who are some of the people who have made the most difference in your life, and in what ways were they important?

   a. _____

   b. _____

   c. _____

   d. _____

   e. _____

2. How do you express your love to others? Check the responses that apply to you, and add any other ways in which you show love, affection, and caring.

   _____ a. by telling the other person that I love him or her
   _____ b. through touching and other nonverbal means
   _____ c. by doing special things for the person
   _____ d. by making myself known to the person
   _____ e. by becoming vulnerable and trusting
   _____ f. by buying the person gifts

   g. _____

   _____

3. How do you express to another person your own need to receive love, affection, and caring?

   _____ a. by telling him or her that I need to be loved
   _____ b. by being open and trusting

   c. _____

   _____

4. List some specific fears that you have concerning loving others.

_____

_____

_____

_____

5. Mention some barriers within yourself that prevent others from loving you or that prevent you from fully receiving their love. (Examples: being overly suspicious, refusing to accept others' love, feeling a lack of self-worth, needing to return their love.)

_____

_____

_____

_____

6. List some qualities you have that you deem lovable. (Examples: my ability to care for others, my sense of humor.)

_____

_____

_____

_____

7. List some specific ways in which you might become a more lovable person. (Examples: increasing my feelings of self-worth, trusting others more, taking better care of my physical appearance.)

_____

_____

_____

_____

Learning to Love and Appreciate Ourselves

In our counseling sessions clients are at times surprised when we ask them what they actually like and appreciate about themselves. They look uncomfortable and embarrassed, for it is obvious that they are not accustomed to speaking positively about themselves. An indirect way of getting them to express some self-appreciation is to ask them questions such as "If your best friends were here, how would they describe you? What positive characteristics would they ascribe to you? What reasons might they give for choosing you as a friend?" By responding to this line of questioning, clients appear to find it easier to talk about how they see themselves in positive ways.

Some people are reluctant to speak of their self-love, because they have been brought up to think of it as purely egocentric. Yet unless we learn how to love ourselves, we'll encounter difficulties in loving others and in allowing them to express their love for us. We can't very well give to others what we don't possess ourselves. And if we can't appreciate our own worth, how can we believe others when they say that they see value in us? The following meditation by Casey and Vanceburg (1985) captures the importance of loving ourselves:

> No one of us is free from the need for love. And most of us search for reassurances of that love from the significant people in our lives. However, the search will be unending until we come to love ourselves. Love of self is assured when we understand our worth, our actual necessity in the larger picture of the events that touch us all. (Meditation of January 17)

Having love for ourselves doesn't imply having an exaggerated picture of our own importance or placing ourselves above others or at the center of the universe. Rather, it implies having respect for ourselves, even though we're imperfect. It entails caring about our life and striving to become the person we are capable of becoming.

Many writers have stressed the necessity of self-love as a condition of love for others. In *The Art of Loving*, Fromm (1956) describes self-love as a respect for our own integrity and uniqueness, and he maintains that it cannot be separated from love and understanding of others. In his book *Love*, Buscaglia (1972) also writes that to love others we must first love ourselves, for we cannot give what we have not learned and experienced ourselves. Buscaglia describes loving oneself as "the discovery of the true wonder of you; not only the present you, but the many possibilities of you" (p. 99).

As we grow to treat ourselves with increasing respect and regard, we increase our ability to fully accept the love that others might want to give us; at the same time, we have the foundation for genuinely loving others. In his book *On Caring*, Mayeroff (1971) says that "if I am unable to care for myself, I am unable to care for another person" (p. 49). To care for ourselves, Mayeroff adds, we need to be responsive to our own needs for growth; we also need to feel at one with ourselves rather than estranged from ourselves. Furthermore, caring for ourselves and caring for others are mutually dependent: "I can only fulfill myself by serving someone or something apart from myself, and if I am unable to care for anyone or anything separate from me, I am unable to care for myself" (p. 48).

In counseling situations we often ask clients who only give to others and who have a difficult time taking for themselves: "Do *you* deserve what you so freely give to others?" "If your own well runs dry, how will you be able to give to others?"

Inauthentic and Authentic Love

"LOVE" THAT STIFLES

It isn't always easy to distinguish between authentic love, which enhances us and those we love, and the kind of "love" that diminishes ourselves and those to whom we attempt to give it. Certainly, there are forms of pseudolove that parade as real love but that cripple not only ourselves but also those we say we love.

The following are some characteristics that may indicate a type of love that stifles. This list isn't rigid or definitive, but it may give you some ideas you can use in thinking about the quality of your love. A person whose love is inauthentic

- needs to be in charge and make decisions for the other person
- has rigid and unrealistic expectations of how the other person must act in order to be worthy of love
- attaches strings to loving and loves conditionally
- puts little trust in the love relationship
- perceives personal change as a threat to the continuation of the relationship
- is possessive
- depends on the other person to fill a void in life
- lacks commitment
- is unwilling to share important thoughts and feelings about the relationship
- resorts to manipulation as a way of getting the other person to respond in a predetermined manner

Most of us can find some of these manifestations of inauthentic love occurring in our relationships, yet this does not mean that our love is necessarily fraudulent. For instance, at times we may be reluctant to let another person know about our private life, may have excessive expectations of the person, and may attempt to impose our agenda. What is essential is to be honest with ourselves and to recognize when we are not expressing genuine love, for then we can change these patterns.

SOME MEANINGS OF AUTHENTIC LOVE

So far, we've discussed mostly what we think love is *not*. Now we'd like to share some of the positive meanings love has for us.

Love means that I *know* the person I love. I'm aware of the many facets of the other person — not just the beautiful side but also the limitations, inconsistencies, and flaws. I have an awareness of the other's feelings and thoughts, and I experience something of the core of that person. I can penetrate social masks and roles and see the other person on a deeper level.

Love means that I *care* about the welfare of the person I love. To the extent that it is genuine, my caring is not a smothering of the person or a possessive clinging. On the contrary, my caring liberates both of us. If I care about you, I'm concerned about your growth, and I hope you will become all that you can become. Consequently, I don't put up roadblocks to what you do that enhances you as a person, even though it may result in my discomfort at times.

Love means having *respect* for the *dignity* of the person I love. If I love you, I can see you as a separate person, with your own values and thoughts and feelings, and I do not insist that you surrender your identity and conform to an image of what I expect you to be for me. I can allow and encourage you to stand alone and to be who you are, and I avoid treating you as an object or using you primarily to gratify my own needs.

Love means having a *responsibility* toward the person I love. If I love you, I'm responsive to most of your major needs as a person. This responsibility does not entail my doing for you what you are capable of doing for yourself; nor does it mean that I run your life for you. It *does* imply acknowledging that what I am and what I do affects you, so that I am directly involved in your happiness and your misery. A lover does have the capacity to hurt or neglect the loved one, and in this sense I see that love entails an acceptance of some responsibility for the impact my way of being has on you.

Love means *growth* for both myself and the person I love. If I love you, I am growing as a result of my love. You are a stimulant for me to become more fully what I might become, and my loving enhances your being as well. We each grow as a result of caring and being cared for; we each share in an enriching experience that does not detract from our being.

Love entails *letting go of fear*. In *Love Is Letting Go of Fear*, Jampolsky (1981) writes about ways that worrying about past guilts and future fears allows little room to enjoy and savor the present. Not judging others is one way that I can let go of fear and experience love. Acceptance means that I am not focused on changing others so that they will conform to my expectations of how they should be.

Love means making a *commitment* to the person I love. This commitment does not entail surrendering our total selves to each other; nor does it imply that the relationship is necessarily permanent. It does entail a willingness to stay with each other in times of pain, uncertainty, struggle, and despair, as well as in times of calm and enjoyment.

Love means that I am *vulnerable*. If I open myself up to you in trust, then I can experience hurt, rejection, and loss. Since you aren't perfect, you have the capacity to hurt me; and since there are no guarantees in love, there is no security that your love will endure. Loving involves a sharing with and an experiencing with the person I love. My love for you implies that I want to spend time with you and share meaningful aspects of your life with you. It also implies that I have a desire to share significant aspects of myself with you. As Maier (1991) reminds us, one of the dimensions of love is our willingness to reveal ourselves to those whom we love. Reverend Maier indicates that Jesus provided us with a good role model for loving. Not only did Jesus share his beautiful sayings, but he shared his own frustrations and struggles, his hopes and fears, and his joys and pains as well. Maier believes that it is a challenge for us to love the way Jesus did, for doing so makes us vulnerable. After all, if we show who and what we are, people could reject us. "So it is difficult, even dangerous, to love by revealing ourselves. It is much easier to pretend to be what we are not and hide the parts that are not so lovely" (Maier, 1991, p. 42).

Love means *trusting* the person I love. If I love you, I trust that you will accept my caring and my love and that you won't deliberately hurt me. I trust that you will find me lovable and that you won't abandon me; I trust the reciprocal nature of our love. If we trust each other, we are willing to be open to each other and can shed masks and pretenses and reveal our true selves.

Love can tolerate *imperfection*. In a love relationship there are times of boredom, times when I may feel like giving up, times of real strain, and times I experience an impasse. Authentic love does not imply perpetual happiness. I can stay during rough times, however, because I can remember what we had together in the past, and I can envision what we will have together in our future if we care enough to face our problems and work them through. We agree with Maier (1991) when he writes that love is a spirit that changes life. Love is a way of life that is creative and that transforms. However, Maier does not view love as being reserved for a perfect world. "Love is meant for our imperfect world where things go wrong. Love is meant to be a spirit that works in painful situations. Love is meant to bring meaning into life where nonsense appears to reign" (p. 47). In other words, love comes into an imperfect world to make it livable.

Love is *freeing*. Love is freely given, not doled out on demand. At the same time, my love for you is not contingent on whether you fulfill my expectations of you. Authentic love does not imply "I'll love you when you become perfect or when you become what I expect you to become." Authentic love is not given with strings attached. There is an unconditional quality about love. Maier (1991, pp. 68–69) believes that the prayer of Saint Francis of Assisi is illustrative of a heart that is filled with unconditional love:

O Lord, make me an instrument of Thy peace.
Where there is hatred, let me sow love;
Where there is injury, pardon;
Where there is discord, union;
Where there is despair, hope;
Where there is darkness, light;
Where there is sadness, joy;
O Lord, grant that we seek not to be consoled, but to console;
not to be understood, but to understand;
not to be loved but to love.
For it is in giving that we receive,
in forgetting that we find ourselves,
in pardoning that we are pardoned,
and in dying that we are born to eternal life.
Amen.

Love is *expansive*. If I love you, I encourage you to reach out and develop other relationships. Although our love for each other and our commitment to each other might preclude certain actions on our parts, we are not totally and exclusively wedded to each other. It is a pseudolove that cements one person to another in such a way that he or she is not given room to grow. Casey and Vanceburg (1985) put this notion well:

> The honest evidence of our love is our commitment to encouraging another's full development. We are interdependent personalities who need one another's presence in order to fulfill our destiny. And yet, we are also separate individuals. We must come to terms with our struggles alone. (Meditation of February 21)

Love means having a *want* for the person I love without having a *need* for that person in order to be complete. If I am nothing without you, then I'm not really free to love you. If I love you and you leave, I'll experience a loss and be sad and lonely, but I'll still be able to survive. If I am overly dependent on you for my meaning and my survival, then I am not free to challenge our relationship; nor am I free to challenge and confront you. Because of my fear of losing you, I'll settle for less than I want, and this settling will surely lead to feelings of resentment.

Love means *identifying* with the person I love. If I love you, I can empathize with you and see the world through your eyes. I can identify with you because I'm able to see myself in you and you in me. This closeness does not imply a continual "togetherness," for distance and separation are sometimes essential in a loving relationship. Distance can intensify a loving bond, and it can help us rediscover ourselves, so that we are able to meet each other in a new way.

Love is *selfish*. I can only love you if I genuinely love, value, appreciate, and respect myself. If I am empty, then all I can give you is my emptiness. If I feel that I'm complete and worthwhile in myself, then I'm able to give to you out of my fullness. One of the best ways for me to give you love is by fully enjoying myself with you.

Love involves *seeing the potential* within the person we love. In my love for another, I view her or him as the person she or he can become, while still accepting who and what the person is now. Goethe's observation is relevant here: by taking people as they are, we make them worse, but by treating them as if they already were what they ought to be, we help make them better.

Love means *letting go* of the illusion of total *control* of ourselves, others, and our environment. The more I strive for complete control, the more out of control I am. Loving implies a surrender of control and being open to life's events. It implies the capacity to be surprised.

A while ago a friend surprised me (Jerry), which jarred me into considering the value of surrendering control. I thought that my friend and I were going on an early morning hike up a mountain trail to watch the sunrise. When we got to the trailhead, to my total surprise, we climbed into a hot-air balloon for a ride that he had arranged. As we floated up into the skies at dawn, we saw the sunrise above the clouds and the mountains. Just before I climbed into the basket of the balloon, I felt a need to allay my anxiety, so I asked the pilot how long he had been doing this and if these balloons ever fell down. Calmly he let us know that he had been doing this for eighteen years and that these balloons fall out of the sky only if the pilot wants them to! With that reassurance, I was able to be present and absorb the beauty of the spectacular mountains, the rising sun, and the peacefulness of being taken by the current. I had absolutely no control over which direction we would move and I learned that the pilot had to allow the wind to move us. It dawned on me that living an overly controlled existence shuts out surprises such as this, and that I could not have experienced this majestic ride unless I was willing to be taken by the current and to trust the pilot and the forces of nature.

We conclude this discussion of the meanings that authentic love has for us by sharing a thought from Fromm's *The Art of Loving* (1956). His description of mature love sums up the essential characteristics of authentic love quite well:

> Mature love is union under the condition of preserving one's integrity, one's individuality. In love this paradox occurs that two beings become one and yet remain two. (pp. 20–21)

Is It Worth It to Love?

Often we hear people say something like "Sure, I need to love and to be loved, but is it *really* worth it?" Underlying the question is a series of other questions: "Can I survive without love? Is the risk of rejection and loss worth taking? Are the rewards of opening myself up as great as the risks?"

It would be comforting to know an absolute answer to these questions, but each of us must struggle to decide for ourselves whether it's worth it to love. Our first task is to decide whether we prefer isolation to intimacy. Of course, our choice is not between extreme isolation and constant intimacy; surely there are degrees of both. But we do need to decide whether to experiment with extending our narrow world to include significant others. We can increasingly open ourselves to others and discover for ourselves what that is like for us; alternatively, we can decide that people are basically unreliable and that it's better to be safe and go hungry emotionally.

Suppose that you feel unable to give love but that you'd like to learn how to become more intimate. You might begin by acknowledging this reality to yourself, as well as to those in your life with whom you'd like to become more intimate. In this way you can take a significant beginning step.

In answering the question of whether it's worth it to you to love, you can challenge some of your attitudes and beliefs concerning acceptance and rejection. We've encountered many people who believe that it isn't worth it to love because of the possibility of experiencing rejection. If you feel this way, you can decide whether to stop at this barrier. You can ask yourself: "What's so catastrophic about being rejected? Will I die if someone I love leaves me? Can I survive the emotional hurt that comes with disappointment in love?" Of course, being rejected is not a pleasant experience, yet we hope this possibility will not deter you from allowing yourself to love someone. If a love relationship ends for you, it would surely be worth it to honestly search for your part in contributing to this situation, without being severely self-critical. If you identify some ways in which you would like to change, you can then learn from this experience.

A client whom we worked with, Elana, had to learn to trust again after being deeply hurt in a relationship. She felt that she had a mutual loving bond with Monte, yet most of her friends had a hard time understanding why she continued the relationship. Elana had an idealized picture of Monte and made excuses for his insensitive behavior. She found herself becoming extremely dependent on him and preoccupied with trying to please him at all costs, even if it meant sacrificing her own happiness to keep peace with him. Elana's friends let her know of their concern for her and tried to convince her that she deserved better treatment. She tended to cut herself off from her friends so she would not have to deal with their feedback. Eventually, she experienced a betrayal by him, which led to a crisis. Even though Elana discontinued her relationship with Monte, she was quite fearful of loving again and her old wounds were reopened each time she met a new man. She had fears of dragging memories of her past betrayal into other relationships. Indeed, she would approach new relationships with fear and distrust, which made it difficult to open herself to love again. With concerted work on her part, Elana became aware of how clinging to her past hampered her ability to receive love and develop friendships. Elana's immediate impulses were to flee from getting close, yet she challenged her fears with the realization that the risk of rejection did not have to keep her helpless and guarded.

Hodge (1967) writes that, as adults, we're no longer helpless and that we can do something about rejection and hurt. We can choose to leave relationships that aren't satisfying, we can learn to survive pain, and we can realize that being rejected doesn't mean that we are fundamentally unlovable. Consider how the last line in Hodge's *Your Fear of Love* may apply to you: "We can discover for ourselves that it is worth the risk to love, even though we tremble and even though we know we will sometimes experience the hurt we fear" (p. 270).

Time Out for Personal Reflection

1. The following are some possible reasons for thinking that it is or isn't worth it to love. Check the ones that fit your own thoughts and feelings.

It's worth it to love, because

_____   of the joy involved when two people love each other.
_____   the rewards are greater than the risks.
_____   a life without love is empty.

List other reasons:

_____

_____

It isn't worth it to love, because

_____   of the pain involved when love is not returned.
_____   the risks are not worth the possible rewards.
_____   it's better to be alone than with someone you might no longer love (or who might no longer love you).

List other reasons:

_____

_____

2. Review our list of the meanings love has for us, and then list some of the meanings love has for you.

_____

_____

_____

_____

3. Think of someone you love. What specifically do you love about that person? (Example: I love his sensitivity.) Then list specific ways that you show your love to this person. (Example: I spend time with her. I enjoy doing things that make her happy.)

_____

_____

_____

Love and Sexuality

Although we treat the issues of love, sexuality, and intimacy in three different chapters, these topics cannot be completely separated. So we hope you'll try to make some connections by integrating the ideas of these chapters and applying them to yourself. The following personal inventory should help get you started.

After you've worked through the questions and indicated the responses that actually apply to you now, you might want to take the inventory again and give the responses that indicate how you'd like to be. Feel free to circle more than one response for a given item or to write your own response on the blank line. You may want to take the inventory again at the end of the course to see whether, or to what degree, any of your beliefs, attitudes, and values concerning love and sexuality have changed.

1. As far as my need for love is concerned,

    a. I can give love, but it's difficult for me to receive love.
    b. I can accept love, but it's difficult for me to give love.
    c. Neither giving nor accepting love is especially difficult for me.
    d. Both giving and accepting love are difficult for me.

    e. _____

2. I feel that I have been loved by another person

    a. only once in my life.
    b. never in my life.
    c. many times in my life.
    d. as often as I've chosen to open up to another.

    e. _____

3. When it comes to self-love and appreciation of myself,

    a. I have a healthy regard and respect for myself.
    b. I find the idea of self-love objectionable.
    c. I encounter great difficulty in appreciating myself.
    d. I'm generally able to love myself, but there are parts of myself that I dislike.

    e. _____

4. I love others because

    a. I want their love and acceptance in return.
    b. I fear being alone if I don't.
    c. I like the feeling of loving another.
    d. I derive joy from giving to another person.

    e. _____

5. To me, love is best described as

    a. giving to another out of my fullness as a person.
    b. thinking more of the other person that I do of myself.
    c. relating to another in the hope that I'll not feel so empty.
    d. caring for another to the same degree that I care about myself.

    e. _____

6. My greatest fear of loving and being loved is

   a. that I will have nothing to give another person.
   b. that I will be vulnerable and may be rejected.
   c. that I might be accepted and then not know what to do with this acceptance.
   d. that I will feel tied down and that my freedom will be restricted.

   e. _____

7. In regard to commitment in a loving relationship, I believe that

   a. without commitment there is no real love.
   b. commitment means I love that person exclusively.
   c. commitment means that I stay with the person in times of crisis and attempt to change things.
   d. commitment is not necessary for love.

   e. _____

8. For me, the relationship between love and sex is that

   a. love often develops *after* a sexual relationship.
   b. sex without love is unsatisfying.
   c. the two must always be present in an intimate relationship with another person of the opposite sex.
   d. sex can be very exciting and gratifying without a love relationship.

   e. _____

9. I could become more lovable by

   a. becoming more sensitive to the other person.
   b. learning to love and care for myself more than I do now.
   c. doing what I think others expect of me.
   d. being more genuinely myself, without roles and pretenses.

   e. _____

10. If I loved a person who did not love me in return, I would

    a. never trust another love relationship.
    b. feel devastated.
    c. convince myself that I really didn't care.
    d. feel hurt but eventually open myself to others.

    e. _____

11. In love relationships I generally

    a. settle for what I have with the other person as long as things are comfortable.
    b. constantly seek to improve the relationship.

    c. am willing to talk openly about things I don't like in myself and in the other person.

    d. am able to express positive feelings but unable to express negative feelings.

    e. _____

12. When it comes to talking about sexuality,

    a. I encounter difficulty, especially with my partner.

    b. I feel free in discussing sexual issues openly.

    c. I usually become defensive.

    d. I'm willing to reveal my feelings if I trust the other person.

    e. _____

13. My attitudes and values toward sexuality have been influenced principally by

    a. my parents.

    b. my friends and peers.

    c. my church.

    d. my school experiences.

    e. _____

14. I think that social norms and expectations

    a. encourage the dichotomy between male and female roles.

    b. impose heavy performance standards on men.

    c. make it very difficult to develop one's own ideas about what constitutes normal sexuality.

    d. clash with my own upbringing.

    e. _____

15. I think that sexual attitudes could be improved by

    a. giving children more information while they are growing up.

    b. teaching principles of religion.

    c. increasing people's knowledge about the physical and emotional aspects of sexuality.

    d. allowing people to freely discuss their sexual values and conflicts in small groups.

    e. _____

Here are a few suggestions of things you can do after you've finished this inventory:

1. You can use any of the items that strike you as points of departure for your journal writing.

2. If you're involved in an intimate relationship, you can ask the other

person to take the inventory and then share and compare your responses. Your responses can be used as a basis for dialogue on these important issues.

3. You can write down other questions that occurred to you as you took this inventory, and you can bring these questions to class.

4. Your class can form small groups in which to discuss the items that had the most meaning for each person.

Chapter Summary

Although we have a need to love and to be loved, most of us encounter barriers to meeting these needs. Our doubt that we are worthy of being loved is perhaps the major roadblock to loving others and receiving their love. Although many of us have been brought up believing that self-love is egotistic, in reality we are not able to love others unless we love and appreciate ourselves. How can we give to others something we do not possess ourselves? Our fear of love is another major impediment to loving. Many people would like guarantees that their love for special people will last as long as they live, but the stark reality is that there are no guarantees. It helps to realize that loving and trembling go together and to accept that we must learn to love in spite of our fears.

There are a number of myths and misconceptions about love that make it difficult to be open to giving and receiving love. A few of these are the myth of eternal love, the myth that love implies constant closeness, the myth of the exclusiveness of love, the myth that true love is selfless, and the myth of falling in love. Although love that is genuine results in the growth of both persons, some "love" is stifling. Not all that poses as real love is authentic, and one of the major challenges is to decide for ourselves the meanings of authentic love. By recognizing our attitudes about loving, we can increase our ability to choose the ways in which we behave in our love relationships.

Activities and Exercises

1. Mention some early decisions that you made regarding your own ability to love or to be loved, such as

   • "I'm not lovable unless I produce."
   • "I'm not lovable unless I meet others' expectations."
   • "I won't love another because of my fears of rejection."
   • "I'm not worthy of being loved."

   Write down some of the messages that you've received and perhaps accepted uncritically. How has your ability to feel loved or to give love been restricted by these messages and decisions?

2. For a period of at least a week, pay close attention to the messages conveyed by the media concerning love. What picture of love do you get from television? What do popular songs portray about love? Make a list of some common myths regarding love that you see promoted by the media, such as

   • Love means that two people never argue or disagree.
   • Love implies giving up one's identity.
   • Love implies constant closeness and romance.
   • Love means rarely having negative feelings toward those you love.

3. How much do you agree with the proposition that you can't fully love others unless you first love yourself? How does this apply to you? In your journal you might want to write some notes to yourself concerning the situations in which you don't appreciate yourself. You might also keep a record of the times and events when you do value and respect yourself.

4. How important is love in your life right now? Do you feel that you love others in the ways you'd like to? Do you feel that you're loved by others in the ways you want to be?

5. Are you an active lover or a passive lover? You might try writing down the ways in which you demonstrate your caring for those you love and then ask them to read your list and discuss with you how they see your style of loving.

6. Select one or more of the following books for further reading on the topics explored in this chapter: Buscaglia, *Love* (1972); Fromm, *The Art of Loving* (1956); Jampolsky, *Love Is Letting Go of Fear* (1981); Peck, *The Road Less Traveled* (1978); Maier, *God's Love Song* (1991).

CHAPTER EIGHT
Sexuality

Prechapter Self-Inventory

Use the following scale to respond: 4 = this statement is true of me *most* of the time; 3 = this statement is true of me *much* of the time; 2 = this statement is true of me *some* of the time; 1 = this statement is true of me *almost none* of the time.

_____ 1. I think that the quality of a sexual relationship usually depends on the general quality of the relationship.

_____ 2. I believe that exercising sexual freedom creates corresponding responsibilities.

_____ 3. I find it easy to talk openly and honestly about sexuality with at least one other person.

_____ 4. For me, sex without love is unsatisfying.

_____ 5. I experience guilt or shame over sexuality.

_____ 6. I have found that gender-role definitions and stereotypes get in the way of mutually satisfying sexual relations.

_____ 7. Sensual experiences do not necessarily have to be sexual.

_____ 8. Performance standards and expectations get in the way of my enjoying sensual and sexual experiences.

_____ 9. I have struggled to find my own values pertaining to sexual behavior.

_____ 10. I believe that I acquired healthy attitudes about sexuality from my parents.

Introduction

People of all ages experience difficulty at times in talking openly about sexual matters. This lack of communication contributes to the perpetuation of myths and misinformation about sexuality. It is true that the media are giving increased attention to all aspects of sexual behavior, to the point of bombarding us with new information and trends. Almost nothing is unmentionable in the popular media. Yet this increased knowledge regarding sexuality does not appear to have resulted in encouraging all people to talk more freely about their own sexual concerns, nor has it always reduced their anxiety about sexuality. For many people sex remains a delicate topic, to the extent that they find it difficult to communicate their sexual wants, especially to a person close to them.

A goal of this chapter is to introduce the idea of learning how to recognize and appropriately express our sexual concerns. Too many people suffer from needless guilt, shame, worries, and inhibition merely because they keep their concerns about sexuality secret, largely out of embarrassment.

Moreover, keeping their concerns to themselves can hinder their efforts to determine their own values regarding sex. This chapter asks you to examine your values and attitudes toward sexuality and to determine what choices *you* want to make in this area of your life.

Myths and Misconceptions about Sexuality

The following list contains statements that we consider to be misconceptions about sex. As you read over this list, ask yourself what your attitudes are and where you developed these beliefs. Are they working for you? Could any of the following statements apply to you? How might some of these statements affect your ability to make free choices concerning sexuality?

- If I allow myself to become sexual, I'll get into trouble.
- Women should be less active than men in sex.
- Women are not as sexually desirable when they initiate.
- By their very nature, men are sexually aggressive.
- Men need to prove themselves through sexual conquests.
- As you get older, you're bound to lose interest in sex.
- If my partner really loved me, I wouldn't have to tell him or her what I liked or wanted. My partner should know what I need intuitively without my asking.
- My partner would be offended and hurt if I told her (him) what I liked and wanted.
- I am not responsible for the level of my sexual satisfaction.
- I can't hope to overcome my negative conditioning I received about sex as I was growing up.
- Acting without any guilt or restrictions is what is meant by being sexually free.
- The more people know about the mechanics of sex, the more they will be satisfied with their sexual relationships.
- Some people find that the only place they get along well together is in bed.
- Being sexually attracted to a person other than my partner implies that I don't really find my partner sexually exciting.
- There is only one right person for me.
- Multiple sexual relationships enhance a primary relationship.
- The inability or unwillingness to engage in multiple sexual relationships indicates a lack of trust in oneself or at least a basic insecurity.
- The more physically attractive a person is, the more sexually exciting he or she is.
- With the passage of time, any sexual relationship is bound to become less exciting or grow stale.

Learning to Talk Openly about Sexual Issues

As in other areas of your life, you may saddle yourself with beliefs about sex that you have not given much thought to. Open discussions with those you are intimate with, as well as an honest exchange of views in your class, can do a lot to help you challenge some of the unexamined attitudes you have about this significant area of your life.

One might expect that people today would be able to discuss openly and frankly the concerns they have about sex. Students will discuss attitudes about sexual behavior in a general way, but they show considerable resistance to speaking of their own sexual concerns, fears, and conflicts. It is of value to simply provide a climate in which people can feel free to examine their personal concerns. In the groups that we lead, we have found it useful to give women and men an opportunity to discuss sexual issues in separate groups and then come together to share the concerns they've discovered. Typically, both men and women appreciate the chance to explore their sexual fears, expectations, secrets, and wishes, as well as their concerns about the normality of their bodies and feelings. Then, when the male and female groups come together, the participants usually find that there is much common ground, and the experience of making this discovery can be very therapeutic. For instance, men may fear becoming impotent, not performing up to some expected standard, being lousy lovers, or not being "man enough." When the men and women meet as one group, the men may be surprised to discover that women worry about having to achieve orgasm (or several of them) every time they have sex and that they, too, have fears about their sexual desirability. When people talk about these concerns in a direct way, much game playing and putting on of false fronts can be dispensed with.

Although it may be helpful for people to be encouraged to talk more openly about sexual concerns, their privacy should be respected and they should not be pushed to disclose personal sexual thoughts, fantasies, and experiences. What seems more relevant is that they know that their fantasies and feelings are not evil and need not cause them to feel guilty. We do not need to know the specifics of a person's sexual fantasy if we are to help this person overcome feelings of guilt. It is probably helpful to most of us to learn that we are not the only ones to have such fantasies. There is a delicate line between being sexually repressed and being indiscriminately open about our sexual lives.

In the past there was clearly a taboo against openly discussing sexual topics. Today, bookstores are flooded with paperbacks devoted to enhancing one's sexuality. Although people may come to a counselor with greater awareness of sexuality, it is clear that many of them have not been able to translate their knowledge into a more satisfying sex life. In fact, their increased awareness of what is normal for women and men may have compounded their problems. They may burden themselves with expectations of what their sex life *should* be like, according to the latest studies. Counselors discover that couples are often very uncomfortable communicating their sexual likes and dislikes, their personal fears, and the shame and guilt they sometimes have about sex. They still operate on the old myth that if their mate really loves them, then he or she should know intuitively what gives them pleasure. To ask for what one wants sexually is often seen as diminishing the value of what is received.

Nevertheless, the outlook in this area is not totally negative. Whereas in the past a couple with sexual problems might have kept such problems locked behind their bedroom door, the trend now is toward a willingness to acknowledge these problems and to seek help. Indeed, many people are able to apply their knowledge about sexuality to enhancing their sex life. Many more are challenging the myths pertaining to sex.

A number of typical concerns are openly aired by both men and women in discussion groups that we have participated in. These concerns might be expressed as follows:

• "I often wonder what excites my partner and what she [he] would like, yet I seldom ask. I suppose it's important for me to learn how to initiate by asking and also how to tell the other person what I enjoy."
• "My fear of getting AIDS keeps me from being involved in sexual relationships."

• "Even if my partner has been tested for the AIDS virus, I am still uneasy because of the chance that he or she will have sex with others."

• "So often I doubt my capacity as a lover. I'd like to know what my partner thinks. Perhaps one thing that I can learn to do is to share this concern with him [her]."

• "I worry about my body. Am I normal? How do I compare with others? Am I too big? too small? Am I proportioned properly? Do others find me attractive? Do I find myself attractive? What can I do to increase my own appeal to myself and to others?"

• "Am I responsible if my partner is dissatisfied?"

• "I am concerned about sexually transmitted diseases."

• "Sex can be fun, I suppose, but often I'm much too serious. It's really difficult for me to be playful and to let go without feeling foolish — and not just in regard to sex. It isn't easy for me to be spontaneous."

• "There are many times when I feel that my partner is bored with sex, and that makes me wonder whether I'm sexually attractive to her [him]."

• "There are times when I desire sex and initiate it, and my partner lets me know in subtle or even direct ways that he [she] isn't interested. Then I feel almost like a beggar. This kind of experience makes me not want to initiate anymore."

• "As a woman, I'd really like to know how other women feel after a sexual experience. Do they normally feel fulfilled? What prevents them from enjoying sex? How do they decide who's responsible when they don't have a positive experience?"

• "As a man, I frequently worry about performance standards, and that gets in the way of my making love freely and spontaneously. It's a burden to me to worry about doing the right things and being sexually powerful, and I often wonder what other men experience in this area."

• "What troubles me is that whenever I want affection or simply would like to be held, my husband assumes that I want sex."

• "There seem to be two extremes in sex: we can be overly concerned with pleasing our partner and therefore take too much responsibility for their sexual gratification, or we can become so involved with our own pleasure that we don't concern ourselves with our partner's feelings or needs. I ask myself how I can discover a balance — how I can be selfish enough to seek my own pleasure yet sensitive enough to take care of my partner's needs."

• "Sometimes I get scared of women [men], and I struggle with myself over whether I should let the other person know that I feel threatened. Will I be perceived as weak? Is it so terrible to be weak at times? Can I be weak and still be strong?"

• "I frequently feel guilty over my sexual feelings, but there are times when I wonder whether I really want to free myself of guilt feelings. What would happen if I were free of guilt? Would I give up all control?"

- "I worry a lot about being feminine [masculine] and all that it entails. I'm trying to separate out what I've been conditioned to believe about the way a woman [man] is supposed to be, yet I still have a hard time deciding for myself the kind of woman [man] I want to be. I want to find my own standards and not be haunted by external standards of what I should be and feel."
- "Can sex be an attempt to overcome my feelings of isolation and separation? There are times when I think I'm running into a sexual relationship because I feel lonely."
- "I've wondered whether we are by nature monogamous. I know I'd like to experience others sexually, but I don't want my mate to have these same experiences."
- "There are times lately when I don't seem to be enjoying sex much. In the past year I haven't been able to experience orgasms, and the man I'm living with thinks it's his fault. What's happening? Why am I not as sexually responsive as I used to be with him?"
- "I feel very open and trusting in talking about my sexuality in this group, and I'd very much like to experience this with my partner. I want to be able to be direct and avoid getting involved in sexual games. I need to learn how to initiate this kind of open dialogue."
- "There are times when I really don't crave intercourse but would still like to be held and touched and caressed. I wish my partner could understand this about me and not take it as a personal rejection when for some reason I simply don't want intercourse."
- "I really felt humiliated when I became impotent—I was sure she saw me as unmanly. I'm glad to learn that this is a common experience for other men and that I'm not abnormal."

Sex and Guilt

GUILT OVER SEXUAL FEELINGS

Most of us have learned certain taboos about sex. We often feel guilty about our *feelings*, even if we don't act them out. Guilt is commonly experienced in connection with homosexual fantasies and impulses, feelings of sexual attraction toward members of one's family, sexual feelings toward people other than one's spouse, enjoyment of sexuality, and too much (or too little) desire for sex. Even though we may intensely fear such feelings, we can and should learn to accept them as legitimate. Moreover, simply having feelings doesn't mean that we're impelled to act on them.

As in the case of shame over our bodies, we need to become aware of our guilt and then to reexamine it to determine whether we're needlessly burdening ourselves. Not all guilt is unhealthy and irrational, of course, but there is a real value in learning to challenge guilt feelings and to rid ourselves of those that are *unrealistic*.

For many of my earlier years, I (Jerry) experienced a great deal of guilt over my sexual feelings. I believe that my guilt was largely due to the influence of a strict religious education that took a strong stand on sexual morality. Even though I've consciously struggled to overcome some of this influence, I still experience traces of old guilt. As in so many other areas, I find that early lessons in regard to sex are difficult to unlearn. Consequently, it has been important for me to continue to challenge old guilt patterns that interfere with my sexual enjoyment, while at the same time developing a personal ethical code that I can live by with integrity and self-respect.

Contrary to Jerry, I (Marianne) did not have to contend that much with guilt over sexuality. Growing up on a farm in Germany allowed me to realize that sexuality is an important aspect of both animal and human life. Living in close proximity with family members, and lacking privacy, I was exposed at an early age to sexual behavior and talk. This helped me to accept sexuality as a natural part of life. Sexual matters were openly discussed and joked about at times. Sex was not a taboo or heavy subject. Although I don't recall feeling guilty over sexual thoughts or feelings, I had clear boundaries regarding the expression of my sexuality. While there may have been a lack of sexual information, I did not receive negative messages pertaining to sexuality. Many of my clients report that they find it impossible to imagine their parents having sex. I knew that sexuality was a part of my parents' lives and that they enjoyed it. I was not burdened with fears about sex.

Many people express some very real fears as they begin to recognize and accept their sexuality. A common fear is that if we recognize or accept our sexual feelings, our impulses will sweep us away, leaving us out of control. It's important to learn that we can accept the full range of our sexual feelings yet decide for ourselves what we will *do* about them. For instance, we remember a man who said that he felt satisfied with his marriage and found his wife exciting but was troubled because he found other women appealing and sometimes desired them. Even though he had made a decision not to have extramarital affairs, he still experienced a high level of anxiety over simply having sexual feelings toward other women. At some level he believed that he might be more likely to *act* on his feelings if he fully accepted that he had them. It was important that he learn to discriminate between having sexual feelings and deciding to take certain actions and that he learn to trust his own decisions.

In making responsible, inner-directed choices about whether to act on sexual feelings, many people find questions such as the following to be helpful guidelines: Will my actions hurt another person or myself? Will my actions limit another person's freedom? Will my actions exploit another's rights? Are my actions consistent with my commitments? Of course, each of us must decide on our own moral guidelines, but it seems unrealistic to expect that we can or should control our feelings in the same way that we can control our actions. By controlling our actions, we define who we are; by trying to deny or banish our feelings, we only become alienated from ourselves.

GUILT OVER SEXUAL EXPERIENCES

Although some people are convinced that in these sexually liberated times college students do not suffer guilt feelings over their sexual behaviors, our observations show us that this is not the case. College students, whether single or married, young or middle-aged, often report a variety of experiences over which they feel guilty. Guilt may be related to masturbation, extramarital (or "extrapartner") affairs, homosexual behavior, sexual practices that are sometimes considered deviant, and the practice of having sex with many partners.

Sex therapists emphasize early sexual learning as a crucial factor in one's later sexual adjustment. They assume that current guilt feelings often stem from both unconscious and conscious decisions that were made in response to verbal and nonverbal messages about sexuality.

Children are often not given the proper words for their body parts and for erotic activities. If parents restrict their vocabulary by referring to the genitals as simply organs of excretion, then children tend to assume that sexual pleasure is "dirty" or unnatural. An acquaintance once was shocked and upset when she heard one of our daughters use the word *penis*. When we asked her how she referred to genitals with her children, she replied, "Of course, I call it a weenie!" Such distortions or omissions of information can create an underlying negative attitude through which later information tends to be filtered.

Peers often fill the void left by parents. However, reliance on the same-sex peer group usually results in learning inaccurate sexual information, which can later lead to fears and guilt over sexual feelings and activities. Most sex information from the peer group is imparted during the early teen years. Many distorted notions are incorporated, such as "If you masturbate, your penis will fall off." "Kissing will get you pregnant." "Babies are born through the navel."

Movies, television, magazines, and newspapers provide information that is often a source of negative learning about sexuality. Material dealing with rape, violent sex, and venereal disease is blatantly presented to children. This slanted information often produces unrealistic and unbalanced attitudes about sexuality and ultimately fosters fears and guilt that can have a powerful impact on the ability to enjoy sex as an adult.

Some ministers of certain churches have contributed to sexual guilt, especially those preachers who shout "hell-and-damnation" sermons. A television evangelist who delivered passionate sermons on the evil and corruption around us shocked many when he was caught going to a prostitute, not once, but on two occasions. To us, this is an example of how repressed sexuality often manifests itself in indirect ways. In Chapter Two we discussed the use of the ego-defense mechanisms as a way of keeping anxiety in check. The behavior of this preacher illustrates defense mechanisms such as repression, denial, projection, and reaction formation.

The main point is that we acquire a sense of guilt over sexual feelings and experiences as a result of a wide diversity of sources of information and *misinformation*. We are not implying that all guilt is neurotic and should therefore be eliminated. When we violate our value system, guilt is a consequence, and in these cases guilt can serve a useful purpose. Ideally, this guilt will not immobilize us but instead will motivate us to change the behavior that is not congruent with our ethical standards. In freeing ourselves of guilt, a first step is becoming aware of early verbal and nonverbal messages about sexuality and gender-role behavior that we received in a cultural context. Once we become aware of such messages, we can explore them to determine in what ways we might want to modify them.

Time Out for Personal Reflection

1. Complete the following statements pertaining to sexuality:

   a. I first learned about sex through _____

   _____

   b. My earliest memory about sex is _____

   _____

   c. The way this memory affects me now is _____

   _____

   d. One verbal sexual message I received from my parents was

   _____

   e. One nonverbal sexual message I received from my parents was

   _____

   f. An expectation I have about sex is _____

   _____

   g. When the topic of sexuality comes up I usually _____

   _____

h. While I was growing up, a sexual taboo I internalized was _____

_____

2. List a couple of the myths and misconceptions that have most affected you personally.

_____

_____

_____

_____

3. Are there any steps you'd like to take toward learning to accept your body and your sexuality more than you do now? If so, what are they?

_____

_____

_____

_____

4. Do you experience guilt over sexual feelings? If so, what specific feelings give rise to guilt?

_____

_____

_____

_____

5. How openly are you able to discuss sexuality in a personal way? Would you like to be more open in discussing your sexuality or sexual issues? If so, what is preventing this openness?

_____

_____

_____

_____

6. What are some personal issues relating to sex that you're willing to discuss in your class group?

_____

_____

_____

Learning to Enjoy Sensuality and Sexuality

Sensual experiences involve the enjoyment of all of our senses and can be enjoyed separately from sexual experiences. People often confuse sensuality with sexuality, especially by concluding that sensuality necessarily leads to sexual experiences. Although sexuality involves sensual experiences, sensuality often does not lead to sexual activity.

As we've seen, performance standards and expectations often get in the way of people's sensual and sexual pleasure, particularly in the case of men. Some men are not content to be themselves but think they must be *supermen*, particularly in the area of sexual attractiveness and performance. They measure themselves by unrealistic standards and may greatly fear losing their sexual power. Instead of enjoying sexual and sensual experiences, they become oriented toward orgasm. For some men, the fact that their partner experiences an orgasm signifies that they have performed adequately. They may expect her always to have an orgasm during intercourse, primarily out of their need to prove their sexual adequacy. For example, Roland stated in his human sexuality class that he would not continue to date a woman who did not have an orgasm with him. Several of the other male students were in full agreement with Roland's attitude. With this type of orientation toward sex, it is not surprising that these men fear so much the problem of impotence.

LISTENING TO OUR BODY

In a chapter entitled "Thank God for Impotence!" Goldberg (1987) maintains that impotence can really be a message that a man doesn't want to have sex with this particular woman at this particular time; it doesn't necessarily mean that he has lost his potency in general. Impotence is best viewed as an outgrowth of the interaction between two persons. The man's inability to maintain an erection needs to be understood in the context of a strained relationship.

Although impotence is one of the most anxiety-provoking situations that men can experience, it paradoxically creates and promotes the only potential they have for making significant changes, for it can lead to cracking their armor. Goldberg contends that impotence is potentially a lifesaving and life-giving response. If the context is properly understood and if the man's fragile masculine self-image is able to tolerate the anxiety over not performing adequately, he has the opportunity to become aware of his flawed emotional interaction. His impotence can thus be the only authentic response he has left to measure the defects in the interchange. Although he is telling himself that he *should* be close, his body is telling the real truth, for it knows that he doesn't want to be close. Impotence is a pathway to his deeper feelings because it represents a central threat to his ego, makes him vulnerable, and motivates him to seek help. If men are able to pay attention to their body signals, they can see that their penis serves as a monitoring device in the relationship. Goldberg likens impotence to a psychological heart attack, which can either result in psychological death or be a catalyst for the man to restructure his patterns of living.

It should be added that sexual dysfunction can occur for any one of a number of reasons, including, in some cases, physical ones. In the majority of cases, however, a problem such as impotence is due to psychological factors. In addition to the lack of desire to have sex with a certain person at a certain time, for example, impotence may result from feelings of guilt, prolonged depression, hostility or resentment, anxiety about personal adequacy, or a generally low level of self-esteem. Most men for whom impotence becomes a problem might be well advised to ask themselves: What is my body telling me?

Some women have difficulty responding sexually, especially experiencing orgasm. Stress is a major factor that can easily interfere with being in a frame of mind that will allow a woman's body to respond. Although her partner may climax and feel some degree of satisfaction, she might be left frustrated. This is particularly true if the couple engages in sex late at night when they are both tired or if they have been under considerable stress. If her body is not responding, it could well be a sign that stress and fatigue are making it difficult for her to relax and give in to a full psychological and physical release. Rather than interpreting her lack of responsiveness as a sign of her sexual inadequacy, she would be wise to pay attention to what her body is expressing. Her body is probably saying "I'm too tired to enjoy this."

ASKING FOR WHAT WE WANT

Paying attention to the messages of our body is only a first step. We still need to learn how to express to our partner *specifically* what we like and don't like sexually. We've found that both women and men tend to keep their sexual preferences and dislikes to themselves instead of sharing them with their partner. They've accepted the misconception that their partner should know intuitively what they like and don't like, and they resist telling their partner what feels good to them out of fear that their lovemaking will become mechanical or that their partner will only be trying to please them.

Often a woman will complain that she doesn't derive as much enjoyment from sex as she might because the man is too concerned with his own pleasure or is orgasm-oriented and sees touching, holding, and caressing only as necessary duties that he must perform to obtain "the real thing." Thus, she may say that he rolls over in bed as soon as he is satisfied, even if she's left frustrated. Although she may require touching and considerable foreplay and afterplay, he may not recognize her needs. Therefore, she needs to express to him what it feels like to be left unsatisfied, but in a way that doesn't feel to him like an attack.

It is not uncommon for a woman to ask a question such as "Does touching always have to lead to sex?" She is probably implying that there is a significant dimension missing for her in lovemaking—namely, the sensual aspect. The case of Tiffani and Kenny illustrates this common conflict in lovemaking. Tiffani complains that anytime she wants to be affectionate with Kenny, he wants to have sexual intercourse. She harbors considerable resentment over his inability to respond to her need for affection without making a sexual demand. When Tiffani senses that Kenny wants to be sexual with her, she tends to start a fight as a way of creating distance. In turn, he feels rejected, humiliated, and angry. For this couple, sex becomes a threatening experience instead of a way of expressing closeness.

Being sensual is an important part of a sexual experience. Sensuality pertains to fully experiencing all of our senses, not just sensations in our genitals. There are many parts of the body that are sensual and that can contribute to our enjoyment of sex. Although there is a great enjoyment in the orgasmic experience, many people are missing out on other sources of enjoyment by not giving pleasure to themselves and their partner with other stimulation.

People sometimes engage in sexual intercourse when what they actually want is to be touched and embraced and to feel sensual in all parts of their body. They may feel deeply frustrated when their need for a sensual experience quickly culminates with an orgasm. If this becomes a pattern, people may find that there is a feeling of emptiness attached to their sex life. Sex then becomes either a duty or a routine event. One or both of the partners are likely to feel used or cheated and eventually may find reasons to avoid sex.

THE SENSATE-FOCUS EXERCISE

One way for couples to become more aware of and to appreciate their sensuality is the sensate-focus exercise. This exercise was originally developed by Masters and Johnson (1980) as a technique in a treatment plan for sexual dysfunctions. The sensate-focus experience involves people's taking time to make contact with each other, paying attention to the sensations of their entire body, learning how to ask for what they want, and receiving pleasure without feeling pressured or guilty. It consists of having the couple forgo sexual intercourse and orgasm for a period of time. This is done so that there is no demand to perform sexually and so that the goal of orgasm is not made the primary one. Instead, the partners limit their erotic activity to gently touching and caressing each other's body. Freed from pressures, both the woman and the man are often able to experience full erotic and sensuous sensations for the first time. The general instructions given to a couple are:

> One of you will be the giver, and the other the receiver. As the receiver your only responsibility is to take and enjoy, and to communicate verbally or nonverbally what is pleasurable. It is important that you do not worry about whether the giver is getting tired or anything else. You are to be selfish and to concentrate on your sensations over your entire body. The giver focuses on the feelings and sensations of giving the partner pleasure. Each of you takes a turn at being in the role of giver and receiver. To prolong the experience of sensuality, avoid touching genitals.

Although this approach might sound simple, it's surprising how many couples have never tried it. These people have restricted the pleasure they could give to their partner and receive for themselves, merely because they didn't think it was right to ask directly for what they wanted.

Sex and Intimacy

Intimacy can be conceived of as a close emotional relationship characterized by a deep level of caring for another person. It is a basic component of all loving relationships. Although intimacy is a part of all loving relationships, it is a mistake to assume that sexuality is a part of all loving and intimate relationships. Chapter Nine explores many forms of intimate relationships that do not involve sex.

Increasing our sexual awareness can include becoming more sensitive to the ways in which we sometimes engage in sex as a means to some end. For instance, sexual activity can be used as a way to actually prevent the development of intimacy. It can also be a way to avoid experiencing our aloneness, our isolation, and our feelings of distance from others. Sex can be an escape into activity, a way of avoiding inner emptiness. When it is used in any of these ways, it can take on a driving or compulsive quality that detracts from its spontaneity and leaves us unfulfilled. Sex used as a way of filling inner emptiness becomes a mechanical act, divorced from any passion, feeling, or caring. Then it only deepens our feelings of isolation and detachment.

In her personal therapy, Evelyn, who's 23 and single, reveals her extreme feelings of isolation and despair. Although she is seen by her friends as outgoing, attractive, and vivacious, she feels an inner emptiness. She has had many sexual partners and sexual conquests, which have only left her feeling even more empty. In all of her sexual experiences she has ended up feeling more removed from her partner. She longs for a relationship in which she can feel both emotional and sexual satisfaction.

Another case illustrates how sexual activity can be used to avoid boredom. Earl, who is middle-aged and married, sought out an affair to bring more vitality to what he felt was a dead life. Although he found excitement in his affair initially, he soon discovered that he could not run from his meaningless existence. Sex proved to be no "cure" for his restlessness in his marriage, his stagnation in his work, and his inability to enjoy leisure activities.

In spite of the fact that we live in an age of sexual liberation, many people do not experience genuine satisfaction in their sexual relationships. Rollo May (1981) develops the thesis that sex without intimacy as a lifestyle leads to enslavement and the emotional deadening of a person. In his clinical experience as a psychotherapist, May has observed that people who engage in sex without intimacy have little capacity for feeling and become sex machines that function mechanically instead of lovingly: "The danger is that these detached persons who are afraid of intimacy will move toward a robot-like existence, heralded by the drying up of their emotions not only on sexual levels, but on all levels, supported by the motto 'Sex does not involve intimacy anyway'" (p. 153). In short, May contends that the trend toward sex without intimacy in our culture is closely associated with the loss of the capacity to feel any emotions.

In our professional work with clients and college students we have observed a trend away from casual sexual encounters without any emotional attachment. Those who have left sexually exclusive relationships may look forward to sex with a variety of partners. For a time, some of them may be drawn to "sport sex" as they experience their newly found "freedom." Many report, however, that they eventually tire of such relationships and find themselves searching for intimacy as a vital part of their sexual involvements. Of course, the impact of AIDS on sexual behavior probably accounts for some of the caution in getting involved with multiple partners. The fear of becoming infected certainly makes casual sex much less attractive than it might otherwise be. As one student put it, "When you are sexually intimate with someone, it could be a life-or-death matter. You are really trusting them with your life."

In our discussions with college students, we find that they are seeking to be loved by a special person, and they want to trust giving their love in return. What they appear to want is much like May's view of intimacy and love. His perspective is that love is a state of being characterized by both a physical and an emotional sharing. To him, "Intimacy is the sharing between two people not only of their bodies, but also of their hopes, fears, anxieties and aspirations" (1981, p. 149).

It might be a good idea to reflect on how sex can be used to either enhance or diminish ourselves and our partner as persons. We can ask ourselves such questions as: Are my intimate relationships based on a need to conquer or exert power over someone else? Or are they based on a genuine desire to become intimate, to share, to experience joy and pleasure, to both give and receive? Asking ourselves what we want in our relationships and what uses sex serves for us may also help us avoid the overemphasis on technique and performance that frequently detracts from sexual experiences. Although technique and knowledge are important, they are not ends in themselves, and overemphasizing them can cause us to become oblivious to the *persons* we have sex with. An abundance of anxiety over performance and technique can only impede sexual enjoyment and rob us of the experience of genuine intimacy and caring.

Time Out for Personal Reflection

1. Complete the following sentences:

   a. To me, being sensual means _____

   _____

   b. To me, being sexual means _____

   _____

   c. Sex without intimacy is _____

   _____

   d. Sex can be an empty experience when _____

   _____

e. Sex can be most fulfilling when _____

_____

2. Look over the following list, quickly checking the words that you associate with sex:

___ fun	___ dirty	___ routine
___ ecstasy	___ shameful	___ closeness
___ procreation	___ joy	___ release
___ beautiful	___ pressure	___ sinful
___ duty	___ performance	___ guilty
___ trust	___ experimentation	___ vulnerability

Now look over the words you've checked and see whether there are any significant patterns in your responses. What can you say by way of summary about your attitudes toward sex?

_____

_____

_____

_____

AIDS: A Crisis of Our Time

If you have not already done so, you will inevitably come in contact with people who have tested positive as carriers of the AIDS virus, people who have AIDS, people who have had sexual contact with those who have tested HIV-positive, people who are close to AIDS patients, and people who have not tested positive but who are worried that they might get the virus (the worried well).

AIDS already affects a wide population with diverse demographic characteristics and will continue to be a major health problem. Unless you are educated about the problem, you are likely to live needlessly in fear. Accurate and updated information is vital if you are to deal with the personal and societal implications of the AIDS epidemic. You need to be able to differentiate between fact and fiction about this disease. Information about some aspects of AIDS seems to be changing daily, so the facts we provide here might be outdated by the time this book is published. We recommend that you contact the national HIV and AIDS hotline (1-800-342-AIDS) for free written material as well as answers to your questions.

We want to express our appreciation to Jerome Wright of California State University at Fullerton for his thoughtful reading of this section on AIDS and his constructive suggestions for refining this discussion.

There is much ignorance and fear of AIDS, fueled by conflicting reports. Misinformation about the ways in which the disease is spread results in apprehension among many people. There is no reason to remain ignorant, because you can get the basic information you need about this disease by contacting some of the sources listed at the end of this section. Reading is a minimum step. You can also attend an AIDS workshop or contact one of the many clinics that are being started all over the country. Our intent is not to provide you with all the relevant facts about AIDS but rather to encourage you to explore your own sexual practices, attitudes, values, and fears pertaining to the problem.

The reality of the AIDS epidemic has significant implications for your choices about sexual behavior. With an increased understanding of AIDS, you are in a better position to make informed and wise choices about expressing your sexuality. In November of 1991 Magic Johnson, a star of the Los Angeles Lakers basketball team, disclosed that he had tested HIV-positive. Although this was sad news, Magic's disclosure has caused increased attention to the problem by the media and has galvanized the campaign against AIDS in the United States. People have seen that the disease can strike even an athletic hero, which is likely to do more to advance the cause of AIDS prevention than years of governmental proclamations (Goldsmith, 1991). There have been many special reports dealing with AIDS on television since Magic's announcement. These reports have dealt with many of the topics that we cover in this section.

BASIC FACTS ABOUT AIDS

What is AIDS? *Acquired immunodeficiency syndrome* is a serious condition that affects the body's ability to fight infection. A diagnosis of AIDS is usually made when a person develops a life-threatening illness not ordinarily found in someone with a normal ability to fight infection. This condition was first reported in the United States in 1981. Although the virus that causes AIDS and related disorders has several different names, the most recent name is human immunodeficiency virus (HIV).

People who have AIDS are vulnerable to serious illnesses that would not be a threat to anyone whose immune system was functioning normally. These illnesses are referred to as "opportunistic" infections or diseases. AIDS weakens the body against invasive agents, so that other diseases can prey on the body.

The two diseases most often found in AIDS patients are a lung infection called Pneumocystis carinii and a rare form of cancer called Kaposi's sarcoma. It is these diseases, not the AIDS virus itself, that can lead to death. According to the U.S. Centers for Disease Control, as of February 1991, there had been 164,129 AIDS cases diagnosed in the country and 102,802 AIDS deaths.

Perhaps the major challenge is helping people with AIDS come to terms with loss. "At its simplest, AIDS is about loss. It is about loss of one's health, vitality, sensuality, and career — and most profoundly, the letting go of the future as one had envisioned it" (Hoffman, 1991, p. 468).

What causes AIDS? At this time, much is known about AIDS, such as how it is transmitted and how it can be avoided. What is not known is how to cure the disease. Infection with HIV does not always lead to AIDS. Research suggests that more than 50 percent of HIV-infected persons may develop AIDS; and almost everyone with the virus will ultimately become ill to some degree within five to ten years after infection. However, the complete natural history of the disease is still not known. Infected individuals may develop illnesses varying in severity from mild to extremely serious. These illnesses are designated AIDS-related complex (ARC).

How is the AIDS virus transmitted? The AIDS virus can be transmitted by sexual intercourse with a person infected with the virus or by sharing needles with an infected person. A woman infected with HIV who becomes pregnant or breast-feeds can pass the virus to the baby. Although some cases have developed through blood transfusions, this risk has been virtually eliminated through testing of donated blood for HIV antibodies. The AIDS virus can be spread by women or by men through heterosexual or homosexual contact. The virus can enter the body through the vagina, penis, rectum, or mouth or through breaks in the skin. The risk of infection with the virus is increased by having multiple sexual partners and by sharing needles among those using drugs. The AIDS virus has been found in a number of body fluids and secretions, such as blood, semen, vaginal secretions, saliva, urine, breast milk, and tears. You don't "catch" AIDS in the same way as a cold or the flu. It cannot be passed through sharing a glass or eating utensils. The AIDS virus is not transmitted through everyday contact with people around you in the workplace, at school, and at social functions. You cannot get AIDS by being near someone who carries the virus. The AIDS virus is hard to get and easily avoided. It is a misconception that it is spread through casual contact or from a mosquito bite, a casual kiss, or a toilet seat.

Who gets AIDS? It is a mistake to view the problem of AIDS as the exclusive concern of any particular group. AIDS has been called an "equal opportunity disease," for it affects a wide segment of society. The AIDS virus has infected people of all ages, races, and social groups. AIDS, unlike people, does not discriminate. It is a myth that AIDS is restricted to the gay male population. Perhaps the largest growth in HIV infection is occurring among women. At the United States Public Health Service National Conference in December of 1990, it was reported that of the estimated 1 million persons in the United States infected with HIV, as many as 140,000 are women. The World Health Organization estimates that 8 to 10 million women worldwide are infected with AIDS. By the year 2000 the number of worldwide cases of AIDS is expected to be 40 million. Most of the public health effort has been focused on persons with high-risk behavior such as bisexual and homosexual men, injection drug users, and blood transfusion recipients. However, efforts must be directed toward reduction of the risk of infection of women, especially women of color, since they are particularly at risk. We need to move away from our stereotypes that only certain kinds of males are at risk and focus our prevention efforts on women as well.

Since 1981 the Centers for Disease Control have been collecting information on AIDS. Approximately 95 percent of those with AIDS belong to one of the following groups:

- sexually active homosexual or bisexual men (73 percent)
- present or past users of intravenous drugs (17 percent)
- patients who had transfusions of blood or blood products (2 percent)
- persons with hemophilia or other coagulation disorders (1 percent)
- heterosexuals who have had sexual contact with someone with AIDS or at risk for AIDS (1 percent)
- infants born to infected mothers (1 percent)

What are the symptoms of AIDS? The AIDS virus may live in the human body for years before symptoms appear. Although many individuals infected with the AIDS virus have no symptoms, some victims develop severe and prolonged fatigue, fever, loss of appetite and weight, diarrhea, swollen lymph glands in the neck, and night sweats. Anyone having one or more of these symptoms for more than two weeks should see a health care provider. Of course, other diseases besides AIDS can cause similar symptoms.

What kind of test is there for AIDS? There is an AIDS antibody test. A positive test result does not mean that the person has AIDS or will get AIDS, for many people who test positive either remain symptom-free or develop less serious illnesses. The antibody test cannot tell whether the individual will eventually develop signs of illness related to the viral infection or, if so, how serious the illness might be. What a positive test result does indicate is that the person has been infected by the AIDS virus, has developed a reaction to it, and can transmit it to others. If you suspect that you have been exposed to the AIDS virus, it is crucial that you get tested. With proper medical attention, it is possible to delay the diseases that stem from AIDS if you are treated early enough. Testing is completely anonymous and it is generally free if you go to the health department of your county.

What are common reactions to testing HIV-positive? People who believe or have discovered that they are carriers of the AIDS virus are typically highly anxious. Both those who have tested positive and those who have contracted AIDS are commonly in need of immediate help. Upon learning of their status, they are liable to experience a gamut of emotional reactions from shock, to anger, to fear and anxiety, to grieving for the loss of their previous sexual freedom and for their uncertain future. Some feel that they have been given a death sentence. They will need to find a support system to help them cope with the troubled times that lie ahead of them.

In addition to feeling anxious, those with AIDS are typically angry. They often feel left alone and without support. This perception may be grounded in reality. In some cases family members actually disown the person with AIDS. For some victims this isolation makes it hard to see any meaning in their plight, and thus they often give in to depression. The sense of hopelessness may develop into anger at having a life-threatening condition.

Victims express their anger by asking, over and over: "What did I do to deserve this? Why me?" This anger is sometimes directed at God for letting this happen, and then they may feel guilty for having reacted this way. Anger is also directed toward others, especially those who are likely to have given them the virus.

Why is a stigma attached to AIDS? Both those who have AIDS and those who have tested HIV-positive struggle with the stigma attached to this disease. The stigma stems from the fact that those who contact AIDS belong primarily to the sexually active homosexual or bisexual male population or are present or past abusers of intravenous drugs. Among the mainstream population there is still a general negative reaction toward people who are homosexual or bisexual, or who are illicit drug users.

For some, the stigma may be worse than the diagnosis itself. They live in fear of being rejected by society in general and by significant persons in their life. Indeed, this stigma may be the filter through which society has viewed the AIDS crisis (Hoffman, 1991). Very often people afflicted with AIDS stigmatize themselves and perpetuate beliefs such as "I feel guilty and ashamed." "I feel that God is punishing me." "I'm a horrible person, and therefore I deserve to suffer." "I'm to blame for getting this disease."

How is AIDS treated? HIV is highly mutable. As a result it is extremely difficult to find an effective vaccine for this virus. Those who carry the virus are likely to have it for the rest of their life. No drugs have been shown to cure AIDS, but an antiviral agent called azidothymidine (AZT) appears to retard the progression of the disease in some patients. Although no treatment has yet been successful in restoring the immune system, doctors have been able to treat the various acute illnesses affecting those with AIDS.

How can AIDS be prevented? Because the AIDS crisis shows no signs of easing, education to stop the spread of the disease is the key to prevention. Individuals can do a lot to avoid contracting the disease. The following recommendations aimed at prevention have been taken from a number of pamphlets:

• All sexually active individuals need to know the basic facts about this disease and how to avoid the risk of infection.
• Talk to your partner(s) about past and present sexual practices and drug use.
• Avoid having sex with multiple partners. The more partners you have, the more you increase your risk.
• Avoid sex with persons with AIDS, with those at risk for AIDS, or with those who have had a positive result on the HIV antibody test.

- Avoid sex with someone you don't know well or with someone you know has had several sexual partners.
- Avoid anal sex, with or without a condom.
- Use condoms and spermicidal barriers to reduce the possibility of transmitting the virus, but realize that they are not 100-percent effective. Rather than thinking in terms of "safe sex," it is helpful to consider practices as "unsafe," "relatively safe," and "safer." The only "safe" behavior consists of choosing not to be sexually active or restricting sex to one mutually faithful, uninfected partner; and not injecting drugs.
- If you use intravenous drugs, don't share needles.
- Avoid using drugs and alcohol, which lessen your judgment.
- Be aware that people who carry the AIDS virus are not always sick and often do not know that they are infected.

Where to go for further information

- *Facts about AIDS.* (U.S. Department of Health and Human Services, 1987.)
- *Understanding AIDS.* (U.S. Department of Health and Human Services, 1988).
- *Women, Sex, and AIDS.* (U.S. Department of Health and Human Services, 1988).
- *Many Teens Are Saying No.* (U.S. Department of Health and Human Services, 1989).
- *AIDS and You.* (U.S. Department of Health and Human Services, 1991).
- *Caring for Someone with AIDS.* (U.S. Department of Health and Human Services, 1991).
- *HIV Infection and AIDS: Are You at Risk?* (U.S. Department of Health and Human Services, 1991).
- *How You Won't Get AIDS.* (U.S. Department of Health and Human Services, 1991).
- *Voluntary HIV Counseling and Testing: Facts, Issues, and Answers.* (U.S. Department of Health and Human Services, 1991).

More information about AIDS and AIDS-related illnesses can be obtained from your doctor; your state or local health department; your local chapter of the American Red Cross; and the Public Health Service's toll-free HIV and AIDS hotline: 1-800-342-AIDS. This national hotline is for anyone with questions about HIV and AIDS. It functions twenty-four hours a day in every state. The information specialists are well trained and they respect privacy. In addition to providing information, they provide referrals to appropriate sources among the more than 8,000 entries in the hotline data base. The hotline is the place to call for free pamphlets and booklets with updated information about HIV and AIDS. Information materials are also available from the National AIDS Clearinghouse by calling 1-800-458-5231.

CONCLUDING COMMENTS

As we have stressed, it is essential that you educate yourself on the major issues surrounding AIDS and that you explore your own attitudes and choices pertaining to sexual behavior. Because information is changing rapidly, it is difficult for people who are at risk to trust what they hear from the medical profession. Some individuals become defensive about education because they don't believe what is presented to them. They also may remain in a state of denial because they do not want to change their sexual lifestyle. Simply having information will not prevent you from getting AIDS, but it will help you make sound behavioral choices. It appears that even though people may not be changing their sexual values, they are seriously considering changing some of their behaviors because of the possibility of contracting the disease.

This discussion is not meant to scare you; rather, its aim is to help you to think about your priorities. Of course, your personal value system needs to be considered in making choices about sexual behavior. The following section, on developing your sexual values, can be helpful as a basis for making sexual choices.

Developing Your Own Sexual Values

The AIDS epidemic poses a challenge to changes in sexual attitudes and behaviors over the last quarter-century that many people have termed a sexual revolution. During that period there has been an open questioning of society's sexual standards and practices, accompanied by the growing belief that individuals can and should decide for themselves what sexual practices are acceptable. Previously, many people did not have to struggle to decide what was moral or immoral, since they took their standards of sexual behavior from external sources. This is not to say that they were necessarily moral, even by their own standards, for they may have been more secretive about their sexual activities and may also have suffered more guilt than many people today.

It is desirable to bring sexual issues into the open and talk freely without guilt and shame, and it is important that sexual behavior be consistent with one's value system. The change in sexual attitudes can give people the freedom to determine their own values and govern their own behavior.

Many people accept external standards, such as those of their church or their parents, and eventually internalize a set of sexual values that they can best live with. Whereas at one time people were afraid to reveal that they had sexual experiences before marriage, now some people are anxious about revealing that they have refrained from sexual intercourse. We are reminded of Elvira, a 23-year-old client, who with some embarrassment revealed that she was a virgin. She and her boyfriend had decided to delay sexual relations until after marriage. But she felt pressure from her peers and was afraid that she was behaving strangely because of the choice she had made. Our hope for Elvira was that she would remain true to her own convictions, rather than surrendering to pressure to behave as others thought she should. There are many others who, like Elvira, make a decision about their sexual behavior based on their values rather than on a fear of pregnancy or venereal disease.

Designing a personal and meaningful set of sexual ethics is not an easy task. It can be accomplished only through a process of honest questioning. Our questioning can start with the values we now have: What is their source? Do they fit in with our views of ourselves in other areas of life? Which of them should we keep in order to live responsibly and with enjoyment? Which should we reject? Achieving freedom doesn't have to mean shedding all our past beliefs or values. Whether we keep or reject them in whole or in part, we can refuse to allow someone besides ourselves to make our decisions for us. It can be tempting to allow others (whether past authorities or present acquaintances) to tell us what is right and wrong and design our life for us, for then we don't have to wrestle with touch decisions ourselves. If we fail to create our own values and choose for ourselves, however, we surrender our autonomy and run the risk of becoming alienated from ourselves. Also, there is the matter of realistic and appropriate guilt when we engage in sexual practices that are not in accordance with our value system. For instance, some people struggle with wanting to act out sexually with many partners, even though this behavior goes against their personal value system. Their struggle is between giving behavioral expression to their sexual desires and feeling guilty because of not living by their values.

In their book *Sexual Awareness: Enhancing Sexual Pleasure*, McCarthy and McCarthy (1984) observe that we have gone from a sexually repressed, ignorant, and inhibited culture to a performance-oriented and confused sexual culture. They assert that the more knowledge people have about sexuality, the better they can choose to integrate sexual expression into their life. Contending that sexuality cannot be value-free, they develop the following guidelines for sexual awareness, sexual functioning, and making choices pertaining to sexual expression:

- Sexuality is a basic part of our existence and is not to be considered inherently evil.
- Our sexuality is a positive and integral part of our personality.
- It is our responsibility to choose how we will express our sexuality. Since sexuality can enhance our life, it should not contribute to anxiety and guilt.
- At its best a sexual relationship involves trust, respect, and concern for our partner.
- An intimate relationship is the most satisfying way to express our sexuality.

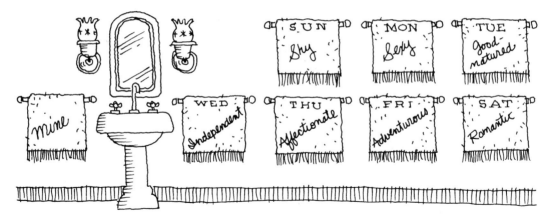

WE CAN ENGAGE IN SELF-DECEPTION BY ADJUSTING OUR BEHAVIOR TO WHAT WE DESIRE AT THE MOMENT.

Developing our own values means assuming responsibility for ourselves, which includes taking into consideration how others may be affected by our choices while allowing them to take responsibility for theirs. We make the assumption that in an adult relationship the parties involved are capable of taking personal responsibility for their own actions. Consequently, it's difficult to be used or manipulated unless we allow others to use or manipulate us. Generally, we cannot be exploited unless we collaborate in this activity. For example, in the case of premarital or extramarital sex, each person must weigh such questions as: Do I really want to pursue a sexual relationship with this person at this time? Is the price worth it? What are my commitments? Who else is involved, and who could be hurt? Might this be a positive or a negative experience? How does my decision fit in with my values generally?

In summary, it's no easier to achieve sexual autonomy than it is to achieve autonomy in the other areas of our life. While challenging our values, we need to take a careful look at ways in which we could easily engage in self-deception by adjusting our behavior to whatever we might desire at the moment. We also need to pay attention to how we feel about ourselves in regard to our past sexual experience. Perhaps, in doing so, we can use our level of self-respect as one important guide to our future behavior. That is, we can each ask: Do I feel enhanced or diminished by my past experience?

Sex can be a positive or a negative force, depending on how it is used. At its best, sex can be a deep source of enjoyment, bring pleasure, enhance one's overall well-being, and express love, caring, and affection. Of course, it can lead to the creation of new life. At its worst, sex can be used to hurt others. Sex is abused when it is manipulative, a punishing force, used to get favors, the tool of aggression and control, aimed at dominating another, and when it evokes guilt. In the following section, we consider some of the ways in which sex is frequently abused and used as a ploy to assume power and control over others.

Time Out for Personal Reflection

1. What influences have shaped your attitudes and values concerning sexuality? In the following list, indicate the importance of each factor by placing a 1 in the blank if it was *very important*, a 2 if it was *somewhat important*, and a 3 if it was *unimportant*. For each item that you mark with a 1 or a 2, indicate briefly the nature of that influence.

_____   parents _____

_____   church _____

_____   friends _____

_____   siblings _____

_____   movies _____

_____   school _____

_____   books _____

_____   television _____

_____   spouse _____

_____   grandparents _____

_____   your own experiences _____

_____   other influential factors _____

_____

2. Try making a list of specific values that you hold regarding sexual issues. As a beginning, respond to the following questions:

   a. How do you feel about promiscuity?

   _____

   _____

   _____

   _____

   b. What is your view of sex outside of marriage?

   _____

   _____

   _____

   _____

   c. Do you think it's legitimate to separate love and sex?

_____

_____

_____

_____

   d. How do you feel about having sex with a person you don't like or respect?

_____

_____

_____

_____

Sexual Abuse and Harassment

In this section, we discuss three topics that relate to each other in that they all involve some form of abuse of sexuality. In each of these cases, power is misused, or a trusting relationship is betrayed for the purpose of gaining control over the individual. Thus, people are robbed of their choice in the situation, except for the choice of how they might react to being violated. Incest, date and acquaintance rape, and sexual harassment all involve depriving individuals of choices, and they also entail abusive power, control, destructiveness, and violence. Another common denominator lies in the reluctance of victims to disclose that they have been wronged. In fact, many of them may suffer from undue guilt over the belief that they were responsible for what occurred. This guilt is exacerbated by segments of society who contribute to the "blaming the victim" syndrome. Victims often carry psychological scars from these experiences that stifle their ability to accept and express the range of their sexuality.

INCEST: A BETRAYAL OF TRUST

In our therapeutic groups we continue to meet many women who are suffering tremendous guilt related to early incestuous experiences. This subject is being given much-deserved attention by both helping professionals and the general public. It appears that incest is far more widespread than ever before thought. It occurs on all social, economic, educational, and professional levels. At least one out of ten children is molested by a trusted family member (Forward & Buck 1988). This number of victims is conservative, since many incidents are never reported. Many women do not remember their incestuous experiences until something triggers a certain memory in their adult years (Maltz & Holman, 1987).

In our personal-growth groups for relatively well-functioning people, we find a startling number of women who report incidents of incest and sexual experimentation with fathers, uncles, stepfathers, grandfathers, and brothers. Black (1987) defines incest as "inappropriate sexual behavior, usually perpetrated by an adult family member with a minor child, brought about by coercion, deception, or psychological manipulation. It includes inappropriate touching, fondling, oral sex, and/or intercourse" (p. 154). The definition used by Vanderbilt (1992) is "any sexual abuse of a child by a relative or other person in a position of trust and authority over the child. It is the violation of the child where he or she lives—literally and metaphorically" (p. 51). Vanderbilt indicates that incest is a felony offense in all fifty states, although its definition varies from state to state, as does the punishment. Although father-daughter incest is the most common type of adult-child incest, sexual relations also occur between mother and daughter, mother and son, and father and son (Forward & Buck, 1988). Although females are more often incest victims, males also suffer the effects of incestuous experiences.

In our groups, many women will bring up the matter because they feel burdened with guilt, rage, hurt, and confusion over having been taken advantage of sexually and emotionally. Some feel both confused and guilty, because even though they feel like a victim, at the same time they see themselves as a conspirator. They may believe that they were to blame, a belief that is often reinforced by others. They may have liked the affection and love they received even though they were probably repulsed by the sexual component. Because children realize that adults have power over them, they tend to be compliant, even in situations that seem strange. Typically, these experiences happen in childhood or early adolescence; the women remember feeling helpless at the time, not knowing how to stop the man, and also being afraid to tell anyone. Some of the reasons children give for not telling others about the abuse include: not knowing that it was wrong, feeling ashamed, being frightened of the consequences of telling, fearing that others might not believe that such abuse occurred, and hoping to protect their siblings from incest. However, once they bring out these past experiences, intense, pent-up emotions surface, such as hatred and rage for having been treated in such a way and feelings of having been raped and used.

In their book *Betrayal of Innocence*, Forward and Buck (1988) describe recurring themes that emerge from the incest experiences of almost every victim. From the victim's perspective, these themes include a desire to be loved by the perpetrator; a tendency to put up little resistance; an atmosphere of secrecy surrounding the incest; feelings of repulsion, fear, and guilt; the experience of pain and confusion; fears of being punished or removed from the home; and feelings of tremendous isolation and of having no one to turn to in a time of need. Most often the victim feels responsible for what occurred.

Children who have been sexually abused by someone in their family feel betrayed and typically develop a mistrust of others who are in a position to take advantage of them. Oftentimes the sexual abuse is only one facet of a dysfunctional family. There may also be physical abuse, neglect, alcoholism, and other problems. These children are often unaware of how psychologically abusive their family atmosphere really is for all the members of the family.

The effects of these early childhood experiences can carry over into adulthood. The woman's ability to form sexually satisfying relationships may be impaired by events that she has kept inside of her for many years. She may resent all men, associating them with the father or other man who initially took advantage of her. If she couldn't trust her own father, then what man can she trust? She may have a hard time trusting men who express affection for her, thinking that they, too, will take advantage of her. She may keep control of relationships by not letting herself be open with men or be sexually playful and free with them. She may rarely or never allow herself to fully give in to sexual pleasure during intercourse. Her fear is that if she gives up her control, she will be hurt again. Her guilt over sexual feelings and her negative conditioning prevent her from being open to enjoying a satisfying sexual relationship. She may blame all men for her feelings of guilt and her betrayal and victimization. She may develop severe problems with establishing and maintaining intimate relationships, not only with her partner, but also with her own children. In adulthood she may marry a man who will later victimize their own children, which perpetuates the pattern of her experiences in growing up. In this way there is a repeating of the dynamics from childhood through adulthood.

We've found that it is therapeutic for most of these women to simply share this burden that they've been carrying alone for so many years. In a climate of support, trust, care, and respect, these women can *begin* a healing process that will eventually allow them to shed needless guilt. Before this healing can occur, they generally need to fully express bottled-up feelings, usually of anger and hatred. A major part of their therapy consists of accepting the reality that they were indeed victims and learning to direct their anger outward, rather than blaming themselves. We stress that what is important is that this catharsis occur in the group in *symbolic* ways. With the assistance of their therapist, they may be able to confront the perpetrator and those who did not protect them. Sometimes the man in question will no longer be alive, or the woman may decide that she does not want to confront the aggressor.

As we mentioned, it is not uncommon for a woman to assume the guilt and responsibility for these inappropriate sexual activities. Even though she may have been only 7 years old, she firmly believes that she should have prevented the abuse from happening. She fails to realize that the adults in her life were violating her and failing to provide the safe environment in which she could have developed and matured as a sexual being. A very moving account that describes a long period of incest between a lonely and disturbed man and his daughter is the subject of *If I Should Die before I Wake* by Michelle Morris (1984). This book depicts the terror experienced by the victim and shows the psychological scars she carried beyond childhood.

The process of recovery from the psychological wounds of incest varies from individual to individual, depending on a number of complex factors. Many incest victims cut off their feelings as a survival tactic. Part of the recovery process involves regaining the ability to feel, getting in touch with buried memories, and speaking truths. They will likely have to deal with questions such as: What is wrong with me? Why did this happen in my life? Why didn't I stop it? What will my future be like? Victims may vacillate between denying the incestuous experiences and accepting what occurred. As they work through their memories surrounding the events, they eventually accept the fact that they were involved in incest. They typically feel sadness and grief, and then rage. If recovery is successful, they are finally able to forgive themselves and find a resolution to being stuck (Vanderbilt, 1992).

According to Forward and Buck (1988), one of the greatest gifts that therapy can bestow is a full and realistic reversal of blame and responsibility from the victim to the victimizers. In her therapeutic practice with victims of incest, Susan Forward attempts to achieve three major goals:

1. Assist the client in externalizing the guilt, rage, shame, hurt, fear, and confusion that are stored up within her.
2. Help the victim place the responsibility for the event(s) primarily with the aggressor and secondarily with the silent partner.
3. Help the client realize that although incest has damaged her dignity and self-esteem, she does not have to remain psychologically victimized for the rest of her life.

Forward's words offer encouragement to those who have suffered from the impact of incest: "Incest is a pervasive and crushing problem for both individuals and society, but it is definitely not a dead-end street. The damage is not irreparable. Self-worth and dignity can definitely be restored. I know this from both personal and professional experience" (p. 6).

Through role playing, release of feelings, and sharing of her conflicts with others in the group, the victim often finds that she is not alone in her plight, and she begins to put these experiences into a new perspective. Although she will never forget these experiences, she can begin the process of letting go of feelings of self-blame. Hopefully, she will be able to get to a place where she is not controlled by these past experiences. In doing so, she is also freeing herself of the control that these sexual experiences (and the feelings associated with them) have had over her ability to form intimate relationships with men.

Again, we have worked with adult men who were incest victims during childhood and adolescence, although they have been far fewer in number. Regardless of one's gender or cultural background, we find the dynamics similar and thus the therapeutic work is much the same for both women and men.

If you are interested in doing further reading on the psychological aspects of incest, including its causes, effects, and treatment approaches, the following books are recommended: Black, *It Will Never Happen to Me* (1987); Finkelhor, *Child Sexual Abuse* (1984); Forward and Buck, *Betrayal of Innocence* (1988); Herman, *Father-Daughter Incest* (1981); Justice and Justice, *The Broken Taboo* (1979); Maltz, *The Sexual Healing Journey* (1991); Maltz and Holman, *Incest and Sexuality* (1987); Meiselman, *Incest* (1978) and *Resolving the Trauma of Incest* (1990); Morris, *If I Should Die before I Wake* (1984); and Rush, *The Best Kept Secret* (1980).

Vanderbilt (1992) lists some self-help resources that can be useful for victims of childhood sexual abuse. Four of them are

- Self-Help Clearinghouse, St. Clare's-Riverside Medical Center, Denville, NJ 07834 (201-625-9565). Publishes *The Self-Help Directory*, a guide to mutual-aid self-help groups and how to form them.
- Incest Survivors Anonymous, P.O. Box 5613, Long Beach, CA 90805-0613 (213-428-5599). Assists in forming 12-step groups.
- SARA (Sexual Assault Recovery Anonymous) Society, P.O. Box 16, Surrey, British Columbia V3T 4W4 Canada (604-584-2626). Provides self-help information for adults and teens who were sexually abused as children.
- National Council on Child Abuse and Family Violence, 1155 Connecticut Avenue NW, Suite 400, Washington, DC 20036 (202-429-6695).

DATE AND ACQUAINTANCE RAPE

In our contacts with college students it has become clear to us that date rape is prevalent on campus. *Acquaintance rape* takes place when a woman is forced to have unwanted sex with someone she knows. This might involve friends, co-workers, neighbors, or relatives. *Date rape* occurs in those situations where a woman is forced to have unwanted intercourse with a person in the context of dating. Some writers consider acquaintance rape and date rape as examples of communication gone awry (Weiten, Lloyd, & Lashley, 1991).

Earlier in this chapter we identified some myths and misconceptions about sexuality. One of these myths that men often operate under is that by nature they are sexually aggressive. Thus men may feel that they are expected to be this way. As a consequence they may misinterpret a woman's "no" as a "maybe" or a sign of initial resistance that can be broken down. Dating partners may not say what they really mean, or they may not mean what they say. This phenomenon is reinforced by the linkage of sex with domination and submission. In our society, masculinity is equated with power, dominance, and sexual aggressiveness, while femininity is associated with pleasing men, sexual passivity, and lack of assertiveness (Basow, 1992).

Both date rape and acquaintance rape can be considered as a betrayal of trust. Much like in incest, when a woman is forced to have sex against her will, her dignity as a person is violated. Not believing that she is in danger, she may make herself vulnerable to a man and then experience hurt. She might have explicit trust in a man she knows, only to discover that he is intent on getting what he wants, regardless of the cost to her. The emotional scars that are a part of date rape are similar to the wounds inflicted by incest. As is the case with incest victims, women who are raped by people they know often take responsibility and blame themselves for what occurred, and therefore they are embarrassed about or afraid of reporting the incident.

Weiten and his colleagues indicate that inadequate communication between dating partners often is a key factor contributing to date rape. They offer the following suggestions to people in dating relationships:

- Recognize that date rape is an act of sexual aggression.
- Beware of using excessive alcohol or drugs, which can lower your resistance and distort your judgment.
- Clarify your values and attitudes about sex before you are in situations where you have to make a decision about sexual behavior.
- Communicate your feelings, thoughts, and expectations about sex in a clear and open manner.
- Listen carefully to each other and respect each other's values, decisions, and boundaries.

Currently, many college campuses offer education directed at the prevention of date rape. The focus of this education is on emphasizing the importance of being consistent and clear about what you want or don't want with your dating partner, as well as providing information about factors contributing to date rape. Many prevention programs are designed for women to increase their awareness of high-risk situations and behaviors and to teach them how to protect themselves. Basow (1992) emphasizes the reality that because men rape, only they can stop rape. It is the man's responsibility to avoid forcing a woman to have sex with him, and he must learn that her "no" really does mean "no." Basow reports that innovative campus programs aimed at men are just beginning, especially programs for men in fraternity groups. It is clear that campus preventive programs need to be designed for both women and men. Both could benefit from discussion groups or workshops on this topic so that they can explore myths and misconceptions that drive certain behavior. Basow believes that all of us are a part of the problem and that all of us need to be a part of the solution. She points out that rape can be viewed as an outgrowth of a culture that glorifies sex and violence; prevention programs need to address ways of changing those attitudes and behaviors that lead to the exploitation of women.

SEXUAL HARASSMENT

Sexual harassment is considered to be repeated and unwanted sexually oriented behavior in the form of comments, gestures, or physical contacts. This phenomenon is of concern on the college campus, in the workplace, and in the military. Women experience sexual harassment more frequently than men. Sexual harassment is an issue of abuse of the power differential between men and women. According to Basow (1992), those who have more power tend to engage in sexual harassment more frequently than those with less power. Basow makes the point that sexual harassment is not gender neutral; rather, it is fairly gender specific. Sexist remarks, sexual bribery, seductive behaviors, and sexual coercion serve as reminders to women that they are not equal human beings. Men sometimes make the assumption that women like sexual attention, when in fact they resent being related to in strictly sexual terms. Sexual harassment diminishes choice, and surely it is not flattering. Harassment reduces people to objects to be demeaned.

As is true in cases of incest and date or acquaintance rape, many incidences of sexual harassment go unreported because the individuals involved often fear the consequences, such as getting fired, being denied a promotion, risking a low grade in a course, and encountering barriers to pursuing their careers. Fear of reprisals is a foremost barrier to reporting. Riger (1991) suggests that it is gender bias in policies and procedures that discourages women from making complaints.

If women do not report sexual harassment, they are contributing to these practices and their credibility may later be questioned. This was dramatically illustrated in the 1991 Senate confirmation hearings of Supreme Court Justice Clarence Thomas. The publicity given to the Clarence Thomas and Anita Hill incident brought sexual harassment to the forefront of public attention. This publicity certainly affected perspectives on unwanted sexual advances on workers and on students. Many industries and businesses as well as universities now have policies and procedures in place to deal with sexual harassment. They also offer workshops to educate employees in this area.

Chapter Summary

Sexuality is a part of our personhood and should not be thought of as an activity divorced from our feelings, values, and relationships. Although our childhood and adolescent experiences do have an impact on the shaping of our present attitudes toward sex and our sexual behavior, we are in a position to modify this area of our life if we are not satisfied with ourselves as sexual beings.

One significant step toward evaluating our sexual attitudes is to become aware of the myths and misconceptions that we may harbor. It helps to review where and how we acquired our views about sexuality. Have the sources of your sexual knowledge and values been healthy models? Have you questioned the ways in which your attitudes affect the way you feel about yourself sexually? Is your sexuality an expression of yourself as a complete person?

Another step toward developing our own sexual views is to learn to be open in talking about our sexual concerns, including fears and desires, with at least one other person whom we trust. Guilt feelings may be based on irrational premises, and we may be burdening ourselves needlessly with feeling guilty about normal feelings and behavior. We may feel very alone when it comes to our sexual feelings, fantasies, fears, and actions. By sharing some of these concerns with others, we are likely to find out that we are not the only ones with such concerns.

If we are successful in dealing with barriers that prevent us from acknowledging, experiencing, and expressing our sexuality, then we increase our chances of learning how to enjoy both sensuality and sexuality. Sensuality can be a significant path toward creating satisfying sexual relationships, and we can learn to become sensual beings even if we decide not to have sexual relationships with others. Sensuality implies a full awareness of and a sensitivity to the pleasures of sight, sound, smell, taste, and touch. We can enjoy sensuality without being sexual, and it is a mistake to conclude that sensuality necessarily leads to sexual behavior. Nevertheless, sensuality is very important in enhancing sexual relationships. Intimacy, or the emotional sharing with a person we care for, is another ingredient of joyful sex. As a habitual style, sex without intimacy tends to lead to a basic sense of frustration, emptiness, and emotional deadness.

The AIDS crisis has had a significant impact on sexual behavior. Although ignorance and fear of AIDS are rampant, education can be the key to dispelling them. There are many myths and misconceptions pertaining to who gets AIDS, how it is transmitted, and the stigma attached to it. Along with a better understanding of this disease, education can put you in a good position to make informed choices in expressing your sexuality.

The place that sex occupies in our life and the attitudes we have toward it are very much a matter of free choice. It is no easier to achieve sexual autonomy than it is to achieve autonomy in other areas of life.

Incest, date or acquaintance rape, and sexual harassment are all forms of sexual abuse that have the capacity to render the victims powerless and helpless. They are all embedded in gender and power dynamics. Incest and date rape are examples of betrayal of trust, sexual aggression, and violence. Those involved do not have much choice in a situation that is foisted upon them. The consequences are potentially dire both physically and psychologically, for the victims often have difficulty in forming trusting relationships and in enjoying sexuality.

The themes explored in the previous chapter on love and in the following chapter — on relationships and lifestyles — are really impossible to separate from the themes in this chapter. Think about love, sex, and relationships as an integrated dimension of a rich and full life.

Activities and Exercises

1. Write down some of your major questions or concerns regarding sexuality. You might consider discussing these issues with a friend, your partner (if you're involved in an intimate relationship), or your class group.

2. In your journal trace the evolution of your sexual history. What were some important experiences for you, and what did you learn from these experiences?

3. List as many common slang words as you are able to think of pertaining to (a) the male genitals, (b) the female genitals, and (c) sexual intercourse. Review this list and ask yourself what sexual attitudes seem to be expressed. What do you think this list implies about your culture's attitude toward sexuality? Explore the hypothesis that the more rigid, uncomfortable, and embarrassed a particular culture is about sex, the more negative are the words used to describe sexual functioning.

4. Incest is a universal taboo. Explore some of the reasons for this taboo. You might investigate cross-cultural attitudes pertaining to incest. Do you view sexual experimentation between siblings during childhood as incest? Discuss.

5. The media are giving increasing attention to the topics of incest and sexual abuse of children. What do you think this current interest in these subjects implies?

6. What sexual modeling did you see in your parents? What attitudes and values about sex did they convey to you, both implicitly and explicitly? What would you most want to communicate to your children about sex?

7. Select one or more of the following books for further reading on the topics explored in this chapter: Forward and Buck, *Betrayal of Innocence* (1988); McCarthy and McCarthy, *Sexual Awareness: Enhancing Sexual Pleasure* (1984).

CHAPTER NINE

Relationships and Lifestyles

Prechapter Self-Inventory

Use the following scale to respond: 4 = this statement is true of me *most* of the time; 3 = this statement is true of me *much* of the time; 2 = this statement is true of me *some* of the time; 1 = this statement is true of me *almost none* of the time.

_____ 1. I consider the absence of conflict and crisis to be a sign of a good relationship.

_____ 2. It's difficult for me to have many close relationships at one time.

_____ 3. If I'm involved in a satisfactory relationship, I won't feel attracted to others besides my partner.

_____ 4. I believe that the mark of a successful relationship is that I enjoy being both with and without the other person.

_____ 5. I would like to find intimacy with one other person.

_____ 6. At times, wanting too much from another person causes me difficulties in the relationship.

_____ 7. I think that an exclusive relationship is bound to become dull, predictable, and unexciting.

_____ 8. I know what I'm looking for in a relationship.

_____ 9. I have what I want in terms of intimacy with others.

_____ 10. I can be emotionally intimate with another person without being physically intimate with that person.

Introduction

Although this chapter focuses mainly on the role that relationships play in our lives, we deal with relationships from a broad perspective, and also with a range of lifestyles. The chapter deals with friendships, marital relationships, intimacy between people who are not married, dating relationships, relationships between parents and children, same-gender relationships as well as opposite-gender relationships, alternative lifestyles, and other meaningful personal relationships.

Marriage is still the dominant relationship in our society, particularly if the term *marriage* is construed broadly to include the many couples who consider themselves committed to each other even though they are not legally married as well as those who are creating relationships that are different in many respects from the traditional marriage. Bellah and his colleagues (1985) found that in today's society most people still want to marry, even though many of them no longer see it as a life requirement. For increasing numbers of people it is not considered disgraceful to be unmarried, and more people are remaining single by choice. There is less pressure to have children, and starting a family tends to be more of a conscious decision than was true in the past. Most of those interviewed believe in love as a basis for an enduring relationship. Love and commitment appear to be highly valued, although maintaining these qualities is difficult. Most people value spontaneity and solidity, freedom and intimacy, and the sharing of thoughts, feelings, values, and life goals. They feel freer than in the past to leave a marriage that is not working, and divorce is seen as one (but not the only) solution to an unhappy marriage.

Whether you choose to marry or not, or whether your preference is a same-gender or an opposite-gender primary relationship, you probably have many different types of relationships. What is true for marriage is largely true for these other relationships as well. Allowing for the differences in relationships, the signs of growth and meaningfulness are much the same, and so are the problems. Consequently, whatever lifestyle you choose, you can use the ideas in this chapter as a basis for thinking about the role relationships play in your life. The aim of the chapter is to stimulate your reflection on what you want from all of your special relationships, and also to invite you to take an honest look at the quality of these relationships.

Types of Intimacy

As we saw earlier, Erikson maintains that the challenge of forming intimate relationships is the major task of early adulthood. Intimacy implies that we are able to share significant aspects of ourselves with others. The issues we raise concerning barriers to intimacy and ways of enhancing intimacy can help you better understand the many different types of relationships in your life. The ideas in this chapter are useful tools in rethinking what kind of relationships you want, as well as in clarifying some new choices that you may want to make. You can take a fresh look at these relationships, including both their frustrations and their delights, and you can think about initiating some changes.

Consider the case of Donald, who told us about how little closeness he had experienced with his father. He saw his father as uncaring, aloof, and preoccupied with his own concerns. Yet Donald deeply wished that he could be physically and emotionally closer to him, and he had no idea how to bring this about. He made the difficult decision to talk to his father and tell him how he felt and what he wanted. His father appeared to listen, and his eyes moistened, but then without saying much he quickly left the room. Donald reported how hurt and disappointed he was that his father had not been as responsive as he had hoped he would be. What Donald was missing were subtle, yet significant, signs that his father had been touched and was not as uncaring as he had imagined. That his father listened to him, that he

responded with even a few clumsy words, that he touched Donald on the shoulder, and that he became emotional were all manifestations that Donald's overtures had been received. Donald needs to understand that his father is probably very uncomfortable in talking personally. His father may well be every bit as afraid of his son's rejection as Donald is of his father's rebuffs. Donald will need to show patience and continue "hanging in there" with his father if he is really interested in changing the way they relate to each other.

The experience Donald had with his father could have occurred in any intimate relationship. We can experience feelings of awkwardness, unexpressed desires, and fears of rejection with our friends, lovers, spouses, parents, or children. A key point is that we have the power to bring about change if we ourselves change and do not insist that the other person make quick and total changes. It is up to us to teach others specific ways of becoming more personal. It does little good to invest our energy in lamenting all the ways in which the other person is not fulfilling our expectations, nor is it helpful to focus on remaking others. Time and again, this chapter will encourage you to focus on your own wants, to look at what you are doing, and to make some decisions about how you can assume increased control of your relationships. When you take a passive stance and simply hope the other person will change in the ways that you would like, you are giving away a sense of your power.

The intimacy we share with another person can be emotional, intellectual, physical, spiritual, or any combination of these. It can be exclusive or nonexclusive, long-term or brief. For example, many of the participants in the personal-growth groups that we conduct become emotionally involved with one another. During the space of a week in which they share their struggles, they develop a meaningful closeness, even though they may not keep in touch once the week is over. This closeness does not come about magically or automatically. They earn it by daring to be different in how they relate. Instead of keeping their thoughts, feelings, and reactions to themselves, they let others know them in ways that they typically do not allow outside of the group setting. The cohesion comes about when people discover that they have very similar feelings and when they are willing to share their pain, anger, frustrations — and their joys. We've observed how reluctant many people are to open themselves up emotionally in such short-term situations, because they want to avoid the sadness of parting. Bonds of intimacy and friendship can be formed in a short period, however, and subsequent distance in space and time need not diminish the quality of the friendships we form. We caution that developing intimacy with people in the group should not be the final goal. What is important is that the members translate this learning to their outside lives.

When we avoid intimacy, we only rob ourselves. We may pass up the chance to really get to know neighbors and new acquaintances, because we fear that either we or our new friends will move and that the friendship will come to an end. Similarly, we may not want to open ourselves to intimacy with sick or dying persons, because we fear the pain of losing them. Although such fears may be natural ones, too often we allow them to cheat us of the uniquely rich experience of being truly close to another person. We can enhance our life greatly by daring to care about others and fully savoring the time we can share with them now.

The idea that we most want to stress is that you can choose the kinds of relationships you want to experience. Often, we fail to make our own choices and instead fall into a certain type of relationship because we think "This is the way it's *supposed* to be." For example, some people marry who in reality might prefer to remain single — particularly women who often feel the pressure to have a family because it's "natural" for them to do so. Sometimes people choose a heterosexual relationship because they think that it is what is expected of them, when they would really prefer a homosexual relationship. Instead of blindly accepting that relationships must be a certain way or that only one type of lifestyle is possible, you have the choice of giving real thought to the question of what types of intimacy have meaning for you.

As you read the remainder of this chapter, spend some time thinking about the quality of all the various kinds of intimacy you are experiencing in your life. Are you involved in the kinds of relationships that you want? How can you enhance your relationships? What are *you* willing to do to improve them? What is your view of a growing relationship?

Time Out for Personal Reflection

1. What do you look for in a person you'd like to form an intimate relationship with? For each item, put a 1 in the space if the quality is *very important* to you, a 2 if it is *somewhat important*, and a 3 if it is *not very important*.

_____	intelligence
_____	character (a strong sense of values)
_____	physical appearance and attractiveness
_____	money and possessions
_____	charm
_____	prestige and status
_____	a strong sense of identity
_____	expressiveness and a tendency to be outgoing
_____	a sense of humor
_____	caring and sensitivity
_____	power
_____	independence
_____	a quiet person
_____	someone who will make decisions for me
_____	someone I can lean on
_____	someone who will lean on me
_____	someone I can't live without
_____	someone who works hard and is disciplined
_____	someone who likes to play and have fun
_____	someone who has values similar to mine
_____	someone I'd like to grow old with

Now list the three qualities that you value most in a person when you are considering an intimate relationship.

_____

_____

_____

2. Why do you think a person might want an intimate relationship with you? Look over the qualities listed above, and then list the qualities you see yourself as having.

_____

_____

_____

3. Identify the kinds of intimate relationships you have chosen so far in your life. If you aren't presently involved in any significant intimate relationships, would you like to be?

_____

_____

_____

4. What do you get from being involved in a significant relationship? Check the responses that apply to you, and add your own on the lines provided.

_____	a feeling of being cared for
_____	a sense of importance
_____	joy in being able to care for another person
_____	excitement
_____	the feeling of not being alone in the world
_____	sharing and companionship

Other:

_____

_____

_____

Meaningful Relationships: A Personal View

In this section we share some of our ideas about the characteristics of a meaningful relationship. Although these guidelines pertain to couples, they are also relevant to other personal relationships, such as those between parent and child and between friends of the same or opposite gender. Take, for example, the guideline "The persons involved are willing to work at keeping their relationship alive." Sometimes parents and children take each other for granted and rarely spend time talking about how they are getting along. Either parent or child may expect the other to assume the major responsibility for their relationship. The same principle applies to friends or to partners in a primary relationship. As you look over our list, adapt it to your own relationships, keeping in mind your particular cultural values. Since the values that are a part of your cultural background play an influential role in your relationships, you will need to adapt them in appropriate ways. As you review our list, ask yourself what qualities *you* think are most important in your relationships.

We see relationships as most meaningful when they are dynamic and evolving rather than fixed or final. Thus, there may be periods of joy and excitement followed by times of struggle, pain, and distance. As long as the persons in a relationship are growing and changing, their relationship is bound to change as well. The following are some of the qualities of a relationship that seem most important to us.

• *Each person in the relationship has a separate identity.* Kahlil Gibran (1923) expresses this thought in *The Prophet*: "But let there be spaces in your togetherness, and let the winds of the heavens dance between you" (p. 16). In *The Dance of Anger*, Harriet Goldhor Lerner (1985) says that making long-term relationships work is difficult because it is necessary to create and maintain a balance between separateness and togetherness. If there is not enough togetherness in a relationship, people in it typically feel isolated and do not share feelings and experiences. If there is not enough separateness, they give up a sense of their own identity and control. They also devote much effort to becoming what the other person expects.

• *Although each person desires the other, each can survive without the other.* This characteristic is an extension of the prior one, and it implies that people are in a relationship by choice. They are not so tightly bound together that if they are separated, one or the other becomes lost and empty. Thus, if a young man says "I simply can't live without my girlfriend," he is indeed in trouble. His dependency should not be interpreted as love but as the seeking of an object to make him feel complete.

• *Each is able to talk openly with the other about matters of significance to the relationship.* The two persons can openly express grievances and let each other know the changes they desire. They can ask for what they want, rather than expecting the other to intuitively know what they want and give it to them. For example, assume that you are not satisfied with how you and your mother spend time together. You can take the first step by letting her know, in a nonjudgmental way, that you would like to talk more personally. Rather than telling her how she is, you can focus more on telling her how you feel in your relationship with her.

• *Each person assumes responsibility for his or her own level of happiness and refrains from blaming the other if he or she is unhappy.* Of course, in a close relationship or friendship the unhappiness of the other person is bound to affect you, but you should not expect another person to *make* you happy, fulfilled, or excited. Although the way others feel will influence your life, they do not create or cause your feelings. Ultimately, you are responsible for defining your goals and your life, and you can take actions to change what *you* are doing if you are unhappy with a situation.

• *The persons involved are willing to work at keeping their relationship alive.* If we hope to keep a relationship vital, we must reevaluate and revise our way of being with each other from time to time. Consider how this guideline fits for your friendships. If you take a good friend for granted and show little interest in doing what is necessary to maintain your friendship, she may soon grow disenchanted and wonder what kind of friend you are.

• *The persons are able to have fun and to play together; they enjoy doing things with each other.* It is easy to become so serious that we forget to take the time to enjoy those we love. One way of changing drab relationships is to become aware of the infrequency of playful moments and then determine what things are getting in the way of enjoying life. Again, think of this guideline as it applies to your close friends.

• *Each person is growing, changing, and opening up to new experiences.* When you rely on others for your personal fulfillment and confirmation as a person, you are in trouble. The best way to build solid relationships with others is to work on developing your own personality. But do not be surprised if you encounter resistance to your growth and change. This resistance can come from within yourself as well as from others.

• *If the relationship contains a sexual component, each person makes some attempt to keep the romance alive.* The two persons may not always experience the intensity and novelty of the early period of their relationship, but they can devise ways of creating a climate of romance and closeness. They may go places they haven't been to before or otherwise vary their routine in some ways. They recognize when their life is getting dull and look for ways to eliminate its boring aspects. In their lovemaking they are sensitive to each other's needs and desires; at the same time, they are able to ask each other for what they want and need.

• *The two persons are equal in the relationship.* People who feel that they are typically the "givers" and that their partner is usually unavailable when they need him or her might question the balance in their relationship. In some relationships one person may feel compelled to assume a superior position relative to the other — for example, to be very willing to listen and give advice yet unwilling to go to the other person and show any vulnerability or need. Lerner (1985) says that women often define their own wishes and preferences as being the same as those of their partner. In this case there surely is no equality in the relationship. Both parties need to be willing to look at aspects of inequality and demonstrate a willingness to negotiate changes.

• *Each person actively demonstrates concern for the other.* In a vital relationship the participants do more than just talk about how much they value each other. Their actions show their care and concern more eloquently than any words. Each person has a desire to give to the other. They have an interest in each other's welfare and a desire to see that the other person is fulfilled.

• *Each person finds meaning and sources of nourishment outside the relationship.* Sometimes people become very possessive in their friendships. A sign of a healthy relationship is that each avoids assuming an attitude of ownership toward the other. Although they may experience jealousy at times, they do not demand that the other person deaden his or her feelings for others. Their lives did not begin when they met each other, nor would their lives end if they should part.

• *Each avoids manipulating, exploiting, and using the other.* Each respects and cares for the other and is willing to see the world through the other's eyes. At times parent-child relationships are strained because either or both parties attempt to manipulate the other. Consider the father who brags about his son, Roger, to others and whose affection is based on Roger's being an outstanding athlete. Roger may feel used if his father is able to talk only of sports. What if he were to decide to quit playing sports? Would he still be earning his father's approval?

• *Each person is moving in a direction in life that is personally meaningful.*
They are both excited about the quality of their lives and their projects.
Applied to couples, this guideline implies that both individuals feel that
their needs are being met within the relationship, but they also feel a sense of
engagement in their work, play, and relationships with other friends and
family members. Goldberg (1987) makes some excellent points pertaining to
these issues:

> Probably the best or healthiest relationships begin without intensely ro-
> mantic feelings, but where there is a genuine basis for being with each other
> on a friendship level and where there is enjoyment of each other's company
> without concern over commitment or future. Add to that a balanced flow of
> power, healthy conflict resolution free of blaming guilt, a sense of being
> known for who you are and knowing your partner, and a relaxed desire to be
> fully present with little need to escape or avoid through distraction, and you
> have a fine potential for growth in a good relationship. (p. 89)

• *If they are in a committed relationship, they maintain this relationship by choice, not simply for the sake of any children involved, out of duty, or because of convenience.* They choose to keep their ties with each other even if things get rough or if they sometimes experience emptiness in their relationship. They share some common purposes and values, and therefore, they are willing to look at what is lacking in their relationship and to work on changing undesirable situations.

• *They are able to cope with anger in their relationship.* Couples often seek relationship counseling with the expectation that they will learn to stop fighting and that conflict will end. This is not a realistic goal. More important than the absence of fighting is learning how to fight cleanly and constructively, which entails an ongoing process of expressing anger and frustrations. It is the buildup of these emotions that creates trouble. If anger is not expressed and dealt with constructively, it will sour a relationship. Stored-up anger usually results in the target person getting more than his or her share of deserved anger. At other times bottled-up anger is let out in indirect ways such as sarcasm and hostility. If the parties in a relationship are angry, they should try to express it in a direct way.

• *Each person recognizes the need for solitude and is willing to create the time in which to be alone.* Each allows the other a sense of privacy. Because they recognize each other's individual integrity, they avoid prying into every thought or manipulating the other to disclose what he or she wants to keep private. Sometimes parents are guilty of not respecting the privacy of their children. A father may be hurt if his daughter does not want to talk with him at any time that *he* feels like talking. He needs to realize that she is a separate person with her own needs and that she may need time alone at certain times when he wants to talk.

• *They do not expect the other to do for them what they are capable of doing for themselves.* They don't expect the other person to make them feel alive, take away their boredom, assume their risks, or make them feel valued and important. Each is working toward creating his or her own autonomous identity. Consequently, neither person depends on the other for confirmation of his or her personal worth; nor does one walk in the shadow of the other.

• *They encourage each other to become all that they are capable of becoming.* Unfortunately, people often have an investment in keeping those with whom they are intimately involved from changing. Their expectations and needs may lead them to resist changes in their partner and thus make it difficult for their partner to grow. If they recognize their fears, however, they can challenge their need to block their partner's progress.

• *Each has a commitment to the other.* Commitment is a vital part of an intimate relationship. It means that the people involved have an investment in their future together and that they are willing to stay with each other in times of crisis and conflict. Although many people express an aversion to any long-term commitment in a relationship, how deeply will they allow themselves to be loved if they believe that the relationship can be dissolved on a whim when things look bleak? Perhaps, for some people, a fear of intimacy gets in the way of developing a sense of commitment. Loving and being loved is both exciting and frightening, and we may have to struggle with the issue of how much anxiety we want to tolerate. Commitment to another person involves risks and carries a price, but it is an essential part of an intimate relationship.

One of the reviewers of this book commented that the primary interest among college students was creating and maintaining friendships, especially intimate relationships. There is no single or easy prescription for success in this case, but developing meaningful relationships entails the willingness to struggle.

Many college students encounter difficulties in keeping their relationships alive. They may say that they don't have enough time to maintain their friendships and other relationships. If this fits for you, realize that your relationships and friendships are likely to dissolve if you neglect them. Time must be devoted to nourishing and revitalizing your relationships if you expect them to last. You can make choices that will increase your chances of developing lasting friendships: be tolerant of differences between your friends and yourself; learn to become aware of conflicts and deal with them constructively; be willing to let the other person know how you are affected in the relationship; stay in the relationship even though you may experience a fear of rejection; check out your assumptions with others instead of deciding for them what they are thinking and feeling; be willing to make yourself vulnerable and to take risks; and avoid the temptation to live up to others' expectations instead of being true to yourself.

In summary, creating and maintaining friendships and intimate relationships requires time, work, and the willingness to ride out hard times. Further, to be a good friend to another, you must first be a good friend to yourself, which implies knowing yourself and caring about yourself. The following "Time Out" asks you to focus on some of the ways in which you see yourself as an alive and growing person, which is the foundation of building meaningful relationships.

Time Out for Personal Reflection

1. What are some ways in which you see yourself as growing? In what ways do you see yourself as resisting personal growth by sticking with old and comfortable patterns, even if they don't work? To facilitate your reflection, look over the following statements, and mark each one

with a "T" or an "F," depending on whether you think it generally applies to you.

_____   If I'm involved in an intimate relationship, I tell the other person what I want.
_____   I'm willing to try new things.
_____   Rather than settling for comfort in a relationship or in life, I ask for more.
_____   If I'm involved in an intimate relationship, I tell the other person what I'm feeling.
_____   I'm engaged in projects that are meaningful to me.

2. List other ways in which you're growing:

   _____

   _____

3. List some ways in which you resist personal growth:

   _____

   _____

4. In what ways do you see the person with whom you're most intimate growing or resisting growth?

   _____

   _____

5. If you're involved in a couple relationship, in what ways do you think you and your partner are growing closer? In what ways are you going in different directions?

   _____

   _____

   _____

   _____

6. Are you satisfied with the relationship you've just described? If not, what would you most like to change? How might you go about it?

   _____

   _____

   _____

   _____

A suggestion: If you're involved in a couple relationship, have your partner respond to the questions on a separate sheet of paper. Then compare your answers and discuss areas of agreement and disagreement.

Dealing with Communication Blocks

A number of barriers to effective communication can inhibit the developing and maintaining of intimate relationships. Some of these barriers are failing to really listen to another person; selective listening—that is, hearing only what you want to hear; being overly concerned with getting your point across without considering the other's views; silently rehearsing what you will say next as you are "listening"; becoming defensive, with self-protection your primary concern; attempting to change others rather than first attempting to understand them; telling others how they are, rather than telling them how they affect you; bringing old patterns into the present and not allowing the other person to change; overreacting to a person; failing to state what your needs are and expecting others to know intuitively; making assumptions about another person without checking them out; using sarcasm and hostility instead of being direct; and speaking in vague terms such as "You manipulate me!"

In most of these cases you tend to be so concerned with getting your point across, defending your view of yourself, or changing another person that you cannot appreciate what the other person is thinking and feeling. These blocks make it very difficult to have what are called I-Thou encounters, in which two persons are open with themselves and each other, expressing what they think and feel and making genuine contact. Instead, the persons who are attempting to communicate typically feel distant from each other.

Deborah Tannen has written two best-selling books on the subject of communication between women and men. In *That's Not What I Meant* (1987), Tannen focuses on how conversational styles can make or break a relationship. She maintains that male-female communication can be considered cross-cultural. The language we use as we are growing up is influenced by our gender, ethnicity, class and cultural background, and location. Boys and girls grow up in different worlds, even if they are part of the same family. Furthermore, they carry many of the patterns they established in childhood into their transactions as adults. For Tannen, these cultural differences include different expectations about the role of communication in relationships. These factors make up our conversational style, and the subtle differences in this style can lead to overwhelming misunderstandings and disappointments. In her other book, *You Just Don't Understand* (1991), Tannen develops the idea that conversational style differences do not explain all the conflicts in relationships between women and men, but many problems result because partners are expressing their thoughts and feelings in different ways. She believes that if we can sort out these differences based on conversational style, then we are better able to confront real conflicts and find a form of communication that will allow for a negotiation of these differences.

Rogers (1961) has written extensively on ways to improve personal relationships. For him, the main block to effective communication is our tendency to evaluate and judge the statements of others. He believes that what gets in the way of understanding another is the tendency to approve or disapprove, the unwillingness to put ourselves in the other's frame of reference, and the fear of being changed ourselves if we really listen to and understand a person with a viewpoint different from our own.

One of Rogers's suggestions for testing the quality of our understanding of someone is as follows: The next time you get into an argument with your partner, your friend, or a small group of friends, just stop the discussion for a moment and, for an experiment, institute this rule: "Each person can speak up for himself *only* after he has restated the ideas and feelings of the previous speaker accurately, and to that speaker's satisfaction" (p. 332). Carrying out this experiment implies that you must strive to genuinely understand another person and achieve his or her perspective. Although this may sound simple, it can be extremely difficult to put into practice. It involves challenging yourself to go beyond what you find convenient to hear, examining your assumptions and prejudices, not attributing to statements meanings that were not intended, and not coming to quick conclusions based on superficial listening. If you are successful in challenging yourself in these ways, you can enter the subjective world of the significant person in your life; that is, you can acquire empathy, which is the necessary foundation for all intimate relationships. Rogers (1980) contends that the sensitive companionship offered by an empathic person is healing and that such a deep understanding is a precious gift to another.

EFFECTIVE PERSONAL COMMUNICATION

Your culture influences both the content and the process of your communication. Some cultures prize direct communication, while other cultures see this behavior as rude and insensitive. In certain cultures direct eye contact is as insulting as the avoidance of eye contact is in other cultures. Harmony within the family is a cardinal value in certain cultures, and it may be inappropriate for adult children to confront their parents. As you read the following discussion, recognize that variations do exist among cultures. Our discussion has a Euro-American slant, which makes it essential that you adapt the principles we present to your own cultural framework. You need to examine the ways that your communication style has been influenced by your culture and then decide if you want to modify certain patterns that you have learned. For example, your culture might have taught you to control your feelings. You might decide to become more emotionally expressive if you discover that this pattern is restricting you in areas of your life where you would like to be freer.

From our perspective, when two persons are communicating meaningfully, they are involved in many of the following processes:

- They are facing each other and making eye contact, and one is listening while the other speaks.
- They do not rehearse their response while the other is speaking. The listener is able to summarize accurately what the speaker has said. ("So you're hurt when I don't call to tell you that I'll be late.")
- The language is specific and concrete. (A vague statement is "I feel manipulated." A concrete statement is "I don't like it when you bring me flowers and then expect me to do something for you that I already told you I didn't want to do.")
- The speaker makes personal statements instead of bombarding the other with impersonal questions. (A questioning statement is "Where were you last night, and why did you come home so late?" A personal statement is "I was worried and scared because I didn't know where you were last night.")
- The listener takes a moment before responding to reflect on what was said and on how he or she is affected. There is a sincere effort to walk in the shoes of the other person. ("It must have been very hard for you when you didn't know where I was last night and thought I might have been in an accident.")
- Although each has reactions to what the other is saying, there is an absence of critical judgment. (A critical judgment is "You never think about anybody but yourself, and you're totally irresponsible." A more appropriate reaction would be "I appreciate it when you think to call me, knowing that I may be worried.")
- Each of the parties can be honest and direct without insensitively damaging the other's dignity. Each makes "I" statements, rather than second-guessing and speaking for the other. ("Sometimes I worry that you don't care about me, and I want to check that out with you, rather than assuming that it's true.")
- There is a respect for each other's differences and an avoidance of pressuring each other to accept a point of view. ("I look at this matter very differently than you do, but I understand that you have your own opinion.")
- There is a congruency (or a matching) between the verbal and nonverbal messages. (If she is expressing anger, she is not smiling.)

- Each person is open about how he or she is affected by the other. (An ineffective response is "You have no right to criticize me." An effective response is "I'm very disappointed that you don't like the work I've done.")
- Neither person is being mysterious, expecting the other to decode his or her messages.

These processes are essential for fostering any meaningful relationship. You might try observing yourself while you are communicating, and take note of the degree to which you practice these principles. Decide if the quality of your relationships is satisfying to you. If you determine that you want to improve certain relationships, it will be helpful to begin by working on one of these skills at a time.

Although communication skills are basic to solid relationships, they alone are not sufficient to enable two persons to understand and work through their difficulties. Goldberg (1987) believes that men and women have trouble communicating mainly because of their polarized and unconscious defenses. Gender-defensive polarization develops because of the gender-role conditioning we discussed in Chapter Four. Both genders often have difficulties in grasping the world of the other. According to Goldberg, if women and men are engaged in defending themselves, they will be using different languages and living in different psychological worlds. He emphasizes that the starting point for effective communication is an absence of gender-defensive polarization.

COMMUNICATING WITH YOUR PARENTS

Parents are powerful people in our lives. We often expect them to change in the way we want and to do so quickly. We often insist that they undo years of unfair treatment or pain that they have caused us. If we persist in this behavior, our parents will eventually withdraw from us. It would be a good idea for us to decide what we want with our parents now. If we decide we want a different kind of life with them in the present, we will probably have to let go of some of our past grudges. It is important to learn how to forgive and to make peace.

If you do want a new relationship, you need to let go of the past. In our personal-growth groups we find that people don't give their parents much room to be imperfect. Time and again they blame their parents for having done or having failed to do something. In the group they express this blame in a symbolic way, such as in role-playing exercises. But before they get involved in a group they might have been engaging in blaming behavior for years.

If you desire intimacy with your parents, it is a good idea to put aside your need to remake them and to accept any small changes that they may make. This recommendation was illustrated earlier in the chapter by the example of

Donald's attempt to confront his father. Furthermore, rather than expecting your parents to make the first move, it would be more realistic to take the first step by initiating the changes in yourself that you are hoping they will make. For example, if you hope for more physical signs of affection between you and your parents, you might initiate touching. If you want more time with your mother and are angry that she doesn't ask for this time, ask yourself what is stopping you from taking this time with her. Persistence in asking for what you want sometimes does pay off. Too many people withdraw quickly when their expectations of others are not fully and immediately met.

Our experience with our personal-growth groups has taught us how central our relationship with our parents is and how it affects all of our other interpersonal relationships. We learn from our parents how to deal with the rest of the world. We are often unaware of the impact our parents had, and continue to have, on us. Our groups are made up of people of various ages, sociocultural backgrounds, life experiences, and vocations, yet many of the members have ongoing struggles with their parents. It is not uncommon to have a 60-year-old man and a 20-year-old woman both expressing their frustration over not being accepted and affirmed by their parents. They are both intent on obtaining parental approval that they are convinced they need.

It is important to recognize the present effect that your parents are having on you and to decide the degree to which you like this effect. On the one hand, you may have problems in letting them be other than they were when you were a child. Although they may continue to treat you as a child, it could be that you behave around them as you did as a child and provoke their response. On the other hand, parents at times are reluctant to give up old parental roles; this does not mean that you cannot be different with them. You might become angry at your parents for the very things you are not willing to do, such as initiating closer contact or making time for the relationship. If you really want to be able to talk with them more intimately, you can take the first step. Again, the principles of effective communication can be applied to enrich the time you spend with your parents.

Gay and Lesbian Relationships as an Alternative Lifestyle

Homosexuality is a fact of life for many people in our society. The challenge is how to help both heterosexuals and homosexuals recognize that homosexuality is a viable alternative lifestyle. The gay liberation movement has made significant strides toward gaining such recognition and acceptance. In many states acknowledged homosexuals are holding public office, yet homosexuality is still a difficult subject for many people.

We include a discussion of this special type of relationship because society has yet to recognize gay and lesbian lifestyles as acceptable. Our intention in including a discussion of gay and lesbian relationships is to dispel the myth that these relationships are basically different from heterosexual relationships. There are common factors underlying all forms of intimate relationships. For example, the guidelines for meaningful relationships that we presented earlier can be applied to friendships, parent-child relationships, and relationships between couples who are married or unmarried, gay or straight.

This section is not designed to be a comprehensive discussion of such a complex issue; rather, it is aimed at dispelling some of the myths and challenging some of the prejudices that lead to homophobia. You may be struggling over making a decision to declare your gay inclinations to others (or to acknowledge and accept them in yourself). You may be affected by the prejudices of others, and you may be trying to clarify your values and decide how you want to behave. We hope that this discussion will assist you in thinking about your views, assumptions, values, and possible prejudices pertaining to this subject.

PSYCHOLOGICAL VIEWS OF HOMOSEXUALITY

There is controversy over the causes of homosexuality. Some experts argue that one's sexual preference is at least partly a function of genetic or physiological factors, and others contend that homosexuality is entirely a learned behavior. Some maintain that there is both an internal predisposition and an environmental dimension to the shaping of one's sexual orientation. And there are those who assert that sexual identity is strictly a matter of choice at some point in one's life. Many gay individuals think that they did not actively choose their sexual orientation, any more than they did their sex. Where they see choice entering the picture is in deciding how they will act on their inclinations. Some will see that they have a choice of keeping their lifestyle a secret or "coming out" and claiming their sexual orientation and affectional preference.

The American Psychiatric Association in 1973 and the American Psychological Association in 1975 stopped calling homosexuality a form of mental illness, endeding a long and bitter dispute. Along with these changes came the challenge to the mental health professions to modify their thinking and practice to reflect a view of homosexuality as an alternative lifestyle. Homosexuality can be regarded as another style of expressing sexuality; this style can be healthy or unhealthy, depending on the person and the social and psychological dynamics. Sociologists hold that the fact that homosexuality is minority behavior is not a sufficient reason for denying it acceptance. In the helping professions, there has been a trend toward treating the *problems* encountered by lesbians and gay men, rather than treating the condition of their sexual orientation (Fassinger, 1991).

Still, in the training workshops that we offer for counselors and other mental health professionals, we are surprised at the number of heterosexual counselors who see their proper role as actively trying to convert gay couples or gay individuals to a heterosexual lifestyle, even if these clients do not have a problem with their sexual orientation. As an example of this attitude, a professor of psychology wrote a letter in response to our discussion of homosexuality in an earlier edition of this book and made the following comment: "I believe that heterosexuality is the only normal sexual orientation. Helping people is possible by educating and teaching them to be normal. The mainstream of most cultures considers homosexuality a deviation. Some believe that most homosexuals were forced to be, because they learned homosexuality at an age when they weren't mature."

Many gay people are not interested in changing their lifestyle but seek counseling for many of the same reasons as do nongay people. In our consulting with counselors we make our views quite clear. We see the counselor's job as helping clients clarify their own values and decide for themselves the course of action to take. We strongly oppose the notion that it is the role of counselors to impose their values on their clients, to tell others how to live, or to make their decisions for them. We believe that it is unethical for counselors who are opposed to homosexuality on moral grounds to work with gay clients if they are unable to retain the objectivity necessary to effectively help them. The ethical course would be to acknowledge their bias and provide referrals to other professionals who are in a position to work with them objectively. If the lifestyle choice of individuals is not causing harm to themselves or others, we maintain that it is not the counselor's job to persuade these individuals to change.

PREJUDICE AND DISCRIMINATION AGAINST LESBIANS AND GAY MEN

In the past many people felt ashamed and abnormal because of their homosexual orientation. Heterosexuals frequently categorized them as deviants and as sick or immoral. For these and other reasons many gay and lesbian individuals were forced to conceal their preferences, perhaps even to themselves. Today, the gay liberation movement is actively challenging the stigma attached to this alternative lifestyle, and those who choose it are increasingly asserting their right to live as they choose, without discrimination. However, just as gay people have won some of their rights and are more willing to disclose their lifestyles, the AIDS crisis has again created animosity, fear, and antipathy toward the homosexual population. Much of the public continues to cling to stereotypes, prejudices, and misconceptions regarding homosexual behavior.

Like any minority group, lesbians and gay men are subjected to discrimination. This discrimination manifests itself when gay people seek employment or a place of residence. For instance, the Department of Defense does not allow openly homosexual individuals in the military. A special issue that lesbians and gay men often bring to counseling is the struggle between concealing their identity versus "coming out." Dealing with other family members is of special importance to gay couples. They may want to be honest with their parents, yet they may fear hurting their parents or receiving negative reactions from them.

In a study designed to examine common psychosocial assumptions pertaining to lesbian mothers, Falk (1989) found that discrimination has persisted in court decisions denying lesbian mothers' petitions for custody of their children. The courts often assume that lesbians are emotionally unstable or unable to perform a maternal role. They also assume that children with lesbian mothers are more likely to be emotionally harmed, that they will be subject to molestation, that their role development will be negatively affected, or that they will themselves become homosexual. Falk came to the conclusion that research has yet to identify significant differences between lesbian mothers and their heterosexual counterparts or the children raised by these groups. Researchers have not been able to establish scientifically that children suffer detrimental results from being raised by lesbian mothers.

HELPING GAY PEOPLE

In their book *Counseling with Gay Men and Woman*, Woodman and Lenna (1980) define the gay liberation movement as a demand for equal rights and equal protection under the law. These rights include the right to choose how to live creatively and socially. The liberation effort has two aims: (1) the recognition of homosexuality as not abnormal or aberrant and (2) the dismantling or restructuring of discriminatory social institutions. This movement has implications on both the individual and collective levels. As individuals, many gay people are no longer willing to remain passive when others define reality in ways that are contrary to their feelings and experiences. Collectively, gay people are banding together by forming organizations to fight institutionalized oppression.

At a recent American Psychological Association annual convention we attended several presentations related to the social and political dimensions of gay and lesbian lifestyles. One example of these programs was an invited symposium entitled "Beyond Stigma: Lesbian and Gay Policy Issues in the 1990s." A panel of five participants addressed concerns related to family life, school life, the struggles for civil rights, job discrimination, and the future of AIDS politics. This dynamic panel dealt with fundamental concerns related to gaining a voice in society. As the symposium presenters addressed some of the political challenges facing gay and lesbian people in the 1990s, it was clear that there is still a critical need for the general public to become educated about gay and lesbian lifestyles.

In basic agreement with the perspective described by Woodman and Lenna is the concept of "homosexuality as beyond deviance" as advocated by Nass and his associates (1984). They write that homosexuals have organized to free themselves from the fears and stigmas of the past, mainly by trying to reeducate the public. According to them, these organized efforts have promoted greater acceptance of homosexual choices by some people, and many gays have been helped to develop a more positive self-image. A further problem consists in the labeling done by both heterosexuals and homosexuals. These authors contend that applying labels to people can restrict their possibilities in developing an identity. They suggest that the phrasing "He is now involved in a homosexual relationship" is preferable to "He is a homosexual." The former statement allows for the possibility that one's sexual orientation is a choice subject to change, rather than a permanent condition. Also, a person has many other dimensions besides sexual orientation, and the label of "gay" or "homosexual" can easily reduce a person's identity to a merely sexual one.

In his very informative book *The New Loving Someone Gay*, the gay psychologist Don Clark (1987) makes some generalizations about the problems facing homosexuals:

- Gay people have learned to feel different. Even though they may be outwardly successful, they often feel devalued.
- Gay people have learned to distrust their own feelings, for many of them have accepted the myth that they have "perverted" feelings.
- Being often "invisible" to others, gay people are subject to daily attacks on their character and ability; they experience antigay jokes and statements, as well as discrimination.
- They feel alone and wrong and fear further lack of support and affection if they reveal what they really think and feel; therefore, they often struggle over keeping their true identity a secret.
- They are likely to experience depression.
- Gay people are often tempted to numb the pain they experience by using drugs and alcohol or to end their pain through suicide.

Clark suggests the following guidelines for those who are interested in being helpful to gay people:

- Help cannot be forced but only offered. Gay people tend to be suspicious of an overture of help until they can sense its personal validity. They will not accept help until trust is established.
- The primary goal in helping gay people should be to encourage them to become more truly themselves through developing self-appreciation and integrity.
- Those who want to help gay people had better discover any homophobic or antigay feelings of their own and seek whatever help may be necessary to rid themselves of these feelings. Growing up in this culture entails some degree of homophobic feelings.
- It is important for you to admit to yourself and others any homosexual feelings of your own as well as your general feelings of attraction to people of the same gender.
- It is essential that you not inform on gay people by telling others what you know, especially their family. To divulge information is a breach of trust.

Clark contends that neglecting these ground rules retards, disrupts, or terminates the helping process with gay people. He also urges us to avoid prejudging gay and lesbian people and instead to accept them as individuals.

TINA AND APRIL: THE STRUGGLE TO BE TRUE TO ONESELF

Tina and April met when they were in their early 20s while attending a teacher credentialing program. Over the years they became close friends and spent more and more time together. Even though neither ever married, both had various relationships with men, for the most part not very satisfying. As their friendship deepened, their interest in male companionship diminished and, when it was there, it seemed to be more in response to a societal "should" than an inner need.

Their families and friends often manifested their concern and disapproval about the closeness of their relationship, which didn't appear "natural" or "normal" to them and which, they thought, might interfere with their "settling down with a good man" and starting a family. So the two women tried to keep their lifestyle a secret for fear of rejection.

At one point, Tina and April's relationship became a sexual one, a fact that brought out many of their self-doubts and vulnerabilities and the concern that, should they become separated, being sexually involved would make the parting even more difficult. Even though the sexual aspect didn't last long because of their concerns and doubts, their relationship continued. But the burden of pretending to be other than they were became increasingly heavy for both of them. They felt insincere and dishonest both toward each other and toward their families and friends, and they found the need to invent pat answers when others were asking them why they were still single almost unbearable. They both felt that, if they had been honest, they would have said instead, "I'm not interested at all in a traditional marriage. I have a significant other, and I wish I didn't have to hide this very important part of my life."

The situation was complicated by the fact that Tina lived in a small rural community near her extended family, which made it almost impossible to maintain a sense of privacy. Although April did not live near her family, she too felt that she couldn't openly acknowledge her relationship with Tina for fear of being rejected by her family, friends, and co-workers.

In her early 30s, April developed severe panic attacks that manifested themselves in acute anxiety over driving, being in a store, or even just going out of her house. She believed she was being watched, and she couldn't bear the thought of her parents' finding out about her relationship with Tina, because she was sure that they would interpret it as the result of their failure to raise her properly. Because of her anxiety attacks, April went into therapy, and soon afterwards her symptoms decreased greatly. She never felt a need to explore her preference for women, but she did spend a good deal of time on the conflict between her need to do what she thought was right for her and her need to give in to external pressures to be "normal."

The two women claim that neither of them knew that she was a lesbian. They were aware, however, of being somewhat "different" from other girls their age when they were going to school; they didn't have the same interest in boys as did most of their friends, and as they matured, they still felt more comfortable with women.

At the age of 40, April and Tina made the decision that they could no longer live with the duplicity and that something had to be done. Either they would go separate ways, or they would share a life and acknowledge their situation openly. They decided to do the latter. After years of struggling, they were finally able to face themselves, each other, and then the other significant people in their lives. Much to their surprise, when they did disclose the truth about their relationship, most of their relatives and friends were supportive and understanding, and some even told them that they knew of their "special" relationship. They felt that a great burden had been lifted from them and began to experience a new sense of peace and happiness. Today Tina and April are living together as a couple, trying to deal with the practical and financial aspects of their life together, but successful in their professions and well liked and respected by their colleagues and friends.

This case illustrates the struggle that many couples like Tina and April go through as they make the choice of how they will live. Many of the issues that concern Tina and April are the same interpersonal conflicts that any couple will eventually face and need to resolve. However, they must also deal with the pressure of being a part of a segment of society whose lifestyle some consider unacceptable. Thus, being involved in a gay or lesbian relationship is not simply a matter of sexual preference, because it involves a whole spectrum of interpersonal and practical issues. All the concerns about friendships, heterosexual relationships, and traditional marriage that we explore in this chapter apply to gay and lesbian relationships as well. Indeed, barriers to effective communication are found in every kind of intimate relationship. The challenge is to find ways of removing the blocks that obstruct communication and intimacy.

CONCLUDING COMMENTS

In categorizing relationships as heterosexual or homosexual, we sometimes forget that sex is not the only aspect of a relationship. Whatever choice we make, we need to examine the bases for it, whether it is the best choice for us, and whether it is compatible with our own values. People might choose or reject certain gender roles because of others' expectations, and in the same fashion people may reject a gay lifestyle merely because others condemn it or adopt it merely because they are unquestioningly following a liberation movement. What we think is important is that you define yourself, that you assume the responsibility and accept the consequences for your own choices, and that you live out your choices with peace and inner integrity.

Time Out for Personal Reflection

1. How do you generally cope with conflicts in your relationship? Check the items that most apply to you.

——————————   open dialogue
——————————   avoidance
——————————   fighting and arguing
——————————   compromising
——————————   getting involved with other people or in projects

    List other ways in which you deal with conflicts in your relationship:

    ———————————————————————————————————————

    ———————————————————————————————————————

    ———————————————————————————————————————

2. List some ways in which you've changed during the period of your relationship. How have your changes affected the relationship?

    ———————————————————————————————————————

    ———————————————————————————————————————

    ———————————————————————————————————————

3. To what extent do you have an identity apart from the relationship? How much do you need (and depend on) the other person? Imagine that he or she is no longer in your life, and write down how your life might be different.

    ———————————————————————————————————————

    ———————————————————————————————————————

    ———————————————————————————————————————

4. What are your reactions to people who have a homosexual lifestyle?

    ———————————————————————————————————————

    ———————————————————————————————————————

    ———————————————————————————————————————

5. How do you feel about homosexual experiences for yourself?

_____

_____

_____

6. What are your views concerning the gay liberation movement? Do you believe that the rights of homosexuals have been denied? Do you think that people who openly profess a gay lifestyle have rights equal to those of heterosexuals and should not be denied a specific job because of their sexual orientation alone?

_____

_____

_____

Separation and Divorce

This section largely pertains to the breakup of an intimate relationship. The principles that we discuss can certainly be applied to separations between people who are friends and also to unmarried people who are involved in an intimate relationship. The fear of being alone forever often keeps people from separating, even when they agree that there is little left in their relationship. People may say something like this: "I know what I have, and at least I have somebody. So maybe it's better to have that than nothing at all." Because of their fears, many remain stuck in stagnant relationships.

FREEING OURSELVES FROM DEADENING WAYS OF BEING TOGETHER

Another alternative to separating or stagnating is to remain in the relationship but challenge both yourself and your partner to create a different way of relating to each other. In speaking to a group of marriage and family therapists at a convention, Sidney Jourard (1975) developed the idea of having several different "marriages" with the same person. His key point was that people should develop new dimensions to intimate relationships. He described marriage as a dialogue that ends as soon as habitual ways of acting set in. He maintained that people are frequently not very creative when it comes to finding new ways of living with each other and that they tend to fall into the same ruts day after day, year after year. We can recognize that, at its best, marriage is a relationship that generates change through dialogue. Instead of

being threatened by change, we can welcome it as necessary for keeping the relationship alive.

Thus, an impasse can become a turning point that enables two people to create a new way of life together. If they both care enough about their investment in each other, and if they are committed to doing the work necessary to change old patterns and establish more productive ones, a crisis can actually save their relationship. People often terminate their relationships without really giving themselves or others a chance to face a particular crisis and work it through. For example, a man begins to see how deadening his marriage is for him and to realize how he has contributed to his own unhappiness in it. As a result of changes in his perceptions and attitudes, he decides that he no longer wants to live with a woman in this deadening fashion. However, rather than deciding to simply end the marriage, he might allow his partner to really see and experience him as the different person he is becoming. Moreover, he might encourage her to change as well, instead of giving up on her too quickly. His progress toward becoming a more integrated person might well inspire her to work actively toward her own internal changes. This kind of work on the part of both persons takes understanding and patience, but they may find that they can meet each other as new and changing persons and form a very different kind of relationship.

Sometimes, of course, ending a relationship is the wisest course. The ending of a relationship can then be an act of courage that makes a new beginning possible. Our concern is only that too many people may not be committed enough to each other to stay together in times of crisis and strug-gle. As a result, they may separate at the very time when they could be making a new start.

WHEN TO SEPARATE OR TERMINATE A RELATIONSHIP

How do two people know when a separation is the best solution? No categori-cal answer can be given to this question. However, before two people decide to terminate their relationship, they might consider at least the following questions:

• Has each of them sought personal therapy or counseling? Perhaps their exploration of themselves would lead to changes that allow them to renew or strengthen their relationship.

• Have they considered seeking relationship counseling? If they do get involved in relationship counseling of any type, is each doing so willingly, or is one of them merely going along to placate the other?

• Are both parties really interested in maintaining their relationship? Perhaps one or both are not interested in keeping the *old* relationship, but it is vital that they both at least want time together. We routinely ask both partners in a significant relationship who are experiencing difficulties to de-cide whether they even want to preserve their relationship. Some of the responses people give include "I don't really know. I've lost hope for any real change, and at this point I find it difficult to care whether we stay together or not." "I'm sure that I don't want to live with this person anymore; I just don't care enough to work on improving things between us. I'm here so that we can separate cleanly and finish the business between us." "Even though we're going through some turmoil right now, I would very much like to care enough to make things better. Frankly, I'm not too hopeful, but I'm willing to give it a try." Whatever their responses, it's imperative that they each know how they feel about the possibility of renewing their relationship.

• Have they each taken the time to be alone, to get themselves in focus, and to decide what kind of life they want for themselves and with others?

• If they are a couple, have they taken time to be with each other for even a weekend? We find that few couples arrange for time alone with each other. It's almost as if many couples fear discovering that they really have little to say to each other. This discovery in itself might be very useful, for at least they might be able to do something about the situation if they con-fronted it; but many couples seem to arrange their lives in such a way that they block any possibilities for intimacy. They eat dinner together with the television set blasting, or they spend all their time together taking care of their children, or they simply refuse to make time to be together.

• If they are married, what do they each expect from the divorce? Fre-quently, problems in a marriage are reflections of internal conflicts within the individuals in that marriage. In general, unless there are some changes within the individuals, the problems they experienced may not end with the divorce. In fact, many who do divorce with the expectation of finding increased joy and freedom discover instead that they are still miserable, lonely, depressed, and anxious. Lacking insight into themselves, they may soon find a new partner very much like the one they divorced and repeat the same dynamics. Thus, a woman who finally decides to leave a man she thinks of as weak and passive may find a similar man to live with again, unless she comes to understand why she needs or wants to align herself with this sort of person. Or a man who contends that he has "put up with" his wife for over twenty years may find a similar person unless he understands what motivated him to stay with his first wife for so long. It seems essential, therefore, that each come to know as clearly as possible why they are divorcing and that they look at the changes they may need to make in themselves as well as in their circumstances.

Sometimes one or both members of a couple identify strong reasons for separating but say that, for one reason or another, they are not free to do so. This kind of reasoning is always worth examining, however, since an attitude of "I couldn't possibly leave" will not help either partner make a free and sound choice. Some of the reasons people give for refusing to call an end to their relationship include the following:

• "I have an investment of fifteen years with this person, and to end our relationship now would mean that these fifteen years have been wasted." A person who feels this way might ask himself or herself: If I really don't see much potential for change, and if my partner has consistently and over a long period of time rebuffed any moves that might lead to improving our relationship, should I stay another fifteen years and have thirty years to regret?

• "I can't leave because of the kids, but I do plan on leaving as soon as they get into high school." Often this kind of thinking burdens children with unnecessary guilt. In a sense, it makes them responsible for the unhappiness of their parents. We would ask: Why place the burden on them if *you* stay in a place where you say you don't want to be? And will you find another reason to cement yourself to your partner once your children grow up?

• "Since the children need both a mother and a father, I cannot consider breaking up our marriage." True, children do need both a father and a mother. But it's worth asking whether they will get much of value from either parent if they see them despising each other. How useful is the model that parents present when they stay together and the children see how little joy they experience? Might they not get more from the two parents separately? Wouldn't the parents set a better and more honest example if they openly admitted that they no longer really chose to remain together?

• One man in a gay relationship may say, "I'm afraid to break off the relationship because I might find that I would be even more lonely than I am now." Certainly, loneliness is a real possibility. There are no guarantees that a new relationship will be established after their relationship is terminated. He might be reluctant to leave the relationship because his parents warned him of the problems he was getting into when he decided on an arrangement of living together. However, he might be more lonely living with someone he doesn't like, must less love, than he would be if he were living alone. Living alone might bring far more serenity and inner strength than remaining in a relationship that is no longer right for him. If he refuses to get out of a relationship because of what his parents might say about his original choice, he is almost certain to experience more alienation that he already does.

- "One thing that holds me back from separating is that I might discover that I left too soon and that I didn't give us a fair chance." To avoid this regret, partners should explore all the possibilities for creating a new relationship *before* making the decision to dissolve their relationship. There does come a point, however, at which a person must finally take a stand and decide, and then we see it as fruitless to brood continually over whether he or she did the right thing.

In summary, we limit our options unnecessarily whenever we tell ourselves that we *can't possibly* take a certain course of action. Before deciding to terminate a relationship, we can ask whether we've really given the other person (and ourselves) a chance to establish something new. By the same token, if we decide that we want to end the relationship but can't, it's worth asking whether we're not simply evading the responsibility for creating our own happiness. Neither keeping a relationship alive and growing nor ending one that no longer is right for us is easy, and it's tempting to find ways of putting the responsibility for our decisions on our children, our mate, or circumstances. We take a real step toward genuine freedom when we fully accept that whatever we decide, the choice is ours to make.

REACTIONS TO ENDING A LONG-TERM RELATIONSHIP

When people do break off a long-term relationship, there is a mixture of feelings, ranging from a sense of loss and regret to relief. Take the example of Betty, an unmarried college student in her mid-20s. She is going through some typical reactions to the breakup of a three-year relationship with her boyfriend. At first, she felt abandoned and was afraid of never finding a suitable replacement. She found herself ruminating over who was at fault. She switched back and forth between blaming herself and blaming him. She felt severe depression, which affected her eating and her sleeping patterns. Then she began to withdraw from other relationships. She told herself that she was not enough as a person, which led to feelings of worthlessness and inadequacy. She went from the extreme of shying away from other relationships, so that she would not get hurt again, to the other extreme of wanting too many new relationships, to take away the hurt. Her feelings and behavior were largely the product of irrational beliefs that she continued to tell herself, such as "This relationship didn't work out, and it proves that I'm a failure and unlovable and that I won't be able to establish and keep any further relationships." "Because things didn't work out between Isaac and me, this is a sure sign that I'll never get along with any man." "If Isaac found me undesirable, it must prove that I'm the kind of person he said I was." "I don't think I can stand the pain of his rejection." It was internal dialogue such as this that kept Betty miserable and kept her from taking any action that could change her situation. The point is that it was not the breakup with Isaac itself that was causing Betty's reactions; rather, her beliefs about and her interpretations of the breakup were giving her trouble.

There are no easy tips for dealing with the end of a long-standing relationship. Each person needs to find a way of doing so that works for him or her. Some people have told us that they found solace in Colgrove and her colleagues' (1976) book *How to Survive the Loss of a Love*.

Time Out for Personal Reflection

Complete the following sentences by writing down the first responses that come to mind. Suggestion: Ask your partner or a close friend to do the exercise on a separate sheet of paper; then compare and discuss your responses.

1. To me, intimacy means _____

   _____

2. The most important thing in making an intimate relationship successful is _____

   _____

3. The thing I most fear about an intimate relationship is _____

   _____

4. When an intimate relationship becomes stale, I usually _____

   _____

5. One of the reasons I need another person is _____

   _____

6. One conflict that I have concerning intimate relationships is

   _____

7. In an intimate relationship, it's unrealistic to expect that _____

_____

8. To me, commitment means _____

_____

9. I have encouraged my partner to grow by _____

_____

10. My partner has encouraged me to grow by _____

_____

On Choosing the Single Life

There are many reasons for remaining single (for a time or throughout your life). A few of these are the desire for personal autonomy, the failure to find a suitable mate, a distrust of marriage perhaps based on the failure of one's parents' marriage, and incompatibility between marriage and a career. Being single is now a more accepted status than it was in the past, and there is a greater recognition of the idea that some people choose to remain unmarried. Being single does not mean that one is deficient in social skills. Attitudes toward never-married people are becoming more positive, and such people are not necessarily seen as losers.

Americans are staying single longer and getting married later than ever before (Carr, 1988). The percentage of single women and men in this country has risen sharply and continues to rise. As far as women are concerned, some of them do not see marriage as a requirement for parenthood or for emotional, social, and economic support. It is clear that more women today are resisting societal pressure to get married and have a family, and more women are waiting until later in life to get involved in a committed relationship. There are intrinsic values and limitations in both a marriage and a single life. What is critical is that we weigh the pros and cons of each and freely make the choice of how we want to live, rather than merely giving in to the pressure to do what we think we "should" do.

DIFFICULTIES IN BEING SINGLE

The following case typifies the problems and challenges that many young women face if they choose a single lifestyle. June likes the advantages of being single, yet she struggles with nagging doubts over whether she is missing more by not getting married, particularly when she has someone in mind whom she is fond of.

June has a successful teaching career at age 27. She earns a good salary, is living in her own house, is free to pursue additional education, and enjoys the freedom of traveling in many countries of the world. She has nobody to answer to in terms of considering changing her career. She says that her many male and female friends provide nourishment to her. She also enjoys many sports and other leisure activities. She feels a sense of accomplishment and independence, something that perhaps not many people her age do.

At times June struggles with the internal pressure of fearing that she will never get married. She also feels external pressure from the man she is now having a close relationship with. But she is also very afraid to give in to his urgings to get married. While she enjoys the intimacy with him, she does not feel ready to commit herself to marriage. Though she does tell herself that she really *should* be ready at her age to take this step, she realizes that the price of getting married would be giving up much of what she values in her single lifestyle.

June judges herself as being too selfish to make compromises and consider her friend's needs and demands. She tells herself at times that perhaps she should be willing to give up more of what she wants so that she could share a life with him. She wonders about her chances for ever marrying if she fails to take this opportunity. Her family is also applying pressure on her to marry and not spoil a good relationship. At this time June is still searching within herself for her answer. Does she really want to get married? Who is telling her that she should get married? Does she equate being single with a lonely life? And does she want to get married because she is afraid of being seen as a spinster?

REWARDS OF THE SINGLE LIFE

On a television program, about twenty single people from various states were interviewed about four main topics: being single by choice, finding oneself suddenly single, the sexual revolution, and longtime single persons who had recently married. Most of those interviewed reported advantages to being single, such as personal freedom, not being responsible for anyone but themselves, and not having to consider how their actions affected others. It was interesting to note, however, that those who said they were single by choice were missing "that one special person," or best friend, whom they could confide in about anything. They noted that they did not like casual relationships as a steady diet. Some of the women mentioned the pressure of time if they wanted to have children.

Those who found themselves suddenly single, either through divorce or death, experienced rejection as a key theme in their life. Although they felt pain over their loss and resented the absence of the security they had had in the relationship, this experience proved to be a catalyst for their growth. Some said: "I have been able to do things alone that I never thought possible." "I can meet many of my needs through a support system." "I have been more independent than I ever dreamed of."

In terms of sex and the single life, many acknowledged that sex was readily available with many partners. Yet most of them did not find that casual sexual relationships were satisfying to them for very long. What was most valued was an emotional relationship as an important adjunct to a sexual relationship.

Among those who had been single for a long time and had recently married, there was agreement that they had enjoyed their single lifestyle and also enjoyed being involved in a primary relationship. None of them remarked that they had married because of societal pressures, nor did any of them claim to have felt odd because of their singlehood. "I was single, not waiting to be married yet open to getting married," one woman said.

Chapter Summary

In this chapter we've encouraged you to think about what characterizes a growing, meaningful relationship and to ask yourself such questions as: Do I have what I want in my various relationships? Do I desire more (or less) intimacy? What changes would I most like to make in my intimate relationships? In each of my relationships, can both the other person and I maintain our separate identities and at the same time develop a strong bond that enhances us as individuals?

The themes explored in this chapter can be applied to all intimate relationships, regardless of one's sexual orientation. Although there is controversy over the cause of homosexuality, it is still a lifestyle of many people. Rather than judging lesbians and gay men because of their sexual orientation, it is helpful to focus on understanding their concerns and struggles that we all share as persons.

A major barrier to developing and maintaining relationships is our tendency to evaluate and judge others. By attempting to change others we typically increase their defensiveness. A key characteristic of a meaningful relationship is the ability of the people involved to listen and to respond to each other. They are able to communicate effectively, and they are committed to staying in the relationship even when communication appears to have broken down. It is important to pay attention to both cultural and gender differences that make up our conversational style. Many misunderstandings are due to different ways that women and men express their thoughts and feelings.

We need to realize that maintaining a relationship entails dedication and hard work. Although there are many sources of conflict in intimate relationships, a major problem is a sense of predictability that comes with knowing another person well. It takes both imagination and effort to think of ways to revise our relationships so that they remain alive. At times people decide that a relationship is "dead," and they give serious consideration to separating. Although this may be a solution for some situations, a relationship that has lost life can also be reinvented. Again, commitment is essential, because time will be required to resolve certain issues that are divisive and that cause conflict.

People can still experience intimacy with others even though they choose the single lifestyle. Today there is a greater acceptance of being single, and this way of living does not have to be thought of as "second best." Although there are difficulties in being single, there are also some distinct advantages and rewards to this lifestyle.

The ideal picture we've drawn of a growing relationship is not a dogmatic or necessarily complete one; nor will your relationships, however good they are, always approximate it. Our hope is that these reflections will stimulate your own independent thinking. You can begin by honestly assessing the present state of your intimate relationships and recognizing how they really are (as opposed to how you wish they were). Then you can begin to consider the choices that can lead to positive change in those areas over which you are dissatisfied. Throughout this chapter we've emphasized that we must actively work on recognizing problems in ourselves and in our relationships if we are to make intimacy as rewarding as it can be. Finally, we've stressed that you can choose the quality of relationships that you want in your life.

Activities and Exercises

Some of the following activities are appropriate for you to do on your own; others are designed for two persons in an intimate relationship to do together. Select the ones that have the most meaning for you, and consider sharing the results with the other members of your class.

1. In your journal write down some reflections on your parents' relationship. Consider such questions as the following:

   • Would you like the same kind of relationship your parents have had? What are some of the things you like best about their relationship? What are some features of their relationship that you would not want in your own relationships?
   • How have your own views, attitudes, and practices regarding intimacy been affected by your parents' relationship?

2. How much self-disclosure, honesty, and openness do you want in your intimate relationships? Reflect in your journal on how much you would share your feelings concerning each of the following with your partner. The discuss how you would like your partner to respond to this same question.

   • your sexual fantasies about another person
   • your secrets
   • your need for support from your partner
   • your angry feelings
   • your dreams
   • your friendships with persons of the opposite sex
   • your ideas on religion and your philosophy of life
   • the times when you feel inadequate as a person
   • the times when you feel extremely close and loving toward your partner
   • the times in your relationship when you feel boredom, staleness, hostility, or detachment

   After you've answered this question for yourself, think about how open you want *your partner* to be with *you*. If your partner were doing this exercise, what answers do you wish he or she would give for each of the preceding items?

3. Over a period of about a week, do some writing about the evolution of your relationship, and ask your partner to do the same. Consider issues such as: Why were we initially attracted to each other? How have we changed since we first met? Do I like these changes? What would I most like to change about our life together? What are the best things we have going for us? What are some problem areas we need to explore? If I could do it over again, would I select the same person? What's the future of our life together? What would I like to see us doing differently? After you've each written about these and any other questions that are significant for you, read each other's work and discuss where you want to go from here. This activity can stimulate you to talk more openly with each other and can also give each of you the chance to see how the other perceives the quality of your relationship.

4. As you look at various television shows, keep a record of the messages you get regarding marriage, family life, and intimacy. What are some common stereotypes? What sex roles are portrayed? What myths do you think are being presented? After you've kept a record for a couple of weeks or so, write down some of the attitudes that you think you have incorporated from television and other media about marriage, family life, and intimacy.

5. Select one or more of the following books for further reading on the topics explored in this chapter: Clark, *The New Loving Someone Gay* (1987);

Dworkin and Gutierrez, *Counseling Gay Men and Lesbians: Journey to the End of the Rainbow* (1992); Lerner, *The Dance of Anger* (1985); Napier, *The Fragile Bond: In Search of an Equal, Intimate, and Enduring Marriage* (1990); and Tannen, *That's Not What I Meant: How Conversational Style Makes or Breaks Relationships* (1987) and *You Just Don't Understand: Women and Men in Conversation* (1991).

CHAPTER TEN
Loneliness and Solitude

Prechapter Self-Inventory

Use the following scale to respond: 4 = this statement is true of me *most* of the time; 3 = this statement is true of me *much* of the time; 2 = this statement is true of me *some* of the time; 1 = this statement is true of me *almost none* of the time.

_____ 1. I stay in unsatisfactory relationships just to avoid being lonely.
_____ 2. Knowing that I am ultimately on my own in the world scares me.
_____ 3. I don't know what to do with my time when I'm alone.
_____ 4. Sometimes when I'm with people I feel lonely and shut out.
_____ 5. I can't escape loneliness completely.
_____ 6. I know the difference between being lonely and being alone.
_____ 7. My childhood was a lonely period in my life.
_____ 8. My adolescent years were lonely ones for me.
_____ 9. Loneliness is a problem for me in my life now.
_____ 10. I generally arrange for time alone so that I can reflect on the way my life is going.

Introduction

A premise of existentialism is that we are ultimately alone. Although the presence of others can surely enhance our life, no one else can completely become us or share our unique world of feelings, thoughts, hopes, and memories. In addition, none of us knows when our loved ones may leave us or die, when we will no longer be able to involve ourselves in a cherished activity, or when the forest we love will be burned or cut down. We come into the world alone, and we will be alone again when the time comes to leave it.

In the last chapter our focus was on intimacy and interpersonal relationships. We now turn to the experience of loneliness and the creative use of solitude. Being with others and being with ourselves are best understood as two sides of the same coin. If we do not like our own company, why should others want to be with us? If we have a good relationship with ourselves and enjoy our solitude, we have a far greater chance of creating solid, give-and-take relationships with others.

We invite you to think of being alone as a natural — and potentially valuable — part of human experience. It is important to distinguish between being alone and being lonely. Casey and Vanceburg (1985) write about being alone, but not lonely, as we search for understanding, serenity, and certainty about the path of life we are traveling. All of us are ultimately alone in the world, but appreciating that aloneness can actually enrich our experience of life. Moreover, we can use times of solitude to look within ourselves, renew our sense of ourselves as the center of choice and direction in our life, and learn to trust our inner resources instead of allowing circumstances or the expectations of others to determine the path we travel. If we fundamentally accept our aloneness and recognize that no one can take away *all* our loneliness, we can deal more effectively with our experiences of loneliness and give ourselves to our projects and relationships out of our freedom instead of running to them out of our fear.

The Value of Loneliness and Solitude

Loneliness and solitude are different experiences, each of which has its own potential value. Loneliness generally results from certain events in our life — the death of someone we love, the decision of another person to leave us for someone else, a move to a new city, a long stay in a hospital. Loneliness can occur when we feel set apart in some way from everyone around us. And sometimes feelings of loneliness are simply an indication of the extent to which we've failed to listen to ourselves and our own feelings. However it occurs, loneliness is generally something that happens to us, rather than something we choose to experience; but we *can* choose the attitude we take toward it. If we allow ourselves to experience our loneliness, even if it is painful, we may be surprised to find within ourselves the sources of strength and creativity.

Unlike loneliness, solitude is something that we often choose for ourselves. In solitude, we make the time to be with ourselves, to discover who we are, and to renew ourselves. Casey and Vanceburg (1985) reveal that solitude is a pathway to self-knowledge:

> It's in our solitude that we come to know ourselves, to appreciate the many nuances that distinguish us from others. It's in the stillness that we detect our soul's inclinations. The privacy of silence offers us the answers we need. The distractions that stood in our way no longer fetter us when we've invited solitude to be our guest. (Meditation of January 10)

In her beautiful and poetic book *Gift from the Sea*, Anne Morrow Lindbergh (1955/1975) describes her own need to get away by herself in order to find her center, simplify her life, and nourish herself so that she can give to others again. She relates how her busy life, with its many and conflicting demands, fragmented her, so that she felt "the spring is dry, and the well is empty" (p. 47).* Through solitude, she found replenishment and became reacquainted with herself:

---

*This and all other quotations from this source from *Gift from the Sea*, by A. M. Lindbergh. Copyright 1955 by Pantheon Books, a division of Random House, Inc.

When one is a stranger to oneself, then one is estranged from others too. If one is out of touch with oneself, then one cannot touch others. . . . Only when one is connected to one's own core is one connected to others. . . . For me, the core, the inner spring, can best be refound through solitude. (pp. 43–44)

If we don't take time for ourselves but instead fill our life with activities and projects, we run the risk of losing a sense of centeredness. As Lindbergh puts it, "Instead of stilling the center, the axis of the wheel, we add more centrifugal activities to our lives — which tend to throw us off balance" (p. 51). Her own solitude taught her that she must remind herself to be alone each day, even for a few minutes, in order to keep a sense of herself that would then enable her to give of herself to others. She expressed this thought in words addressed to a seashell she took with her from an island where she had spent some time alone:

You will remind me that I must try to be alone for part of each year, even a week or a few days; and for part of each day, even for an hour or for a few minutes, in order to keep my core, my center, my island-quality. You will remind me that unless I keep the island-quality intact somewhere within me, I will have little to give my husband, my children, my friends or the world at large. (p. 57)

In much the same way as Lindbergh describes solitude as a way of discovering her core and putting her life in perspective, Clark Moustakas (1977) relates that a critical turning point in his life occurred when he discovered that loneliness could be the basis for a creative experience. He came to see that his personal growth and changed relationship with others were related to his feelings of loneliness. Accepting himself as a lonely person gave him the courage to face aspects of himself that he had never dared to face before and taught him the value of listening to his inner self. For him, solitude became an antidote to loneliness. He writes: "In times of loneliness, my way back to life with others required that I stop listening to others, that I cut myself off from others and deliberately go off alone, to a place of isolation" (p. 109). In doing so, Moustakas became aware of how he had forsaken himself and of the importance of returning to himself. This process of finding himself led him to find new ways of relating to others: "In solitude, silent awareness and self-dialogues often quickly restored me to myself, and I was filled with new energy and the desire to renew my life with others in real ways" (p. 109).

Solitude can thus provide us with the opportunity to sort out our life and gain a sense of perspective. It can give us time to ask significant questions, such as: How much have I become a stranger to myself? Have I been listening to myself, or have I been distracted and overstimulated by a busy life? Am I aware of my sense experiences, or have I been too involved in doing things to be aware of them?

Quiet time that allows for personal reflection is seen as a blessing by some and a curse by others. According to Travis and Ryan (1988), for those who want to escape from their loneliness, silence is threatening, because it forces them to reflect and touch deep parts of themselves. But silence also has a value: "Learning to be comfortable with silence is learning to be comfortable alone with yourself. It is one of the healthiest habits one can cultivate. Religious teachers speak of the necessity of silence for encountering the voice of God. In the silence of the mind, the heart speaks" (p. 61).

Many of us fail to experience solitude because we allow our life to become more and more frantic and complicated. Unless we make a conscious effort to be alone, we may find that days and weeks go by without our having the chance to be with ourselves. Moreover, we may fear that we will alienate others if we ask for private time, so we alienate ourselves instead. Perhaps we fear that others will think us odd if we express a need to be alone. Indeed, others may sometimes fail to understand our need for solitude and try to bring

us into the crowd or "cheer us up." People who are close to us may feel vaguely threatened, as if our need for time alone somehow reflected on our affection for them. Their own fears of being left alone may lead them to try to keep us from taking time away from them. It is not uncommon to feel uneasy about wanting and taking time alone for ourselves. We may feel a need to make up excuses if we want to decline an invitation to be with others so that we can have some time alone. Claiming what we need and want for ourselves can involve a certain risk; if we fail to take that risk, however, we give up the very thing solitude could provide — a sense of self-direction and being centered.

Most of us need to remind ourselves that we can tolerate only so much intensity with others and that ignoring our need for distance can breed resentment. For instance, a mother and father who are constantly with each other and with their children may not be doing a service either to their children or to themselves. Eventually they are likely to resent their "obligations." Unless they take time out, they may be there bodily and yet not be fully present to each other or to their children.

In summary, we hope that you will welcome time alone. Once you fully accept it, your aloneness can become the source of your strength and the foundation of your relatedness to others. Taking time to *be* alone gives us the opportunity to think, plan, imagine, and dream. It allows us to listen to ourselves and to become sensitive to what we are experiencing. In solitude we can come to appreciate anew both our separateness from and our relatedness to the important people and projects in our lives.

Learning to Confront the Fear of Loneliness

Many people fear being lonely. If we associate the lonely periods in our life with pain and struggle, we may think of loneliness only as a condition to be avoided as much as possible. Furthermore, we may identify being alone with being lonely and either actively avoid having time by ourselves or fill such time with distractions and diversions. We may associate being alone with rejection of self and being cut off from others. Paradoxically, out of fear of rejection and loneliness, we may even make ourselves needlessly lonely by refusing to reach out to others or by holding back parts of ourselves in our intimate relationships. On the other hand, because of our fear of loneliness, we sometimes deceive ourselves by convincing ourselves that we can overcome loneliness by anchoring our life to another's life. The search for relationships, especially ones in which we think we will be taken care of, is often motivated by the fear of being isolated.

Some of the ways in which we attempt to escape from facing and coping with loneliness are as follows:

- We busy ourselves in work and activities, so that we have little time to think or to reflect by ourselves.
- We schedule every moment and overstructure our life, so that we have no opportunity to think about ourselves and what we are doing with our life.
- We strive for perfect control of our environment so that we won't have to cope with the unexpected.
- We surround ourselves with people and become absorbed in social functions, in the hope that we won't have to feel alone.
- We try to numb ourselves with television, loud music, alcohol, or drugs.
- We immerse ourselves in helping others and in our "responsibilities."
- We eat compulsively, hoping that doing so will fill our inner emptiness and protect us from the pain of being lonely.
- We make ourselves slave to routine, become stuck in a narrow and predictable rut, becoming machines that don't feel much of anything.
- We go to bars and other centers of activity, trying to lose ourselves in a crowd. By escaping into crowds we are hoping to avoid coming to terms with deeper layers of our inner world.

Most of us lead a hectic life in a crowded, noisy environment. We are surrounded by entertainments and escapes, which makes it impossible to hear the voice within us. Paradoxically, in the midst of our congested cities and with all the activities available to us, we are often lonely because we are alienated from ourselves. The predicament of many people in our society is that of the alienated person described by the Josephsons in their book *Man Alone: Alienation in Modern Society* (1962): "The alienated man is everyman and no man, drifting in a world that has little meaning for him and over which he exercises no power, a stranger to himself and to others" (p. 11). Although this quote is thirty years old, it is still timely.

In her book *Crisis in Intimacy*, Carr (1988) develops the notion that the fear of separation often leads us to search for closeness with others. Thus, we may see the quest of intimacy as an antidote to the human condition of loneliness. Carr writes that the key struggle is keeping our separate identity yet at the same time fusing our life and identity with another. "Maintaining a separate identity in the context of an intimate relationship is the prevailing concern today — one to be wrestled with again and again" (p. 9).

Stella is a young woman who often fears separateness from others, even though she immerses herself in many relationships and activities. Outsiders tend to envy her "fun-filled" life and often wish they were in her place. In a moment of candor, however, she will admit that she feels her life to be empty and that she is in a desperate search for substance. She is petrified when she has to spend any time alone in her apartment. Stella schedules her life so that she spends as little time by herself as possible. She has a long list of phone numbers to call, just in case her panic overwhelms her. Her stereo or television is typically blaring so that she is unable to pay attention to any resources within herself. It is her mistaken belief that being alone implies that people don't want to be with her that drives her to seek reassurance from others. Stella wants so much to fill the inner void with confirmation by others. Because she feels shaky about her own worth, she looks outside of herself for security yet never finds it. In her therapy she is learning to stay with being uncomfortable with herself long enough to meet those facets of herself that she fears. Only with the courage to plunge into what she fears is the abyss within herself can she find new resources.

In some ways Stella illustrates the quiet desperation that is captured in Edward Arlington Robinson's poem "Richard Cory" (1897):

> Whenever Richard Cory went down town,
> We people on the pavement looked at him:
> He was a gentleman from sole to crown,
> Clean favored, and imperially slim.
> And he was always human when he talked;
> But still he fluttered pulses when he said,
> "Good morning," and he glittered when he walked.
> And he was rich — yes, richer than a king —

And admirably schooled in every grace:
In fine, we thought that he was everything
To make us wish that we were in his place.
So on we worked and waited for the light,
And went without the meat, and cursed the bread;
And Richard Cory, one calm summer night,
Went home and put a bullet through his head.

There is a loneliness in living in ways that belie the way we present ourselves to the world, as the cases of Stella and Richard Cory demonstrate. Pretending to others to be what we are not, as well as anchoring our life to others as a way of avoiding facing ourselves, results in our losing a sense of selfhood and feeling alienated.

If we want to get back into contact with ourselves, we can begin by looking at the ways in which we have learned to escape being lonely. We can examine the values of our society and question whether they are contributing to our estrangement from ourselves and to our sense of isolation. We can ask whether the activities that fill our time actually satisfy us or whether they leave us hungry and discontented. To truly confront loneliness, ironically, we may have to spend more time alone, strengthening our awareness of ourselves as the true center of meaning and direction in our life.

Creating Our Own Loneliness through Shyness

Shyness is both a personality trait and a lifestyle that can lead to loneliness. Shy people tend to be easily frightened, timid, inhibited, uncomfortable in social situations, and relatively unassertive. Some specific characteristics that identify shy individuals are timidity in expressing themselves; being overly sensitive to how others are perceiving and reacting to them; getting embarrassed easily; and experiencing bodily symptoms such as blushing, upset stomach, anxiety, and racing pulse (Weiten, Lloyd, & Lashley, 1991).

Shyness has become a popular topic in both the media and the field of psychology. For example, Phil Zimbardo, founder of the shyness clinic at Stanford University, made an appearance on the "20/20" television program. According to Zimbardo (1987), shyness is an almost universal experience. Eighty percent of those questioned reported that they had been shy at some point in their lives. Of those, more than 40 percent considered themselves shy at that time. This means that four out of every ten people you meet, or 84 million Americans, are shy. Shyness exists on a continuum. That is, some people see themselves as *chronically* shy, whereas others are shy with certain people or in certain situations.

Shyness often leads directly to feelings of loneliness. Zimbardo believes that shyness can be a social and a psychological handicap as crippling as many physical handicaps. He lists the following as some of the consequences of shyness.

- It prevents people from expressing their views and speaking up for their rights.
- It makes it difficult to think clearly and to communicate effectively.
- It holds people back from meeting new people, making friends, and getting involved in many social activities.
- It often results in feelings such as depression, anxiety, and loneliness.

You may be aware that shyness is a problem for you and that you are creating your own loneliness, at least in part. You may well be asking What can I do about it? For one thing, being shy is not necessarily only negative. We are not suggesting that you try to make yourself into an extroverted personality if this is not the person you are. You can, however, challenge those personal fears that keep you from expressing yourself the way you'd like to. It is likely that one reason for your shyness is not having the interpersonal skills that make it possible to express your feelings and thoughts. You can put yourself in situations where you will be forced to make contact with people and to engage in social activities, even if you are intimidated.

It helps to understand the context of your shyness, especially to identify those social situations that bring out your shy behavior. Also, it is useful to pinpoint the reasons or combination of factors underlying your shyness. According to Zimbardo (1987), there are a constellation of factors explaining shyness, such as being overly sensitive to negative feedback from others; fearing rejection; lacking self-confidence and specific social skills; being frightened of intimacy; and personal handicap. A good way to identify those factors that contribute to your shyness is to keep track in your journal of those situations that elicit your shy behavior. It is also helpful to write down the symptoms you experience and what you actually do in such situations. Pay attention to what you tell yourself when you are in difficult situations. For example, your "self-talk" may be negative, actually setting you up to fail. You may say silently to yourself: "I'm ugly, so who would want anything to do with me?" "I'd better not try something new, because I might look like a fool." "I'm afraid of being rejected, so I won't even approach a person I'd like to get to know." "If people really knew what I was like, they wouldn't like what they saw." "Others are constantly evaluating and judging me, and I'm sure I won't measure up to what they expect." These are the very statements that are likely to keep you a prisoner of your shyness and prevent you from making contact with others. You can do a lot yourself to control how your shyness affects you by learning to challenge your self-defeating beliefs and by substituting constructive statements. Realize that learning new ways of thinking about yourself entails much work. It involves self-discipline in pushing yourself to test out your new beliefs by acting in new ways.

If shyness is a problem for you and if it is something that you'd like to change about yourself, we encourage you to monitor your thoughts, feelings, and actions to become more aware of the effects of shyness in your life. One way to understand your own shyness and learn some ways of dealing with it would be to read Zimbardo's excellent book *Shyness* (1987).

Time Out for Personal Reflection

1. Do you try to escape from your loneliness? In what ways? Check any of the following statements that you think apply to you.

_____   I bury myself in work.
_____   I constantly seek to be with others.
_____   I drink excessively or take drugs.
_____   I schedule every moment so that I'll have very little time to think about myself.
_____   I attempt to avoid my troubles by watching television or listening to music.
_____   I eat compulsively.
_____   I sleep excessively to avoid the stress in my life.
_____   I become overly concerned with helping others.
_____   I rarely think about anything if I can help it; I concentrate on playing and having fun.

List other specific ways in which you sometimes try to avoid loneliness:

_____

_____

_____

2. Would you like to change any of the patterns you've just identified? If so, what are they? What might you do to change them?

_____

_____

_____

3. Is shyness a problem for you? In what ways might you be creating your own loneliness through your shyness?

_____

_____

_____

4. Do you see time spent alone as being valuable to you? If so, in what ways?

_____

_____

_____

_____

5. Have you experienced periods of creative solitude? If so, what were some of the positive aspects of these experiences?

_____

_____

_____

_____

6. List a few of the major decisions you've made in your life. Did you make these decisions when you were alone or when you were with others?

_____

_____

_____

_____

A journal suggestion: If you find it difficult to be alone, without distractions, for more than a few minutes at a time, try being alone for a little longer than you're generally comfortable with. During this time you might simply let your thoughts wander freely, without hanging on to one line of thinking. In your journal describe what this experience is like for you.

_____

Loneliness and Our Life Stages

How we deal with feelings of loneliness can depend to a great extent on our experiences of loneliness in childhood and adolescence. Later in life we may feel that loneliness has no place or that we can and should be able to avoid it. It's important to reflect on our past experiences, because they are often the basis of our present feelings about loneliness. In addition, we may fear loneliness less if we recognize that it is a natural part of living in every stage of life. Once we have accepted our ultimate aloneness and the likelihood that we will feel lonely at many points in our life, we may be better able to take responsibility for our own loneliness and recognize ways in which we may be contributing to it.

LONELINESS AND CHILDHOOD

Reliving some of our childhood experiences of loneliness can help us come to grips with present fears about being alone or lonely. The following are some typical memories of lonely periods that people we've worked with in therapy have relived:

- A woman recalls the time her parents were fighting in the bedroom and she heard them screaming and yelling. She was sure that they would divorce, and in many ways she felt responsible. She remembers living in continual fear that she would be deserted.
- A man recalls attempting to give a speech in the sixth grade. He stuttered over certain words, and children in the class began to laugh at him. Afterward, he developed extreme self-consciousness in regard to his speech, and he long remembered the hurt he had experienced.
- An African-American man recalls how excluded he felt in his all-White elementary school and how the other children would talk about him in derisive ways. As an adult he can still cry over these memories.
- A woman recalls the fright she felt as a small child when her uncle made sexual advances toward her. Although she didn't really understand what was happening, she remembers the terrible loneliness of feeling that she couldn't tell her parents for fear of what they would do.
- A man recalls the boyhood loneliness of feeling that he was continually failing at everything he tried. To this day, he resists undertaking a task unless he is sure he can handle it, for fear of rekindling those old feelings of loneliness.
- A woman vividly remembers being in the hospital as a small child for an operation. She remembers the loneliness of not knowing what was going on or whether she would be able to leave the hospital. Since no one talked with her, she was all alone with her fears.

As we try to relive these experiences, we should remember that children do not live in a logical, well-ordered world. Our childhood fears may have been greatly exaggerated, and the feeling of fright may remain with us even though we may now think of it as irrational. Unfortunately, being told by adults that we were foolish for having such fears may only have increased our loneliness while doing nothing to lessen the fears themselves.

At this point you may wonder: Why go back and recall childhood pain and loneliness? Why not just let it be a thing of the past? It is important that we reexperience some of the pain we felt as children to see whether we are still carrying it around with us now. We can also look at some of the decisions we made during these times of extreme loneliness and ask whether these decisions are still appropriate.

Frequently, strategies we adopted as children remain with us into adulthood, when they are no longer appropriate. For instance, suppose that your family moved to a strange city when you were 7 years old and that you had to go to a new school. Kids at the new school laughed at you, and you lived through several months of anguish. You felt desperately alone in the world. During this time you decided to keep your feelings to yourself and build a wall around yourself so that others couldn't hurt you. Although this experience is now long past, you still defend yourself in the same way, because you haven't *really* made a new decision to open up and trust some people. In this way old fears of loneliness might contribute to a real loneliness in the present. If you allow yourself to experience your grief and work it through, emotionally as well as intellectually, you can overcome past pain and create new choices for yourself.

Time Out for Personal Reflection

Take some time to decide whether you're willing to recall and relive a childhood experience of loneliness. If so, try to recapture the experience in as much detail as you can, reliving it in fantasy. Then reflect on the experience, using the following questions as a starting point.

1. Describe in a few words the most intense experience of loneliness you recall having as a child.

   _____

   _____

   _____

   _____

2. How do you think the experience affected you then?

   _____

   _____

   _____

   _____

3. How do you think the experience may still be affecting you now?

   _____

   _____

   _____

   _____

Journal suggestions: Consider elaborating on this exercise in your journal. Here are a few questions you might reflect on: How did you cope with loneliness as a child? How has this influenced the way you deal with loneliness in your life now? If you could go back and put a new ending on your most intense childhood experience of loneliness, what would it be? You might also think about times in your childhood when you enjoyed being alone. Write some notes to yourself about what these experiences were like for you. Where did you like to spend time alone? What did you enjoy doing by yourself? What positive aspects of these times do you recall?

LONELINESS AND ADOLESCENCE

For many people loneliness and adolescence are practically synonymous. Adolescents often feel that they are all alone in their world, that they are the first ones to have had the feelings they do, and that they are separated from others by some abnormality. Bodily changes and impulses alone are sufficient to bring about a sense of perplexity and loneliness, but there are other stresses to be undergone as well. Adolescents are developing a sense of identity. They strive to be successful yet fear failure. They want to be accepted and liked, but they fear rejection, ridicule, or exclusion by their peers. Most adolescents know the feeling of being lonely in a crowd or among friends. They often have fears of being ostracized. Conformity can bring acceptance, and the price of nonconformity can be steep.

As you recall your adolescent years—and in particular the areas of your life that were marked by loneliness—you might reflect on the following questions:

- Did I feel included in a social group? Or did I sit on the sidelines, afraid of being included and wishing for it at the same time?
- Was there at least one person whom I felt I could talk to—one who really heard me, so that I didn't feel desperately alone?
- What experience stands out as one of the loneliest times during these years? How did I cope with my loneliness?
- Did I experience a sense of confusion concerning who I was and what I wanted to be as a person? How did I deal with my confusion? Who or what helped me during this time?
- How did I feel about my own worth and value? Did I believe that I had anything of value to offer anyone or that anyone would find me worth being with?
- How did my culture affect the way I viewed loneliness? Did I learn that loneliness is a natural condition? Or did I pick up the message that loneliness is a disease to cure?

As you reflect on your adolescence, add your own questions to the list we've suggested. Then try to discover some of the ways in which the person you now are is a result of your experiences of loneliness as an adolescent. Do you shrink from competition for fear of failure? In social situations are you afraid of being left out? Do you feel some of the isolation you did then? If so, how do you deal with it? How might you have changed the way you deal with loneliness?

Time Out for Personal Reflection

1. Describe the most intense experience of loneliness of your adolescent years.

   _____

   _____

   _____

   _____

2. How did you cope with the loneliness you've just described?

   _____

   _____

   _____

   _____

3. What effect do you think the experience you've described has on you today?

   _____

   _____

   _____

   _____

LONELINESS AND YOUNG ADULTHOOD

In our young-adult years we experiment with ways of being, and we establish lifestyles that may remain with us for many years. We may be struggling with the question of what to do with our life, what intimate relationships we want to establish, and how we will chart our future. Dealing with all the choices that face us at this time of life can be a lonely process.

How we come to terms with our own aloneness at this time can have significant effects on the choices we make — choices that, in turn, may deter-

mine the course of our life for years to come. For instance, if we haven't learned to listen to ourselves and to depend on our own inner resources, we might succumb to the pressure to choose a relationship or a career before we're really prepared to do so, or we might look to our projects or partners for the sense of identity that we ultimately can find only in ourselves. Alternatively, we may feel lonely and establish patterns that only increase our loneliness. This last possibility is well illustrated by the case of Saul.

Saul was in his early 20s when he attended college. He claimed that his chief problem was his isolation, yet he rarely reached out to others. His general manner seemed to say "Keep away." Although he was enrolled in a small, informal class in self-awareness and personal growth, he quickly left after each session, depriving himself of the chance to make contact with anyone.

One day, as I (Jerry) was walking across the campus, I saw Saul sitting alone in a secluded spot, while many students were congregated on the lawn, enjoying the beautiful spring weather. Here was a chance for him to do something about his separation from others; instead, he chose to seclude himself. He continually told himself that others didn't like him and, sadly, made his prophecy self-fulfilling by his own behavior. He made himself unapproachable and, in many ways, the kind of person people would avoid.

In this time of life we have the chance to decide on ways of being toward ourselves and others as well as on our vocation and future plans. If you feel lonely on the campus, we'd like to challenge you to ask yourself what *you* are doing and can do about your own loneliness. Do you decide in advance that the other students and instructors want to keep to themselves? Do you assume that there already are well-established cliques to which you cannot belong? Do you expect others to reach out to you, even though you don't initiate contacts yourself? What fears might be holding you back? Where do they seem to come from? Are past experiences of loneliness or rejection determining the choices you make now?

Often we create unnecessary loneliness for ourselves by our own behavior. If we sit back and wait for others to come to us, we give them the power to make us lonely. As we learn to take responsibility for ourselves in young adulthood, one area we can work on is taking responsibility for our own loneliness and creating new choices for ourselves.

LONELINESS AND MIDDLE AGE

Many changes occur during middle age that can result in new feelings of loneliness. Although we may not be free to choose some of the things that occur at this time in our life, we *are* free to choose how we relate to these events. Among some possible changes and crises of middle age are the following:

- Our significant other may grow tired of living with us and decide to leave. If this happens, we must decide how to respond. Will we blame ourselves and become absorbed in self-hate? Will we refuse to see any of our own responsibility for the breakup and simply blame the other person? Will we decide never to trust anyone again? Will we mourn our loss and, after a period of grieving, actively look for another person to live with?
- Our life may not turn out the way we had planned. We may not enjoy the success we had hoped for, we may feel disenchanted with our work, or we may feel that we passed up many fine opportunities earlier. But the key point is what we can do about our life *now*. What choices will we make in light of this reality? Will we slip into hopelessness and berate ourselves endlessly about what we could have done and should have done? Will we allow ourselves to stay trapped in meaningless work and empty relationships, or will we look for positive options for change?
- Our children may leave home, and with this change we may experience emptiness and a sense of loss. If so, what will we do about this transition? Will we attempt to hang on? Can we let go and create a new life with new meaning? When our children leave, will we lose our desire to live? Will we look back with regret at all that we could have done differently, or will we choose to look ahead to the kind of life we want to create for ourselves now that we don't have the responsibilities of parenthood?
- Up to this time in our life, we may have been absorbed in work and family responsibilities. We may have an overwhelming sense of regret over all the time we missed with friends and the time we did not have for recreation, and we may feel a strong desire to change our lives in the direction of integrating leisure time with work.

These are just a few of the changes that many of us confront during midlife. Although we may feel that events are not in our control, we can still choose the ways in which we respond to these life situations. To illustrate, we'd like to present a brief example that reflects the loneliness many people experience after a divorce and show how the two persons involved made different decisions about how to deal with their loneliness.

Amy and Gary had been married for over twenty years before their recent divorce, and they have three children in their teens. Amy is 43; Gary is 41. Although they have both experienced a good deal of loneliness since their divorce, they have chosen different attitudes toward their loneliness. For his part, Gary felt resentful at first and believed that somehow they could have stayed together if only Amy had changed her attitude. He lives alone in a small apartment and sees his teenagers on weekends. He interprets the divorce as a personal failure, and he still feels a mixture of guilt and resentment. He hates to come home to an empty apartment, with no one to talk to and no one to share his life with. In some ways he has decided not to cultivate other relationships, because he still bears the scars of his "first failure." He wonders whether women would find him interesting once they got to know him, and he fears that it's too late to begin a new life with someone else.

Gary declines most of his friends' invitations, interpreting their concern as pity. He says that at times he feels like climbing the walls, that he sometimes wakes up at night in a cold sweat and feels real pangs of abandonment and loneliness. He attempts to numb his feelings by burying himself in his work, but he cannot rid himself of the ache of loneliness. Gary seems to have decided on some level not to let go of his isolation. He has convinced himself that it isn't really possible for him to develop a new relationship. His own attitude limits his options, because he has set up a self-fulfilling prophecy: he convinces himself that another woman would not want to share time with him, and, as a consequence, others pick up the messages that he is sending out about himself.

For her part, Amy had many ambivalent feelings about divorcing. After the divorce she experienced panic and aloneness as she faced the prospect of rearing her children and managing the home on her own. She wondered whether she could meet her responsibilities and still have time for any social life for herself. She wondered whether men would be interested in her, particularly in light of the fact that she had three teenagers. She anguished over such questions as: Will I be able to have another life with someone else? Do I want to live alone? Can I take care of my emotional needs and still provide for the family? Unlike Gary, Amy decided to date several people — when she felt like it, and because she felt like it. At first she was pressured by her family to find a man and settle down. She decided, however, to resist this pressure, and she has chosen to remain single for the time being. She intends to develop a long-term relationship only if she feels it is what she wants after she has had time to live alone. Although she is lonely at times, she doesn't feel trapped and resists being a victim of her feelings.

Experiences like those of Gary and Amy are very common among middle-aged people. Many find themselves having to cope with feelings of isolation and abandonment after a divorce. Some, like Gary, may feel panic and either retreat from people or quickly run into a new relationship to avoid the pain of separation. If they don't confront their fears and their pain, they may be controlled by their fear of being left alone for the rest of their lives. Others, like Amy, may go through a similar period of loneliness after a divorce yet refuse to be controlled by a fear of living alone. Although they might want a long-term relationship again some day, they avoid rushing impulsively into a new relationship to avoid feelings of pain or loneliness.

LONELINESS AND THE LATER YEARS

Our society emphasizes productivity, youth, beauty, power, and vitality. As we age, we may lose some of our vitality and sense of power or attractiveness. Many people face a real crisis when they reach retirement, for they feel that they're being put out to pasture—that they aren't needed anymore and that their lives are really over. Loneliness and hopelessness are experienced by anyone who feels that there is little to look forward to or that he or she has no vital place in society, and such feelings are particularly common among older adults.

The loneliness of the later years can be accentuated by the losses that come with age. There can be some loss of sight, hearing, memory, and strength. Older people may lose their jobs, hobbies, friends, and loved ones. A particularly difficult loss is the death of a spouse with whom one has been close for many years. In the face of such losses a person may ultimately ask what reason remains for living. It may be no coincidence that many old people die soon after their spouses have died or shortly after their retirement.

In his thought-provoking book *Learn to Grow Old*, Paul Tournier (1972) writes that the way we live earlier in life determines the quality of our years during old age and retirement. For him, growing old and retiring does not mean being condemned to loneliness. He believes that we need to prepare ourselves in the present for a meaningful life of work and leisure in our later years.

The pangs of aloneness or the feelings that life is futile reflect a drastic loss of meaning rather than an essential part of growing old. Viktor Frankl (1969) has written about the "will to meaning" as a key determinant of a person's desire to live. He notes that many of the inmates in the Nazi concentration camp where he was imprisoned kept themselves alive by looking forward to the prospect of being released and reunited with their families. Many of those who lost hope simply gave up and died, regardless of their age.

At least until recently our society has compounded the elderly person's loss of meaning by grossly neglecting the aged population. The number of institutions and convalescent homes in which old people are often left to vegetate testifies to this neglect. It's hard to imagine a lonelier existence than the one many of these people are compelled to suffer. In contrast, there are those cultures that revere the elderly, and in these cases growing old is not a condemnation to isolation.

Sometimes, however, older people choose a lonely existence, rather than participating in the activities and human relationships that could be open to them. One of our daughters works as an activity director at an apartment complex for people over 65. There are opportunities for living a more vital life, yet the residents differ greatly in how much they take advantage of these opportunities. Cindy observes that there is a small core of people who are highly visible and willing to participate in the many recreational and educational activities available. She also notices that others need to be drawn out and encouraged to become involved, whereas still others never participate and keep themselves isolated. She has discovered that those people who are active and have family involvement inevitably tend to be happier and more outgoing than those without such social relationships.

Rudy is an example of an older man who feels basically lost and does not seem able to find a direction that brings him satisfaction. He is an 85-year-old man whose wife died fifteen years ago and who remained in his large house. He reports that he has real difficulty in being at home for any length of time. He leaves the house early in the morning in his pickup truck, in which he spends most of his day doing crossword puzzles, except for the time he spends walking a few miles. When he finally returns home late at night he faces the loneliness that he attempted to escape from early in the morning. He has few friends, dates women much younger than himself, and always worries that they are out to get his money. A solitary pleasure is his going to the races. Although he has occasional contact with extended family at holiday gatherings, he rarely initiates contact with them during the rest of the year. He shies away from people out of his fear of burdening them. What he fails to realize is how much he still has to offer and how much others could benefit from their association with him. His inability to recognize and appreciate what he could offer to others keeps him a prisoner of his loneliness.

Those who specialize in the study of aging often make the point that if we have led a rich life in early adulthood, we have a good chance of finding richness in our later years. Certainly, if we have learned to find direction from within ourselves, we will be better equipped to deal with the changes that aging brings. A few years ago we had the good fortune to meet an exceptional man, Dr. Ewald Schnitzer, who retired from the University of California at Los Angeles in 1973 and moved to Idyllwild, California, a place that he considers his last and happiest home. He provides an outstanding model of how to productively face old age.

Schnitzer lives alone by preference and continues to find excitement and meaning in art, philosophy, music, history, hiking, writing, and traveling. He believes that his entire life has prepared him well for his later years. He has learned to be content when he is alone, he finds pleasure in the company of people, animals, and nature, and he enjoys many memories of his rich experiences. He recently has assumed a grandfatherlike role with two children of a neighboring couple. He takes great pleasure in being part of these children's lives. He can live fully now, without dreading the future. This spirit of being fully alive is well expressed in his book *Looking In* (1977): "It would be painful should frailty prevent me from climbing mountains. Yet, when that time comes, I hope I find serenity in wandering through valleys, looking at the realm of distant summits not with ambition but with loving memories" (p. 88). At age 82 he is still hiking in the mountains, although his hikes are less strenuous than earlier.

Schnitzer exemplifies accepting the fact of aging yet recognizing that each stage of life brings its unique challenges and potentialities for creating a meaningful existence:

> I am writing this as I stand on the threshold of old age. Like everybody at this stage I have to face the fact of my bodily decline. I am saying this with a tinge of sadness but without a trace of despair. For it has always seemed to me that each age has its own possibilities and challenges, and I have often taken heart from this remark of Roger Fry's: "It is a wonderful thing to recognize the advanced age of a person less by the infirmity of his body than by the maturity of his soul." (p. 87)

We conclude this discussion of the later years—and, in a sense, this entire chapter on loneliness and solitude—by returning to the example of Anne Morrow Lindbergh. In her later years her lifelong courage in facing aloneness enabled her to find new and rich meaning in her life. We were extremely impressed with this woman when we first read her book *Gift from the Sea*, but our respect increased when we read the "Afterword" in the book's twentieth-anniversary edition (1975). There, she looks back at the time when she originally wrote the book and notes that she was then deeply involved in family life. Since that time her children have left and established their own lives. She describes how a most uncomfortable stage followed her middle years, one that she hadn't anticipated when she wrote the book. She writes that she went from the "oyster-bed" stage of taking care of a family to the "abandoned-shell" stage of later life. This is how she describes the essence of the "abandoned-shell" stage:

> Plenty of solitude, and a sudden panic at how to fill it, characterized this period. With me, it was not a question of simply filling up the space or the time. I had many activities and even a well-established vocation to pursue. But when a mother is left, the lone hub of a wheel, with no other lives revolving around her, she faces a total reorientation. It takes time to re-find the center of gravity. (p. 134)

In this stage she did make choices to come to terms with herself and create a new role for herself. She points out that all the exploration she did earlier in life paid off when she reached the "abandoned-shell" stage. Here again, earlier choices affect current ones.

Before her husband, Charles, died in 1974, Lindbergh had looked forward to retiring with him on the Hawaiian island of Maui. His death changed her life abruptly but did not bring it to an end. Its continuity was preserved in part by the presence of her five children and twelve grandchildren; moreover, she continued to involve herself in her own writing and in the preparation of her husband's papers for publication. Here is a fine example of a woman who has encountered her share of loneliness and learned to renew herself by actively choosing a positive stance toward life.

Time Out for Personal Reflection

Complete the following sentences by writing down the first response that comes to mind.

1. The loneliest time in my life was when _____

_____

2. I usually deal with my loneliness by _____

_____

3. I escape from loneliness by _____

_____

4. If I were to be left and abandoned by all those who love me,

_____

5. One value I see in experiencing loneliness is _____

_____

6. My greatest fear of loneliness is _____

_____

7. I have felt lonely in a crowd when _____

_____

8. When I'm with a person who is lonely, _____

_____

9. For me, being with others _____

_____

10. I feel loneliest when _____

_____

11. The thought of living alone the rest of my life _____

_____

Chapter Summary

We have a need to be with others that is best satisfied through many forms of intimate relationships. Yet another essential dimension of the human experience is to be able to function alone creatively. Unless we can enjoy our own company, we will have difficulty finding real joy in being with others. Being with others and being with ourselves are two sides of the same coin.

Some people fail to reach out to others and make significant contact because they are timid in social situations and are relatively unassertive. Many people report that they are troubled by shyness or have had problems with being shy in the past. Shyness can lead to feelings of loneliness, yet shy people can challenge the fears that keep them unassertive. Shyness is not a disorder that needs to be "cured," nor are all aspects of being shy negative. What is important is to recognize that certain attitudes and behaviors can create much of the loneliness we sometimes experience.

As you will recall from earlier chapters on the developmental stages, each period of life presents unique tasks to be mastered. Loneliness can be best understood from a developmental perspective. There are particular circumstances that often result in loneliness as we pass through childhood, adolescence, young adulthood, middle age, and the later years. Most of us have experienced loneliness during our childhood and adolescent years, and these experiences can have a significant influence on our present attitudes, behavior, and relationships. It helps to be able to recognize our feelings about events that are associated with each of these turning points.

Experiencing loneliness is part of being human, for ultimately we are alone. We can grow from such experiences if we understand them and use them to renew our sense of ourselves. Moreover, we don't have to remain victimized by early decisions that we made as a result of past loneliness. We do have choices. We can choose to face loneliness and deal with it creatively, or we can choose to try to escape from it. We have some choice concerning whether we will feel lonely or whether we will make connections with others. We can design our activities so that we reject others before they can reject us, or we can risk making contact with them.

Activities and Exercises

1. Allocate some time each day in which to be alone, and reflect on anything you wish. Note down in your journal the thoughts and feelings that occur to you during your time alone.
2. If you have feelings of loneliness when you think about a certain person who has been or is now significant to you, write a letter to that person expressing all the things you're feeling (you don't have to mail the letter). For instance, tell that person how you miss him or her or write about your sadness, your resentment, or your desire for more closeness.
3. Imagine that you are the person you've written your letter to, and write a reply to yourself. What do you imagine that person would say to you if he or she received your letter? What do you fear (and what do you wish) he or she would say?
4. If you sometimes feel lonely and left out, you might try some specific experiments for a week or so. For example, if you feel isolated in most of your classes, why not make it a point to get to class early and initiate contact with a fellow student? If you feel anxious about taking such a step, try doing it in fantasy. What are your fears? What is the worst thing you can imagine might happen? Record your impressions in your journal. If you decide to try reaching out to other people, record in your journal what the experience is like for you.
5. Recall some periods of loneliness in your life. Select important situations in which you experienced loneliness, and spend some time recalling the details of each situation and reflecting on the meaning each of these experiences has had for you. Now you might do two things:

      a. Write down your reflections in your journal. How do you think your past experiences of loneliness affect you now?

      b. Select a friend or a person you'd like to trust more, and share this experience of loneliness.

6. Many people rarely make time exclusively for themselves. If you'd like to have time to yourself but just haven't gotten around to arranging it, consider going to a place you haven't been to before or to the beach, desert, or mountains. Reserve a weekend just for yourself; if this seems too much, then spend a day completely alone. The important thing is to remove yourself from your everyday routine and just be with yourself without external distractions.

7. Try spending a day or part of a day in a place where you can observe and experience lonely people. You might spend time near a busy downtown intersection, in a park where old people congregate, or in a large shopping center. Try to pay attention to expressions of loneliness, alienation, and isolation. How do people seem to be dealing with their loneliness? Later, you might discuss your observations in class.

8. Imagine yourself living in a typical rest home — without any of your possessions, cut off from your family and friends, and unable to do the things you now do. Reflect on what this experience would be like for you; then write down some of your reactions in your journal.

9. Select one or more of the following books for further reading on the topics explored in this chapter. Lindbergh, *Gift from the Sea* (1975); Moustakas, *Loneliness* (1961).

Death

and

Loss

Prechapter Self-Inventory

Use the following scale to respond: 4 = this statement is true of me *most* of the time; 3 = this statement is true of me *much* of the time; 2 = this statement is true of me *some* of the time; 1 = this statement is true of me *almost none* of the time.

_____ 1. The fact that I must die makes me take the present moment seriously.

_____ 2. I don't like funerals, because they make me dwell on a painful subject.

_____ 3. If I had a terminal illness, I'd want to know how much time I had left to live, so I could decide how to spend it.

_____ 4. Because of the possibility of losing those I love, I don't allow myself to get too close to others.

_____ 5. If I live with dignity, I'll be able to die with dignity.

_____ 6. One of my greatest fears of death is the fear of the unknown.

_____ 7. I've had losses in my life that in some ways were like the experience of dying.

_____ 8. There are some ways in which I'm not really alive emotionally.

_____ 9. I'm not especially afraid of dying.

_____ 10. I fear the deaths of those I love more than I do my own.

Introduction

Your awareness of death enables you to give meaning to your life. The reality of your finiteness can stimulate you to look at your priorities and to ask what you value most. In this way your willingness to come to terms with your death can teach you how to really live. To run from death is to run from life, for as Gibran (1923) writes, "Life and death are one, even as the river and the sea are one" (p. 71). Are you living *now* the way you want? Do you have goals you have yet to meet? What do you most want to be able to say that you have experienced or accomplished before you die?

In this chapter we invite you to look at your attitudes and beliefs about your own death, the deaths of those you love, and other forms of significant loss. Although the topic of this chapter might seem to be morbid or depressing, an honest understanding and acceptance of death and loss can lay the groundwork for a rich and meaningful life. If we fully accept that we have only a limited time in which to live, we can make choices that will make the most of the time we have.

We also ask you to consider the notion of death in a broader perspective and to raise such questions as: What parts of me aren't as alive as they might be? In what emotional ways am I dead or dying? What will I do with my awareness of the ways in which I'm not fully alive? Finally, we discuss the importance of fully experiencing your grief when you suffer serious losses.

This discussion of death and loss has an important connection with the themes of the previous chapter, loneliness and solitude. When we emotionally accept the reality of our eventual death, we experience our ultimate aloneness. This awareness of our mortality and aloneness helps us realize that our actions do count, that we do have choices concerning how we live our life, and that we must accept the final responsibility for how well we are living.

This chapter is also a bridge to the next chapter, which deals with meaning and values. The awareness of death is a catalyst for the human search for meaning in life. Our knowledge that we will die can encourage us to ask ourselves whether we're living by values that create a meaningful existence; if not, we have the time and opportunity to change our way of living. As Siegel (1989) puts it: "Facing death is often the catalyst that enables people to reach out for what they want" (p. 241).

Our Fears of Death

We may fear many aspects of death, including leaving behind those we love, losing ourselves, encountering the unknown, coping with the humiliation and indignity of a painful or long dying, and growing distant in the memories of others. For many people it's not so much death itself as the experience of dying that arouses fears. Here, too, it is a good idea to ask what our fears are really about and to confront them honestly, as Schnitzer (1977) does in *Looking In*:

> Death is feared because it seems to condemn us to utter loneliness and to the loss of identity. But consciousness also vanishes, and what is there to be feared when it is totally gone? "To fear death means pretending to know what we don't know," Plato once said. What we are afraid of is not death but dying, the phase that confronts us with the loss of our world and its familiar beings — the only home we know. And that indeed must be painful. There may be agony, both physical and mental. At that last stage we will be much more in need of braveness. (p. 89)

Siegel (1988) believes that the pain and fear of dying come primarily from unresolved conflict and unfinished business. One of Siegel's patients told him, "Death is not the worst thing. Life without love is far worse" (p. 207). Perhaps we fear dying because we might realize that we have never really lived.

At this point you might pause to reflect on your own fears of death and dying. What expectations seem to arouse the greatest fears in you? Do your religious beliefs assist you in dealing with your fear of dying? Do your fears involve death itself, or the experience of dying? How might your fears be affecting how you choose to live now? Have you had someone close to you die? If so, how did the experience of that person's death affect your feelings about death and dying?

If you consider yourself relatively young, you might ask: Why should this topic interest me? I've got lots of time left, so why think about morbid subjects? Even the very young can be at least temporarily shocked into the realization that they could die at any time. This happens when a classmate dies in an automobile accident, by drowning, by suicide, from cancer or AIDS, or by some act of violence. Although it is not necessary to morbidly focus on your death, it is important for you to deal with your fears of it and to consider what death means to you in terms of *living fully* now.

Death and the Meaning of Life

The existentialists view the acceptance of death as vitally related to the discovery of meaning and purpose in life. One of our distinguishing characteristics as human beings is our ability to grasp the concept of the future and, thus, the inevitability of death. Our ability to do so gives meaning to our existence, for it makes our every act and moment count.

Rather than living in fear of our mortality, we can actually view death as a challenge and as an opportunity. Siegel (1989) maintains that death is not a failure, but failing to live fully is the worst outcome. His writings and lectures are permeated with the assumption that the knowledge of our eventual death is what gives meaning to life. For Siegel, the realization that we will die is a wake-up call to appreciate the urgency and beauty of each day. He writes: "The greatest gift of all is that we don't live forever. It makes us face up to the meaning of our existence. It also enables people who never took time for themselves in life to take that time, at last, before they die" (p. 234).

The Stoics of ancient Greece had a dictum: "Contemplate death if you would learn how to live." Seneca commented that "no man enjoys the true taste of life but he who is willing and ready to quit it." And Saint Augustine said "It is only in the face of death that man's self is born." Thus, it is in facing the reality of our death that we find meaning in life. As Travis and Ryan (1988) point out, death is a highly creative force and a meaning-filled fact of life. The highest spiritual values of life spring forth from the study of and reflection on death. Although we can prolong life through wellness practices, death is our natural inheritance. Travis and Ryan also contend that finding meaning is perhaps the most difficult task we come to grips with, especially within the context of accepting our mortality. Some of the guidelines they offer are

• Learn to look within yourself, listen to your inner wisdom, and trust what you find.
• Pay attention to what is happening now, rather than living in the past or in the future.
• In relationships with others, strive to honestly be the person you are, rather than being what you think others expect of you.
• Learn to face death and pain, rather than running from them.

A sharply defined example of facing the reality of death, and of giving meaning to what is left of life, is provided by those who are terminally ill. Their confrontation with death causes them to do much living in a relatively brief period of time. The pressure of time almost forces them to choose how they will spend their remaining days. Irvin Yalom (1980) found that cancer patients in group therapy had the capacity to view their crisis as an opportunity to instigate change in their lives. Once they discovered that they had cancer, their inner changes included

- a rearrangement of life's priorities, paying little attention to trivial matters
- a sense of liberation: the ability to choose to do those things they really wanted to do
- an increase sense of living in the moment: no postponement of living until some future time
- a vivid appreciation of the basic facts of life—for example, noticing changes in the seasons and other aspects of nature

- a deeper communication with loved ones than before the crisis
- fewer interpersonal fears, less concern over security, and more willingness to take risks (p. 35)

The irony of the situation is well summed up by one of the patients: "What a tragedy that we had to wait till now, till our bodies were riddled with cancer, to learn these truths" (p. 165). This example serves to make a central point: when we confront the reality that life does not go on forever, life becomes more precious. Siegel (1988) echoes this view that confronting death makes it possible to love life. He reminds us that we have a choice and encourages us to choose love and life. "We have an infinite number of choices ahead, but a finite number of endings. They are destruction and death or love and healing. If we choose the path of love we save ourselves and our universe" (p. 225).

The meaning of our life, then, depends on the fact that we are finite beings. What we do with our life counts. We can choose to become all that we are capable of becoming and make a conscious decision to fully affirm life, or we can passively let life slip by us. We can settle for letting events happen to us, or we can actively choose and create the kind of life we want. If we had forever to actualize our potentials, there would be no urgency about doing so. Our time is invaluable precisely because it is limited.

Cultural and religious beliefs affect the way in which people view death. Some belief systems emphasize making the most of this life, for it is viewed as the *only* existence. Other belief systems focus on the natural continuity and progression of this temporal life into an afterlife. Just as our beliefs and values affect our fear of death, so do they affect the meaning we attribute to death. Regardless of your philosophical views on the meaning of life and death, there is still a wide range of choices open to you to maximize the quality of your present life. The reality of death provides a catalyst for you to examine the meaning of your life and how well you are living.

Time Out for Personal Reflection

1. What fears do you experience when you think about your own death? Check any of the following statements that apply to you:

_____	I worry about what will happen to me after death.
_____	I'm anxious about the way I will die.
_____	I wonder whether I'll die with dignity.
_____	I fear the physical pain of dying.
_____	I worry most about my loved ones who will be left behind.
_____	I'm afraid that I won't be able to accomplish all that I want to accomplish before I die.
_____	I worry about my lack of control over how and when I will die.
_____	I fear ceasing to exist.

_____   I worry about being forgotten.
_____   I worry about all the things I'll miss after I die.

List any other fears you have about death or dying.

_____

_____

_____

_____

2. How well do you think you're living your life? List some specific things you aren't doing now that you'd like to be doing. List some things you think you'd be likely to do if you knew that you had only a short time to live.

_____

_____

_____

_____

3. We've asked students to write a brief description of what they might do if they knew they had only 24 hours left to live. If you're willing to, write down what occurs to you when you think about this possibility.

_____

_____

_____

_____

4. In what ways does the fact that you will die give meaning to your life now?

_____

_____

_____

_____

5. In what ways do you think your fears about death and dying might be affecting the choices you make now?

_____

_____

_____

Suicide: Ultimate Choice or Ultimate Cop-Out?

Suicide is one of the leading causes of death in the United States, and it is on the increase. Suicide ranks among the top five causes of death for White males aged 10 to 55 and is the second-ranked cause of death for all males aged 15 to 24 (DeSpelder & Strickland, 1983).

People who attempt suicide simply do not want to go on in deadening patterns, or they see life as unbearable. They may feel that the chances of change are slim. Although there are options for living differently, they are unable to see any. Is suicide an ultimate choice or an ultimate cop-out? This question is a complex one, and there is no easy answer. What seems essential is that we make conscious choices about how fully we are willing to live, realizing that we must pay a price for being alive. At the same time, for some people ending their lives does seem like a cop-out, the result of not being willing to struggle or of being too quick to give up without exploring other possibilities. Shneidman (1984) indicates that a major shortcoming of suicide is that it answers a remediable challenge with a permanent negative solution.

Consider the following questions as a way of clarifying your views on suicide:

1. *What does your personal experience reveal?* At times you may have felt a deep sense of hopelessness, and you may have questioned whether it was worth it to continue living. Have you ever felt really suicidal? If so, what was going on in your life that contributed to your desire to end it? What factor or factors kept you from following through with taking your life? Would this act have been motivated by the feeling that you had no choices?

2. *What hidden meanings does suicide have?* Taking one's life is such a powerful act that we must look to some of its underlying messages and symbolic meanings:

- A cry for help: "I cried out, but nobody heard me!"
- A form of self-punishment: "I don't deserve to live."
- An act of hostility: "I'll get even with you; see what you made me do."
- An attempt to control and exert power over people: "I will make others suffer for the rest of their lives for having rejected me."
- An attempt to be noticed: "Maybe now people will talk about me and feel sorry for the way they treated me."
- A relief from a terrible state of mind: "Life is too stressful, and I'm fed up."
- An escape from a difficult or impossible situation: "I hate living in an alcoholic family, and death seems like one way to end this situation."
- A relief from hopelessness: "I see no way out of the despair I feel. Ending my life will be better than hating to wake up each morning."
- An end to pain: "I suffer extreme physical pain, which will not end. Suicide will put an end to this nightmare."

3. *Can suicide be an act of mercy?* There have been victims of painful and terminal illnesses who decided *when* and *how* to end their lives. Rather than dying with cancer and enduring extreme pain, some people have actually called their family together and then taken some form of poison. Of recent interest in the news is the physician from Michigan known as the "suicide doctor," who designed a "suicide machine" to assist terminally ill people in making the choice to end their lives. Although this doctor faced murder or manslaughter charges, he maintained that he was providing people with a means of choosing to end their lives when there was no more hope. And recently the CBS program "60 Minutes" had a feature on a person who was devoting his life to assisting people with AIDS to die. He was about to be prosecuted when he himself died of AIDS. These recent events that have made major news represent an outcry of some people saying, "I want nobody to keep me alive when my quality of life has diminished." People fear being kept alive at all costs when they are ready to die. The hospital machines can obstruct this readiness. Lawyers report an increase in the number of people asking for living wills, in which they give directions about when to unplug life-supporting equipment. What are your thoughts about a person's choice to end his or her life when it is certain that there is no chance of recovery? What are your thoughts about a living will for yourself?

These are simply a few issues on the important topic of suicide as a choice. See if you can come up with some other questions that will help you formulate your own opinions on the meanings of suicide, as well as alternatives to this final act.

SUICIDE AMONG ADOLESCENTS

Suicide rates have increased alarmingly for youths between the ages of 15 and 24. Although suicide accounts for approximately 2 percent of all deaths in the United States, it accounts for more than 15 percent of the deaths among adolescents (Bongar, 1991). Over the past three decades, the suicide rate for 15- to 19-year-olds has shown a dramatic increase of 312 percent (Berman & Jobes, 1991). What is more, underreporting of suicidal deaths is probably common for youths. Many "accidental" deaths of adolescents are regarded by experts as having involved suicidal motives, either conscious or unconscious.

Several factors contribute to suicide among young people. Family supports are often lacking. When faced with the stresses of the adolescent years, such as personal failure or the breakup of relationships, young people may feel abandoned and may contemplate suicide as a way out of hopelessness. Hawton (1986) writes that youths who attempt suicide are facing more problems than others. These problems include poor relationships with parents; school or work difficulties; unhappiness in dating; and social isolation. According to Hawton, the main feelings that precede adolescent attempts at suicide are anger against a significant person; feeling lonely or unwanted; being worried about the future; feeling as though one has failed in life; and being ashamed of something.

Although there is no typical suicidal adolescent, there are risk factors that are linked to adolescent suicide, some of which include the presence of mood disorders, antisocial behaviors, social isolation and alienation, withdrawal, extreme loneliness, and supersensitiveness (Berman & Jobes, 1991). Most explanations of adolescent suicide involve a combination of a background of depression and a current traumatic or stressful experience as the trigger. A few of these experiences that can increase the chances of a suicide include the death of a family member; the divorce or separation of parents; chronic illness or personal injury; and an adolescent's own pregnancy, abortion, or birth of a baby. Generally, suicide is not a simple act and can best be understood as the result of a combination of factors.

Youths who attempt suicide typically feel that they have little power to change the direction of their lives. They see little meaning in life and feel trapped in their desperate situation, which leads to a state of chronic depression. Young people often explain attempts to end their lives as a way of escaping from unbearable stress. Although more alternatives are available to them than they recognize, their belief system includes two possibilities: living with their hopelessness in a situation they cannot change, or suicide as an escape from the pain of powerlessness and hopelessness.

Unfortunately, a modeling effect occurs when adolescents take their own lives. The phenomenon of serial suicide has made headlines from time to time. Some youths seem to feel that suicide is one way of getting recognition, even through death. There is also the problem of romanticizing the lives of adolescents who dramatically put an end to their existence. We are thinking about a popular high school student who was a star athlete and who shocked the entire school and community when he committed suicide. In some ways he became idealized after his death. There is a danger in giving too much attention to suicides, for other distressed youths can learn that it is a way to draw attention to themselves.

REACTIONS TO SUICIDE

When a family member commits suicide, the immediate reaction is generally shock and distress, followed by a range of feelings such as denial, anger, shame, guilt, and fear (Hawton, 1986). When family members are in denial, they may invent reasons that will contribute to their refusal to accept the death as a suicide. Anger is quite common, often directed toward the deceased: "Why did you shut me out and leave me?" It can also be aimed at medical agencies, friends, and other family members. There may be a sense of shame because of the stigma of suicide. Guilt is often experienced over what the survivors could and should have done to prevent the tragedy. "Maybe if I had been more sensitive and caring," they might feel, "this terrible thing wouldn't have happened." They also experience fear over the possibility of this act's being repeated by another family member or, perhaps, even by themselves.

In a discussion of how to help survivors deal with their reactions to youth suicide, Hawton (1986) emphasizes the significant role of counseling. The nature of the unfinished business, how it is handled, and how the survivor is affected by it all have an impact on the grief process. Typically, those who are left behind experience a deep sense of abandonment, loneliness, and isolation. If the family members are willing to seek counseling (either individually or as a family), they can be taught how to express feelings that they might otherwise have kept buried inside. Counseling encourages them to talk about the things they may be rehearsing over and over in their heads, and it can help them to talk about their feelings with one another. Counseling helps them correct distortions they may hold, prepare for their future, learn to let go of regrets and blame, and give expression to their anger. Because of their deep sadness, it may be difficult for family members to become aware of, much less express to one another, the anger that they have a right to feel.

Freedom in Dying

The process of dying involves a gradual diminishing of the choices available to us. Even in dying, however, we still have choices concerning how we handle what is happening to us. The following account deals with the dying of Jim Morelock, a student and close friend of mine (Jerry's).*

Jim is 25 years old. He is full of life—witty, bright, honest, and actively questioning. He had just graduated from college as a human services major and seemed to have a bright future when his illness was discovered.

About a year and a half ago, Jim developed a growth on his forehead and underwent surgery to have it removed. At that time, his doctors believed that the growth was a rare disorder that was not malignant. Later, more tumors erupted, and more surgery followed. Several months ago, Jim found out that the tumors had spread throughout his body and that even with cobalt treatment, he would have a short life. Since that time he has steadily grown weaker and has been able to do less and less; yet he has shown remarkable courage in the way he has faced this loss and his dying.

Some time ago Jim came to Idyllwild, California, and took part in the weekend seminar that we had with the reviewers of this book. On this chapter, he commented that although we may not have a choice concerning the losses we suffer in dying, we do retain the ability to choose our attitude toward our death and the way we relate to it.

*This account is being repeated as it appeared in this book's first edition. Many readers have commented to us about how touched they were as they read about Jim's life and his death, and in this way he seems to have lived on in one important respect.

Jim has taught me a lot during these past few months about this enduring capacity for choice, even in extreme circumstances. Jim has made many critical choices since being told of his illness. He chose to continue taking a course at the university, because he liked the contact with the people there. He worked hard at a boat dock to support himself, until he could no longer manage the physical exertion. He decided to undergo cobalt treatment, even though he knew that it most likely would not result in his cure, because he hoped that it would reduce his pain. It did not, and Jim has suffered much agony during the past few months. He decided not to undergo chemotherapy, primarily because he didn't want to prolong his life if he couldn't really live fully. He made a choice to accept God in his life, which gave him a sense of peace and serenity. Before he became bedridden, he decided to go to Hawaii and enjoy his time in first-class style.

Jim has always had an aversion to hospitals — to most institutions, for that matter — so he chose to remain at home, in more personal surroundings. As long as he was able, he read widely and continued to write in his journal about his thoughts and feelings on living and dying. With his friends, he played his guitar and sang songs that he had written. He maintained an active interest in life and in the things around him, without denying the fact that he was dying.

More than anyone I have known or heard about, Jim has taken care of unfinished business. He made it a point to gather his family and tell them his wishes, he made contact with all his friends and said everything he wanted to say to them, and he asked Marianne to deliver the eulogy at his funeral services. He clearly stated his desire for cremation; he wants to burn those tumors and then have his ashes scattered over the sea — a wish that reflects his love of freedom and movement.

Jim has very little freedom and movement now, for he can do little except lie in his bed and wait for his death to come. To this day he is choosing to die with dignity, and although his body is deteriorating, his spirit is still very much alive. He retains his mental sharpness, his ability to say a lot in a very few words, and his sense of humor. He has allowed himself to grieve over his losses. As he puts it, "I'd sure like to hang around to enjoy all those people that love me!" Realizing that this isn't possible, Jim is saying good-bye to all those who are close to him.

Throughout this ordeal, Jim's mother has been truly exceptional. When she told me how remarkable Jim has been in complaining so rarely despite his constant pain, I reminded her that I'd never heard her complain during her months on duty. I have been continually amazed by her strength and courage, and I have admired her willingness to honor Jim's wishes and accept his beliefs, even though at times they have differed from her own. She has demonstrated her care without smothering him or depriving him of his free spirit and independence. Her acceptance of Jim's dying and her willingness to be fully present to him have given him the opportunity to express openly whatever he feels. Jim has been able to grieve and mourn because she has not cut off this process.

This experience has taught me much about dying and about living. Through him, I have learned that I don't have to do that much for a person who is dying other than to be with him or her by being myself. So often I have felt a sense of helplessness, of not knowing what to say or how much to say, of not knowing what to ask or not to ask, of feeling stuck for words. Jim's imminent death seems such a loss, and it's very difficult for me to accept it. Gradually, however, I have learned not to be so concerned about what to say or to refrain from saying. In fact, in my last visit I said very little, but I feel that we made significant contact with each other. I've also learned to share with him the sadness I feel, but there is simply no easy way to say good-bye to a friend.

Jim is showing me that his style of dying will be no different from his style of living. By his example and by his words, Jim has been a catalyst for me to think about the things I say and to evaluate my own life.

Time Out for Personal Reflection

1. If you were close to someone during his or her dying, how did the experience affect your feelings about your life and about your own dying?

   _____

   _____

   _____

   _____

2. How would you like to be able to respond if a person who is close to you were dying?

   _____

   _____

   _____

   _____

3. If you were dying, what would you most want from the people who are closest to you?

   _____

   _____

   _____

   _____

   _____

The Stages of Dying

Death and dying have become topics of widespread discussion among psychologists, psychiatrists, physicians, sociologists, ministers, and researchers. Whereas these topics were once taboo for many people, they are now the focus of seminars, courses, and workshops. A number of books, many that are listed in "References and Suggested Readings" at the end of the book, give evidence of this growing interest.

Dr. Elisabeth Kübler-Ross is a pioneer in the contemporary study of death and dying. In her widely read books *On Death and Dying* (1969) and *Death: The Final Stage of Growth* (1975), she treats the psychological and sociological aspects of death and the experience of dying. Thanks to her efforts, many people have become aware of the almost universal need the dying have to talk about their impending death and to complete their business with the important people in their life. She has shown how ignorance of the dying process and of the needs of dying people — as well as the fears of those around them — can rob the dying of the opportunity to fully experience their feelings and arrive at a resolution of them.

A greater understanding of dying can help us come to an acceptance of death, as well as to be more helpful and present to those who are dying. For this reason, we describe the five stages of dying that Kübler-Ross has delineated, based on her research with terminally ill cancer patients. She emphasizes that these are not neat and compartmentalized stages that every person passes through in an orderly fashion. At times a person may experience a combination of these stages, perhaps skip one or more stages, or go back to an earlier stage he or she has already experienced. In general, however, Kübler-Ross found this sequence: denial, anger, bargaining, depression, and acceptance.

To make this discussion of the stages of dying more concrete, we give the example of Ann, a 30-year-old cancer patient. Ann was married and the mother of three children in elementary school. Before she discovered that she had terminal cancer, she felt that she had much to live for, and she enjoyed life.

DENIAL

Ann's first reaction to being told that she had only about a year to live was shock. She refused to believe that the diagnosis was correct, and even after obtaining several other medical opinions she still refused to accept that she was dying. In other words, her initial reaction was one of *denial*.

Even though Ann was attempting to deny the full impact of reality, it would have been a mistake to assume that she didn't want to talk about her feelings. Her husband also denied her illness and was unwilling to talk to her about it. He felt that talking bluntly might only make her more depressed and lead her to lose all hope. He failed to recognize how important it would have been to Ann to feel that she *could* bring up the subject if she wished. On some level she knew that she could not talk about her death with her husband.

During the stage of denial the attitudes of a dying person's family and friends are critical. If these people cannot face the fact of their loved one's dying, they cannot help him or her move toward an acceptance of death. Their own fear will blind them to signs that the dying person wants to talk about his or her death and needs support. In the case of Ann it would not necessarily have been a wise idea to force her to talk, but she could have been greatly helped if those around her had been available and sensitive to her when *she* stopped denying her death and showed a need to be listened to.

ANGER

As Ann began to accept that her time was limited by an incurable disease, her denial was replaced by anger. Over and over she wondered why *she* — who had so much to live for — had to be afflicted with this dreadful disease. Her anger mounted as she thought of her children and realized that she would not be able to see them grow and develop. During her frequent visits to the hospital for radiation treatment, she directed some of her anger toward doctors "who didn't seem to know what they were doing" and toward the "impersonal" nurses.

During the stage of anger it's important that others recognize the need of dying people to express their anger, whether they direct it toward their doctors, the hospital staff, their friends, their children, or God. If this displaced anger is taken personally, any meaningful dialogue with the dying will be cut off. Moreover, people like Ann have reason to be enraged over having to suffer in this way when they have so much to live for. Rather than withdrawing support or taking offense, the people who surround a dying person can help most by allowing the person to fully express the pent-up rage inside. In this way they help the person to ultimately come to terms with his or her death.

BARGAINING

Kübler-Ross (1969) sums up the essence of the bargaining stage as follows: "If God has decided to take us from this earth and he did not respond to any angry pleas, he may be more favorable if I ask nicely" (p. 72). Basically, the stage of bargaining is an attempt to postpone the inevitable end.

Ann's ambitions at this stage were to finish her college studies and graduate with her bachelor's degree, which she was close to obtaining. She also hoped to see her oldest daughter begin junior high school in a little over a year. During this time she tried any type of treatment that offered some hope of extending her life.

DEPRESSION

Eventually Ann's bargaining time ran out. No possibility of remission of her cancer remained, and she could no longer deny the inevitability of her death. Having been subjected to radiation treatment, chemotherapy, and a series of operations, she was becoming weaker and thinner, and she was able to do less and less. Her primary feelings became a great sense of loss and a fear of the unknown. She wondered about who would take care of her children and about her husband's future. She felt guilty because she was demanding so much attention and time and because the treatment of her illness was depleting the family income. She felt depressed over losing her hair and her beauty.

It would not have been helpful at this stage to try to cheer Ann up or to deny her real situation. Just as it had been important to allow her to fully vent her anger, it was important now to let her talk about her feelings and to make her final plans. Dying people are about to lose everyone they love, and only the freedom to grieve over these losses will enable them to find some peace and serenity in a final acceptance of death.

ACCEPTANCE

Kübler-Ross found that if patients have had enough time and support to work through the previous stages, most of them reach a stage at which they are neither depressed nor angry. Because they have expressed their anger and mourned the impending loss of those they love, they are able to become more accepting of their death. Kübler-Ross (1969) comments: "Acceptance should not be mistaken for a happy stage. It is almost devoid of feelings. It is as if the pain has gone, the struggle is over, and there comes a time for 'the final rest before the long journey,' as one patient phrased it" (p. 100).

Of course, some people never achieve an acceptance of their death, and some have no desire to. Ann, for example, never truly reached a stage of acceptance. Her final attitude was more one of surrender, a realization that it was futile to fight any longer. Although she still felt unready to die, she did want an end to her suffering. It may be that if those close to her had been more open to her and accepting of her feelings, she would have been able to work through more of her anger and depression.

THE SIGNIFICANCE OF KÜBLER-ROSS'S STAGES

It needs to be reemphasized that Kübler-Ross's description of the dying process is not meant to be rigid and should not be interpreted as a natural progression that is expected in most cases. Just as people are unique in the way they live, they are unique in the way they die; it is a mistake to use these stages as the standard by which to judge whether a dying person's behavior is normal or right. The value of the stages is that they describe and summarize in a general way what many patients experience and therefore add to our understanding of dying. Sometimes practitioners who work with the termi-

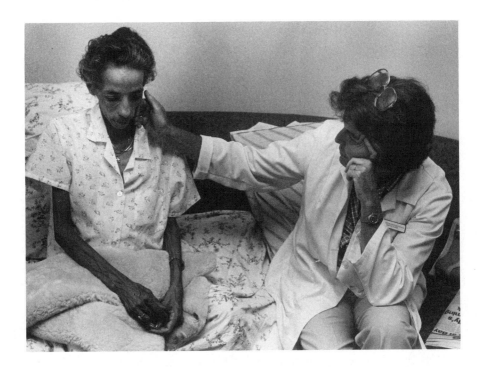

nally ill forget that the stages of dying do not progress neatly, even though they cognitively know this reality. One practitioner told us: "Although I had read Kübler-Ross's book and knew the stages that a dying person was supposed to go through, many of my terminal patients had not read the same book!"

Kalish (1985) comments that many doctors and nurses regard the stage progression as something that everyone will naturally follow. Patients who do not make it to the acceptance stage are sometimes viewed as failures. For example, some nurses get angry at patients who take "backward" steps by going from depression to anger, or they question patients about why they have "stayed so long in the anger stage." Kalish emphasizes that people die in a variety of ways and have a variety of feelings during this process: hope, anger, depression, fear, envy, relief, and anticipation. Those who are dying move back and forth from mood to mood. Therefore, these stages should not be used as a method of categorizing, and thus dehumanizing, the dying; they are best used as a frame of reference for helping them.

THE HOSPICE MOVEMENT

There is a trend toward more direct involvement of family members in caring for a dying person. An example of this is the hospice program. The term *hospice* was originally used to describe a waiting place for travelers during the Middle Ages. Later, hospices were established for children without parents, the incurably ill, and the elderly. It was during the nineteenth century that a Catholic religious order began developing hospices for dying persons (Kalish, 1985). In recent years hospices have spread rapidly through Europe and North America.

The hospice movement came about in response to what many people perceived to be inadequate care for the dying in conventional hospitals. In recent years hospice programs have become a part of some of these hospitals. The hospice movement also gives permission to those who are losing a significant person to feel their full range of emotions during the bereavement process. Hospice centers typically offer a variety of counseling services for those who survive the death of a loved one. Many of these survivors need the reassurance that they are not "going crazy," even though they may believe that they are.

According to Kalish (1985), the recent hospice movement has changed the attitude toward a dying person from "There is nothing more that we can do to help" to "We need to do what we can to provide the most humane care." This involves viewing patients and their family members as a unit. Care givers do not separate the person who is dying from his or her family. Whenever possible, patients are kept at home as long as they wish. Both volunteers and a trained staff provide health-care aid, including helping the patient and the family members deal with psychological and social stresses. Hospices aim to provide services that help dying patients experience a sense of self-worth and dignity and to provide support for the family members so that they can prepare for the eventual separation. Although research on these programs are preliminary, hospice patients are more mobile and tend to report less general anxiety and fewer bodily symptoms than those being given traditional care. The spouse is able to spend more time in visiting and caring for the patient (Kalish, 1985).

Although a hospice is a humanitarian way of helping people die with dignity, hospice facilities are not always welcomed in the community. One situation involved intense neighborhood objections to a hospice house for people dying of AIDS. Some of the residents had concerns about their property values falling, and others had reactions to bringing people who were afflicted with AIDS into their community.

Grieving over Death, Separation, and Other Losses

In a way that is similar to the stages of dying, people go through stages of grief in working through death and various other losses. Grief work refers to the exploration of feelings of sorrow, anger, and guilt over the experience of a significant loss. This process is often not an easy or simple one. Some people are never able to accept the death of a child or a spouse. They may get stuck by denying their feelings and by not facing and working through their pain over the loss. At some point in the grief process, people may feel numb, or that they are functioning on automatic pilot. Once this numbness wears off, almost like novocaine, the pain seems to intensify. People who are going through this pain need to learn that they might well get worse before they feel better. To put to rest unresolved issues and unexpressed feelings, people need to express their anger, regrets, guilts, and frustrations. When they attempt to deny their pain, they inevitably wind up being stuck and are unable to express a range of feelings. This unexpressed pain tends to eat away at them both physically and psychologically and prevents them from accepting the reality of the death of a loved one. We are reminded of a woman who reported that she was overcome with emotions and could not stop crying at the funeral of an acquaintance. What surprised her was the way her reaction contrasted with her "strength and composure" over the death of her husband. What she didn't realize was that she had not allowed herself to grieve over the loss of her husband and that years later she was having a delayed grief reaction.

ALLOWING YOURSELF TO GRIEVE

Grief is a necessary and natural process after a significant loss. However, there are forces in many cultures that make it very difficult for people to experience a complete grief process after they have suffered a loss. For example, in American society, there appears to be a cultural norm that fosters an expectation of a "quick cure," and oftentimes others cannot understand why it is taking "such a long time" for a grieving person to "get back to normal." As is the case with any emotion that does not get expressed, unresolved grief lingers in the background and prevents people from letting go of losses and from forming new relationships. Also, unresolved grief is considered a key factor in the onset of a variety of physical illnesses. Siegel (1988, 1989) cites numerous examples of people who developed cancer after a significant loss through death or divorce.

Most writers on the psychological aspects of death and loss agree that grieving is necessary. A common denominator of all of their theories is that there is a general process of moving from a stage of depression to recovery. Although people may successfully work through their feelings pertaining to loss, it can be expected that the loss may always be with them. In successful grieving, however, people are not immobilized by the loss, nor do they close themselves off from other involvements. Another commonality in all these theories is that they recognize that not all people go through the grieving process at the same rate, nor do all people move neatly and predictably from one stage to another.

A chronic state of depression and a restricted range of feelings suffered by some people are often attributed to some unresolved reaction to a significant loss. Such individuals often fear that the pain will consume them and that it is better to shut off their feelings. What they fail to realize is that they pay a price for this denial in the long run. This price involves excluding feelings of closeness and joy. At times these people can go on for years without ever expressing emotions over their loss, being convinced that they have adequately dealt with it. Yet they might find themselves being flooded with emotions for which they have no explanation. They may discover that another's loss opens up old wounds that they thought were successfully healed.

Grief might be over many types of losses besides a death, such as the breakup of a relationship, the loss of one's career, and children's leaving home. In learning to resolve grief, regardless of its source, people need to be able to talk about what they are telling themselves internally and what they are feeling. They typically need to express their feelings over the lack of fairness about their situation. They may eventually face up to the fact that there is no rational reason that will explain their loss.

If people who are experiencing a bereavement process are able to express the full range of their thoughts and feelings, they stand a better chance of adjusting to a new environment. Indeed, part of the grief process involves making basic life changes and experiencing new growth. If they have gone through the necessary cycle of bereavement, they are better equipped to become reinvested with a new purpose and a new reason for living.

What major losses have you had, and how have you coped with them? Have you lost a family member, a close friendship, a job that you valued, a spouse through divorce, a material object that had special meaning, a place where you once lived, a pet, or your faith in some person or group? Are there any similarities in how you responded to these different types of loss? Did you successfully work through your feelings about the losses? Did you shut off your feelings of grief because they were too intense? Or did you allow yourself to express your feelings to someone close to you? In recalling a particular loss, are the feelings still as intense as they were then?

A husband's grief over the death of his wife. Charles, 65, lost his wife, Betsy, to cancer after a year's battle. During the last few months of Betsy's life, members of the local hospice organization helped Charles care for her at home. Before her death she expressed a desire to talk to him about her impending death. He could not tolerate the reality of her illness and her dying, however, and he refused to talk with her. Even though Betsy has been dead for some time, Charles suffers pangs of guilt and regret for not having complied with his wife's final request. He reports that he rarely sleeps through the night and that he gets up early in the morning and looks for tasks to keep him busy. It is difficult for him to be in the house where he and his wife lived together for almost forty-five years, because her memories are everywhere. Although his friends and neighbors are supportive, he is concerned that he not be a burden on anybody. He often refuses invitations from distant friends, for he finds driving alone too painful. He often wishes that he had died instead of Betsy, for she would have been better able to deal with his loss than he is able to cope with her death. His friends continue to encourage him to talk about his feelings and not to isolate himself by retreating into inactivity and depression. Charles may eventually be able to create a new life without Betsy and emotionally come to terms with the reality that she is no longer in his life.

C. S. Lewis, in *A Grief Observed* (1961), poetically compares grief to a long and winding valley where any bend may reveal a totally new landscape. He writes about his own grief over observing the death of his wife from cancer:

> And grief still feels like fear. Perhaps, more strictly, like suspense. Or like waiting; just hanging about waiting for something to happen. It gives life a permanently provisional feeling. It doesn't seem worth starting anything. I can't settle down. I yawn, I fidget, I smoke too much. Up until this I always had too little time. Now there is nothing but time. Almost pure time, empty successiveness. (p. 29)

A young woman's denial of grief. Kelly is a 19-year-old community college student who recently enrolled in a course on death and dying. She let her instructor know privately that the course was touching her emotionally and confronting her with facing the death of her father five years before. She told him that when her father died in an airplane crash, she simply refused to believe that he was actually dead. Kelly convinced herself that he had gone away on a long vacation and would someday return to her. Very few tears were shared in the family, his name was rarely mentioned, no reminiscing was done by any of the family members, and none of them visited his grave. With her peers Kelly never acknowledged her father's death. Only a few close friends knew that she was without a father.

Kelly describes herself as never feeling extremely happy or very sad. She envies people whom she sees as spontaneous, joyous, and, as she puts it, "really able to laugh." Since she began the class on death and dying, she has surprised herself with occasional crying spells, and she notices that she is often angry at the slightest provocation. She gave her instructor some poetry that she had recently written pertaining to how much she was missing her father. She has a desire to go and visit his grave but says that she is afraid of doing so. Kelly is just now, years after her father's death, beginning to allow herself to grieve over her loss. As she permits herself to feel her pain, she will also be able to experience more joy in her life.

A young man's acceptance of grief. Tony, who is 17 years old, told Marianne about the sudden death of his 57-year-old grandfather from a heart attack. He talked a lot about the kind of man his grandfather was and said he regretted their not having had more contact. He is experiencing much sadness over his recent loss. It was interesting to hear his description of and reaction to his grandfather's funeral. Because his grandfather was well known, a surprisingly large crowd attended the funeral. Many people eulogized and spoke about the man. As Tony put it, there were many tears, and it was extremely difficult for him to witness all this emotionality. He asserts that when he dies, he does not want a funeral, because he wants to avoid putting people in such a painful position. What he does not realize is that although it is indeed difficult for him to feel his own pain and observe the pain of others, it is this very process that will enable him to deal more effectively with the loss of his grandfather. Even though Tony reacted negatively to the funeral, unlike Kelly he is not denying his feelings of grief over his loss.

Most cultures have rituals that are designed to help people with this grieving process. Examples are the funeral practices of the Irish, the Jewish, the Russians, and others, whereby painful feelings are actually triggered and released. Many cultures have a formal mourning period (usually a year). In these cultures an obvious pattern is the direct involvement of people in the funeral process.

In the American culture those who suffer from a loss are typically "protected" from any direct involvement in the burial. People are praised for not displaying overt signs of grief. For example, Jacqueline Kennedy was admired for the strength and composure she displayed at her husband's funeral. Many of our rituals make it easy for us to deny our feelings of loss and therefore keep us from coming to terms with the reality of that loss. It has become clear that these practices are not genuinely helpful. The current trend is to provide ways of involving people directly in the dying process of their loved ones (such as the hospice movement) and the funeral process as well.

How our family dealt with a death. Earlier I (Jerry) wrote about Jim Morelock's dying. Let me share some of the stages our family went through in dealing with Jim's loss. When Jim first told me that his cancer was terminal, it was difficult for me to believe. I had thoughts that somehow he would win the battle. It was hard for me to understand why he would have to die, since he had so much to live for and to offer others. Although at times I was able to accept the reality of his impending death, there were other times when I would ask "Why him?" Together we talked about his dying, even though that was difficult. I took the opportunity to say good-bye to him.

At a memorial service many of Jim's friends recounted special times we had had with him. About a year later some close friends of his came to our home, and we planted an apple tree in his memory. We again reminisced and shared the ways in which we were missing him. As the years go by, the pain over his death becomes less intense. I find I bring him to my awareness in certain situations. He has now been dead for sixteen years, yet his memory is still with me.

Our daughters developed a very special relationship with Jim over the years, seeing him as their big brother. During some visits he was very frank with them about his cancer, including telling them he might die. As he put it to them after one of his operations, "Well, I've won this battle, but that doesn't mean I've won the war yet." Cindy and Heidi were 9 and 10 at the time he was dying. They coped with his condition by talking to him, to us, to his mother, and to each other. Cindy wrote a detailed story with an unhappy ending. Heidi dreamed that she had "magic" ice cream that could cure anything. When she told us about her dream, she sadly added, "But there isn't any magic, is there?" Every doll that they had was operated on for cancer. These were the symbolic and direct ways in which our daughters dealt with the dying of a special friend. As parents we made ourselves available to them by listening to them and supporting them, yet we did not offer them false hope.

Even though it has been about sixteen years since Jim died, we still remember him and talk about him at times when we get together with people who knew him. We maintain contact with his mother and with some mutual friends. We share memories and recount some of the lessons each of us learned about living and dying through our contact with Jim. Marianne played an important role in being with Jim during the time he was dying. Jim taught her many lessons about how to relate to a dying person, which was of great value to her as she helped her father go through his dying. One key lesson was the importance of helping dying people retain a sense of dignity in the face of their losses. Another lesson pertained to listening to what the dying person is communicating, both verbally and nonverbally. Marianne also learned how essential it is to encourage the dying person to talk and to complete any unfinished business. Although dying is not easy, for the person dying or those who are assisting in this process, it is crucial that all concerned feel the freedom to talk about what they are experiencing.

STAGES OF GRIEF OVER A DIVORCE OR A SIGNIFICANT LOSS

The five stages of dying described by Kübler-Ross seem to have an application to the severing of relationships and other significant losses, experiences that bear some similarity to dying. To illustrate, we describe a divorce in terms of the five stages. Of course, you can broaden this concept to see whether it applies to separation from your parents, the experience of breaking up with a girlfriend or boyfriend, or the process of seeing your children mature and leave home. In fact, these stages appear to apply to those who are left behind when someone they love commits suicide, as discussed earlier. The stages can also provide understanding of the process one goes through after losing a job and facing the anxieties of unemployment. Although not all people who experience divorce, the breakup of a long-term relationship, or the loss of someone they love necessarily go through the stages in the same way, we've found that many people do experience a similar questioning and struggling.

Denial. Many people who are divorcing go through a process of denial and self-deception. They may try to convince themselves that the state of their marriage isn't all that bad, that nobody is perfect, and that things would be worse if they did separate. Even after the decision is made to divorce, they may feel a sense of disbelief. If it was the other person who initiated the divorce, the remaining partner might ask: Where did things go wrong? Why is she [he] doing this to me? How can this be happening to me?

Anger. Once people accept the reality that they are divorcing, they frequently experience anger and rage. They may say: "I gave a lot, and now I'm being deserted. I feel as if I've been used and then thrown away." Many people feel cheated and angry over the apparent injustice of what is happening to them. Just as it is very important for dying people to express any anger they feel, it's also important for people who are going through the grief associated with a divorce or other loss to express their anger. If they keep it bottled up inside, it is likely to be turned against themselves and may take the form of depression, a kind of self-punishment.

Bargaining. Sometimes people hope that a separation will give them the distance they need to reevaluate things and that they will soon get back together again. Although separations sometimes work in this way, it is often futile to wish that matters can be worked out. Nevertheless, during the bargaining stage one or both partners may try to make concessions and compromises that they hope will lead to a reconciliation.

Depression. In the aftermath of a decision to divorce, a sense of hopelessness may set in. As the partners realize that a reconciliation isn't possible, they may begin to dwell on the emptiness and loss they feel. They may find it very difficult to let go of the future they had envisioned together. They may spend much time ruminating over what their lives might have been like if they had made their relationship work. It is not uncommon for people who divorce to turn their anger away from their spouse and toward themselves. Thus, they may experience much self-blame and self-doubt. They may say to themselves: Maybe I didn't give the relationship a fair chance. What could I have done differently? I wonder where I went wrong? Why couldn't I do something different to make our relationship work? Depression can also be the result of the recognition that a real loss has been sustained. It is vitally important that people fully experience and express the grief (and anger) they feel over their loss. Too often people deceive themselves into believing that they are finished with their sadness (or anger) long before they have given vent to their intense feelings. Unresolved grief (and anger) tends to be carried around with a person, blocking the expression of many other feelings. For instance, if grief isn't worked through, it may be extremely difficult for a person to form new relationships, because in some ways he or she is still holding on to the past relationship.

Acceptance. If people allow themselves to mourn their losses, the process of grief work usually leads to a stage of acceptance. In the case of divorce, once the two persons have finished their grieving, new possibilities begin to open up. They can begin to accept that they must make a life for themselves without the other person and that they cannot cling to resentments that will keep them from beginning to establish that life. They can learn from their experience and apply that knowledge to future events.

In summary, these stages are experienced in different ways by each person who faces a significant loss. Some people, for example, express very little anger; others may not go through a bargaining stage. Nevertheless, the value of a model such as this one is that it provides some understanding of how we can learn to cope with the various losses in our life. Whatever the loss may be and whatever stage of grieving we may be experiencing, it seems to be crucial that we freely express our feelings. Otherwise, we may not be able to achieve acceptance.

Being "Dead" Psychologically and Socially

We find it valuable to broaden the conception of death and dying to include being "dead" in a variety of psychological and social ways. What is dead or dying in us may be something we want to resurrect, or it may be something that *should* die in order to make way for new growth.

Brugh Joy (1979, 1990) believes that most of us live a highly restricted life, which means that many aspects of our being lie dormant. His workshops and books are designed to tilt people from their narrow vision of reality to a set of possibilities that is truly without limits. He writes about people who are ready to open themselves to an awakening process that allows them to be fully alive across the range of human experience. Such individuals "know at the deepest level of their awareness that they are ready for change from unfulfilling, culturally conditioned life patterns into states of consciousness that commit them to a path of self-realization . . . [and] are beginning to become aware that their intimate limitations are nothing but the restrictions set by their own minds" (Joy, 1979, p. 9).

Casey and Vanceburg (1985) reminds us that "being alive is our invitation to act in fresh, inventive ways" (Meditation of February 27). It is not easy to act in fresh and inventive ways if we cling to the safety of old patterns. Sometimes growth requires that we be willing to let go of old and familiar ways of being, and we may need to mourn their loss before we can really move on. You may have experienced a letting go of the security of living with your parents, for example, in exchange for testing your independence by living alone and supporting yourself. In the process you may have lost something that was valuable to you, even if it was incompatible with your further development and growth. The following questions may help you to decide whether you're living as fully as you'd like to be.

ARE YOU CAUGHT UP IN DEADENING ROLES?

Our roles and functions can eventually trap us. Instead of fulfilling certain roles while maintaining a separate sense of identity, we may get lost in our roles and in the patterns of thought, feeling, and behavior that go with them. As a result, we may neglect important parts of ourselves and thus limit our options of feeling and experiencing. Moreover, we may feel lost when we're unable to play a certain role. Thus, a supervisor may not know how to behave when he or she isn't in a superior position to others, an instructor may be at loose ends when there are no students to teach, or a parent may find life empty when the children have grown.

Do you feel caught in certain roles? Do you depend on being able to identify with those roles in order to feel alive and valuable? Have you made the mistake of believing that who you are is expressed by a single role, no matter how much you value that role? Who and what would you be if your roles were stripped away one by one? Are you able to renew yourself by finding innovative ways of being and thinking? At this time in your life you might find that you're so caught up in the student role that you have little time or energy left for other parts of your life. When our roles begin to deaden us, we can ask whether we've taken on a function or identity that others have defined, instead of listening to our own inner promptings.

ARE YOU ALIVE TO YOUR SENSES AND YOUR BODY?

Your body expresses to a large degree how alive you are. It shows signs of your vitality or reveals your tiredness with life. Since your body doesn't lie, you can use it as an indication of the degree to which you're affirming life. As you look at your body, ask yourself: Do I like what I see? Am I taking good care of myself physically, or am I indifferent to my own bodily well-being? What am I expressing by my posture? What does my facial expression communicate?

You can also become deadened to the input from your senses. You may become oblivious to fragrances or eat foods without tasting or savoring them. Perhaps you rarely stop to notice the details of your surroundings. By contrast, taking time to be alive to your senses can help you feel renewed and interested in life. You might ask yourself: What sensations have particularly struck me today? What have I experienced and observed? What sensory surprises have enlivened me?

CAN YOU BE SPONTANEOUS AND PLAYFUL?

Is the "child" part of you living, or have you buried it away inside? Can you be playful, fun, curious, explorative, spontaneous, inappropriate, silly? As an adult, it is likely that you take yourself too seriously at times and lose the ability to laugh at yourself. Siegel (1988) emphasizes the value of laughter, play, and humor in healing and staying healthy. Humor shakes us out of our patterned ways and promotes new perspectives. In his therapy groups for cancer patients, Siegel helps them release the child within, for those who cannot play and laugh are the ones who experience the most difficulty in healing. If you find that you're typically realistic and objective to the point that it's difficult for you to be playful or light, you might ask what inner messages are blocking your ability to let go. Are you inhibited by a fear of being wrong? Are you afraid of being called silly or of meeting with others' disapproval? If you want to, you can begin to challenge the messages that say: "Don't!" "You should!" "You shouldn't!" You can experiment with new behavior and run the risk of seeming silly or of "not acting your age." Then *you* can decide whether you like your new behavior and want to be like a child more often.

ARE YOU ALIVE TO YOUR FEELINGS?

We can deaden ourselves to most of our feelings—the joyful ones as well as the painful ones. We can decide that feeling involves the risk of pain and that it's best to *think* our way through life. In choosing to cut off feelings of depression or sadness, we will most likely cut off feelings of joy. Closing ourselves to our lows usually seems to mean closing ourselves to our highs as well.

Sometimes we find it difficult to recognize our flat emotional state, so insulated have we made ourselves. To begin assessing how alive you are emotionally, you might ask yourself such questions as the following:

- Do I let myself feel my sadness and grieve over a loss?
- Do I try hard to cheer people up when they're sad or depressed, instead of allowing them to experience their feelings?
- Do I let myself cry if I feel like crying?
- Do I ever feel ecstasy and true joy?
- Do I let myself feel close to another person?
- Do I suppress certain emotions? Do I hide my feelings of insecurity, fear, dependence, tenderness, anger, boredom?
- Do I keep myself from showing my feelings out of fear?

ARE YOUR RELATIONSHIPS ALIVE?

Our relationships with the significant people in our lives have a way of becoming stale and deadening. It's easy to get stuck in habitual and routine ways of being with another person and to lose any sense of surprise and spontaneity. This kind of staleness is particularly common in long-term relationships. Of course, breaking out of predictable patterns in relationships can be fraught with anxiety. We have to decide whether we want security or vitality in our relationships. As you look at the significant relationships in your life, think about how alive both you and the other person in each relationship feel with each other. Do you give each other enough space to grow? Does the relationship energize you, or does it sap you of life? Are you settling into a comfortable, undemanding relationship? If you recognize that you aren't getting what you want in your friendships or intimate relationships, ask what *you* can do to revitalize them. Focus on how you can change yourself rather than getting others to change. You can also consider what specific things you'd like to ask from the other person. Simply talking about relationships can do a lot to bring new life into them.

ARE YOU ALIVE INTELLECTUALLY?

Children typically display much curiosity about life, yet somehow they often lose this interest in figuring out problems as they grow older. By the time we reach adulthood, we can easily become caught up in our activities, devoting little time to considering *why* we're doing them and whether we even *want* to be doing them. It's also easy to allow our intellectual potential to shrivel up, either by limiting our exposure to the environment or by failing to follow our curiosity.

This would be a good time for you to reassess the degree to which you keep yourself intellectually active in your classes. In the initial chapter we focus on ways that you can integrate mental and emotional dimensions of learning. One way of keeping mentally alert is by reflecting on how you can apply whatever you are learning in your classes to your personal development. How might you apply the notion of staying intellectually alive as a student? Have you given up on asking any real and substantive questions that you'd like to explore? Have you settled for merely going to classes and collecting the units you need to obtain a degree? Are you indifferent to learning? Are you open to learning new things? Are you changing as a learner?

ARE YOU ALIVE SPIRITUALLY?

As a healer, Bernie Siegel (1988) views spirituality as encompassing the belief in some meaning or order in the universe. From his perspective, there is a loving and intelligent force behind creation. Regardless of what label is used for this force, contact with it allows us the possibility of finding peace and resolving seeming contradictions between the inner world and the outer. Siegel claims that spirituality means accepting what is. He writes:

> Spirituality means the ability to find peace and happiness in an imperfect world, and to feel that one's own personality is imperfect but acceptable. From the peaceful state of mind come both creativity and the ability to love unselfishly, which go hand in hand. Acceptance, faith, forgiveness, peace, and love are the traits that define spirituality for me. These characteristics always appear in those who achieve unexpected healing of serious illness. (p. 178)

How do you define spirituality for yourself? How do your spiritual beliefs give your life meaning and value? To what extent does spirituality play a role in your life now?

Siegel (1988) talks about "spiritual flat tires," referring to unexpected events that can have positive or negative outcomes, depending on how we respond to these situations. As a healer, Siegel has made it his mission to teach people about the inseparable link between mind and body. He finds that people who survive catastrophic illnesses use occasional spiritual flat tires to get refocused and to redirect their lives. Although they may have delays and redirections on the path of life, they don't experience such events as fatal mistakes. Siegel puts the matter of spiritual vitality poetically:

> My advice is to live your life. Allow that wonderful inner intelligence to speak through you. The blueprint for you to be your authentic self lies within. In some mystical way the microscopic egg that grew to be you had the program for your physical, intellectual, emotional, and spiritual development. Allow the development to occur to its fullest; grow and bloom. Follow your bliss and be what you want to be. Don't climb the ladder of success only to find it's leaning against the wrong wall. Do not let your age limit your future growth as a human being. (p. xii)

Accepting Siegel's message can go a long way in helping us to live fully, rather than merely exist.

Time Out for Personal Reflection

1. How alive do you feel psychologically and socially? Check any of the following statements that apply to you.

_____	I feel alive and energetic most of the time.
_____	My body expresses aliveness and vitality.
_____	I feel intellectually curious and alive.
_____	I have significant friendships that are a source of nourishment for me.
_____	I can play and have fun.
_____	I allow myself to feel a wide range of emotions.
_____	I'm keenly aware of the things I see, smell, taste, and touch.
_____	I feel free to express who I am; I'm not trapped by my roles.

2. When do you feel most alive?

_____

_____

_____

_____

3. When do you feel least alive?

_____

_____

_____

_____

4. What specific things would you most like to change about your life so that you could feel more alive? What can you do to make these changes?

_____

_____

_____

_____

Taking Stock: How Well Are You Living Life?

It seems tragic that some people never really take the time to evaluate how well they are living life. Imagine for a moment that you're one of those people who get caught up in the routine of daily existence and never assess the quality of their living. Now assume that you are told that you have only a limited time to live. You begin to look at what you've missed and how you wish things had been different; you begin to experience regrets over the opportunities that you let slip by; you review the significant turning points in your life. You may wish now that you had paused to take stock at many points in your life, instead of waiting until it was too late.

One way to take stock of your life is to imagine your own death, including the details of the funeral and the things people might say about you. As an extension of this exercise, you might try actually writing down your own eulogy or obituary. This can be a powerful way of summing up how you see your life and how you'd like it to be different. In fact, we suggest that you try writing three eulogies for yourself. First, write your "actual" eulogy — the one you would give at your own funeral, if that were possible. Second, write the eulogy that you *fear* — one that expresses some of the negative things someone could say of you. Third, write the eulogy that you would *hope* for — one that expresses the most positive aspects of your life so far. After you've written your three eulogies, seal them in an envelope and put them away for a year or so. Then do the exercise again, and compare the two sets of eulogies to see what changes have occurred in your view of your life.

Postscript: Taking Time

Before he died on August 10, 1977, Jim Morelock gave me (Jerry) a poster showing a man walking in the forest with two small girls. At the top of the poster were the words "Take Time." Jim knew me well enough to know how I tend to get caught up in so many activities that I sometimes forget to simply take time to really experience and enjoy the simple things in life. As I write this, I'm also remembering what one student wrote to me as we were writing what we hoped and wished for each person in the class. On one of my slips of paper was written, "I hope you will take the time to smell a rose." In another class one student gave each person an epitaph. Mine read: "Here lies Jerry Corey — a man who all his life tried to do too many things at once." I promised myself that I'd make a poster with those words on it and place it on my office wall as a reminder to slow down and enjoy life. I think many of us could use reminders like these frequently — especially since it took me almost a semester to get around to putting that poster up! In closing this chapter, the simple message is *Take time*.

I wrote the preceding paragraph for the first edition of this book. Now, 16 years later, am I taking time to do fewer things at once and to enjoy life? Although I have been a slow learner in this respect, I am learning about the value of taking time for what is important. I am reassessing priorities and deciding on what I want besides accomplishments. I am seeing that there is a whole other dimension besides the concrete, rational, and logical world that I have been so comfortable in most of my life. Just now, at age 55, am I beginning to appreciate the many ways in which life continues to teach me important lessons if I pay attention. It's a constant process to look at the things I say and the things I do to determine if I am living in accordance with my nature. Still I do not find it easy to balance my work and leisure, nor have I discovered a way to do all of the things that I say are important to me. It is still a struggle to avoid crowding my life with more activities than I am possibly able to manage. It is also risky to even consider being open to modifying some ways that have led to apparent success. A part of me knows that there is more to life than I've allowed myself to sample, yet another part of me resists opening myself to untapped inner and outer resources.

Although Marianne and I work together in writing and doing workshops, I value spending personal time with her alone, as well as with our family and friends. Because I value my health and enjoy biking and hiking, I *make* the time for these activities, even though it means working less. Although I still have some trouble in taking as much time as I would like for fun, play, and relaxation, I am clearly improving in this respect. Yet, I become anxious as I experience the weeks, months, and years passing too quickly. Within the past year or so, I have been asking myself more often: Is what I am doing now what I *really* want to be doing? And before I accept a work project, I am lingering a bit longer and asking myself: Do I want to accept this project, and what will I have to give up to make time for this new project? Recently I have spent time reflecting on the difference between taking time for doing things and time simply for being. I am also learning how to appreciate the value of making time for quiet reflection, internal focusing, and getting centered, all of which are key in learning to listen to the wisdom within my inner being. It becomes a matter of looking at my behavior so that I can determine the extent to which I am living in accordance with my priorities and by conscious choices.

Chapter Summary

In this chapter we've encouraged you to devote some time to reflecting on your eventual death, because doing so can lead you to examine the quality and direction of your life and help you find your own meaning in living. The acceptance of death is closely related to the acceptance of life. Recognizing and accepting the fact of death gives us the impetus to search for our own answers to questions such as: What is the meaning of my life? What do I most want from life? How can I create the life I want to live? In addition, we've encouraged you to assess how fully alive you are right now.

Although terminally ill people show great variability in how they deal with their dying, a general pattern of stages has been identified: denial, anger, bargaining, depression, and acceptance. These same stages can apply to other types of loss, such as separation and divorce. People go through stages of grief in working through their losses. Grieving is necessary if we are to recover from any significant loss. Unless we express and explore feelings of sorrow, anger, and guilt over our losses, we are likely to remain stuck in depression and a feeling of numbness.

If we can honestly confront our fears of death, we have a chance to work on changing the quality of our life and to make real changes in our relationships with others and with ourselves. We often live as though we had forever to accomplish what we want. Few of us ever contemplate that this may be the last day we have. The realization that there is an end to our life can motivate us to get the most from the time we have. The fact of our finality can also be an impetus to take care of unfinished business. Thus, it is crucial that we live in a manner that will lead to few regrets. The more we fail to deal with immediate realities, the greater the likelihood that we will fear death.

Activities and Exercises

1. For at least a week take a few minutes each day to reflect on when you feel alive and when you feel "dead." Do you notice any trends in your observations? What can you do to feel more alive?

2. If you knew you were going to die within a short time, in what ways would you live your life differently? What might you give up? What might you be doing that you're not doing or experiencing now?

3. Imagine yourself on your deathbed. Write down whom you want to be there, what you want them to say to you, and what you want to say to them. Then write down your reactions to this experience.

4. For about a week write down specific things you see, read, or hear relating to the denial or avoidance of death in our culture.

5. Let yourself reflect on how the death of those you love might affect you. Consider each person separately, and try to imagine how your life today would be different if that person were not in it. In your journal you might respond to such questions as: Do I now have the relationships with my loved ones that I want to have? What's missing? What changes do I most want to make in my relationships?

6. Consider making some time alone in which to write three eulogies for yourself: one that you think *actually* sums up your life, one that you *fear* could be written about you, and one that you *hope* could be written about you. Write the eulogies as if you had died today; then seal them in an envelope, and do the exercise again in the future — say, in about a year. At that time you can compare your eulogies to see in what respects your assessment of your life and your hopes and fears have changed.

7. After you've written your three eulogies, you might write down in your journal what the experience was like for you and what you learned from it. Are there any specific steps you'd like to take *now* in order to begin living more fully?

8. Investigate what type of hospice program, if any, your community has. Who is on the staff? What services does it offer? For a description of hospice programs in various communities, you can write to the National Hospice Organization, 765 Prospect Street, New Haven, CT 06511.

9. Select one or more of the following books for further reading on the topics explored in this chapter: Siegel *Love, Medicine, and Miracles* (1988); Siegel, *Peace, Love, and Healing* (1989); Kalish, *Death, Grief, and Caring Relationships* (1985); Kübler-Ross, *On Death and Dying* (1969) and *Death: The Final Stage of Growth* (1975).

Meaning and Values

Prechapter Self-Inventory

Use the following scale to respond: 4 = this statement is true of me *most of the time*; 3 = this statement is true of me *much* of the time; 2 = this statement is true of me *some* of the time; 1 = this statement is true of me *almost none* of the time.

_____ 1. At this time in my life I have a sense of meaning and purpose that gives me direction.

_____ 2. Most of my values are similar to those of my parents.

_____ 3. I have challenged and questioned most of the values I now hold.

_____ 4. Religion is an important source of meaning for me.

_____ 5. I generally live by the values I hold.

_____ 6. My values and my views about life's meaning have undergone much change over the years.

_____ 7. The meaning of my life is based in large part on my ability to have a significant impact on others.

_____ 8. I let others influence my values more than I'd like to admit.

_____ 9. I value my dreams.

_____ 10. I have a clear sense of who I am and what I want to become.

Introduction

In this chapter we encourage you to look critically at the *why* of your existence, to clarify the sources of your values, and to reflect on questions such as these: In what direction am I moving in my life? What do I have to show for my years on this earth so far? Where have I been, where am I now, and where do I want to go? What steps can I take to make the changes I have decided on?

Many who are fortunate enough to achieve power, fame, success, and material comfort nevertheless experience a sense of emptiness. Although they may not be able to articulate what is lacking in their lives, they know that something is amiss. The astronomical number of pills and drugs consumed to allay the symptoms of this "existential vacuum"—depression and anxiety—is evidence of our failure to find values that allow us to make sense of our place in the world. In *Habits of the Heart*, Bellah and his colleagues (1985) found among the people they interviewed a growing interest in finding purpose in their lives. Although our achievements as a society are enormous, we seem to be hovering on the very brink of disaster, not only from internal conflict but also from societal incoherence. Bellah and his associates assert that the core problem with our society is that we have put our own good, as individuals and as groups, ahead of the common good.

The need for a sense of meaning is manifested by the increased interest in religion, especially among young people in college. A student told us recently that in her English class of twenty students, four of them had selected religion as a topic for a composition dealing with a conflict in their lives. Other signs of the search for meaning include the widespread interest in Eastern and other philosophies, the use of meditation, the number of self-help and inspirational books published each year, the experimentation with different lifestyles, and even the college courses in personal adjustment!

The paradox of our contemporary society is that although we have the benefits of technological progress, we are still not satisfied. We have become increasingly troubled about ourselves and our place in the world, we have less certainty about morality, and we are less sure that there is any meaning or purpose in the universe (Carr, 1988, p. 167). It seems fair to say that we are caught up in a crisis of meaning and values.

Our Search for Identity

The discovery of meaning and values is essentially related to our achievement of identity as a person. The quest for identity involves a commitment to give birth to ourselves by exploring the meaning of our uniqueness and humanity. A major problem for many people is that they have lost a sense of self, because they have directed their search for identity outside themselves. In their attempt to be liked and accepted by everyone, they have become finely tuned to what *others* expect of them but alienated from their *own* inner desires and feelings. As Rollo May (1973) observes, they are able to *respond* but not to *choose*. Indeed, May sees inner emptiness as the chief problem in contemporary society; too many of us, he says, have become "hollow people" who have very little understanding of who we are and what we feel. He cites one person's succinct description: "I'm just a collection of mirrors, reflecting what everyone expects of me" (p. 15).

Moustakas (1975) describes the same alienation from self that May talks about. For Moustakas, alienation is "the developing of a life outlined and determined by others, rather than a life based on one's own inner experience" (p. 31). If we become alienated from ourselves, we don't trust our own feelings but respond automatically to others as we think they want us to respond. As a consequence, Moustakas writes, we live in a world devoid of excitement, risk, and meaning.

As mentioned in the previous chapter, in order to find out who we are, we may have to let parts of us die. We may need to shed old roles and identities that no longer give us vitality. Doing so may require a period of mourning for our old selves. Most people who have struggled with shedding immature and dependent roles and assuming a more active stance toward life know that such rebirth isn't easy and that it may entail pain as well as joy.

Jourard (1971) makes a point that we find exciting. He maintains that we begin to cease living when meaning vanishes from life. Yet too often we are encouraged to believe that we have only *one* identity, *one* role, *one* way to be,

LIFE MAY HAVE MANY DIFFERENT MEANINGS BETWEEN CHILDHOOD AND OLD AGE

and *one* purpose to fulfill in a lifetime. This way of thinking can be figuratively deadly, for when our one ground for being alive is outgrown or lost, we may begin to die psychologically instead of accepting the challenge of reinventing ourselves anew. To keep ourselves from dying spiritually, we need to allow ourselves to imagine new ways of being, to invent new goals to live for, to search for new and more fulfilling meanings, to acquire new identities, and to reinvent our relationships with others. In essence, we need to allow parts of us to die in order to experience the rebirth that is necessary for growth.

Achieving identity doesn't necessarily mean stubbornly clinging to a certain way of thinking or behaving. Instead, it may involve trusting ourselves enough to become open to new possibilities. Nor is an identity something we achieve for all time; rather, we need to be continually willing to reexamine our patterns and our priorities, our habits and relationships. Above all, we need to develop the ability to listen to our inner selves and trust what we hear. To take just one example, some students for whom academic life has become stale and empty have chosen to leave it in response to their inner feelings. Some have opted to travel and live modestly for a time, taking in new cultures and even assimilating into them for a while. They may not be directly engaged in preparing for a career and, in that sense, "estab-lishing" themselves, but they are achieving their own identities by being open to new experiences and ways of being. For some of them, it may take real courage to resist the pressure to settle down in a career or "complete" their education.

Our search for identity involves asking three key existential questions, none of which has easy or definite answers: Who am I? Where am I going? Why?

The question Who am I? is never settled once and for all, for it can be answered differently at different times in our life. We need to revise our life, especially when old identities no longer seem to supply a meaning or give us direction. As we have seen, we must decide whether to let others tell us who we are or to take a stand and define ourselves.

Where am I going? This issue relates to our plans for a lifetime and the means we expect to use in attaining our goals. Like the previous question, this one demands periodic review. Our life goals are not set once and for all. Again, do we show the courage it takes to decide for ourselves where we are going, or do we look for a guru to show us where to go?

Asking the question Why? and searching for reasons are characteristics of being human. We face a rapidly changing world in which old values give way to new ones or to none at all. Part of shaping an identity implies that we are actively searching for meaning, trying to make sense of the world in which we find ourselves.

At this point you might pause to assess how you experience your identity at this time in your life. The following "Time Out" may help you do so.

Time Out for Personal Reflection

1. In the space below list the things that you most like to do or the ac-tivities that have the most meaning for you.

   _____

   _____

   _____

   _____

2. How often do you do or experience each of the things you've just listed?

   _____

   _____

   _____

   _____

3. Does anything prevent you from doing the things you value as frequently as you'd like? If so, what?

_____

_____

_____

_____

4. What are some specific actions you can take to increase the amount of meaningful activity in your life?

_____

_____

_____

_____

5. Who are you? Try completing the sentence "I am . . ." ten different ways by quickly writing down the words or phrases that immediately occur to you. Use the spaces provided below.

I am:

_____   _____

_____   _____

_____   _____

_____   _____

_____   _____

Our Quest for Meaning and Purpose

Humans are the only creatures we know of who can reflect on their existence and, based on this capacity for self-awareness, exercise individual choice in defining their lives. With this freedom, however, come responsibility and a degree of anxiety. If we truly accept that the meaning of our life is largely the product of our own choosing and the emptiness of our life the result of our failure to choose, our anxiety is increased. To avoid this anxiety, we may refuse to examine the values that govern our daily behavior or to accept that we are, to a large degree, what we have chosen to become. Instead, we may make other people or outside institutions responsible for the direction of our life. We pay a steep price for thus choosing a sense of security over our own freedom — the price of denying our basic humanness.

One obstacle in the way of finding meaning is that the world itself may appear meaningless. It's easy, when we look at the absurdity of the world in which we live, to give up the struggle or to seek some authoritative source of meaning. Yet creating our own meaning is precisely our challenge and task as human beings.

Yalom (1980) cites a number of psychotherapists who appear to agree on one major point: many clients who enter psychotherapy do so because they lack a clear sense of meaning and purpose in life. Yalom states the crisis of meaninglessness in its most basic form: "How does a being who needs meaning find meaning in a universe that has no meaning?" (p. 423). Along with Frankl, Yalom concludes that humans require meaning to survive. To live without meaning and values provokes considerable distress, and in its severe form it may lead to the decision for suicide. Humans apparently have a need for some absolutes in the form of clear ideals to which they can aspire and guidelines by which they can direct their actions.

Viktor Frankl is a European psychiatrist who has dedicated his professional life to the study of meaning in life. The approach to therapy that he developed is known as *logotherapy*, which means "therapy through meaning," or "healing through meaning." According to Frankl (1963, 1965, 1969, 1978), what distinguishes us as humans is our search for purpose. The striving to find meaning in our lives is a primary motivational force. Humans can choose to live and even die for the sake of their ideals and values. In his book *Man's Search for Meaning* (1963), Frankl shows how some element of choice is always possible. Frankl notes that "everything can be taken from a man but one thing: the last of the human freedoms — to choose one's attitude in any given set of circumstances, to choose one's own way" (p. 104). Frankl is fond of pointing out the wisdom of Nietzsche's words: "He who has a *why* to live for can bear with almost any *how*" (1963, p. 164). Drawing on his experiences in the death camp at Auschwitz, Frankl asserts that inmates who had a vision of some goal, purpose, or task in life had a much greater chance of surviving than those who had no sense of mission. We are constantly confronted with choices, and the decisions we make or fail to make influence the meaning of our lives.

This relationship between choice and meaning is dramatically illustrated by Holocaust survivors who report that although they did not choose their circumstances, they could at least choose their attitude toward their plight. Consider the example of Dr. Edith Eva Eger, a 64-year-old clinical psychologist who practices in La Jolla, California, who was interviewed about her experiences as a survivor of a Nazi concentration camp (see Glionna, 1992). At one point, Eger weighed only forty pounds, yet she refused to engage in cannibalism that was taking place. She said, "I chose to eat grass. And I sat on the ground, selecting one blade over the other, telling myself that even under those conditions I still had a choice — which blade of grass I would eat." Although Eger lost her family to the camps and had her back broken by one of the guards, she eventually chose to let go of her hatred. She finally came to the realization that it was her captors who were the imprisoned ones. As she put it: "If I still hated today, I would still be in prison. I would be giving Hitler and Mengele their posthumous victories. If I hated, they would still be in charge, not me." Her example supports the notion that even in the most dire situations, it is possible to give a new meaning to such circumstances by our choice of attitudes.

FINDING MEANING BY TRANSCENDING PERSONAL INTERESTS

Carr (1988) concludes that what most of us want is to make a difference in the world. The process of becoming self-actualizing begins as a personal search. Although self-acceptance is a prerequisite for meaningful interpersonal relationships, there is a quest to go beyond self-centered interests. Ultimately, we want to establish connections with others in society, and we want to make a contribution. Likewise, Bellah and his colleagues (1985) conclude that meaning in life is found through intense relationships with others, not through an exclusive and narrow pursuit of self-realization. In their interviews with many people they found a desire to move beyond the isolated self. Our common life requires more than an exclusive concern with material accumulation. These authors maintain that a reconstituting of the social world is required, involving a transformation of consciousness.

DEVELOPING A PHILOSOPHY OF LIFE

A philosophy of life is made up of the fundamental beliefs, attitudes, and values that govern a person's behavior. Many students have said that they hadn't really thought much about their philosophy of life. However, the fact that we've never explicitly defined the components of our philosophy doesn't mean that we are completely without one. All of us do operate on the basis of general assumptions about ourselves, others, and the world. Thus, the first step in actively developing a philosophy of life is to formulate a clearer picture of our present attitudes and beliefs.

We have all been developing an implicit philosophy of life since we first began, as children, to wonder about life and death, love and hate, joy and fear, and the nature of the universe. We probably didn't need to be taught to be curious about such questions; raising them seems to be a natural part of human development. If we were fortunate, adults took the time to engage in dialogue with us, instead of discouraging us from asking questions and deadening some of our innate curiosity.

During the adolescent years the process of questioning usually assumes new dimensions. Adolescents who have been allowed to question and think for themselves as children begin to get involved in a more advanced set of issues. Many of the adolescents we've encountered in classes and workshops have at one time or another struggled with questions such as the following:

- Are the values that I've believed in for all these years the values I want to continue to live by?
- Where did I get my values? Are they still valid for me? Are there additional sources from which I can derive new values?

- Is there a God? What is the nature of the hereafter? What is my conception of a God? What does religion mean in my life? What kind of religion do I choose for myself? Does religion have any value for me?
- What do I base my ethical and moral decisions on? Peer-group standards? Parental standards? The normative values of my society?
- What explains the inhumanity I see in our world?
- What kind of future do I want? What can I do about actively creating this kind of future?

These are only a few of the questions that many adolescents think about and perhaps answer for themselves. However, a philosophy of life is not something we arrive at once and for all during our adolescent years. The development of a philosophy of life continues as long as we live. As long as we remain curious and open to new learning, we can revise and rebuild our conceptions of the world. Life may have a particular meaning for us during adolescence, a new meaning during adulthood, and still another meaning as we reach old age. Indeed, if we don't remain open to basic changes in our views of life, we may find it difficult to adjust to changed circumstances.

Keeping in mind that developing a philosophy of life is a continuing activity of examining and modifying the values we live by, you may find the following suggestions helpful as you go about formulating and reforming your own philosophy:

- Frequently create time to be alone in reflective thought.
- Consider what meaning the fact of your eventual death has for the present moment.
- Make use of significant contacts with others who are willing to challenge your beliefs and the degree to which you live by them.
- Adopt an accepting attitude toward those whose belief systems differ from yours, and develop a willingness to test your own beliefs.

We strongly recommend that you take the time to look at the outline in the "Activities and Exercises" section at the end of this chapter. This outline will help you clarify some key aspects of your philosophy of life, as will the following "Time Out."

Time Out for Personal Reflection

Complete the following sentences by writing down the first responses that come to mind:

1. My parents have influenced my values by _____

_____

2. Life would hardly be worth living if it weren't for _____

_____

3. One thing that I most want to say about my life at this point is

_____

4. If I could change one thing about my life at this point, it would be

_____

5. If I had to answer the question Who am I? in a sentence, I'd say

_____

_____

6. What I like best about me is _____

_____

7. I keep myself alive and vital by _____

_____

8. I'm unique, in that _____

_____

9. When I think of my future, I _____

_____

10. I feel discouraged about life when _____

_____

11. My friends have influenced my values by _____

_____

12. My beliefs have been influenced by _____

_____

13. I feel most powerful when _____

_____

14. If I don't change, _____

_____

15. I feel good about myself when _____

_____

16. To me, the essence of a meaningful life is _____

_____

17. I suffer from a sense of meaninglessness when _____

_____

RELIGION AND MEANING: A PERSONAL VIEW

Religious faith can be a powerful source of meaning and purpose. Religion helps many people make sense out of the universe and the mystery of our purpose in living. Like any other potential source of meaning, religious faith seems most authentic and valuable when it enables us to become as fully human as possible. This means that religion helps us get in touch with our own powers of thinking, feeling, deciding, willing, and acting. You might consider reflecting on the following questions about your religion to determine whether it is a constructive force in your life:

- Does my religion provide me with a set of values that is congruent with the way I live my life?
- Does my religion assist me in better understanding the meaning of life and death?
- Does my religion allow tolerance for others who see the world differently from me?
- Does my religion provide me with a sense of peace and serenity?
- Is my religious faith something that I actively choose or passively accept?
- Do my religious beliefs help me live life fully and treat others with respect and concern?
- Does my religion help me integrate my experience and make sense of the world?
- Does my religion encourage me to exercise my freedom and to assume the responsibility for the direction of my own life?
- Are my religious beliefs helping me become more of the person I'd like to become?
- Does my religion encourage me to question life and keep myself open to new learning?

As you take time for self-examination, how able are you to answer these questions in a way that is meaningful and satisfying to you? If you are honest with yourself, perhaps you will find that you have not really critically evaluated the sources of your spiritual and religious beliefs. Although you may hesitate to question your belief system out of a fear of weakening or undermining your faith, the opposite might well be true: demonstrating the courage to question your beliefs and values might strengthen them. As we have mentioned, increasing numbers of people seem to be deciding that a religious faith is necessary if they are to find an order and purpose in life. At the same time, many others insist that religion only impedes the quest for meaning or that it is incompatible with contemporary beliefs in other areas of life. What seems essential is that our acceptance or rejection of religious faith come authentically from within ourselves and that we remain open to new experience and learning, whatever points of view we decide on.

It is perhaps worth emphasizing that a "religion" may take the form of a system of beliefs and values concerning the ultimate questions in life rather than (or in addition to) membership in a church. People who belong to a church may not be "religious" in this sense, and others may consider themselves religious even though they are atheists or agnostics. Like almost anything else in human life, religion (or irreligion) can be bent to worthwhile or base purposes.

In my own experience, I (Jerry) have found religion most valuable when it is a challenge to broaden my choices and potential, rather than a restrictive influence. Until I was about 30, I tended to think of my religion as a package of ready-made answers for all the crises of life and was willing to let my church make many key decisions for me. I now think that I was experiencing too much anxiety in many areas of life to take full responsibility for my choices. My religious training had taught me that I should look to the authority of the church for ultimate answers in the areas of morality, value, and purpose. Like many other people I was encouraged to learn the "correct" answers and conform my thinking to them. Now, when I think of religion as a positive force, I think of it as being *freeing*, in the sense that it encourages me to trust myself, to discover the sources of strength and integrity within myself, and to assume responsibility for my own choices.

Although as an adult I've questioned and altered many of the religious teachings with which I was raised, I haven't discarded many of my past moral and religious values. Many of them served a purpose earlier in my life and, with modification, are still meaningful for me. However, whether or not I continue to hold the beliefs and values I've been taught, it seems crucial to me that I be willing to subject them to scrutiny. If they hold up under challenge, I can reincorporate them; by the same token, I can continue to examine the new beliefs and values I acquire.

My (Marianne's) religious faith has always been a positive force in my life. Sometimes people who are religious suffer from feelings of guilt and fears of damnation. This saddens me greatly, for if this is the case, religion ceases being a positive and powerful force in one's life. For me, religion helps me with an inner strength on which I can rely and that helps me to overcome difficulties that life presents. Although religion was encouraged in my childhood, it was never forced on me. It was a practice that I wanted to emulate because I saw the positive effects it had on the people in my life. Religion was practiced more than it was preached. The questions that we asked you to reflect on earlier are ones that I pose to myself as well. I want to be sure that I am aware of my beliefs and the necessity for making changes if I am not satisfied with my answers.

VALUES FOR OUR CHILDREN

When our daughters Heidi and Cindy were growing up, we hoped they would come to share some important values with us. We hoped that they would

- have a positive and significant impact on the people in their lives
- be willing to dare and not always choose caution over risk
- form their own values rather than unquestioningly adopting ours

- like and respect themselves and feel good about their abilities and talents
- be open and trusting, rather than fearful or suspicious
- respect and care for others
- continue to have fun as they grew older
- be able to express their feelings and always feel free to come to us and share meaningful aspects of their lives
- remain in touch with their power and refuse to surrender it
- be independent and have the courage to be different from others if they wanted to be
- have an interest in a religion that they freely chose
- be proud of themselves, yet humble
- respect the differences in others
- not compromise their values and principles for material possessions
- develop a flexible view of the world and be willing to modify their perspective based on new experiences
- give back to the world by contributing to make it a better place to live
- make a difference in the lives of others

Our daughters graduated from college a couple of years ago, and our hopes for them continue to be manifested. We enjoy sharing in their lives and being with them. They are now more independent from us, yet they continue to value time with us and invite us to be involved in their lives. Although their lives are not problem-free, they typically show a willingness to face and deal with their struggles and are succeeding in making significant choices for themselves. If you have children or expect to have children someday, you might pause to think about the values you would like them to develop, as well as the part that you will need to play in offering them guidance.

BECOMING AWARE OF HOW YOUR VALUES OPERATE

Your values influence what you do; your daily behavior is an expression of your basic values. We encourage you to make the time to continue examining the source of your values to determine if they are appropriate for you at this time in your life. Furthermore, it is essential that you be aware of the significant impact your value system has on your relationships with others. In our view, it is not appropriate for you to push your values on others, to assume a judgmental stance toward those who have a different world view, or to strive to convert others to adopt your perspective on life. Indeed, if you are secure in your values and basic beliefs, you will not be threatened by those who have a different set of beliefs and values.

In *God's Love Song*, Maier (1991) wonders how anyone can claim to have found the only way, not only for himself or herself but also for everyone else. We strongly agree with his view that there is a unique way for each person, however different that may be from the way of anyone else. As a minister, Sam Maier teaches that diversity shared not only is beautiful but also fosters understanding, caring, and the creation of community. He puts this message in a powerful and poetic way:

> It is heartening to find communities where the emphasis is placed upon each person having the opportunity to:
> - share what is vital and meaningful out of one's own experience;
> - listen to what is vital and meaningful to others;
> - not expect or demand that anyone else do it exactly the same way as oneself. (p. 3)

Reverend Maier's message is well worth contemplating. Although you might clarify a set of values that seem to work for you, we would hope that you respect the values of others that may be quite different from yours. It is not that one is right and the other is wrong. The diversity of cultures, religions, and world views implies a necessity not only to tolerate differences but also to embrace diverse paths toward meaning in life.

Whatever your own values are, they can be further clarified and strengthened if you entertain open discussion of various viewpoints and cultivate a nonjudgmental attitude toward diversity. You might raise questions such as:

- Where did I develop my values?
- Are my values open to modification?
- Have I challenged my values, and am I open to being challenged by others?
- Do I insist that the world remain the same now as it was earlier in my life?
- Do I feel so deeply committed to any of my values that I'm likely to push my friends and family members to accept them?
- How would I communicate my values to others without imposing those values?
- How do my own values and beliefs affect my behavior?
- Am I willing to accept people who hold different values?
- Do I avoid judging others if they think, feel, or act in different ways from myself?

Time Out for Personal Reflection

1. At this time, what are some of the principal sources of meaning and purpose in your life?

   _____

   _____

   _____

   _____

2. Have there been occasions in your life when you've allowed other people or institutions to make key choices for you? If so, give a couple of examples.

_____

_____

_____

_____

3. What role, if any, has religion played in your life?

_____

_____

_____

_____

4. If you were to create a new religion, what virtues and values would you include? What would be the vices and sins?

_____

_____

_____

_____

5. What are some of the values you'd most like to see your children adopt?

_____

_____

_____

_____

6. The following is a list of some of the things different people value. Rate the importance of each one for you, using a five-point scale, with *1* meaning *extremely important* and *5* meaning *very unimportant*.

_____   companionship
_____   family life
_____   security
_____   being financially and materially successful
_____   enjoying leisure time
_____   work
_____   learning and getting an education

	appreciation of nature
_____	competing and winning
_____	loving others and being loved
_____	a relationship with God
_____	self-respect and pride
_____	being productive and achieving
_____	enjoying an intimate relationship
_____	having solitude and private time to reflect
_____	having a good time and being with others
_____	laughter and a sense of humor
_____	intelligence and a sense of curiosity
_____	opening up to new experiences
_____	risk taking and personal growth
_____	being approved of and liked by others
_____	being challenged and meeting challenges well
_____	courage
_____	compassion
_____	being of service to others

Now go back over your list, and circle the things you'd like to have more of in your life. You might think of what keeps you from having or doing the things that you value most.

Dreams as a Pathway to Self-Understanding

People have been fascinated with dreams and have regarded them as significant since ancient times. But dreams have been the subject of scientific investigation only since the mid-nineteenth century. Freud pioneered the scientific study of dreams and made significant discoveries about their meaning and functioning. The first edition of his classic book on this subject, *The Interpretation of Dreams*, was published in 1900 (Freud, 1900/1965).

DREAMS AS AN INDICATOR OF MEANING

When we give guest lectures in both high school and college psychology classes, we get many questions from students about the meaning of their dreams. They frequently ask about particular dreams that they or friends have had. We are cautious about interpreting dreams in this setting, of course, but we generally tell students that dreams are an expression of their inner lives. Dreams are not mysterious but rather can reveal significant clues to events that have meaning for us. If we train ourselves to recall our dreams and discipline ourselves to explore their meanings, we can get a good sense of our struggles, wants, goals, purposes, conflicts, and interests. Dreams can shed a powerful light on our past, present, and future dynamics and on our attempt to identify meaning. They are messages that deserve to be listened to and respected. Dreams can offer you a pathway toward a better understanding of yourself and the choices that are open to you.

In a comparison of dream recallers (those who recall at least one dream a month) and those who do not remember their dreams, Rainwater (1979) reports some interesting differences. Those who do not recall dreams tend to be more inhibited, more conformist, more self-controlled, and more likely to deny or avoid unpleasant situations and confrontations in their daily lives than people who do recall their dreams.

If you are interested in recalling your dreams, Rainwater suggests that you make a contract with yourself to write them down in a journal as soon as you awaken. You may merely jot down fleeting impressions or feelings. Even writing down fragments of a dream, however, often leads to remembering other details. Other suggestions are offered later in this section.

Until recently, I (Jerry) did not frequently have dreams that I could remember. Recently, I attended a conference where an exploration of our dreams was a central part of the program. I began to record whatever fragments of dreams I could recall, and interestingly, during this conference I started to recall some vivid and rich dreams. I have made it a practice to record in my journal any dreams upon awakening, along with my impressions and reactions to the dreams. It helps me to share my dreams with Marianne or other friends, especially in comparing impressions others have to my dreams. I also find it useful to consider that all the images in my dreams are manifestations of some dimension within me. In Gestalt fashion, I typically allow myself to reflect on the ways that people in my dreams represent parts of myself. Becoming the various images in the dream is a way for me to bring unconscious themes forward. What I am finding is that my dreams have a pattern and that they are shorthand ways of understanding conflicts in my life, decisions to be made at crossroads, and themes that tend to recur from time to time. Even a short segment of a dream often contains layers of messages that make sense when I look at what is going on in my waking state.

APPROACHES TO EXPLORING THE MEANING OF DREAMS

We will briefly consider four ways of understanding and working with dreams. These approaches all need to be understood in light of the other basic ideas that are integral to each theory.

Freud's approach to dreams. In a preface that first appeared in the 1932 edition of *The Interpretation of Dreams*, Freud maintained that the book ranked among his most significant contributions to psychology: "It contains, even according to my present-day judgment, the most valuable of all the discoveries it has been my good fortune to make. Insight such as this falls to one's lot but once in a lifetime" (1900/1965, p. xxxii).

Freud writes that dreams represent, in disguised or symbolic form, repressed desires, fears, conflicts, and wishes. Dreams can be understood as repressed wishes, which are buried because they are intolerably painful. The most important of these wishes have their roots in early childhood and are largely sexual and aggressive in nature. Because certain feelings have been repressed (and have been locked in the unconscious), they can surface only in disguised fashion during sleep when the defenses are lowered. Freud calls the repressive agent the *censor*, which is less vigilant during sleep (Hall, 1984).

Freud sees dreams as the "royal road to the unconscious," for in them one's unconscious wishes, needs, and fears are expressed. Dreams have both a *manifest* (or conscious) content and a *latent* (or hidden) content. The manifest content is the dream as it appears to the dreamer; the latent content consists of the disguised, unconscious motives that represent the hidden symbolic meaning of the dream. According to Freud, there are consistent symbols in dreams that allow for an interpretation of their meaning. Although dream symbols have an apparent universality, dreams must be interpreted in an individual context. Symbols are specific to each dreamer, they reveal conflicts in a condensed and intensified form, and they derive their meaning from what is going on in the dreamer's life.

The Freudian approach to dream interpretation emphasizes expression of repressed sexual wishes and fears. For example, Freud writes that steps, ladders, and staircases represent sexual intercourse. Elongated objects are said to represent the male genitals, while enclosed spaces are symbolic of the female genitals. Indeed, Freud sees sexuality as a primary motivation underlying much of human behavior: "It is fair to say that there is no group of ideas that is incapable of representing sexual facts and wishes" (Freud, 1900/1965, p. 406). Other symbols or events, along with their latent psychoanalytic meaning, including bathing as birth, beginning a journey as dying, king and queen as parents, being naked in a crowd as a desire to be noticed, flying as a desire to be admired, and falling as a desire to return to an earlier developmental period where one was taken care of and was safe (Schultz, 1990). If you want to do some ambitious reading on the meaning of dreams, consult *The Interpretation of Dreams*.

Jung's approach to dreams. Carl Jung, the Swiss psychiatrist, was greatly influenced by Freud's *Interpretation of Dreams*. Jung's theory assigned great value to dreams. According to Hall (1984), he believed that many dreams contained messages from the deepest layers of the unconscious, which he thought of as the source of creativity. Jung called this deep layer the *collective unconscious*, for it is the same in every person in every culture. Dreams reflect not only an individual's personal unconscious but also the collective unconscious. This means that some dreams deal with an individual's relationship to a larger whole such as the family, universal humanity, and generations over time. The contents of the collective unconscious are called *archetypes*, which are expressed in the form of images and inherited from past generations. Examples of some of the archetypes with which Jung was concerned are magic, the hero, the child, God, the demon, the animal, the earth mother, power, birth, rebirth, death, and the wise old man. Other important archetypes include the *persona*, the *anima* and the *animus*, and the *shadow*. The persona is the mask, or public face, that we wear to protect ourselves. The animus and the anima, as we have seen, represent both the biological and psychological aspects of masculinity and femininity, which are thought to coexist in both sexes. The shadow has the deepest roots and is the most dangerous and powerful of the archetypes. It represents our "dark side," the thoughts, feelings, and actions that are socially reprehensible and that we tend to disown by projecting them outward. In a dream all of these parts can be considered a manifestation of who and what we are.

As a way of identifying the expression of an archetype in a dream, Jung would ask dreamers to say what each part of the dream reminded them of. A certain element of a dream could then be amplified by the dreamer and also by the therapist through references to mythology, art, religion, and literature (Hall, 1984).

Jung agreed with Freud that dreams provide a pathway into the unconscious, but he differed with Freud on the causes of dreams. Jung writes that dreams have two purposes: They are prospective, in that they help people prepare themselves for the experiences and events they anticipate in the near future. Dreams also serve a compensatory function; that is, they work to bring about a balance between opposites within the person. They compensate for the overdevelopment of one facet of the individual's personality (Schultz, 1990).

Jung views dreams more as an attempt to express than a try to repress and disguise. They are a creative effort of the dreamer in struggling with contradiction, complexity, and confusion. The aim of the dream is resolution and integration. According to Jung, each part of the dream can be understood as some projected quality of the dreamer. His method of interpreting dreams draws on a series of dreams obtained from a person. For Jung, dreams form a coherent series in the course of which the meaning gradually unfolds. If you are interested in further reading, we suggest Jung's (1961) *Memories, Dreams, Reflections.*

Brugh Joy (1990) draws heavily from Jungian concepts in his work with dreams in his conferences. Exploration of dream material is such a fundamental, honest, and candid revelation about people that Joy says he cannot imagine working with individuals who are interested in psychological and spiritual development without focusing on dreams. Joy believes that the personal and collective unconscious patterns control all aspects of our conscious behavior, for underneath the conscious layer exists the dance of the unconscious forces, which are revealed in dreams. Joy states: "Dreams are like looking at an incredibly detailed and often complex blueprint of one's individual makeup, with emphasis on patterns that are presently active or are going to be activated. Dreams reveal the selves that dance our lives at both the unconscious and conscious levels. Dreams are a threshold to understanding universal principles of Life in general, and they have collective as well as individual significance" (p. 185).

Adler's approach to dreams. Alfred Adler's theory of dreams cannot be understood apart from the rest of his basic theory, which is considerably more optimistic than Freud's. Adler saw us as the actor, creator, and artist of our life. We are not the victims of fate but are creative, active, choice-making beings whose every action has purpose and meaning. Movement toward life goals is what is important. What we are doing currently and our anticipation of the future is far more important than what happened to us in the past. Adlerians focus on intentions and what individuals are striving to accomplish.

Adler viewed dreams as an expression of an individual's unique strivings toward goals and purposes. Although he agreed with Freud on the great value of dreams in understanding people, he disagreed with Freud's methods of interpreting dreams. Along with Jung, Adler did not believe that dreams fulfilled wishes or revealed deeply hidden conflicts. Instead, he thought that dreams involve the meaning surrounding current life problems. In this sense, Adlerians view dreams as rehearsals for possible future courses of action. If we want to postpone action, we tend to forget our dreams (Mosak, 1989). Adlerians pay particular attention to childhood dreams, as well as recurrent and recent dreams. According to Mosak, dreams are weathervanes for counseling, bringing problems to the surface and pointing to the person's goals. They are reminders of what the person is about and what the person expects and is planning to do. Dreams clarify our views of self and the world, and they remind us of our life goals and guide us toward accomplishing these goals. Thus, there is no fixed symbolism to interpret dreams; one cannot understand dreams without considering the dreamer.

Adler did find that there were common interpretations for some dreams. Like Freud, he reported that many people had dreams of falling or flying. However, he disagreed with Freud's interpretation of such dreams in a sexual context. According to Adler, a dream involving falling might indicate a fear of losing self-esteem or prestige. Dreams of flying often indicate an upward striving or ambition. Dreamers who are being chased could be feeling a sense of weakness in relation to others. Dreaming of being naked might be indicative of fears of giving oneself away (Schultz, 1990).

If you have an interest in pursuing Adlerian concepts and practices in general, we recommend *Understanding Life-Style: The Psycho-Clarity Process* (Powers & Griffith, 1987).

Perls's approach to dreams. Fritz Perls, the father of Gestalt therapy, discovered some ingenious methods of assisting people to come to a better understanding of themselves by becoming friends with their dreams. According to Perls (1970), the dream is the most spontaneous expression of the existence of the human being; it is a piece of art that individuals chisel out of their lives. It represents an unfinished situation, but it is more than an incomplete situation, an unfulfilled wish, or a prophecy. Every dream contains an existential message about oneself and one's current struggle. Everything is to be found in dreams if all the parts are understood and assimilated. Perls maintains that if dreams are properly worked with, the existential message becomes clearer. In agreement with Jung's view, he sees each element in the dream as a part of the dreamer. However, these parts are to some extent disowned, and they are projected into the world. "We have emptied a part of ourselves into the world; therefore we must be left with holes, with emptiness. If we want to own these parts of ourselves again we have to use special techniques by which we can reassimilate those experiences" (Perls, 1970, p. 27). For Perls, dream work serves as an excellent way to discover personality voids by revealing missing parts.

Unlike the Freudian approach, Gestalt therapy does not aim to uncover, interpret, and explore unconscious meanings. Instead, it brings the dream back to life and relives it as though it were happening now. The suggested format includes making a list of all the details of the dream, remembering each person, event, and mood in it, and then becoming each of these parts by acting and inventing dialogue. All of the different parts of a dream are seen as expressions of contradictory and inconsistent aspects of one's own self. Thus, by engaging in a dialogue between these opposing aspects, one gradually becomes more aware of the range of one's own feelings. Perls saw dreams as "the royal road to integration." By avoiding analyzing and interpreting the dream and focusing instead on becoming and experiencing it in all its aspects, the dreamer gets closer to the existential message of the dream.

Perls shares two examples of encouraging a client to take on the roles of objects in his dreams:

> Two of my favorite examples of this are from the same man. In one dream, he leaves my office, crosses the street into Central Park, and walks over the bridle path. I ask him to play the bridle path, and he answers, "What! And let everybody tramp and shit on me?" In another dream, he left his attaché case on the stairs. I asked him to be the attaché case. He said, "Well, I've got a thick hide, in a thick skin. I've got secrets and nobody is supposed to get to my secrets. I keep them absolutely safe." See how much he tells us about himself by playing, identifying with the objects in his dream? (pp. 28–29)

Of all the approaches to understanding and exploring the personal meanings of your dreams, we think that the Gestalt approach is the most useful as a route to translating the existential messages they are giving to you. If you have an interest in recalling and exploring the possible meanings of your dreams, the Gestalt approach offers you practical methods.

Rainwater (1979) offers some useful guidelines for dreamers to follow in exploring their dreams:

- Be the landscape or the environment.
- Become all the people in the dream. Are any of them significant people?
- Be any object that links and joins, such as telephone lines and highways.
- Identify with any mysterious objects, such as an unopened letter or an unread book.
- Assume the identity of any powerful force, such as a tidal wave.
- Become any two contrasting objects, such as a younger person and an older person.
- Be anything that is missing in the dream. If you don't remember your dreams, then speak to your missing dreams.
- Be alert for any numbers that appear in the dream, become these numbers, and explore associations with them.

Rainwater suggests that in working with a dream you notice how you feel when you wake up. Is your feeling state one of fear, joy, sadness, frustration, surprise, anger? Identifying the feeling tone may be the key to finding the meaning of the dream. As you play out the various parts of your dream, pay attention to what you say, and look for patterns. By identifying your feeling tone and themes that emerge, you will get a clearer sense of what your dreams are telling you. In working with dreams in Gestalt style, you can focus on questions such as the following:

+ What are you doing in the dream?
+ What are you feeling?
+ What do you want in the dream?
+ What are your relationships with other objects and people in the dream?
+ What kind of action can you take now? What is your dream telling you?

If you want to select just one book that illustrates the Gestalt approach to working with dreams, we highly recommend reading *Gestalt Therapy Verbatim* (Perls, 1969). Another useful book for working with dreams (and other topics such as journal writing, autobiography, meditation, and physical health) is Janet Rainwater's (1979) *You're in Charge! A Guide to Becoming Your Own Therapist*.

EXAMPLES OF INTERPRETATIONS OF DREAMS

In one of her therapy sessions, Julie reported the following dream: "There is a well-dressed wheezing baby. I forget to feed the baby. I do everything for the baby. It is a very beautiful baby." This dream illustrates how dreamers select unconscious symbols that powerfully represent core struggles in their lives. In the context of Julie's life struggle the dream had a powerful meaning.

What Julie realized as she explored the possible meanings of her dream was that she was doing everything right, she was giving a lot to others, yet she was forgtting to take care of herself in the process of giving. A detail like the "wheezing baby" was significant, especially in light of the fact that she suffered from asthma, particularly when she became anxious. She discovered that the baby who went unfed was her. She had not been taking the time to nurture herself. As she "became" the baby and took on its personality, she became aware, and was horrified, that she was doing everything for the baby except feeding it. As a result of paying attention to what her dreams were telling her, she began to express more and more of her pain and buried feelings. She became aware of a great deal of repressed pain in her life and of the many ways in which she was neglecting herself. "I haven't been able to breathe so freely in a long time," she said at one point.

The following dream was explored by Ruby during a therapy session: "There is a monkey sitting on top of a horse bent over, holding on desperately. The horse is galloping with great speed along the beach. On top of the monkey are three monkeys weighing the first monkey down." When the therapist asked Ruby what her mood had been when she awakened, she replied that she had felt scared and burdened. As the therapist worked with Ruby's dream, she was asked if the number 3 had any particular significance to her. She quickly said "No, it doesn't." Later she admitted that she had a husband and two children. She was asked to associate with and play out various parts of her dream, including the following:

- "I am the speeding horse. I'm running out of control, and I can't stop." The galloping horse had some meaning in terms of her fears that her life was getting away from her. She had fears that she was aging and that if she didn't do what she most wanted to do, she would soon have no time left.
- "I am the sand, and I'm being stomped on." Ruby's pattern was to allow people to walk all over her and not to assert herself with them.
- "I'm the monkey, holding on desperately. I have three monkeys on my back that are holding me down." She identified the three monkeys as her husband, her son, and her daughter, all of whom could be "monkeys on her back."

As part of her therapeutic work Ruby symbolically talked to each of the monkeys in terms that she had never used with her husband and children. She told them that she wanted to be involved in their lives and give to them, but not to the extent of denying herself in the process. She also decided that she would periodically let them know how they were affecting her and would not allow herself to store up resentments. Since all three of them were adults, she wanted them to take on increased responsibility for themselves. Toward the end of one of her therapy sessions, after she had done considerable work with her dream, Ruby shared the following imagery. She had the image of a horse gracefully galloping along the beach. The monkey was sitting up, and there were no monkeys on its back. She felt very serene and at peace with herself.

As you can see, dreams are a rich source of meaning. If you listen closely to them, they will challenge you to look at ways in which you may want to change your life. I (Marianne) recently had a dream that challenged me to examine the way I was living. The dream occurred during a time when I was feeling personally and professionally overextended. I was giving out more than I was taking for myself. I make it a practice to write down and do Gestalt work with most of my dreams. Here is my dream, which occurred while I was in Germany:

> My mother has cooked me a very special meal and I am looking forward to eating it. There are many people there. By the time I go to get my food, everyone else has eaten the meal, and none is left for me! I am very angry, resentful, and hurt that there is no more food.

The meaning of this dream was obvious to me. The overriding message as that I was not taking care of myself or nurturing myself in my life at that time. I was consciously aware that I was working hard and not relaxing enough, yet the dream served to confront me even more with the importance of recognizing the direction in which I was going.

As you have seen, there are many different ways of interpreting and listening to dreams. There are different theoretical perspectives on interpreting the meaning of dreams. However, all of them seem to agree that dreams provide us with information about ourselves and add to our awareness of ways in which we can live more fully by making better choices for ourselves.

DREAMING OF A VISION THAT COULD BE YOURS

We like to encourage people to dream when they are awake as well as when they are asleep. We are reminded of Don Quixote's phrase "to dream the impossible dream." We have found that people often limit their vision of what they might become by not allowing themselves to formulate dreams. If you allow yourself to create dreams, a range of choices will unfold for you. We have met many people who continue to surprise themselves with what they have in their lives, for at one time they would not have imagined such possibilities, even in their wildest dreams. Some of their dreams became reality for them. Although we encourage this process of having a vision of what you want, we add that this is merely the beginning. Once you have a clearer picture of the person whom you want to become, of the relationships you want with others, and of the kind of world you would like to help create, it is essential to make choices and take action. Our main point is that too many restrict their vision of the possible by not allowing themselves the luxury of reflecting on their impossible dream.

Where to Go from Here: Continuing Your Personal Growth

In this final section we ask you to consider the personal meaning that this book and this course have held for you. Throughout the book you've been continually invited to look at some new choices you'd like to make. And one of the final challenges is to determine where you will go from here. Now that you've finished this book and are completing this course, will you stop here? Or will this be a commencement, a new beginning in the best sense? If you've invested yourself in the process of questioning your life and finding ways to have a different life, this is a prime time to make a commitment to yourself to actively put to use what you've been learning about yourself.

As you consider what experiences for continued personal growth you are likely to choose at this time, be aware that your meaning in life is not cast in concrete. As you change, you can expect that what brings meaning to your life will also change. The projects that you were deeply absorbed in as an adolescent may hold little meaning for you today. And where and how you discover meaning today may not be the pattern for some future period.

You can deliberately choose experiences that will help you actualize your potentials. Perhaps you remember reading a book or seeing a film that had a profound impact on you and really seemed to put things in perspective. Certainly, reading books that deal with significant issues in your life can be a growth experience in itself, as well as an encouragement to try new things.

Often, we make all sorts of resolutions about what we'd like to be doing in our life or about experiences we want to share with others, and then we fail to carry them out. Is this true of you? Are there activities you value yet rarely get around to doing? Perhaps you tell yourself that you prize making new friendships; yet you find that you do very little to actually initiate any contacts. Or perhaps you derive satisfaction from growing vegetables or puttering in your garden and yet find many reasons to neglect this activity. You might tell yourself that you'd love to take a day or two just to be alone and yet never get around to arranging it. When you stop to think about it, aren't there choices you could be making right now that would make your life a richer one? How would you really like to be spending your time? What changes are you willing to make today, this week, this month, this year?

In addition to activities that you enjoy but don't engage in as often as you'd like, there are undoubtedly many new things you might consider trying out as ways of adding meaning to your life and developing your potentials. You might consider making a contract with yourself to start now on a definite

plan of action, instead of putting it off until next week or next year. Some of the ways in which many people choose to challenge themselves to grow include the following:

- finding hobbies that develop new sides of themselves
- going to plays, concerts, and museums
- taking courses in pottery making, wine tasting, guitar playing, and innumerable other special interests
- getting involved in exciting work projects or actively pursuing forms of work that will lead to the development of hidden talents
- spending time alone to reflect on the quality of their lives
- initiating contacts with others and perhaps developing an intimate relationship

- enrolling in continuing-education courses or earning a degree primarily for the satisfaction of learning
- doing volunteer work and helping to make others' lives better
- experiencing the mountains, the desert, and the ocean—by hiking, sailing, and so on
- becoming involved in religious activities or pursuing a spiritual path that is meaningful to them
- traveling to new places, especially to experience different cultures
- keeping a journal in which they record feelings and dreams
- sharing some of their dreams with a person they trust

Any list of ways of growing is only a sample, of course; the avenues to personal growth are as various as the people who choose them. Growth can occur in small ways, and there are many things that you can do on your own (or with friends or family) to continue your personal development. Perhaps the greatest hindrance to our growth as a person is our failure to allow ourselves to imagine all the possibilities that are open to us. What follow are a few resources for continued personal growth.

A READING PROGRAM

One excellent way to keep alive your motivation for self-exploration is by reading good books, including selected self-help books. We caution you to beware of those self-help books that offer quick and sure solutions, that promise a prescription for eternal happiness, or that give you steps to follow to find guaranteed success in any and all of your personal endeavors. We've provided a variety of self-help references in the "References and Suggested Readings" section at the end of this book that should give you a fine start on developing a personal reading program. Many students and clients tell us how meaningful selected books have been for them in putting into perspective some of the themes they have struggled with.

A WRITING PROGRAM

Along with setting up a reading and reflection program for yourself, another way to build on the gains that you have made up to this point is to continue the practice of journal writing. If you have begun a process of personal writing in this book or in a separate notebook, keep up with this practice. Even devoting a short period a few times each week to reflecting on how your life is going and then recording some of your thoughts and feelings is most useful in providing you with an awareness of patterns in your behavior. Without being self-critical you can learn to observe what you are feeling, thinking, and doing; then you have a basis for determining the degree to which you are successfully changing some old patterns that were not working for you.

SELF-DIRECTED BEHAVIOR CHANGE

Now that you have finished this book, you have probably identified a few specific areas where you could do further work. If you recognize that you are not as assertive as you'd like to be in various social situations, for example, you can begin by doing some reading on the topic of assertiveness training. Of course, there are other areas you can target. If you decide that you are frequently tense and that you do not generally react well to stress, you can construct a self-change program that will involve practicing relaxation methods and breathing exercises. The main point is that you identify some target areas for change, that you set realistic goals, that you develop some specific techniques for carrying out your goals, and that you practice selected behaviors that will help you make those changes that you want to make.

SUPPORT GROUPS

You can keep your programs of reading, writing, and self-directed change going by yourself. In addition to these avenues that you can pursue alone, consider how you can reach out to others as a source of continued challenge and support. Assume that you are having a difficult time in working through the loss of a loved one. Doing selected reading on death and loss as well as writing down your feelings in your journal can be of some help; if in addition you interact with a small group of others who have experienced loss, you can receive the empathy and support necessary to assist you in mourning and expressing your grief.

Most colleges and community mental health centers offer a variety of self-help groups that are facilitated by a person who has coped or is coping with a particular life issue. A good support group will help you see that you are not alone in your struggle. The experience can also provide you with alternatives that you may not be considering. Other examples of support groups include those that deal with rape or incest, consciousness-raising groups for women and for men, groups for reentry students, groups for people concerned about gay and lesbian issues, and medical self-help groups. As is the case with self-help books, you are advised to proceed with some caution in joining a support group. These groups do have the potential for negative outcomes, especially if you get in a group where people are quick to give you ready-made advice and tell you what you should do. Beware of "support" groups in which people have an ax to grind and tell you how you should feel, think, and behave.

COUNSELING

We hope you'll keep the options open for yourself to seek professional counseling as an avenue of personal growth. You don't have to be in a crisis to benefit from either individual or group counseling. You may find that you can only do so much by yourself in effectively making the changes you desire.

SOME FINAL COMMENTS

We'd like to end with a reminder of our comment in Chapter One that this book is best considered an unfinished project. It is unfinished in that we hope that you will reread at least portions of it and that you will continue to reflect on the topics we've covered. If you are keeping a journal, there is plenty of material for further reflection in the "Time Out" sections and the "Activities and Exercises" after each chapter. Certain topics will have more appeal than others, so you can return to these chapters and see how any of your views and attitudes change over time. As authors, we also consider our book an unfinished project in that our perspectives continue to evolve as we do. The spirit, general tone, and message of this fifth edition of *I Never Knew I Had a Choice* are basically the same as in the original version; however, with each of the five editions, we have developed topics differently, in light of the changes in our times and our personal changes as well.

Now that you are finishing reading and reflecting on *Choice* and now that your course is coming to an end, we hope that you will not forget either the course or the book and that you won't see your work as finished. Rather, we hope that you are somewhat more aware of personal issues than you were when you began the course and that you are eager to continue on the path of self-examination and reflection. We find that our students and people who attend our workshops sometimes expect dramatic transformations and feel disappointed if they do not make major changes in their lives. We often tell them that it is not the big changes that are necessarily significant, but it is the willingness to take initial steps that lead to continued growth. Remember that it is essential to begin with yourself, as you can only change your own ways of thinking, feeling, and doing. Don't set yourself up to accomplish herculean feats, but instead look at subtle ways of increasing your personal freedom. Throughout this book we have encouraged you to open yourself to taking risks in thinking about yourself and others in new ways. Personal change is an ongoing process that really does not come to an end until you do. We sincerely wish you well in your commitment to take the steps necessary, no matter how small, in your journey to becoming the person you were meant to be. Remember that a journey of a thousand miles begins with the first step — so start walking!

Time Out for Personal Reflection

1. Check any of the following activities that you think you might like to pursue in the near future as a way of continuing your personal development:

_____   take another psychology course
_____   take a class in Eastern philosophies
_____   learn to practice yoga

_____   join a consciousness-raising group
_____   get involved in some type of self-control program (for example, to lose
              weight or stop smoking)
_____   attend a massage workshop
_____   learn relaxation exercises

2. What are some of the reasons that you haven't previously done the things you've listed? Check any of the following responses that fit you:

_____   I haven't known about some of the available resources.
_____   I haven't been able to afford some of the activities I've listed.
_____   I'm afraid of failing.
_____   I'm hesitant about trying new things.
_____   I haven't had the time.

3. What are some things you'd like to do more often, or begin doing, that would not demand the use of professional resources? Check any of the following that fit you:

_____   play more often
_____   spend more time alone
_____   exercise more frequently
_____   do more reading
_____   keep a detailed daily journal
_____   attend church more often
_____   be more open in my intimate relationships
_____   take better care of my body
_____   increase my enjoyment of sex and sensuality
_____   do things for other people
_____   cultivate more hobbies
_____   develop the practice of meditation

4. List any other things that you'd like to do, either by yourself or with others:

_____

_____

_____

_____

5. How open are you to seeking professional help, either in times of personal crisis or as a way to expand your self-understanding? When might you make use of counseling?

_____

_____

_____

Chapter Summary

Seeking meaning and purpose in life is an important part of being human. Meaning is not automatically bestowed on you but instead is the result of your active thinking and choosing. We've encouraged you to recognize your own values and to ask both how you acquired them and whether you can affirm them for yourself out of your own experience and reflection. This task of examining your values and purposes is one that lasts a lifetime.

If you are secure about your value system, you will also be flexible and open to new life experiences. At various times in your life you may look at the world somewhat differently, which will indicate a need to modify some of your values. This is not to say that you will change your values without giving the matter considerable thought. Being secure about your values also implies that you do not need to impose them on other people. We hope that you will be able to respect values of others that may differ from your own. You can learn to accept other people who have a different world view from yours without necessarily approving of all of their behavior. If you are clear about the meaning in your own life, and if you have developed a philosophy of life that provides you with purpose and direction, you will be more able to interact with others who might hold different value systems. Being able to talk openly with these people can be a useful avenue for your own personal growth.

You can take a number of steps on your own if you are interested in actualizing your potentials. A few of these activities include meditation, keeping a journal, reading, travel, finding hobbies, and setting up a program of self-directed behavioral change. Many people find value in getting involved in a support group composed of peers who are struggling with a particular issue in their lives. This can be done in conjunction with setting up a program for self-change. Especially important is learning how to pay attention to your dreams as an indicator of the meaning and direction of your current life. You can also reach out to others by establishing meaningful relationships with them.

Activities and Exercises

1. Ask a few close friends what gives their lives meaning. How have they found their identities? What projects give them a sense of purpose? How do they think their lives would be different without this source of meaning?

2. Now that the course is coming to an end, discuss with other students what topics have meant the most to you. What did you learn about yourself from reading the book and taking the course? What do you think you will do with what you learned? Do you intend to make any specific behavioral changes? What questions were raised that are still open for you?

3. Writing a paper that describes your philosophy of life can help you integrate your thoughts and reflections on the topics raised in this chapter and throughout this book. Ideally, this paper will represent a critical analysis of who you are now and the factors that have been most influential in contributing to that person. If you attempted to write at least a part of your philosophy of life as you began this book, you have a basis for comparison if you now revise your philosophy of life. The following outline for your paper is very comprehensive, and writing such a paper can be a major project in a course. As you review the outline, you might select only one or two of the major topics and use them as a focus of your paper. Feel free to use or omit any part of the outline, and modify it in any way that will help you to write a paper that is personally significant. You might also consider adding poetry, excerpts from other writers, and pictures or works of art. If you take this project seriously, the assignment can help you clarify your goals for the future and the means to obtain them.

I. Who are you now? What influences have contributed to the person you are now?
   A. Influences during childhood:
      1. your relationship with your parents
      2. your relationship with your siblings
      3. important turning points
      4. successes and failures
      5. personal conflicts
      6. family expectations
      7. impact of school and early learning experiences
      8. your relationships with friends
      9. experiences of loneliness
      10. other
   B. Influences during adolescence:
      1. impact of your family and your relationship with your parents
      2. school experiences
      3. personal struggles
      4. critical turning points
      5. influence of your peer group
      6. experiences of loneliness
      7. successes and failures, and their impact on you
      8. influential adults other than parents
      9. your principal values
      10. other
   C. Love and sex:
      1. your need for love
      2. your fear of love
      3. the meaning of love for you
      4. dating experiences and their effect on you
      5. your view of sex roles

       6. expectations of others and their influence on your sex role
       7. attitudes toward the opposite sex
       8. meaning of sexuality in your life
       9. your values concerning love and sex
     10. other

  D. Intimate relationships and family life:
       1. the value you place on marriage
       2. how children fit in your life
       3. the meaning of intimacy for you
       4. the kind of intimate relationships you want
       5. areas of struggle for you in relating to others
       6. your views of marriage
       7. your values concerning family life
       8. how social expectations have influenced your views
       9. sex roles in intimate relationships
     10. other

  E. Death and meaning:
       1. your view of an afterlife
       2. religious views and your view of death
       3. the way death affects you
       4. sources of meaning in your life
       5. the things you most value in your life
       6. your struggles in finding meaning and purpose
       7. religion and the meaning of life
       8. critical turning points in finding meaning
       9. influential people in your life
     10. other

II. Whom do you want to become?
  A. Summary of your present position:
       1. how you see yourself now (strengths and weaknesses)
       2. how others perceive you now
       3. what makes you unique
       4. your relationships with others
       5. present struggles
  B. Your future plans for an occupation:
       1. nature of your work plans and their chances for success
       2. kind of work that is meaningful to you
       3. how you chose or will choose your work
       4. what work means to you
       5. what you expect from work
  C. Your future with others:
       1. the kind of relationships you want
       2. what you need to do to achieve the relationships you want
       3. plans for marriage or an alternative
       4. place for children in your future plans

D. Future plans for yourself:
1. how you would like to be ten years from now
   a. what you need to do to achieve your goals
   b. what you can do now
2. your values for the future
3. your view of the good life
   a. ways to achieve it
   b. how your view of the good life relates to all aspects of your life
4. choices you see as being open to you now
   a. choices in work
   b. choices in school
   c. value choices
   d. other areas of choice in your life

4. Select one or more of the following books for further reading on the topics explored in this chapter: Burke and Miranti, *Ethical and Spiritual Values in Counseling* (1992); Frankl, *Man's Search for Meaning* (1963); Joy, *Joy's Way* (1979) and *Avalanche* (1990).

References and Suggested Readings*

ADLER, A. 1958). *What life should mean to you.* New York: Capricorn.

ADLER, A. (1964). *Social interest: A challenge to mankind.* New York: Capricorn.

ADLER, A. (1969). *The practice and theory of individual psychology.* Paterson, NJ: Littlefield.

ALBRECHT, K. (1979). *Stress and the manager.* Englewood Cliffs, NJ: Prentice-Hall.

AMERICAN RED CROSS. (1986, May). *AIDS: The facts* (pamphlet). Washington, DC: U.S. Public Health Service.

AMERICAN RED CROSS. (1986, October). *AIDS, sex, and you* (pamphlet). Washington, DC: U.S. Public Health Service.

*BASOW, S. A. (1992). *Gender: Stereotypes and roles* (3rd ed.). Pacific Grove, CA: Brooks/Cole.

BATESON, M. C. (1990). *Composing a life.* New York: Plume.

*BECKER, E. (1973). *The denial of death.* New York: Free Press.

*BELLAH, R. N., MADSEN, R., SULLIVAN, W. M., SWIDLER, A., & TIPTON, S. M. (1985). *Habits of the heart: Individualism and commitment in American life.* New York: Harper & Row.

*BENSON, H. (1976). *The relaxation response.* New York: Avon Books.

*BENSON, H. (1984). *Beyond the relaxation response.* New York: Berkeley Books.

*BERMAN, A. L., & JOBES, D. A. (1991). *Adolescent suicide: Assessment and intervention.* Washington, DC: American Psychological Association.

BERNE, E. (1975). *What do you say after you say hello?* New York: Bantam Books.

BETTELHEIM, B. (1967). *The empty fortress: Infantile autism and the birth of self.* New York: Free Press.

*BLACK, C. (1987). *It will never happen to me.* New York: Ballantine.

*BLOOMFIELD, H. H., WITH FELDER, L. (1983). *Making peace with your parents.* New York: Ballantine.

*An asterisk before a book or article indicates that we highly recommend it as supplementary reading.

*BLOOMFIELD, H. H., WITH FELDER, L. (1985). *Making peace with yourself.* New York: Ballantine.

*BLY, R. (1990). *Iron John: A book about men.* New York: Random House.

BLY, R. (1991a). Father hunger in men. In K. Thompson (Ed.), *To be a man: In search of the deep masculine* (pp. 189–192). Los Angeles: Tarcher.

BLY, R. (1991b). The need for male initiation. In K. Thompson (Ed.), *To be a man: In search of the deep masculine* (pp. 38–42). Los Angeles: Tarcher.

BLY, R. (1991c). What men really want. In K. Thompson (Ed.), *To be a man: In search of the deep masculine* (pp. 16–23). Los Angeles: Tarcher.

BOLLES, R. N. (1978). *The three boxes of life.* Berkeley, CA: Ten Speed Press.

*BOLLES, R. N. (1992). *What color is your parachute?* Berkeley, CA: Ten Speed Press.

BONGAR, B. (1991). *The suicidal patient: Clinical and legal standards of care.* Washington, DC: American Psychological Association.

BRAZIER, C. (1991). Men should embrace feminism. In K. Thompson (Ed.), *To be a man: In search of the deep masculine* (pp. 94–96). Los Angeles: Tarcher.

BRENNECKE, J. H., & AMICK, R. G. (1980). *The struggle for significance* (3rd ed.). Encino, CA: Glencoe.

*BURKE, M. T., & MIRANTI, J. G. (1992). *Ethical and spiritual values in counseling.* Alexandria, VA: The Association for Religious and Value Issues in Counseling.

*BURNS, D. D. (1981). *Feeling good: The new mood therapy.* New York: New American Library.

*BURNS, D. D. (1985). *Intimate connections.* New York: American Library.

*BUSCAGLIA, L. (1972). *Love.* Thorofare, NJ: Charles B. Slack.

BUSCAGLIA, L. (1982a). *Living, loving, and learning.* New York: Ballantine.

BUSCAGLIA, L. (1982b). *Personhood: The art of being fully human.* New York: Fawcett.

*CARNEY, C. G., & WELLS, C. F. (1991). *Discover the career within you.* (3rd ed.). Pacific Grove, CA: Brooks/Cole.

*CARR, J. B. (1988). *Crisis in intimacy: When expectations don't meet reality.* Pacific Grove, CA: Brooks/Cole.

*CASEY, K., & VANCEBURG, M. (1985). *The promise of a new day: A book of daily meditations.* New York: Harper/Hazelden.

CHAPMAN, W. (1980). *Counselor's handbook for SIGI.* Princeton, NJ: Educational Testing Service.

*CHARLESWORTH, E. A., & NATHAN, R. G. (1984). *Stress management: A comprehensive guide to wellness.* New York: Ballantine.

CLARK, D. (1987). *The new loving someone gay.* Berkeley, CA: Celestial Arts.

COLGROVE, M., BLOOMFIELD, H. H., & MCWILLIAMS, P. (1976). *How to survive the loss of a love.* New York: Bantam Books.

COREY, G. (1990). *Theory and practice of group counseling.* (3rd ed.). Pacific Grove, CA: Brooks/Cole.

COREY, G. (1991). *Theory and practice of counseling and psychotherapy* (4th ed.). Pacific Grove, CA: Brooks/Cole.

COREY, M., & COREY, G. (1993). *Becoming a helper.* (2nd ed.). Pacific Grove, CA: Brooks/Cole.

CORNEUA, G. (1991). *Absent fathers, lost sons: The search for masculine identity.* Boston: Shambhala.

COWAN, C., & KINDER, M. (1985). *Smart women, foolish choices.* New York: New American Library.

DASS, R. (1978). *Journey of awakening: A meditator's guidebook.* New York: Bantam Books.

DAVIS, M., ESHELMAN, E. R., & MCKAY, M. (1980). *The relaxation and stress reduction workbook.* Richmond, CA: New Harbinger Publications.

DESPELDER, L., & STRICKLAND, A. (1983). *The last dance: Encountering death and dying.* Palo Alto, CA: Mayfield.

DOWLING, C. (1981). *The Cinderella complex.* New York: Pocket Books.

DRUMMOND, R. J. (1988). *Appraisal procedures for counselors and helping professionals.* Columbus, OH: Charles E. Merrill.

DRUMS, SWEAT, AND TEARS. (1991, June 24). *Newsweek,* pp. 46–51.

*DWORKIN, S. H., & GUTIERREZ, F. J. (Eds.). (1992). *Counseling gay men and lesbians: Journey to the end of the rainbow.* Alexandria, VA: American Association for Counseling and Development.

*ELKIND, D. (1984). *All grown up and no place to go.* Reading, MA: Addison-Wesley.

*ELLIS, A. (1988). *How to stubbornly refuse to make yourself miserable about anything—Yes, anything!* Secaucus, NJ: Lyle Stuart.

ELLIS, A., & HARPER R. A. (1975). *A new guide to rational living.* Englewood Cliffs, NJ: Prentice-Hall.

*EMERY, G. (1981). *A new beginning: How you can change your life through cognitive therapy.* New York: Simon & Schuster.

*EMMONS, M. L., & ALBERTI, R. E. (1991). *Accepting each other: Individuality and intimacy in your loving relationships.* San Luis Obispo, CA: Impact.

ERIKSON, E. (1963). *Childhood and society* (2nd ed.). New York: Norton.

ERIKSON, E. (1982). *The life cycle completed.* New York: Norton.

FALK, P. J. (1989). Lesbian mothers: Psychosocial assumptions in family law. *American Psychologist, 44,* 941–947.

FARRELL, W. (1975). *The liberated male.* New York: Bantam Books.

FARRELL, W. (1991). We should embrace traditional masculinity. In K. Thompson (Ed.)., *To be a man: In search of the deep masculine* (pp. 10–16). Los Angeles: Tarcher.

FASSINGER, R. E. (1991). The hidden minority: Issues and challenges in working with lesbian women and gay men. *The Counseling Psychologist, 19,* 157–176.

FINKELHOR, D. (1984). *Child sexual abuse: New theory and research.* New York: Free Press.

*FORWARD, S., & BUCK, C. S. (1988). *Betrayal of innocence: Incest and its devastation.* New York: Penguin.

FORWARD, S., & TORRES, J. (1987). *Men who hate women and the women who love them.* New York: Bantam Books.

*FRANKL, V. (1963). *Man's search for meaning.* New York: Washington Square Press.

FRANKL, V. (1965). *The doctor and the soul.* New York: Bantam Books.

FRANKL, V. (1969). *The will to meaning: Foundation and applications of logotherapy.* New York: New American Library.

FRANKL, V. (1978). *The unheard cry for meaning.* New York: Bantam Books.

FREUD, S. (1949). *An outline of psychoanalysis.* New York: Norton.

FREUD, S. (1965). *The interpretation of dreams.* New York: Avon. (Original work published 1900)

FRIEDMAN, M., & ROSENMAN, R. H. (1974). *Type A behavior and your heart.* Greenwich, CT: Fawcett.

FRIEDMAN, M., & ULMER, D. (1985). *Treating Type A behavior and your heart.* New York: Ballantine.

*FROMM, E. (1956). *The art of loving.* New York: Harper & Row.

GERSON, K. (1987). What do women want from men? Men's influence on women's work and family choices. In M. S. Kimmel (Ed.), *Changing men: New directions in research on men and masculinity.* Newbury Park, CA: Sage Publications.

*GIBRAN, K. (1923). *The prophet.* New York: Knopf.

*GLASSER, W. (1985). *Control therapy: A new explanation of how we control our lives.* New York: Harper & Row.

GLIONNA, J. M. (1992, January 12). Dance of life. *Los Angeles Times,* pp. A3, A27.

GOLDBERG, H. (1976). *The hazards of being male.* New York: Nash.

GOLDBERG, H. (1979). *The new male.* New York: New American Library.

*GOLDBERG, H. (1987). *The inner male: Overcoming roadblocks to intimacy.* New York: New American Library.

GOLDSMITH, M. F. (1991). Global full-court press against HIV, AIDS spurred by player's infection. *Journal of the American Medical Association, 266,* 2801–2802.

GORDON, D. (1972). *Overcoming the fear of death.* New York: Penguin.

GOULD, R. L. (1978). *Transformations: Growth and change in adult life.* New York: Simon & Schuster.

GOULDING, M., & GOULDING, R. (1979). *Changing lives through redecision therapy.* New York: Brunner/Mazel.

GOULDING, R., & GOULDING, M. (1978). *The power is in the patient.* San Francisco: TA Press.

GRUSZNSKI, R., & BANKOVICS, G. (1990). Treating men who batter: A group approach. In D. Moore & F. Leafgren (Eds.), *Problem-solving strategies and intervention for men in conflict* (pp. 201–211). Alexandria, VA: American Association for Counseling.

HAAS, E. M. (1981). *Staying healthy with the seasons.* Berkeley, CA: Ten Speed Press.

HALL, C. S. (1984). Dreams. In R. J. Corsini (Ed.), *Encyclopedia of psychology: Vol. 1* (pp. 388–390). New York: Wiley.

HALL, C. S., & NORDBY, V. J. (1973). *A primer of Jungian psychology.* New York: New American Library.

HAMACHEK, D. E. (1988). Evaluating self-concept and ego development within Erikson's psychosocial framework: A formulation. *Journal of Counseling and Development, 66,* 354–360.

HAMACHEK, D. (1990). Evaluating self-concept and ego status in Erikson's last three psychosocial stages. *Journal of Counseling and Development, 68,* 677–683.

HARLOW, H. F., & HARLOW, M. K. (1966). Learning to love. *American Scientist, 54,* 244–272.

HAVIGHURST, R. (1972). *Developmental tasks and education* (3rd ed.). New York: David McKay.

HAWTON, K. (1986). *Suicide and attempted suicide among children and adolescents.* Newbury Park, CA: Sage Publications.

*HENDRICK, S., & HENDRICK, C. (1992). *Liking, loving, and relating* (2nd ed.). Pacific Grove, CA: Brooks/Cole.

HERMAN, J. (1981). *Father-daughter incest.* Cambridge, MA: Harvard University Press.

HERR, E. L., & CRAMER, S. H. (1988). *Career guidance and counseling through the life span* (3rd ed.). Boston: Scott, Foresman.

HODGE, M. (1967). *Your fear of love.* Garden City, NY: Doubleday.

HOFFMAN, M. A. (1991). Counseling the HIV-infected client: A psychosocial model for assessment and intervention. *The Counseling Psychologist, 19,* 467–542.

HOLLAND, J. L. (1985). *Making vocational choices: A theory of vocational personalities and work environments* (2nd ed.). Englewood Cliffs, NJ: Prentice-Hall.

HOLMES, T. H., & RAHE, R. H. (1967). The social readjustment rating scale. *Journal of Psychosomatic Research, 11,* 213–218.

HOLMES, T. S., & HOLMES, T. H. (1970). Short-term intrusions into the life-style routine. *Journal of Psychosomatic Research, 14,* 121–132.

HOTELLING, K. (1991). Sexual harassment: A problem shielded by silence. *Journal of Counseling and Development, 69,* 497–501.

HOWARD, S. (1991). Organizational resources for addressing sexual harassment. *Journal of Counseling and Development, 69,* 507–511.

ISAACSON, L. E. (1986). *Career information in counseling and career development* (4th ed.). Boston: Allyn & Bacon.

IVEY, A. E. (1990). *Developmental strategies for helpers: Individual, family, and network interventions.* Pacific Grove, CA: Brooks/Cole.

JAMES, M., & JONGEWARD, D. (1971). *Born to win: Transactional analysis with Gestalt experiments.* Reading, MA: Addison-Wesley.

JAMPOLSKY, G. G. (1981). *Love is letting go of fear.* New York: Bantam Books.

JOSEPHSON, E., & JOSEPHSON, M. (Eds.). (1962). *Man alone: Alienation in modern society.* New York: Dell.

JOURARD, S. (1971 *The transparent self: Self-disclosure and well-being* (rev. ed.). New York: Van Nostrand Reinhold.

JOURARD, S. (1975, July). Marriage is for life. *Journal of Marriage and Family Counseling,* pp. 199–208.

*JOY, W. B. (1979). *Joy's way: A map for the transformational journey.* Los Angeles: Tarcher.

JOY, W. B. (1990). *Avalanche: Heretical reflections on the dark and the light.* New York: Ballantine.

JUNG, C. G. (1961). *Memories, dreams, reflections.* New York: Vintage Books.

JUSTICE, B., & JUSTICE, R. (1979). *The broken taboo: Sex in the family.* New York: Human Sciences Press.

*KALISH, R. A. (1985). *Death, grief, and caring relationships* (2nd ed.). Pacific Grove, CA: Brooks/Cole.

KAVANAUGH, R. (1972). *Facing death.* New York: Nash.

*KEEN, S. (1991). *Fire in the belly: On being a man.* New York: Bantam Books.

KIMMEL, M. S. (Ed.). (1987a). *Changing men: New directions in research on men and masculinity.* Newbury Park, CA: Sage Publications.

KIMMEL, M. S. (1987b). Rethinking "masculinity": New directions in research. In M. S. Kimmel (Ed.), *Changing men: New directions in research on men and masculinity* (pp. 9–24). Newbury Park, CA: Sage Publications.

KOPP, S. (1972). *Mirror, mask, and shadow: The risks and rewards of self-acceptance.* New York: Bantam Books.

*KÜBLER-ROSS, E. (1969). *On death and dying.* New York: Macmillan.

KÜBLER-ROSS, E. (1975). *Death: The final stage of growth.* Englewood Cliffs, NJ: Prentice-Hall.

KÜBLER-ROSS, E. (1981). *Living with death and dying.* New York: Macmillan.

LAIDLAW, T. A., MALMO, C., & ASSOCIATES. (1990). *Healing voices: Feminist approaches to therapy with women.* San Francisco: Jossey-Bass.

*LERNER, H. G. (1985). *The dance of anger: A woman's guide to changing the patterns of intimate relationships.* New York: Harper & Row.

LEVINSON, D. J. (1978). *The seasons of a man's life.* New York: Knopf.

LEWIS, C. S. (1961). *A grief observed.* New York: Seabury Press.

*LINDBERGH, A. (1975). *Gift from the sea* (twentieth-anniversary ed.). New York: Pantheon. (Originally published in 1955)

LOCK, R. D. (1992a). *Taking charge of your career direction: Career planning guide, Book 1* (2nd ed.). Pacific Grove, CA: Brooks/Cole.

LOCK, R. D. (1992b). *Job search: Career planning guide, Book 2* (2nd ed.). Pacific Grove, CA: Brooks/Cole.

LOCK, R. D. (1992c). *Student activities for taking charge of your career direction and job search* (2nd ed.). Pacific Grove, CA: Brooks/Cole.

LOTT, B. (1987). *Women's lives: Themes and variations in gender learning.* Pacific Grove, CA: Brooks/Cole.

MACHLOWITZ, M. (1980). *Workaholics: Living with them, working with them.* Reading, MA: Addison-Wesley.

MAIER, S. (1991). *God's love song.* Corvallis, OR: Postal Instant Press.

MALTZ, W. (1991). *The sexual healing journey: A guide for women and men survivors of sexual abuse.* New York: HarperCollins.

MALTZ, M., & HOLMAN, B. (1987). *Incest and sexuality: A guide to understanding and healing.* Lexington, MA: D. C. Health.

MASLACH, C. (1982). *Burnout: The cost of caring.* Englewood Cliffs, NJ: Prentice-Hall.

Maslow, A. (1968). *Toward a psychology of being.* New York: Van Nostrand Reinhold.

Maslow, A. (1970). *Motivation and personality* (2nd ed.). New York: Harper & Row.

Maslow, A. (1971). *The farther reaches of human nature.* New York: Viking.

*Mason, L. J. (1985). *Guide to stress reduction.* Berkeley, CA: Ten Speed Press.

Masters, W. H., & Johnson, V. E. (1980). *Human sexual inadequacy.* New York: Bantam Books.

May, R. (1973). *Man's search for himself.* New York: Dell.

May, R. (1974). *Love and will.* New York: Dell.

May, R. (1981). *Freedom and destiny.* New York: Norton.

May, R. (1983). *Discovery of being.* New York: Norton.

Mayeroff, M. (1971). *On caring.* New York: Harper & Row.

McCarthy, B., & McCarthy, E. (1984). *Sexual awareness: Enhancing sexual pleasure.* New York: Carroll & Graf.

Meichenbaum, D., Price, R., Phares, E. J., McCormick, N., & Hyde, J. (1989). *Exploring choices: The psychology of adjustment.* Glenview, IL: Scott, Foresman.

Meiselman, K. C. (1978). *Incest: A psychological study of causes and effects with treatment recommendations.* San Francisco: Jossey-Bass.

Meiselman, K. C. (1990). *Resolving the trauma of incest: Reintegration therapy with survivors.* San Francisco: Jossey-Bass.

Mencke, R., & Hummel, R. L. (1984). *Career planning for the 80's.* Pacific Grove, CA: Brooks/Cole.

Mornell, P. (1979). *Passive men, wild women.* New York: Ballantine.

Morris, M. (1984). *If I should die before I wake.* New York: Dell.

Mosak, H. H. (1989). Adlerian psychotherapy. In R. J. Corsini & D. Wedding (Eds.), *Current psychotherapies* (4th ed.) (pp. 64–116). Itasca, IL: F. E. Peacock.

Moses, A. E., & Hawkins, R. O. (1982). *Counseling lesbian women and gay men: A life-issues approach.* St. Louis: C. V. Mosby.

*Moustakas, C. (1961). *Loneliness.* Englewood Cliffs, NJ: Prentice-Hall.

Moustakas, C. (1972). *Loneliness and love.* Englewood Cliffs, NJ: Prentice-Hall.

Moustakas, C. (1975). *Finding yourself, finding others.* Englewood Cliffs, NJ: Prentice-Hall.

Moustakas, C. (1977). *Turning points.* Englewood Cliffs, NJ: Prentice-Hall.

Naisbitt, J. (1984). *Megatrends.* New York: Warner Books.

Naisbitt, J., & Aburdene, P. (1990). *Megatrends 2000.* New York: Morrow.

*Napier, A. Y. (1990). *The fragile bond: In search of an equal, intimate, and enduring marriage.* New York: Harper & Row.

Nass, G. D., Libby, R. W., & Fisher, M. P. (1984). *Sexual choices: An introduction to human sexuality* (2nd ed.). Boston: Jones & Bartlett.

Nelson, R. C. (1963). Knowledge and interests concerning sixteen occupations among elementary and secondary school students. *Educational and Psychological Measurements, 23,* 741–754.

*Newman, B. M., & Newman, P. R. (1991). *Development through life: A psychological approach* (5th ed.). Pacific Grove, CA: Brooks/Cole.

Norwood, R. (1985). *Women who love too much: When you keep wishing and hoping he'll change.* New York: Simon & Schuster.

Orsborn, C. (1986). *Enough is enough: Exploring the myth of having it all.* New York: Putnam.

Patterson, C. H. (1985). *The therapeutic relationship: Foundations for an eclectic psychotherapy.* Pacific Grove, CA: Brooks/Cole.

*Peck, M. S. (1978). *The road less traveled: A new psychology of love, traditional values, and spiritual growth.* New York: Simon & Schuster.

*Peck, M. S. (1987). *The different drum: Community making and peace.* New York: Simon & Schuster.

Perls, F. S. (1969). *Gestalt therapy verbatim.* New York: Bantam Books.

Perls, F. S. (1970). Four lectures. In J. Fagan & I. L. Shepherd (Eds.), *Gestalt therapy now* (pp. 14–38). New York: Harper & Row.

Powell, J. (1969). *Why am I afraid to tell you who I am?* Niles, IL: Argus.

Powers, R. L., & Griffith, J. (1987). *Understanding life-style: The psycho-clarity process.* Chicago: American Institute of Adlerian Studies.

*Rainwater, J. (1979). *You're in charge! A guide to becoming your own therapist.* Los Angeles: Guild of Tutors Press.

*Rice, P. L. (1992). *Stress and health* (2nd ed.). Pacific Grove, CA: Brooks/Cole.

Riger, S. (1991). Gender dilemmas in sexual harassment policies and procedures. *American Psychologist, 46,* 497–505.

Robinson, E. A. (1897). *The children of the night.* New York: Scribner's.

Robinson, F. P. (1970). *Effective study* (4th ed.). New York: Harper & Row.

Rogers, C. R. (1961). *On becoming a person: A therapist's view of psychotherapy.* Boston: Houghton Mifflin.

Rogers, C. R. (1980). *A way of being.* Boston: Houghton Mifflin.

Rogers, C. R. (1983). *Freedom to learn for the 80's.* Columbus, OH: Charles E. Merrill.

Rubin, T. I. (1969). *The angry book.* New York: Macmillan.

Rush, F. (1980). *The best kept secret: Sexual abuse of children.* Englewood Cliffs, NJ: Prentice-Hall.

Russell, J. M. (1991). *Perversion, eating disorders, and sex roles.* Paper presented at a meeting of the International Federation of Psychoanalytic Societies, Stockholm, Sweden.

San Francisco AIDS Foundation. (1990). *AIDS in the workplace* (pamphlet). San Francisco: Impact AIDS.

Satir, V. (1975). *Self-esteem.* Berkeley, CA: Celestial Arts.

Satir, V. (1985). *Meditations and inspirations.* Berkeley, CA: Celestial Arts.

Schafer, W. (1992). *Stress management for wellness* (2nd ed.). Orlando, FL: Harcourt Brace Jovanovich College Publishers.

Schnitzer, E. (1977). *Looking in.* Idyllwild, CA: Strawberry Valley Press.

Schopen, A., & Freeman, B. (1992). Meditation: The forgotten Western tradition. *Counseling and Values, 36,* 123–134.

*SCHULTZ, D. (1990). *Theories of personality* (4th ed.). Pacific Grove, CA: Brooks/Cole.

SCHUTZ, W. (1972). *Here comes everybody*. New York: Harper & Row.

SHARF, R. S. (1992). *Applying career development theory to counseling*. Pacific Grove, CA: Brooks/Cole.

SHARF, R. S. (1993). *Occupational information overview*. Pacific Grove, CA: Brooks/Cole.

SHEEHY, G. (1976). *Passages: Predictable crises of adult life*. New York: Dutton.

SHEEHY, G. (1981). *Pathfinders*. New York: Morrow.

SHNEIDMAN, E. S. (Ed.). (1984). *Death: Current perspectives*. Palo Alto, CA: Mayfield.

*SIEGEL, B. (1988). *Love, medicine, and miracles*. New York: Harper & Row.

*SIEGEL, B. (1989). *Peace, love, and healing: Bodymind communication and the path to self-healing: An exploration*. New York: Harper & Row.

*SIGELMAN, C. K., & SHAFFER, D. R. (1991). *Life-span human development*. Pacific Grove, CA: Brooks/Cole.

STEINER, C. (1975). *Scripts people live: Transactional analysis of life scripts*. New York: Bantam Books.

STOLTZ-LOIKE, M. (1992). *Dual career couples: New perspectives in counseling*. Alexandria, VA: American Association for Counseling and Development.

*TANNEN, D. (1987). *That's not what I meant: How conversational style makes or breaks relationships*. New York: Ballantine.

*TANNEN, D. (1991). *You just don't understand: Women and men in conversation*. New York: Ballantine.

TERKEL, S. (1975). *Working*. New York: Avon.

THOMPSON, K. (Ed.). (1991). *To be a man: In search of the deep masculine*. Los Angeles: Tarcher.

TOURNIER, P. (1972). *Learn to grow old*. New York: Harper & Row.

*TRAVIS, J. W., & RYAN, R. S. (1988). *Wellness workbook* (2nd ed.). Berkeley, CA: Ten Speed Press.

U. S. DEPARTMENT OF HEALTH AND HUMAN SERVICES. (1987). *Facts about AIDS* (pamphlet). Washington, DC: U. S. Government Printing Office.

U. S. DEPARTMENT OF HEALTH AND HUMAN SERVICES. (1988). *Understanding AIDS* (pamphlet). Washington, DC: U. S. Government Printing Office.

U. S. DEPARTMENT OF HEALTH AND HUMAN SERVICES. (1988). *Women, sex, and AIDS* (pamphlet). Washington, DC: U. S. Government Printing Office.

U. S. DEPARTMENT OF HEALTH AND HUMAN SERVICES. (1989). *Many teens are saying no* (pamphlet). Washington, DC: U. S. Government Printing Office.

U. S. DEPARTMENT OF HEALTH AND HUMAN SERVICES. (1991). *AIDS and you* (pamphlet). Washington, DC: U. S. Government Printing Office.

U. S. DEPARTMENT OF HEALTH AND HUMAN SERVICES. (1991). *Caring for someone with AIDS* (pamphlet). Washington, DC: U. S. Government Printing Office.

U. S. DEPARTMENT OF HEALTH AND HUMAN SERVICES. (1991). *HIV infection and AIDS: Are you at risk?* (pamphlet). Washington, DC: U. S. Government Printing Office.

U. S. DEPARTMENT OF HEALTH AND HUMAN SERVICES. (1991). *How you won't get AIDS* (pamphlet). Washington, DC: U. S. Government Printing Office.

U. S. DEPARTMENT OF HEALTH AND HUMAN SERVICES. (1991). *Voluntary HIV counseling and testing: Facts, issues, and answers* (pamphlet). Washington, DC: U. S. Government Printing Office.

VANDERBILT, H. (1992, February). Incest: A four-part chilling report. *Lear's*, pp. 49–77.

WATSON, D. L., & THARP, R. G. (1989). *Self-directed behavior: Self-modification for personal adjustment* (5th ed.). Pacific Grove, CA: Brooks/Cole.

*WEITEN, W., LLOYD, M. A., & LASHLEY, R. L. (1991). *Psychology applied to modern life: Adjustment in the 90s* (3rd ed.). Pacific Grove, CA: Brooks/Cole.

WOLFE, S. M., FUGATE, L., HULSTRAND, E. P., & KAMIMOTO, L. E. (1988). *Worst pills best pills*. Washington, DC: Public Citizen Health Research Group.

WOODMAN, N. J., & LENNA, H. R. (1980). *Counseling with gay men and women: A guide for facilitating positive lifestyles*. San Francisco: Jossey-Bass.

WRIGHT, L. (1988). The Type A behavior pattern and coronary artery disease. *American Psychologist, 43,* 2–14.

*YALOM, I. D. (1980). *Existential psychotherapy*. New York: Basic Books.

*ZIMBARDO, P. G. (1987). *Shyness*. New York: Jove.

Index

PHOTO CREDITS

TO THE OWNER OF THIS BOOK:

We hope that you have enjoyed *I Never Knew I Had a Choice* (5th edition) and found it meaningful. We'd like to know as much about your experiences with the book as you care to offer. Your comments can help us make it better for future readers. Thank you.

School: _____

Your instructor's name: _____

1. What did you like *most* about this book? _____

   _____

2. What did you like *least* about this book? _____

   _____

3. How much personal value did you find in the "Time Out for Personal Reflection" sections?

   _____

   _____

4. Of how much interest and value were the end-of-chapter "Activities and Exercises"?

   _____

5. Specific topics in the book you thought were most relevant and important: _____

   _____

6. Specific suggestions for improving the book: _____

   _____

   _____

7. Some ways you used this book in class: _____

   _____

8. Some ways you used this book out of class: _____

   _____

9. The name of the course in which you used this book: _____

   _____

10. In a separate letter, if you care to write one, please let us know what other comments about the book you'd like to make. We welcome your suggestions!

Optional:

Your name: _____ Date: _____

May Brooks/Cole quote you, either in promotion for *I Never Knew I Had a Choice* or in future publishing ventures?

Yes: _____ No: _____

Sincerely,
Gerald Corey
Marianne Schneider Corey

||||||

NO POSTAGE
NECESSARY
IF MAILED
IN THE
UNITED STATES

BUSINESS REPLY MAIL

FIRST CLASS   PERMIT NO. 358   PACIFIC GROVE, CA

POSTAGE WILL BE PAID BY ADDRESSEE

ATT: *Gerald Corey and Marianne Schneider Corey*

Brooks/Cole Publishing Company
511 Forest Lodge Road
Pacific Grove, California 93950-9968

|||||||||||||||||||||||||||||||||||||||||||||